Hayate
the Combat Butler

30

KENJIRO HATA

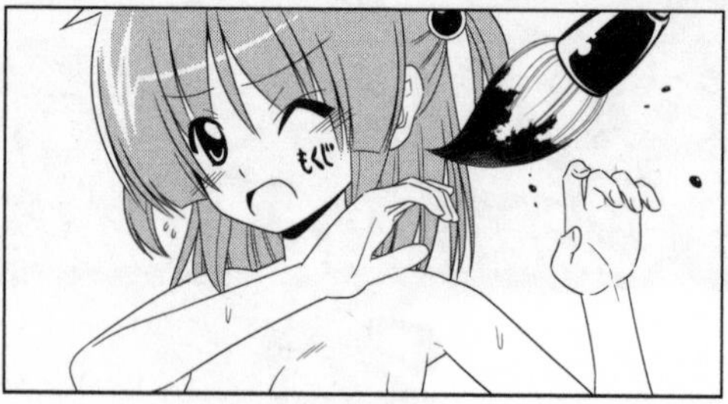
もくじ

*The text on her face spells "Table of Contents."

ハヤテのごとく! Hayate the combat butler 30

Kenjiro Hata

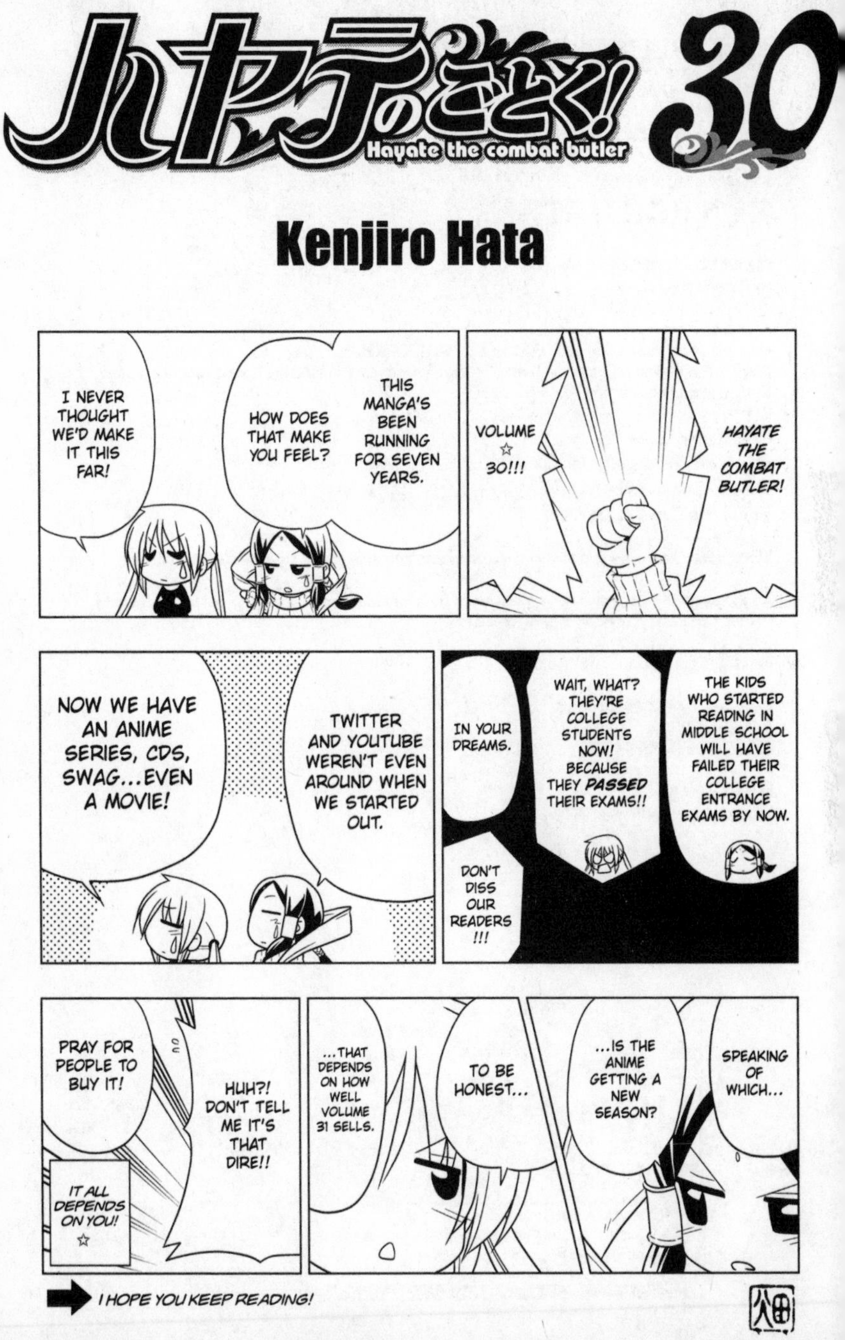
HAYATE THE COMBAT BUTLER!
VOLUME ☆ 30!!!
THIS MANGA'S BEEN RUNNING FOR SEVEN YEARS.
HOW DOES THAT MAKE YOU FEEL?
I NEVER THOUGHT WE'D MAKE IT THIS FAR!
THE KIDS WHO STARTED READING IN MIDDLE SCHOOL WILL HAVE FAILED THEIR COLLEGE ENTRANCE EXAMS BY NOW.
WAIT, WHAT? THEY'RE COLLEGE STUDENTS NOW! BECAUSE THEY *PASSED* THEIR EXAMS!!
IN YOUR DREAMS.
DON'T DISS OUR READERS!!!
TWITTER AND YOUTUBE WEREN'T EVEN AROUND WHEN WE STARTED OUT.
NOW WE HAVE AN ANIME SERIES, CDS, SWAG...EVEN A MOVIE!
SPEAKING OF WHICH...
...IS THE ANIME GETTING A NEW SEASON?
TO BE HONEST...
...THAT DEPENDS ON HOW WELL VOLUME 31 SELLS.
HUH?! DON'T TELL ME IT'S THAT DIRE!!
PRAY FOR PEOPLE TO BUY IT!
IT ALL DEPENDS ON YOU! ☆

➡ *I HOPE YOU KEEP READING!*

HAYATE THE COMBAT BUTLER
VOL. 30
Shonen Sunday Edition

STORY AND ART BY
KENJIRO HATA

HAYATE NO GOTOKU! Vol. 30
by Kenjiro HATA
© 2005 Kenjiro HATA
All rights reserved.
Original Japanese edition published by SHOGAKUKAN.
English translation rights in the United States of America, Canada, the United Kingdom and
Ireland arranged with SHOGAKUKAN.

Translation/John Werry
Touch-up Art & Lettering/John Hunt
Design/Yukiko Whitley
Editor/Shaenon K. Garrity

Printed in the U.S.A.

Published by VIZ Media, LLC
P.O. Box 77010
San Francisco, CA 94107

10 9 8 7 6 5 4 3 2 1
First printing, September 2017

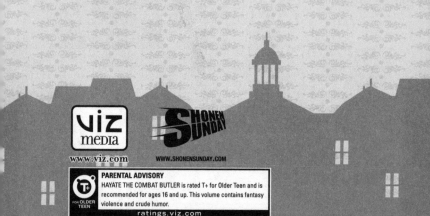

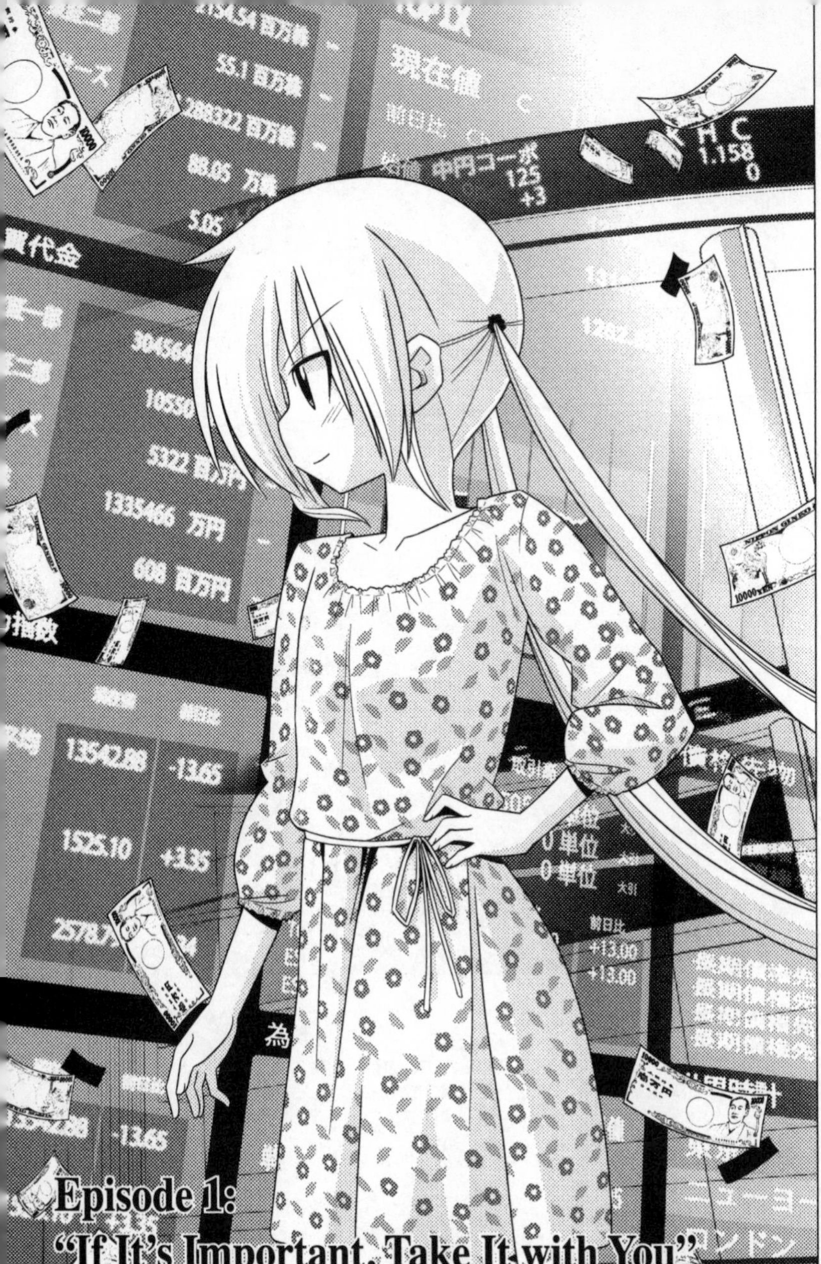

Episode 1: "If It's Important, Take It with You"

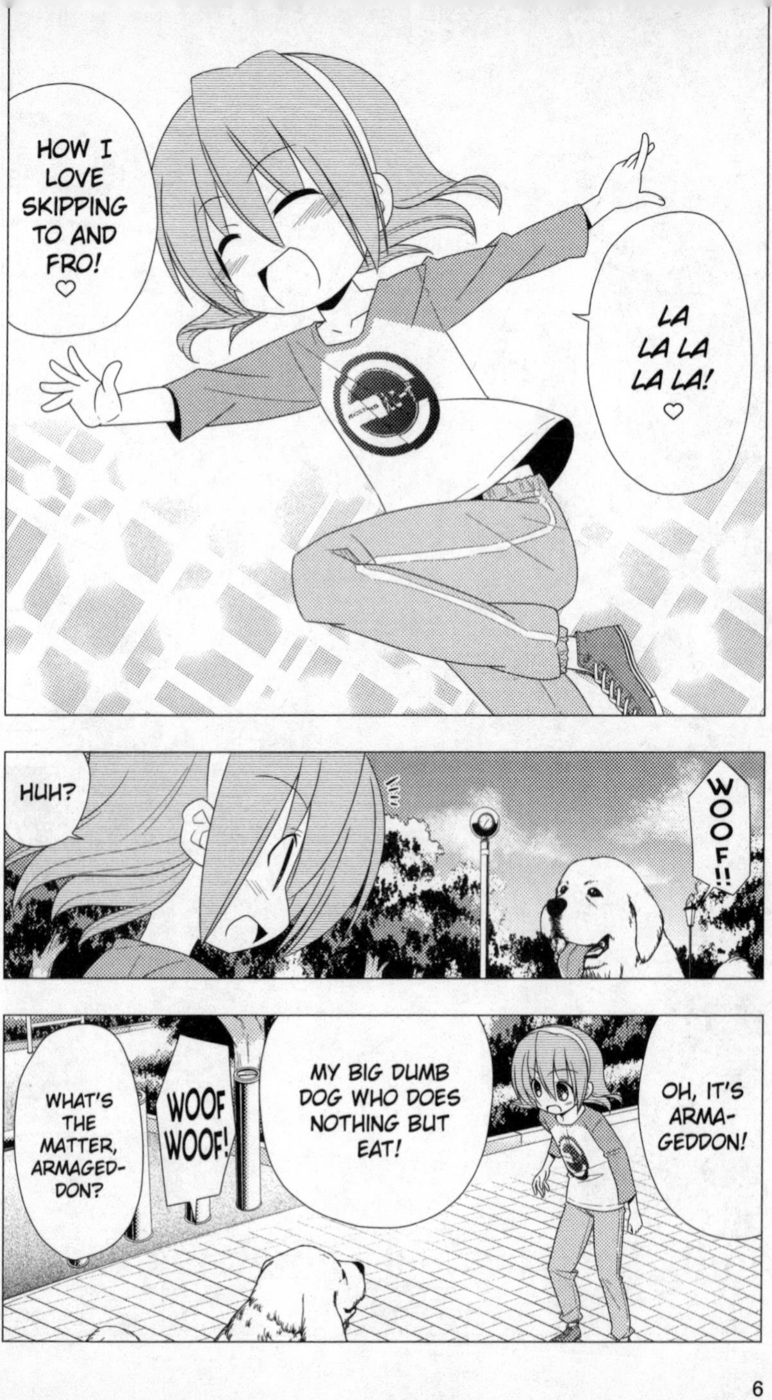
LA LA LA LA LA! ♡
HOW I LOVE SKIPPING TO AND FRO! ♡
WOOF!!
HUH?
OH, IT'S ARMAGEDDON!
MY BIG DUMB DOG WHO DOES NOTHING BUT EAT!
WOOF WOOF!
WHAT'S THE MATTER, ARMAGEDDON?

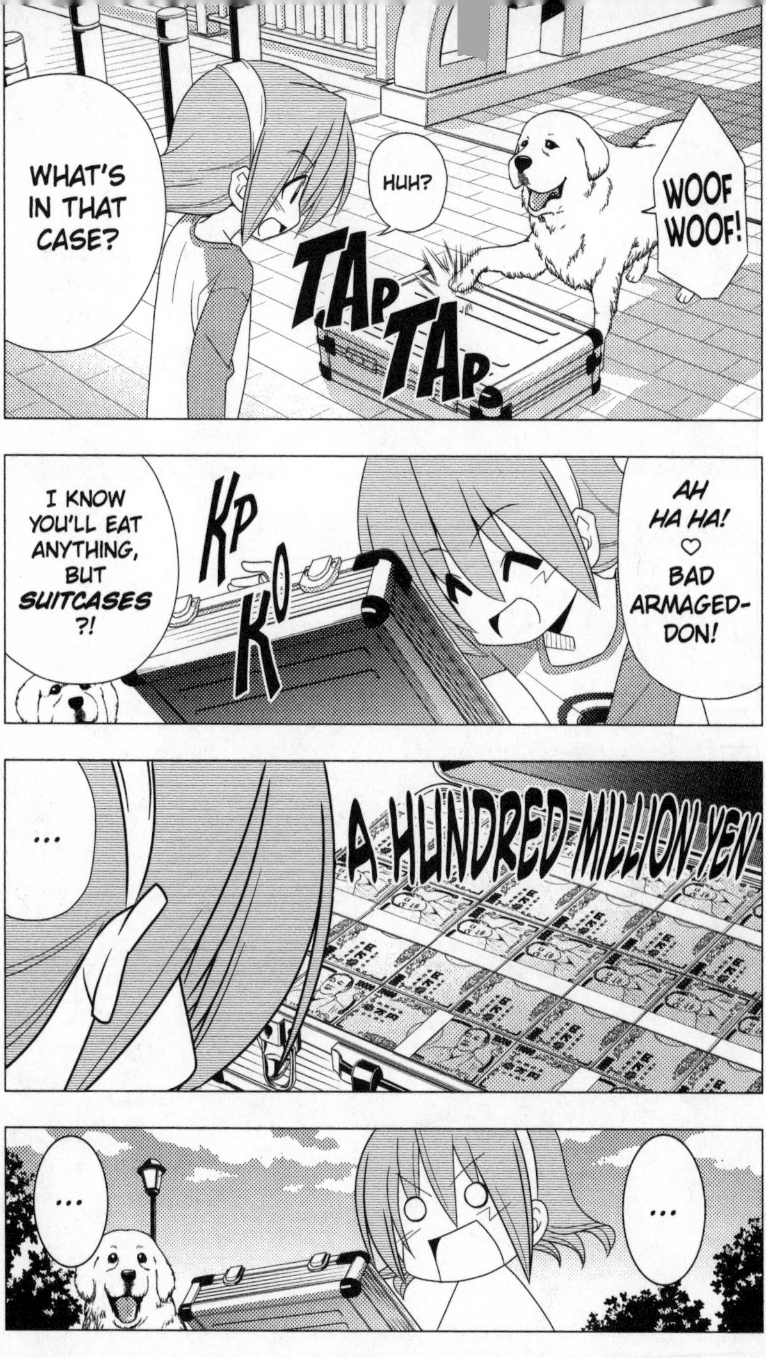
WOOF WOOF!
HUH?
TAP TAP
WHAT'S IN THAT CASE?
AH HA HA! ♡ BAD ARMAGED-DON!
KPOK
I KNOW YOU'LL EAT ANYTHING, BUT SUITCASES ?!
A HUNDRED MILLION YEN
...
...
...

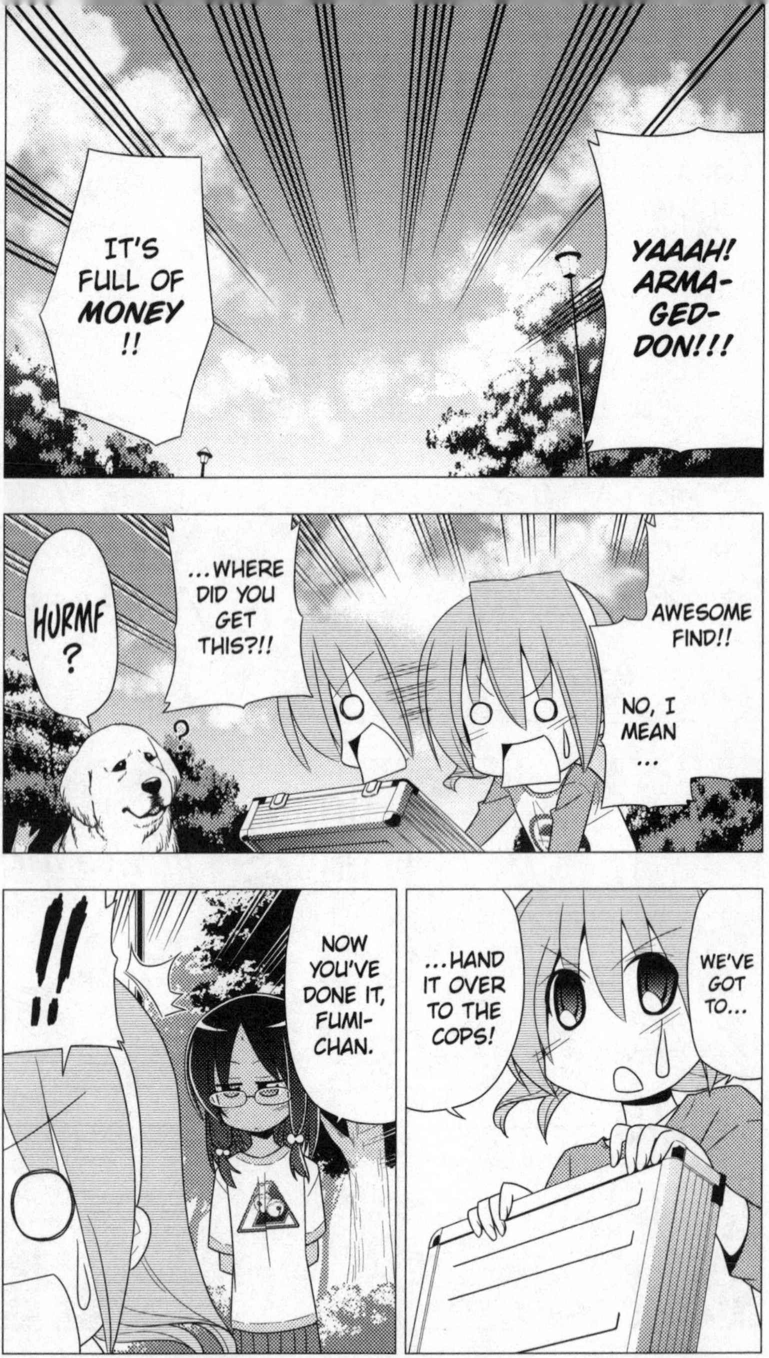
YAAAH! ARMA-GED-DON!!!
IT'S FULL OF MONEY !!
AWESOME FIND!!
NO, I MEAN ...
...WHERE DID YOU GET THIS?!!
HURMF ?
?
WE'VE GOT TO...
...HAND IT OVER TO THE COPS!
NOW YOU'VE DONE IT, FUMI-CHAN.
!!

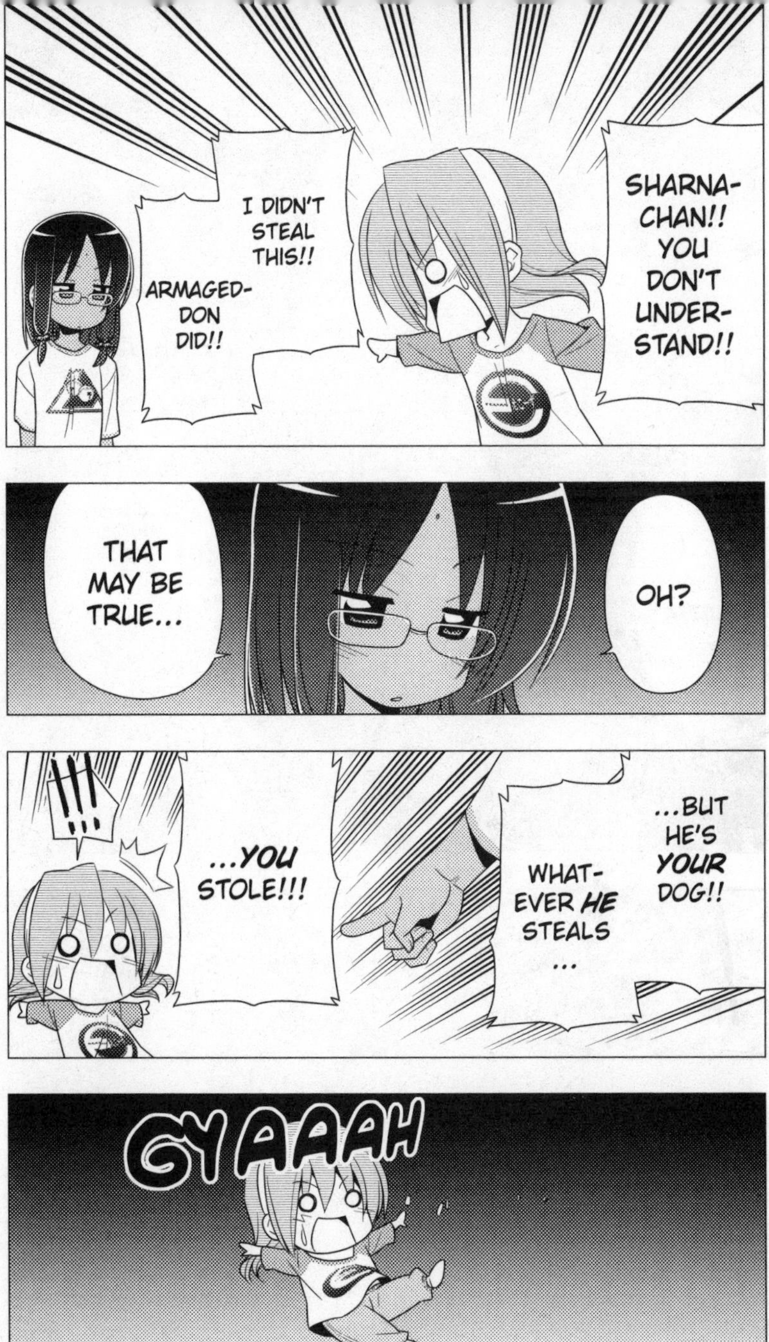
SHARNA-CHAN!! YOU DON'T UNDER-STAND!!
I DIDN'T STEAL THIS!!
ARMAGED-DON DID!!
OH?
THAT MAY BE TRUE...
...BUT HE'S *YOUR* DOG!!
WHAT-EVER *HE* STEALS ...
...*YOU* STOLE!!!
!!!
GYAAAH

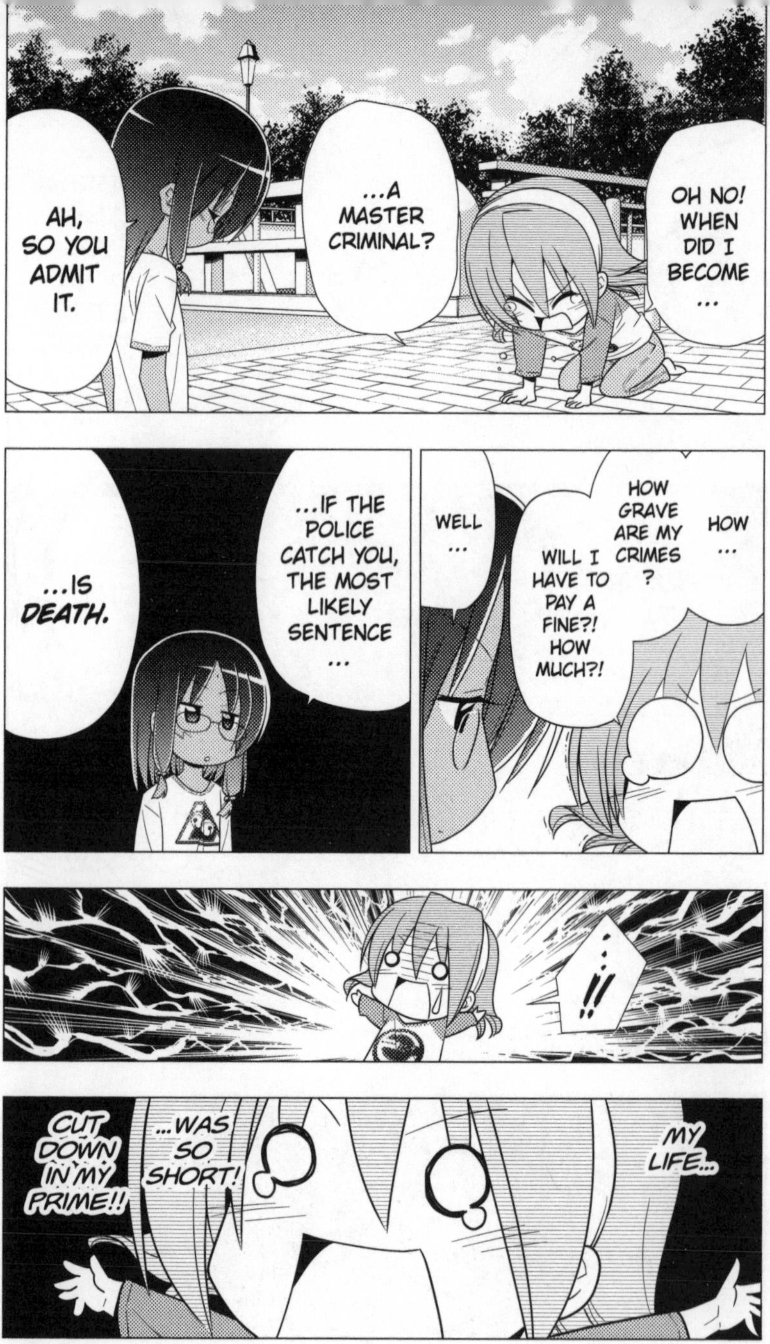
OH NO! WHEN DID I BECOME ...
...A MASTER CRIMINAL?
AH, SO YOU ADMIT IT.
HOW ...
HOW GRAVE ARE MY CRIMES ?
WILL I HAVE TO PAY A FINE?! HOW MUCH?!
WELL ...
...IF THE POLICE CATCH YOU, THE MOST LIKELY SENTENCE ...
...IS DEATH.
...!!
MY LIFE...
...WAS SO SHORT!
CUT DOWN IN MY PRIME!!

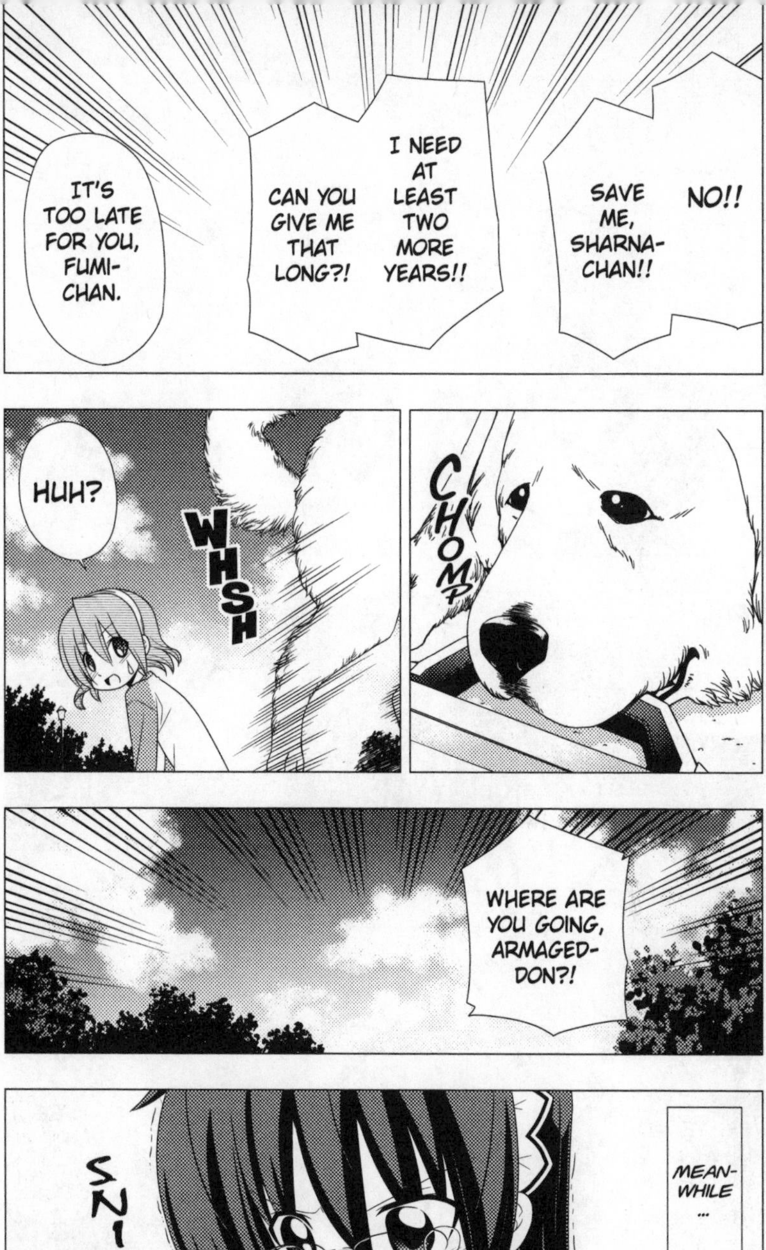
NO!!
SAVE ME, SHARNA-CHAN!!
I NEED AT LEAST TWO MORE YEARS!!
CAN YOU GIVE ME THAT LONG?!
IT'S TOO LATE FOR YOU, FUMI-CHAN.
CHOMP
HUH?
WHSH
WHERE ARE YOU GOING, ARMAGED-DON?!
MEAN-WHILE ...
SNIFF

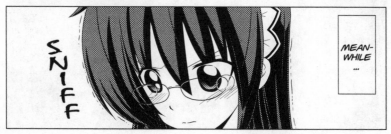

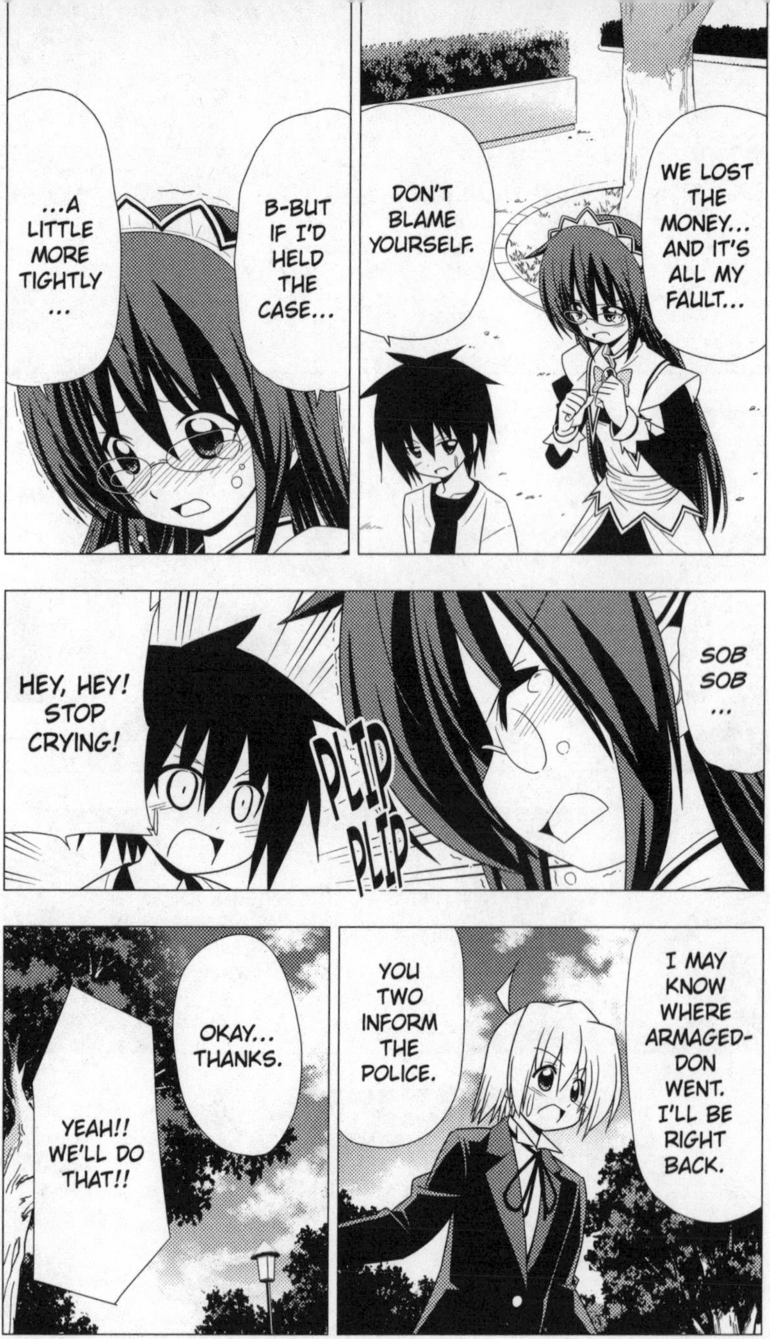
WE LOST THE MONEY... AND IT'S ALL MY FAULT...
DON'T BLAME YOURSELF.
B-BUT IF I'D HELD THE CASE...
...A LITTLE MORE TIGHTLY ...
SOB SOB ...
PLIP PLIP
HEY, HEY! STOP CRYING!
I MAY KNOW WHERE ARMAGED-DON WENT. I'LL BE RIGHT BACK.
YOU TWO INFORM THE POLICE.
OKAY... THANKS.
YEAH!! WE'LL DO THAT!!

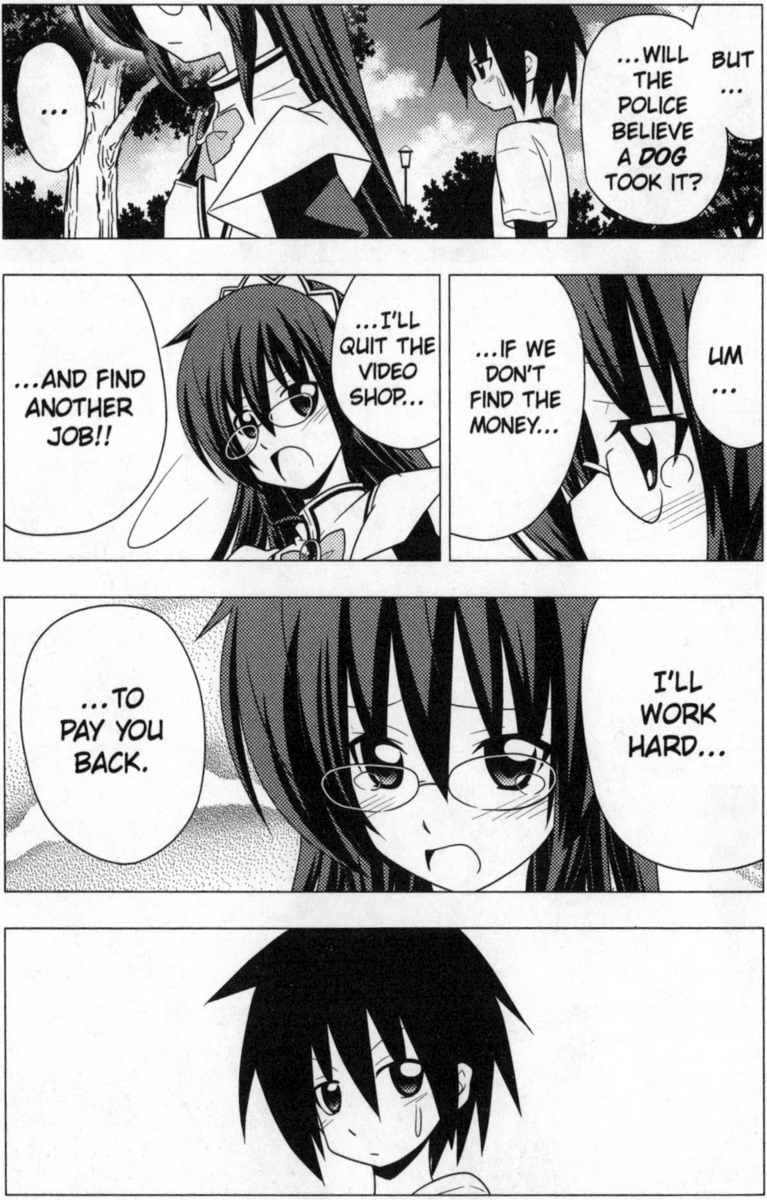
BUT ...
...WILL THE POLICE BELIEVE A *DOG* TOOK IT?
...
UM ...
...IF WE DON'T FIND THE MONEY...
...I'LL QUIT THE VIDEO SHOP...
...AND FIND ANOTHER JOB!!
I'LL WORK HARD...
...TO PAY YOU BACK.

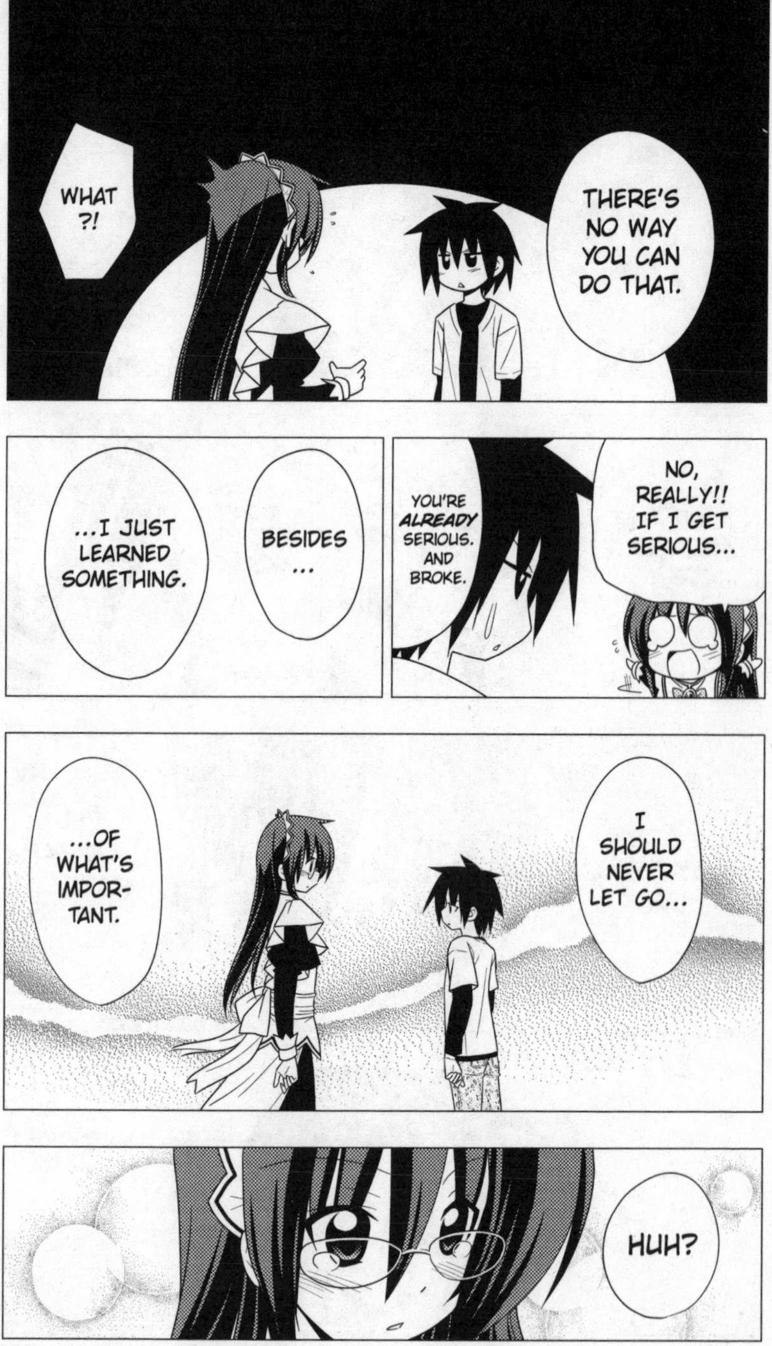
THERE'S NO WAY YOU CAN DO THAT.
WHAT ?!
NO, REALLY!! IF I GET SERIOUS...
YOU'RE ALREADY SERIOUS. AND BROKE.
BESIDES ...
...I JUST LEARNED SOMETHING.
I SHOULD NEVER LET GO...
...OF WHAT'S IMPOR-TANT.
HUH?

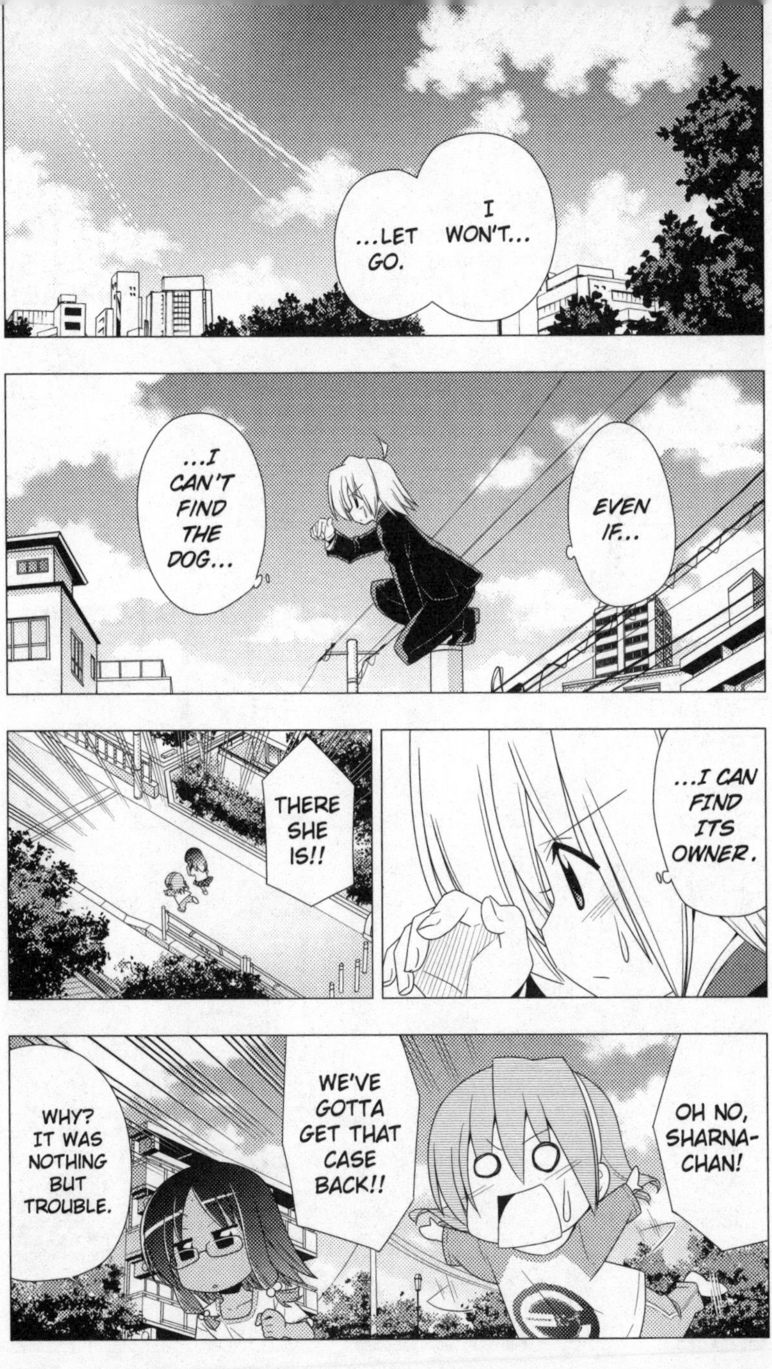
I WON'T...
...LET GO.
EVEN IF...
...I CAN'T FIND THE DOG...
...I CAN FIND ITS OWNER.
THERE SHE IS!!
OH NO, SHARNA-CHAN!
WE'VE GOTTA GET THAT CASE BACK!!
WHY? IT WAS NOTHING BUT TROUBLE.

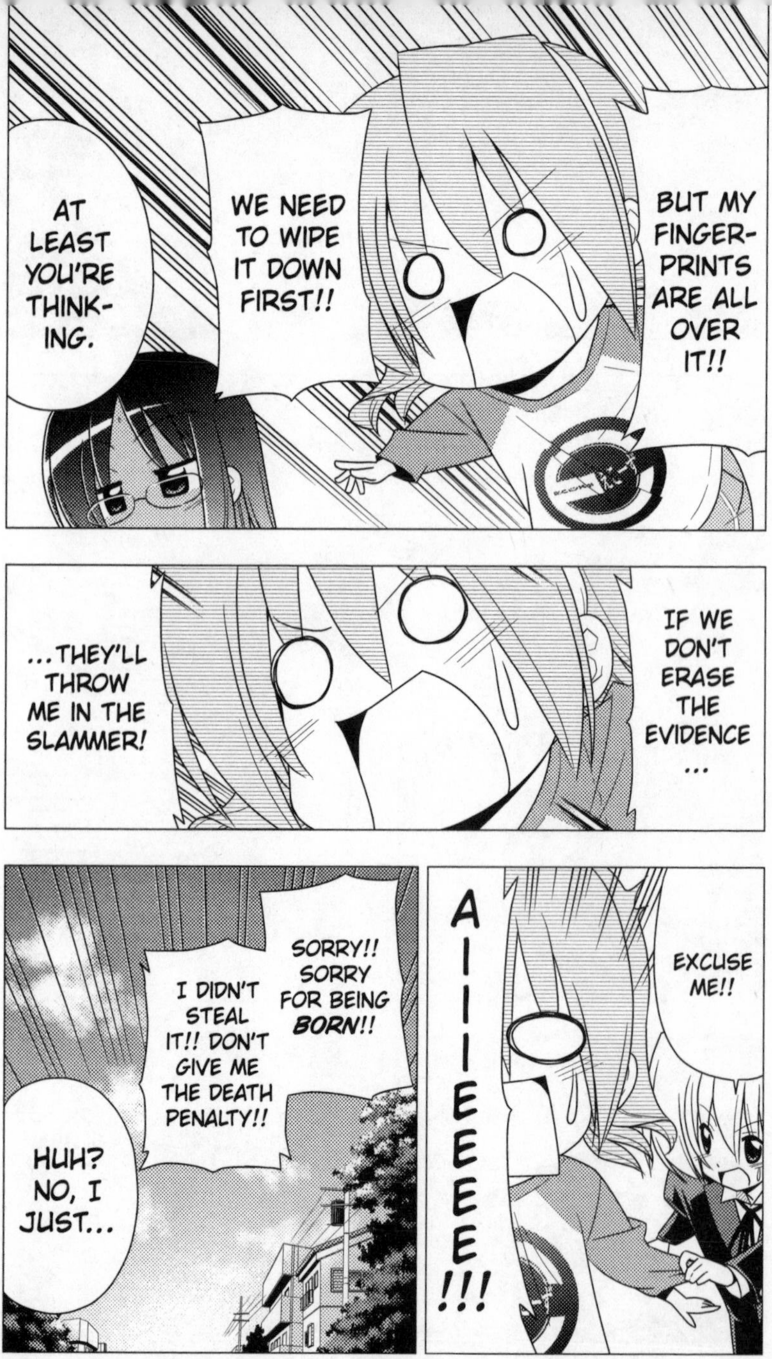
BUT MY FINGER-PRINTS ARE ALL OVER IT!!
WE NEED TO WIPE IT DOWN FIRST!!
AT LEAST YOU'RE THINKING.
IF WE DON'T ERASE THE EVIDENCE...
...THEY'LL THROW ME IN THE SLAMMER!
EXCUSE ME!!
AIIIEEEE!!!
SORRY!! SORRY FOR BEING *BORN*!!
I DIDN'T STEAL IT!! DON'T GIVE ME THE DEATH PENALTY!!
HUH? NO, I JUST...

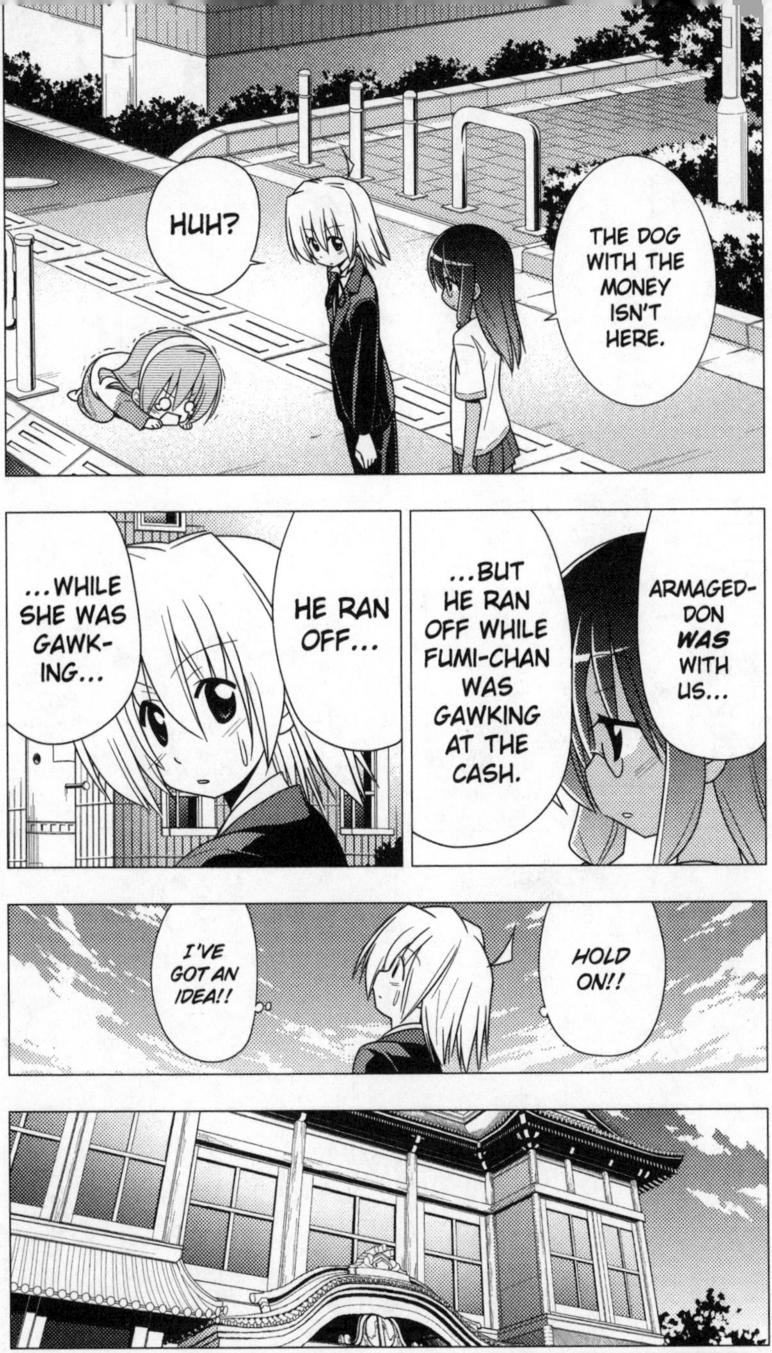
THE DOG WITH THE MONEY ISN'T HERE.
HUH?
ARMAGED-DON *WAS* WITH US...
...BUT HE RAN OFF WHILE FUMI-CHAN WAS GAWKING AT THE CASH.
HE RAN OFF...
...WHILE SHE WAS GAWK-ING...
HOLD ON!!
I'VE GOT AN IDEA!!

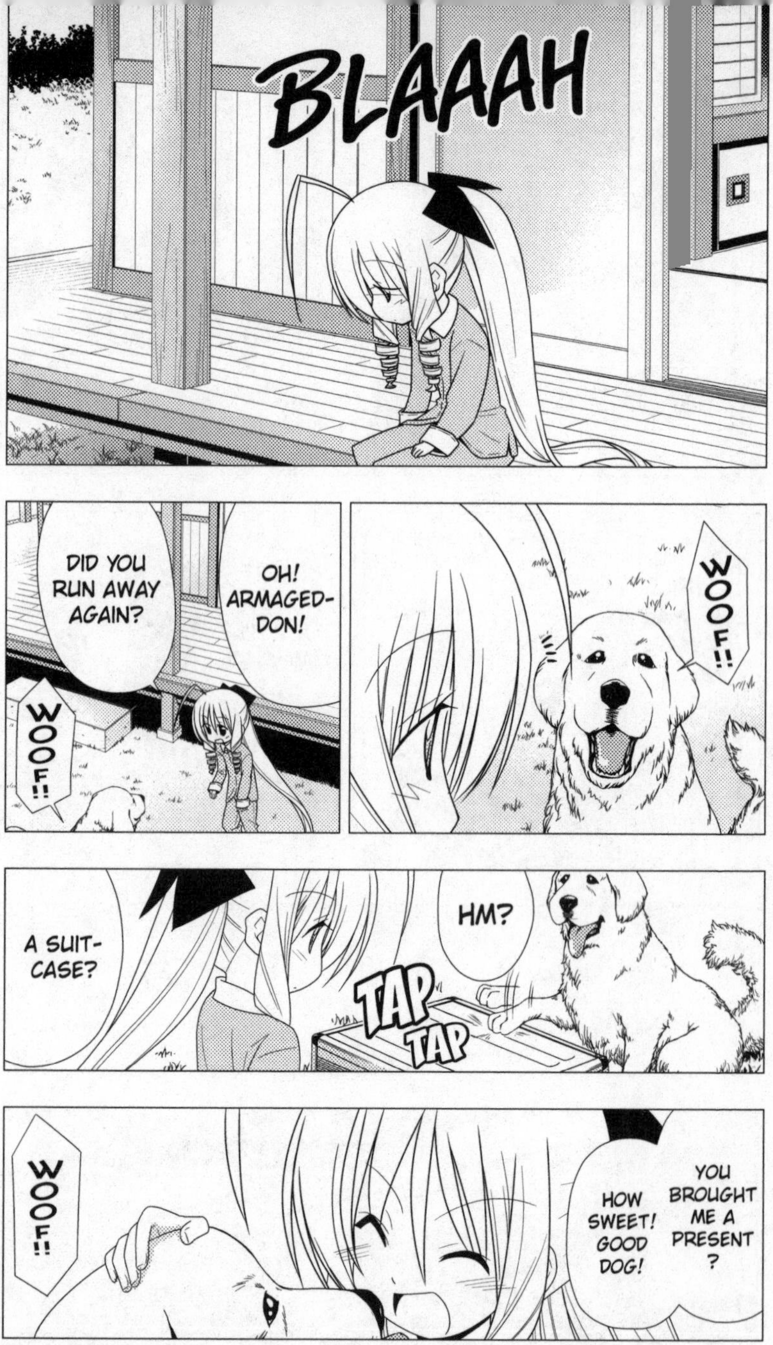
BLAAAH
OH! ARMAGED-DON!
DID YOU RUN AWAY AGAIN?
WOOF!!
WOOF!!
HM?
TAP TAP
A SUIT-CASE?
YOU BROUGHT ME A PRESENT?
HOW SWEET! GOOD DOG!
WOOF!!

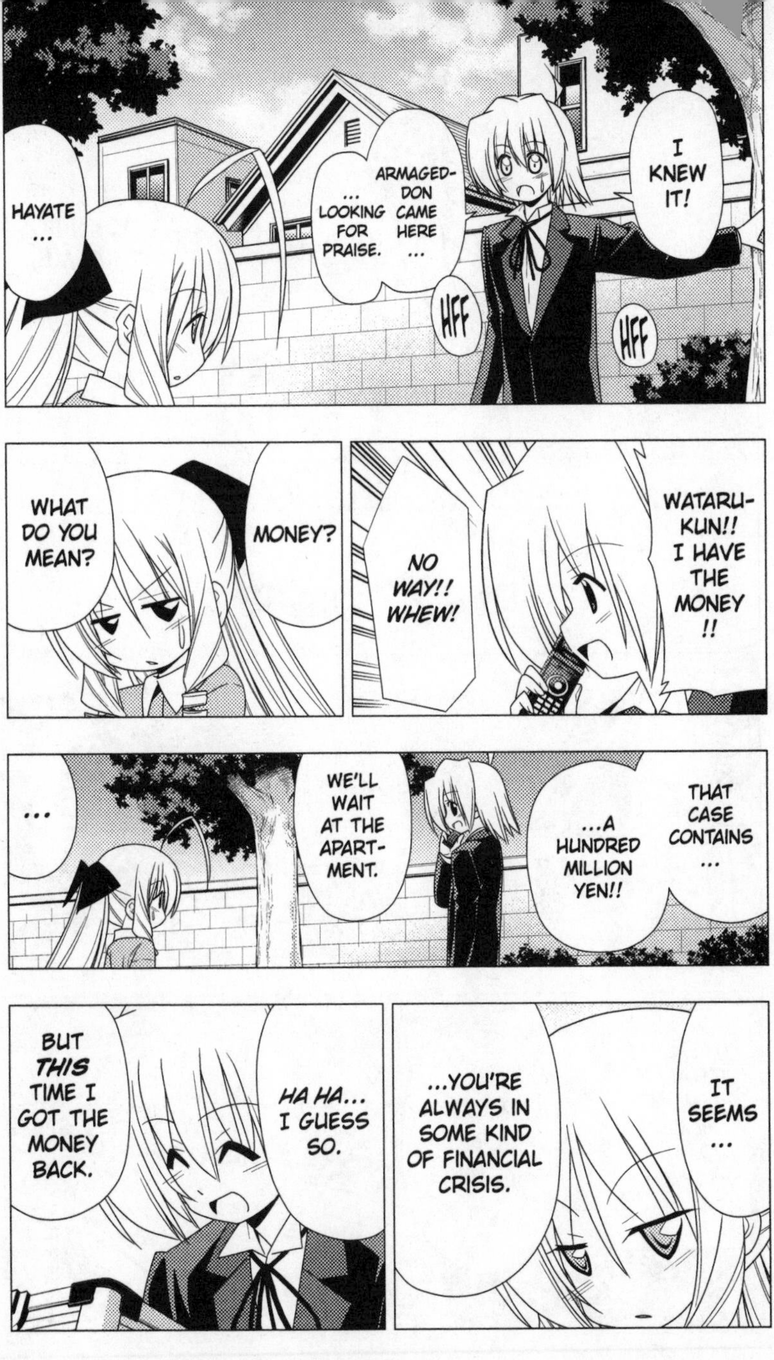
I KNEW IT!
ARMAGED-DON CAME HERE ... ... LOOKING FOR PRAISE.
HFF
HFF
HAYATE ...
WATARU-KUN!! I HAVE THE MONEY !!
NO WAY!! WHEW!
MONEY?
WHAT DO YOU MEAN?
THAT CASE CONTAINS ...
...A HUNDRED MILLION YEN!!
WE'LL WAIT AT THE APART-MENT.
...
IT SEEMS ...
...YOU'RE ALWAYS IN SOME KIND OF FINANCIAL CRISIS.
HA HA... I GUESS SO.
BUT *THIS* TIME I GOT THE MONEY BACK.

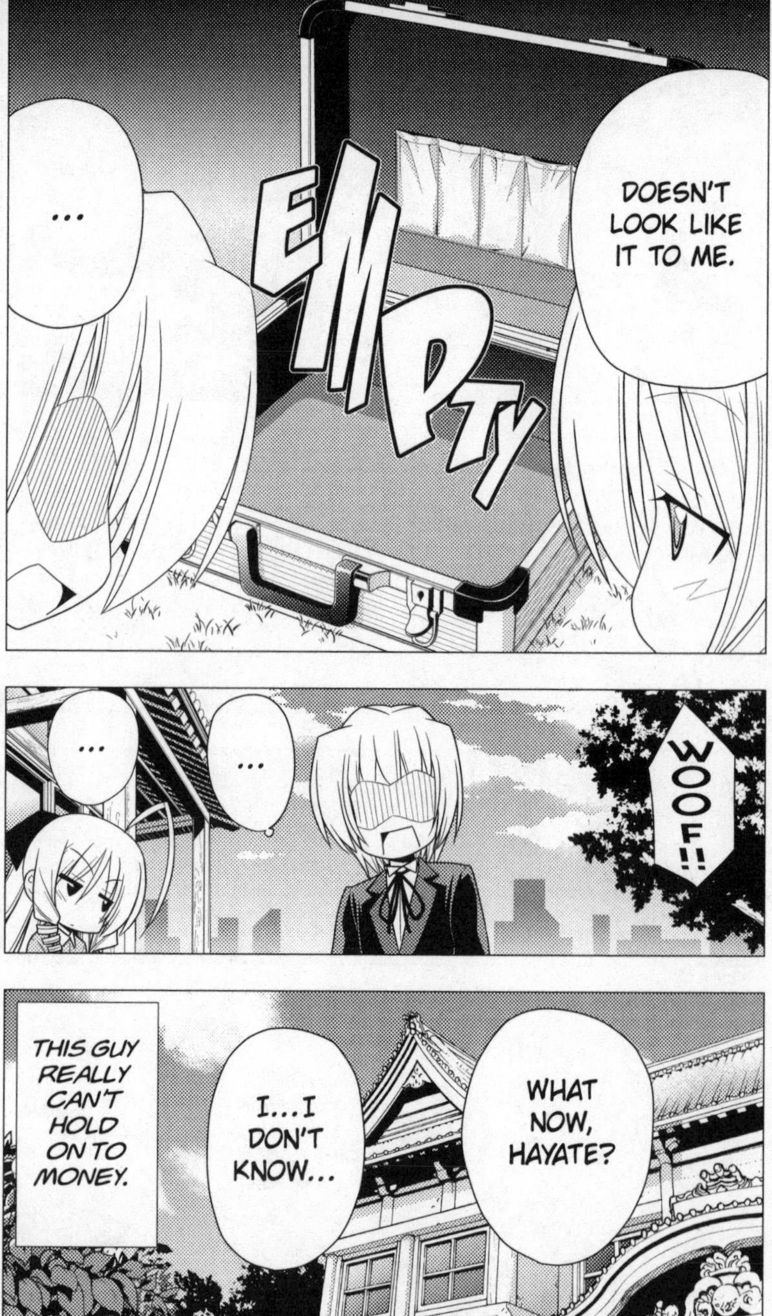
DOESN'T LOOK LIKE IT TO ME.
EMPTY
...
WOOF!!
...
...
WHAT NOW, HAYATE?
I...I DON'T KNOW...
THIS GUY REALLY CAN'T HOLD ON TO MONEY.

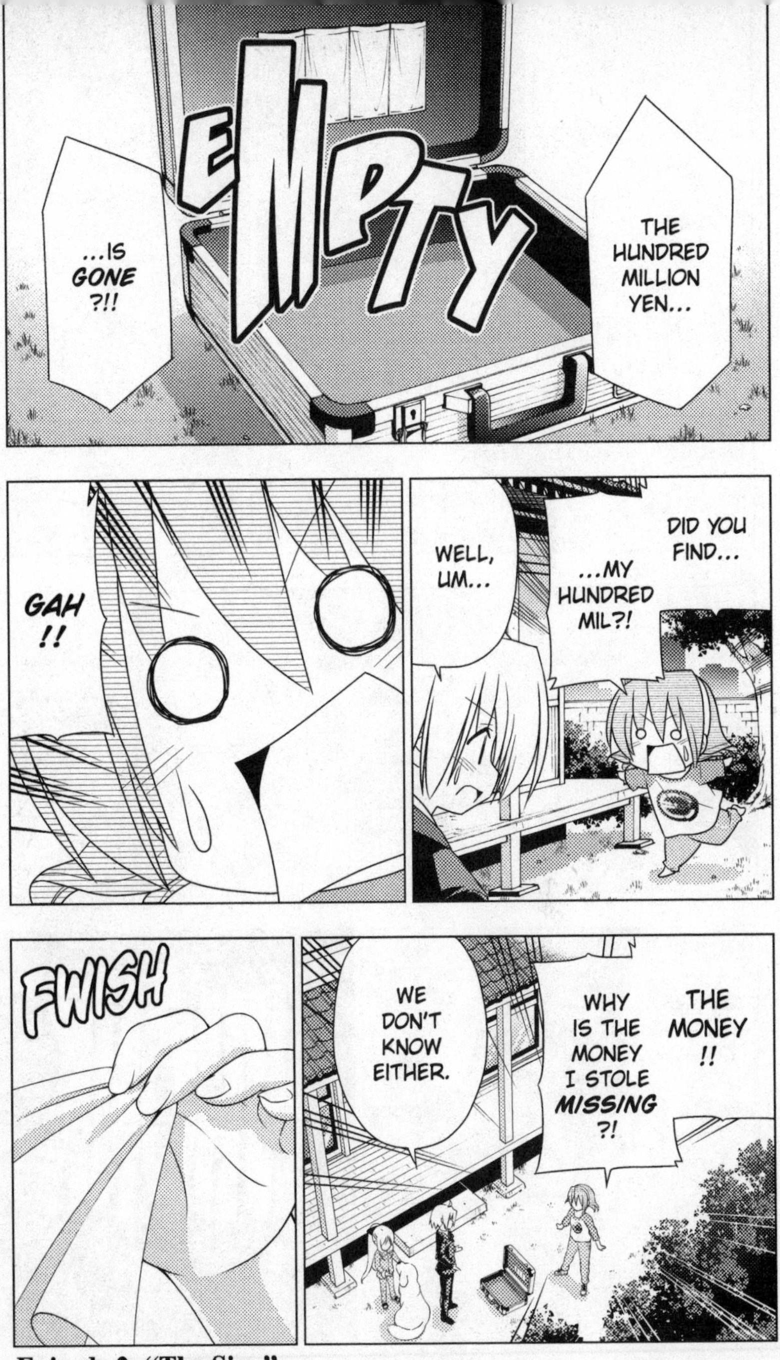
THE HUNDRED MILLION YEN...
EMPTY
...IS GONE ?!!
DID YOU FIND...
...MY HUNDRED MIL?!
WELL, UM...
GAH !!
THE MONEY !!
WHY IS THE MONEY I STOLE MISSING ?!
WE DON'T KNOW EITHER.
FWISH

Episode 2: “The Sign”

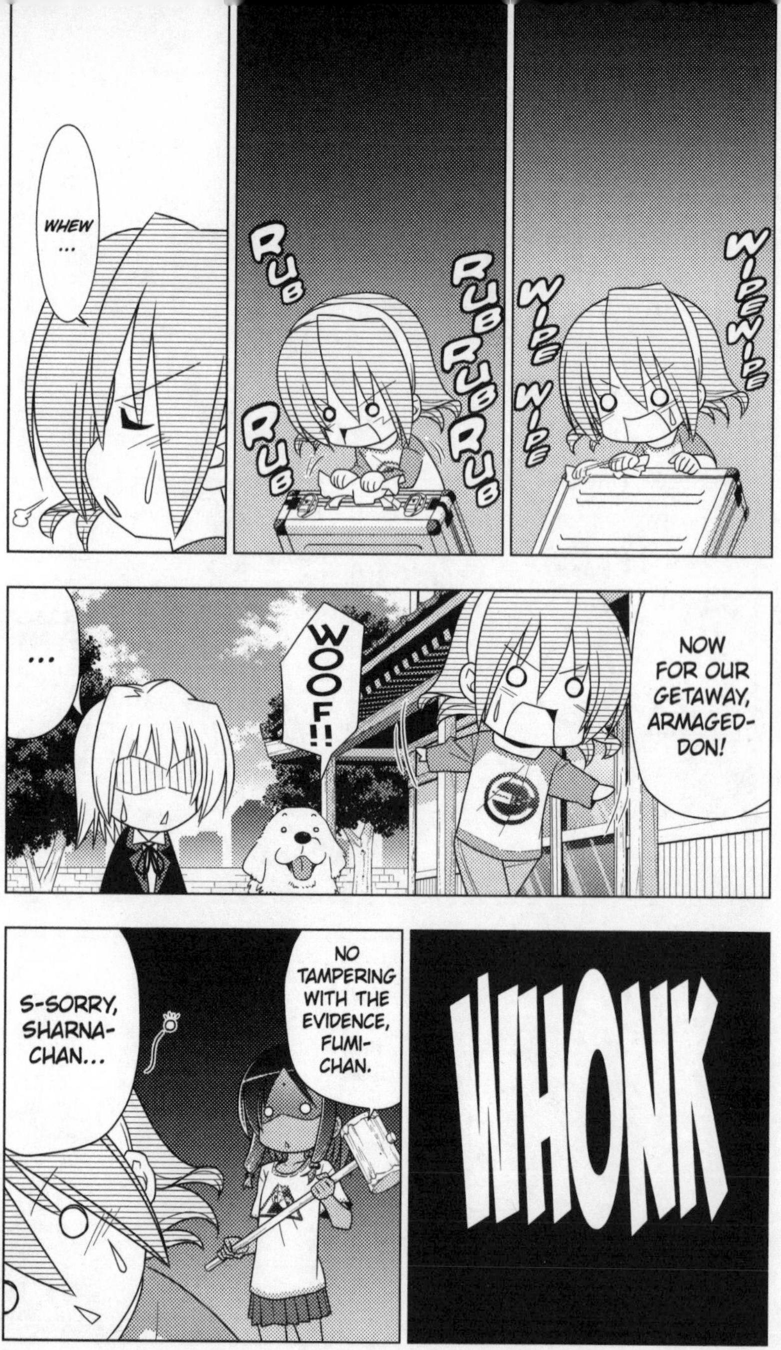

WIPEWIPE
WIPE WIPE
RUBRUBRUBRUB
RUB
RUB
WHEW...
NOW FOR OUR GETAWAY, ARMAGED-DON!
WOOF!!
...
WHONK
NO TAMPERING WITH THE EVIDENCE, FUMI-CHAN.
S-SORRY, SHARNA-CHAN...

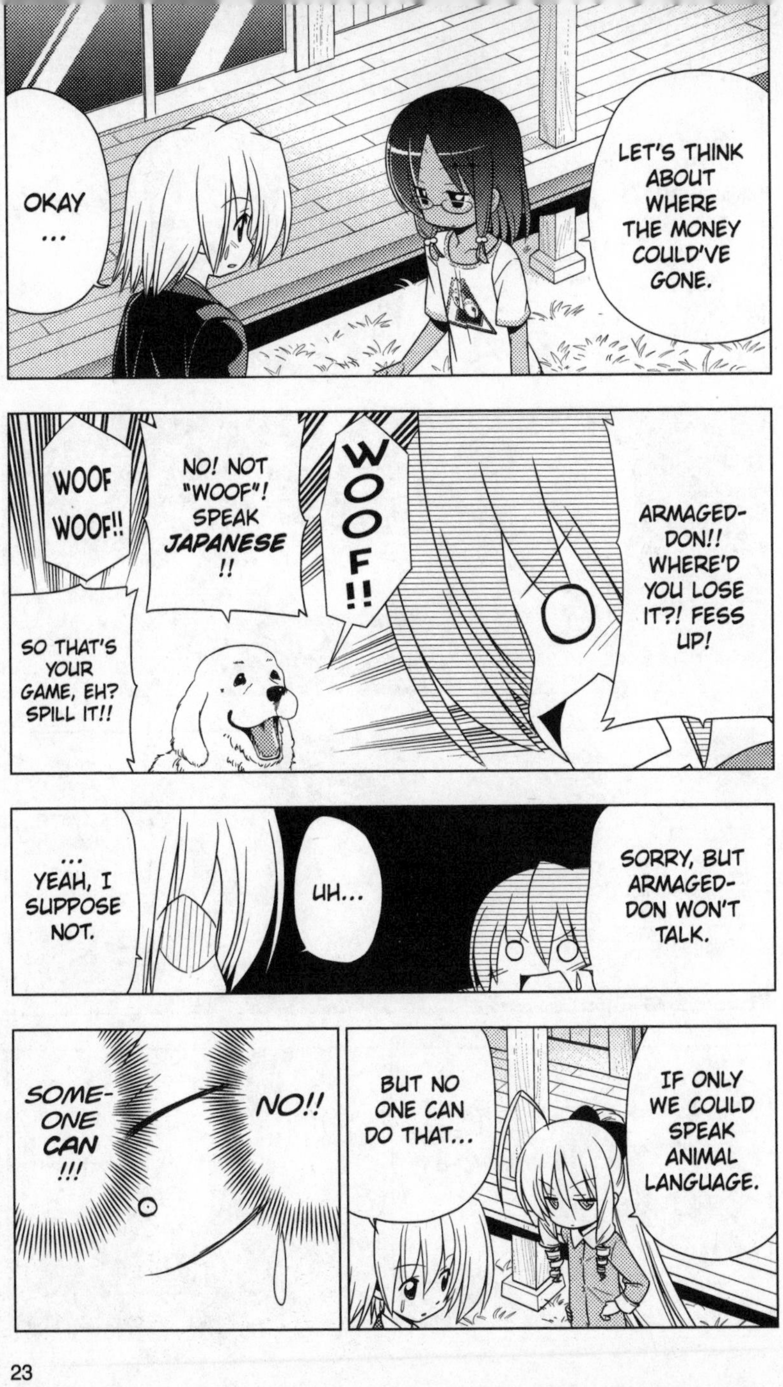
LET'S THINK ABOUT WHERE THE MONEY COULD'VE GONE.
OKAY ...
ARMAGED-DON!! WHERE'D YOU LOSE IT?! FESS UP!
WOOF!!
NO! NOT "WOOF"! SPEAK JAPANESE!!
WOOF WOOF!!
SO THAT'S YOUR GAME, EH? SPILL IT!!
SORRY, BUT ARMAGED-DON WON'T TALK.
UH...
... YEAH, I SUPPOSE NOT.
IF ONLY WE COULD SPEAK ANIMAL LANGUAGE.
BUT NO ONE CAN DO THAT...
NO!!
SOME-ONE CAN!!!

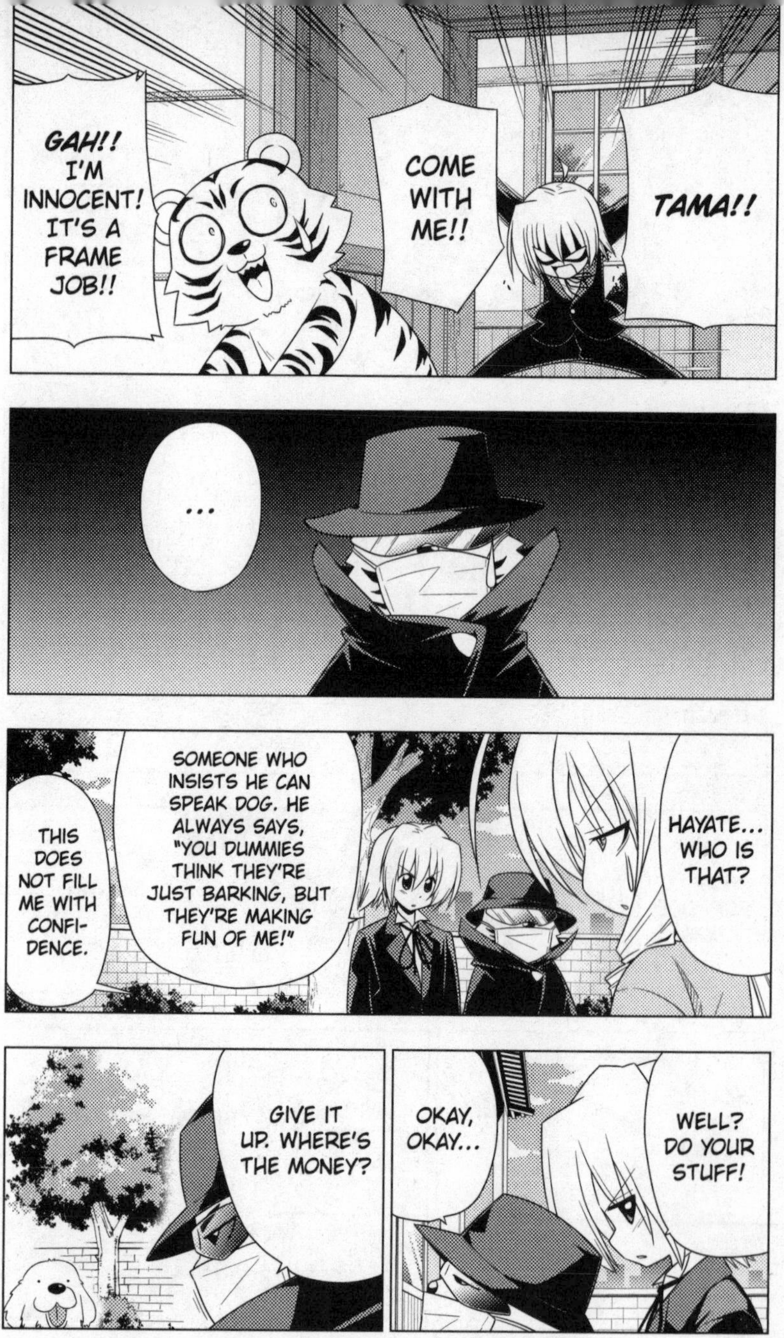
TAMA!!
COME WITH ME!!
GAH!! I'M INNOCENT! IT'S A FRAME JOB!!
...
HAYATE... WHO IS THAT?
SOMEONE WHO INSISTS HE CAN SPEAK DOG. HE ALWAYS SAYS, "YOU DUMMIES THINK THEY'RE JUST BARKING, BUT THEY'RE MAKING FUN OF ME!"
THIS DOES NOT FILL ME WITH CONFI-DENCE.
WELL? DO YOUR STUFF!
OKAY, OKAY...
GIVE IT UP. WHERE'S THE MONEY?

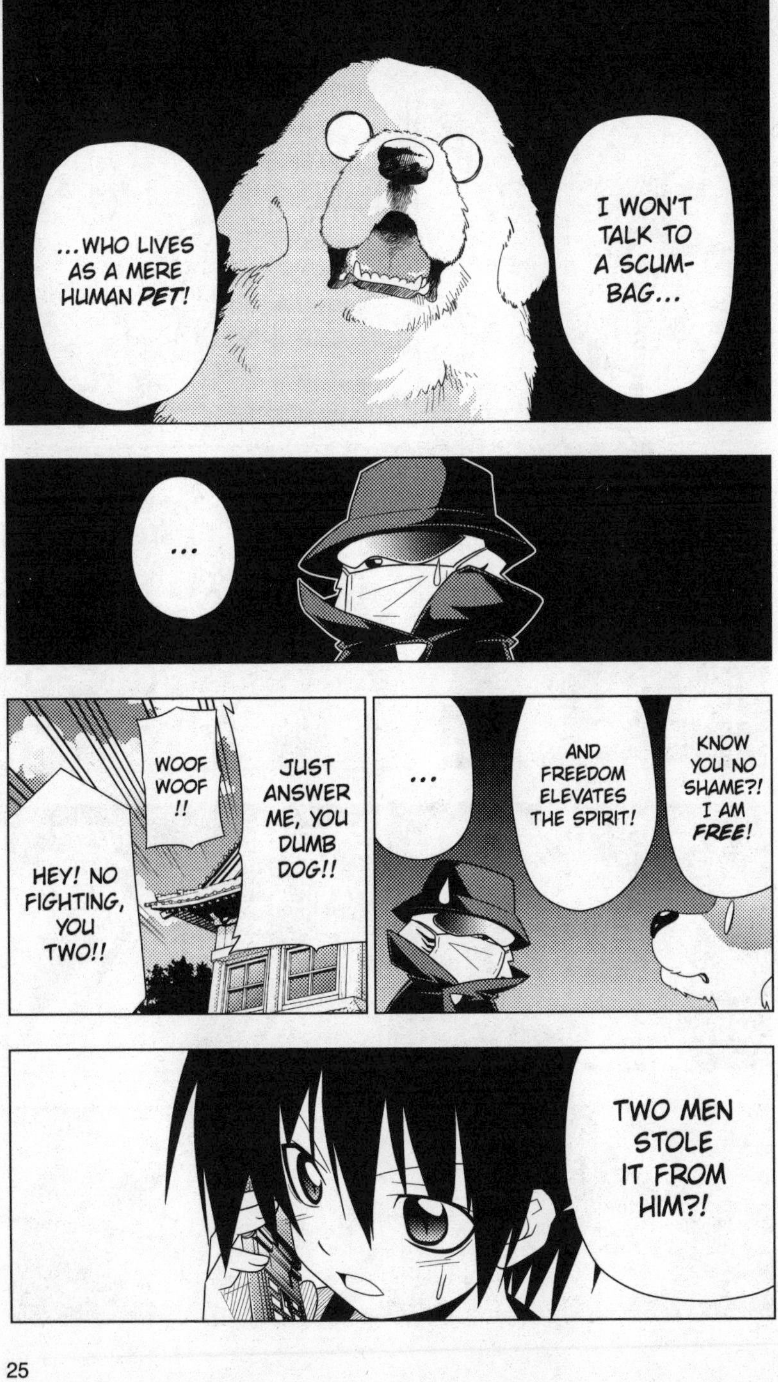
I WON'T TALK TO A SCUM-BAG...
...WHO LIVES AS A MERE HUMAN PET!
...
KNOW YOU NO SHAME?! I AM FREE!
AND FREEDOM ELEVATES THE SPIRIT!
...
JUST ANSWER ME, YOU DUMB DOG!!
WOOF WOOF !!
HEY! NO FIGHTING, YOU TWO!!
TWO MEN STOLE IT FROM HIM?!

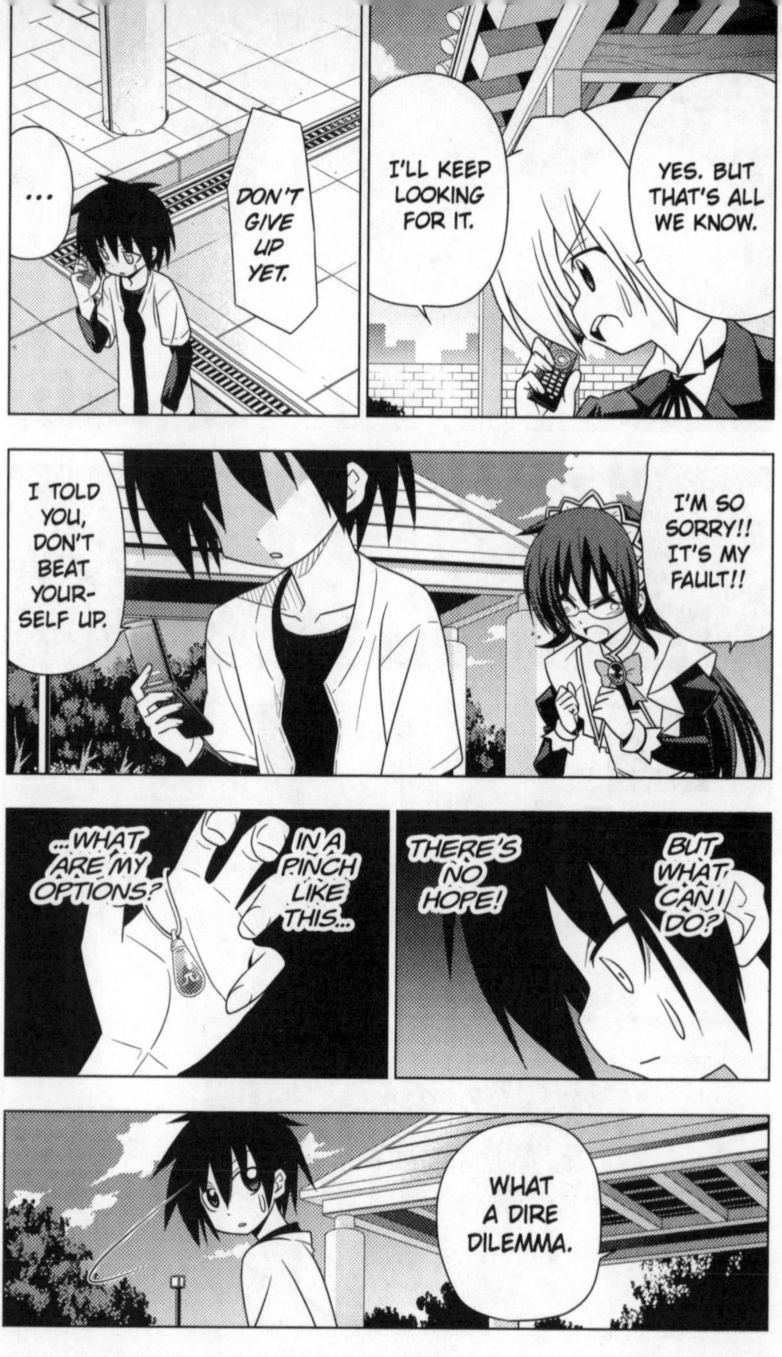
YES. BUT THAT'S ALL WE KNOW.
I'LL KEEP LOOKING FOR IT.
DON'T GIVE UP YET.
...
I'M SO SORRY!! IT'S MY FAULT!!
I TOLD YOU, DON'T BEAT YOUR-SELF UP.
BUT WHAT CAN I DO?
THERE'S NO HOPE!
IN A PINCH LIKE THIS...
...WHAT ARE MY OPTIONS?
WHAT A DIRE DILEMMA.

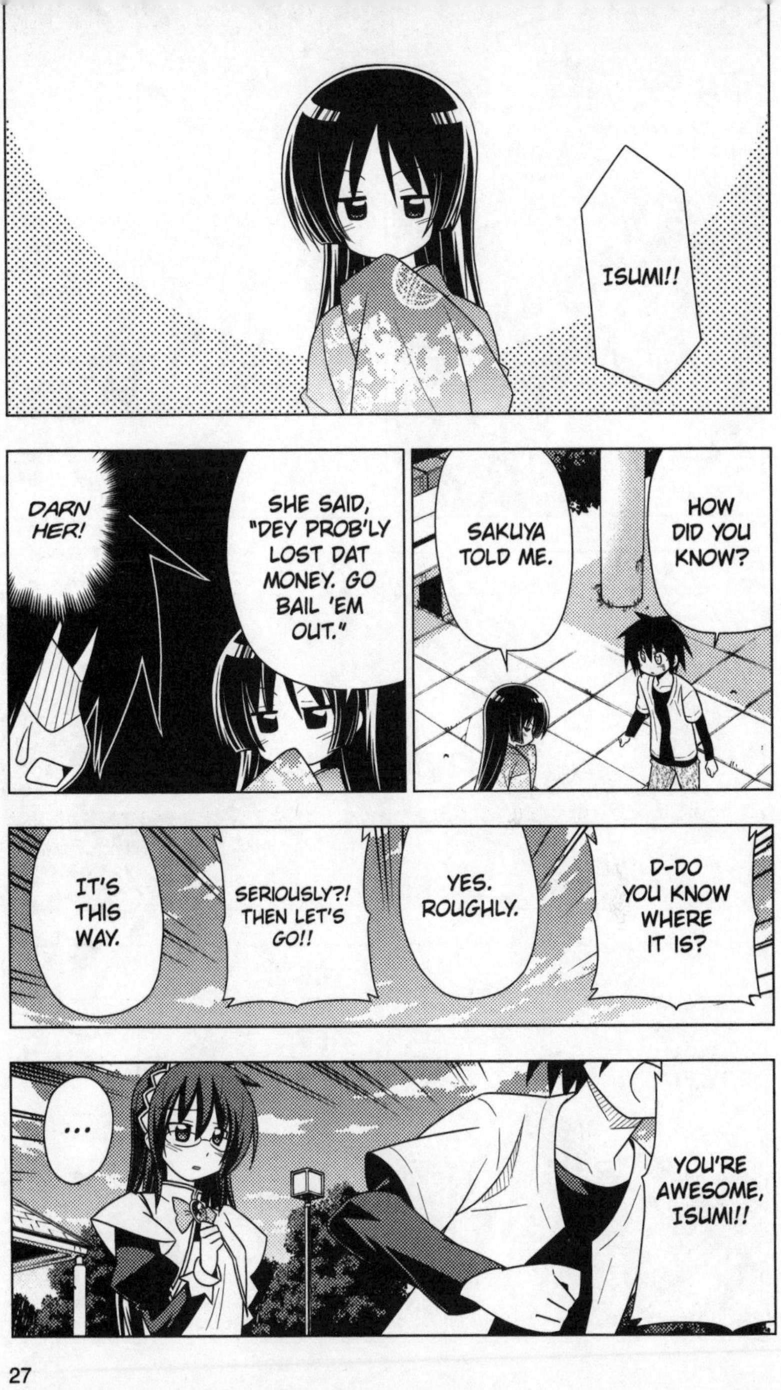
ISUMI!!
HOW DID YOU KNOW?
SAKUYA TOLD ME.
SHE SAID, "DEY PROB'LY LOST DAT MONEY. GO BAIL 'EM OUT."
DARN HER!
D-DO YOU KNOW WHERE IT IS?
YES. ROUGHLY.
SERIOUSLY?! THEN LET'S GO!!
IT'S THIS WAY.
YOU'RE AWESOME, ISUMI!!
...

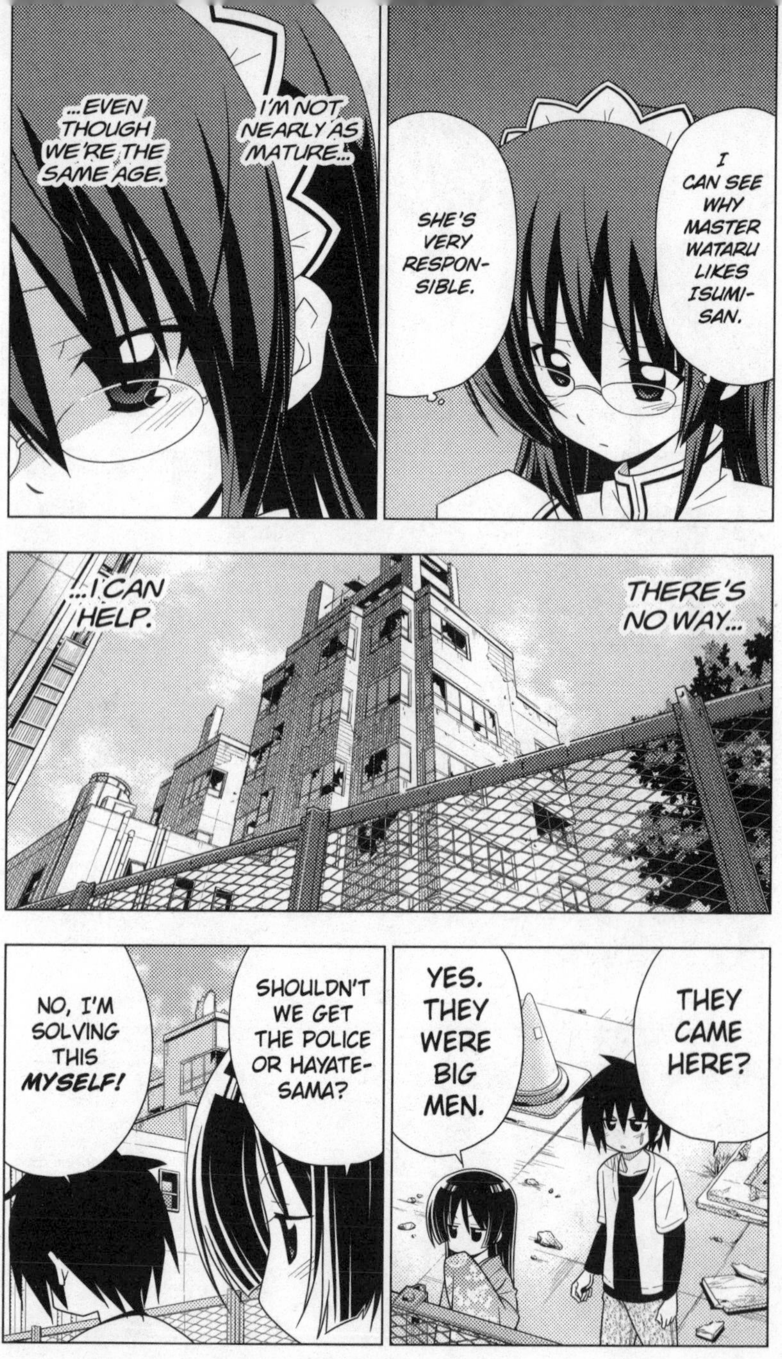
I CAN SEE WHY MASTER WATARU LIKES ISUMI-SAN.
SHE'S VERY RESPONSIBLE.
I'M NOT NEARLY AS MATURE...
...EVEN THOUGH WE'RE THE SAME AGE.
THERE'S NO WAY...
...I CAN HELP.
THEY CAME HERE?
YES. THEY WERE BIG MEN.
SHOULDN'T WE GET THE POLICE OR HAYATE-SAMA?
NO, I'M SOLVING THIS *MYSELF!*

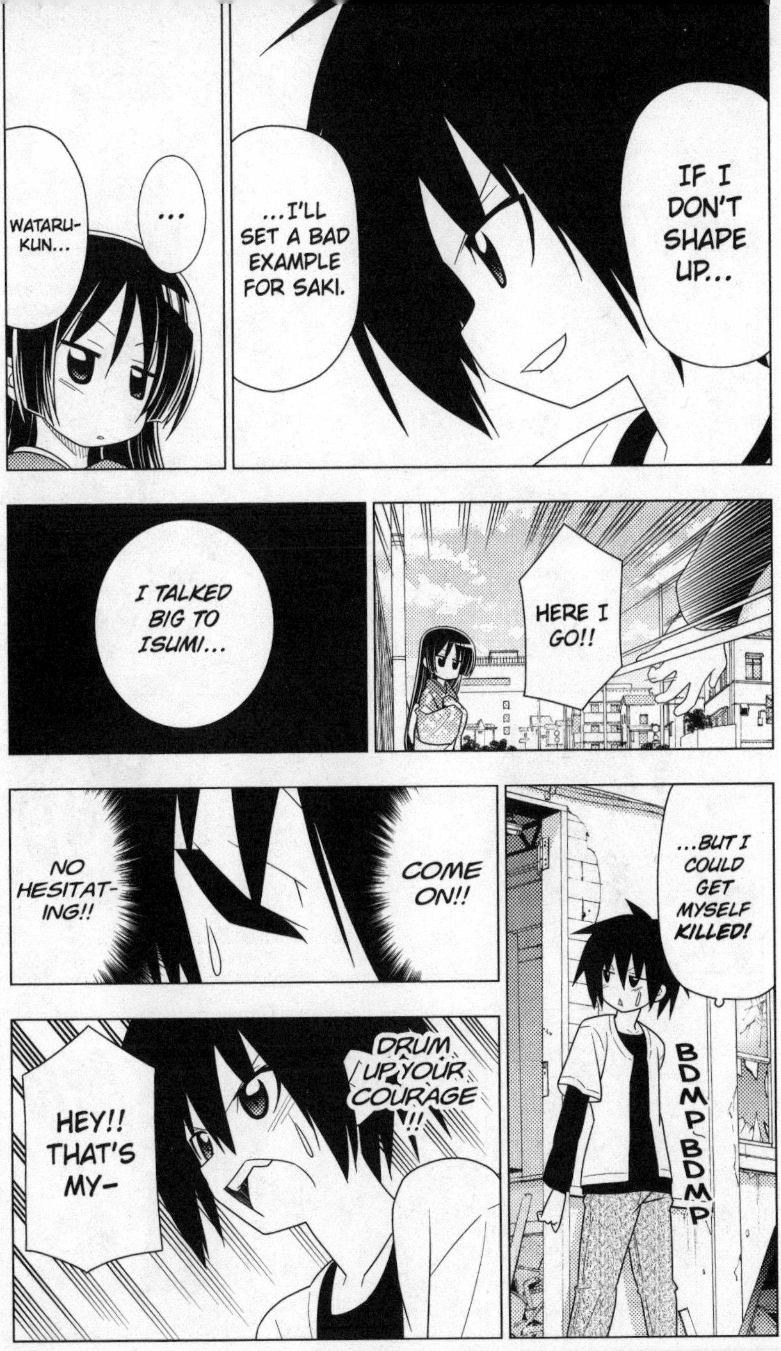
IF I DON'T SHAPE UP...
...I'LL SET A BAD EXAMPLE FOR SAKI.
...
WATARU-KUN...
HERE I GO!!
I TALKED BIG TO ISUMI...
...BUT I COULD GET MYSELF KILLED!
BDMP BDMP
COME ON!!
NO HESITATING!!
DRUM UP YOUR COURAGE!!
HEY!! THAT'S MY-

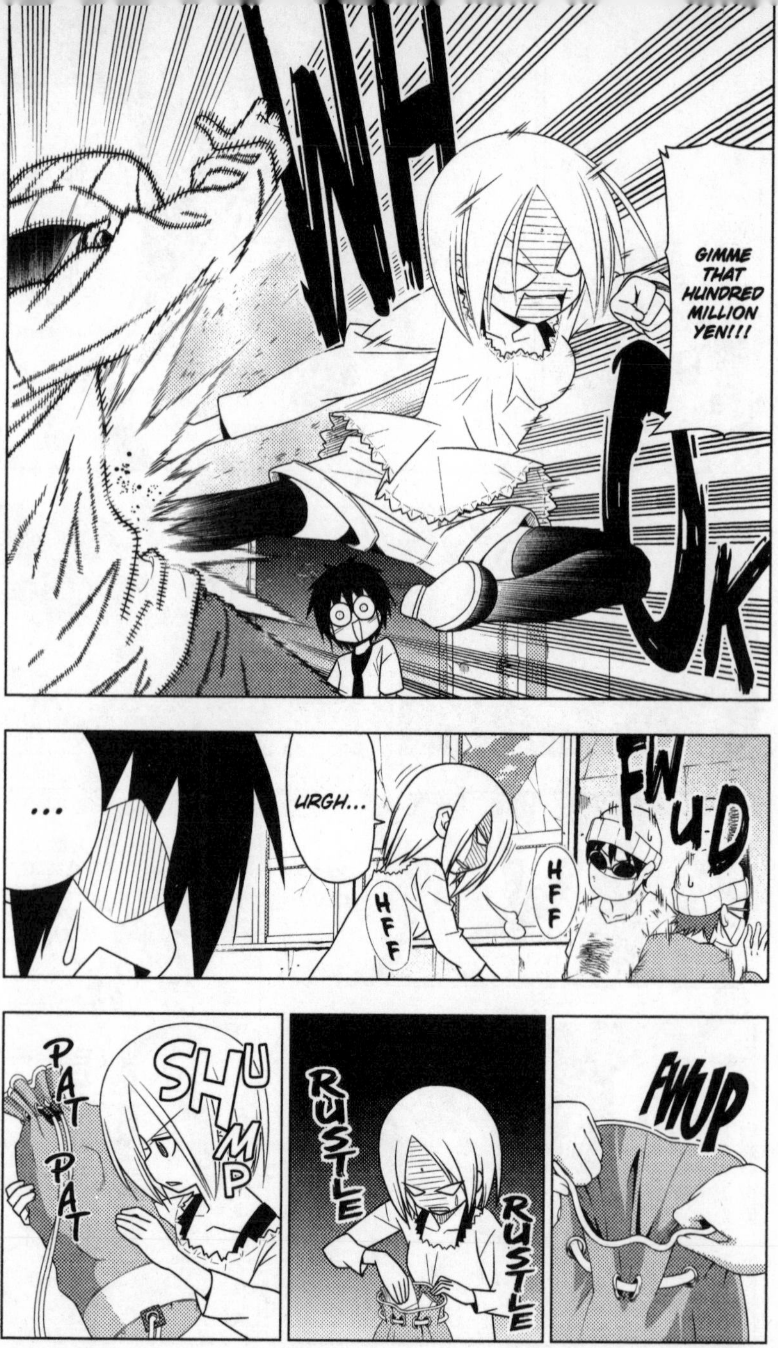
GIMME THAT HUNDRED MILLION YEN!!!
WHUK
FWUD
HFF
URGH...
HFF
...
FWUP
RUSTLE
RUSTLE
SHUMP
PAT PAT

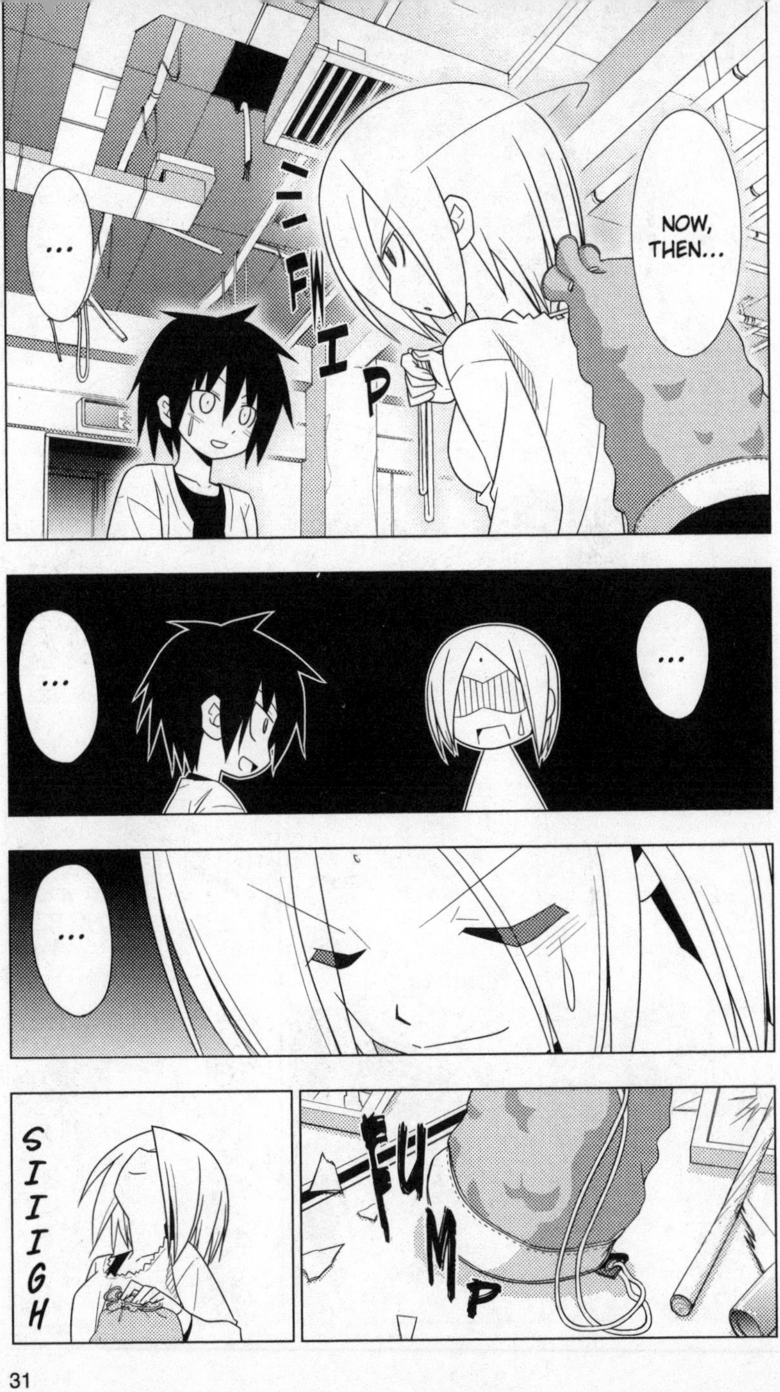
NOW, THEN...
FWIP
...
...
...
...
FUMP
SIIIGH

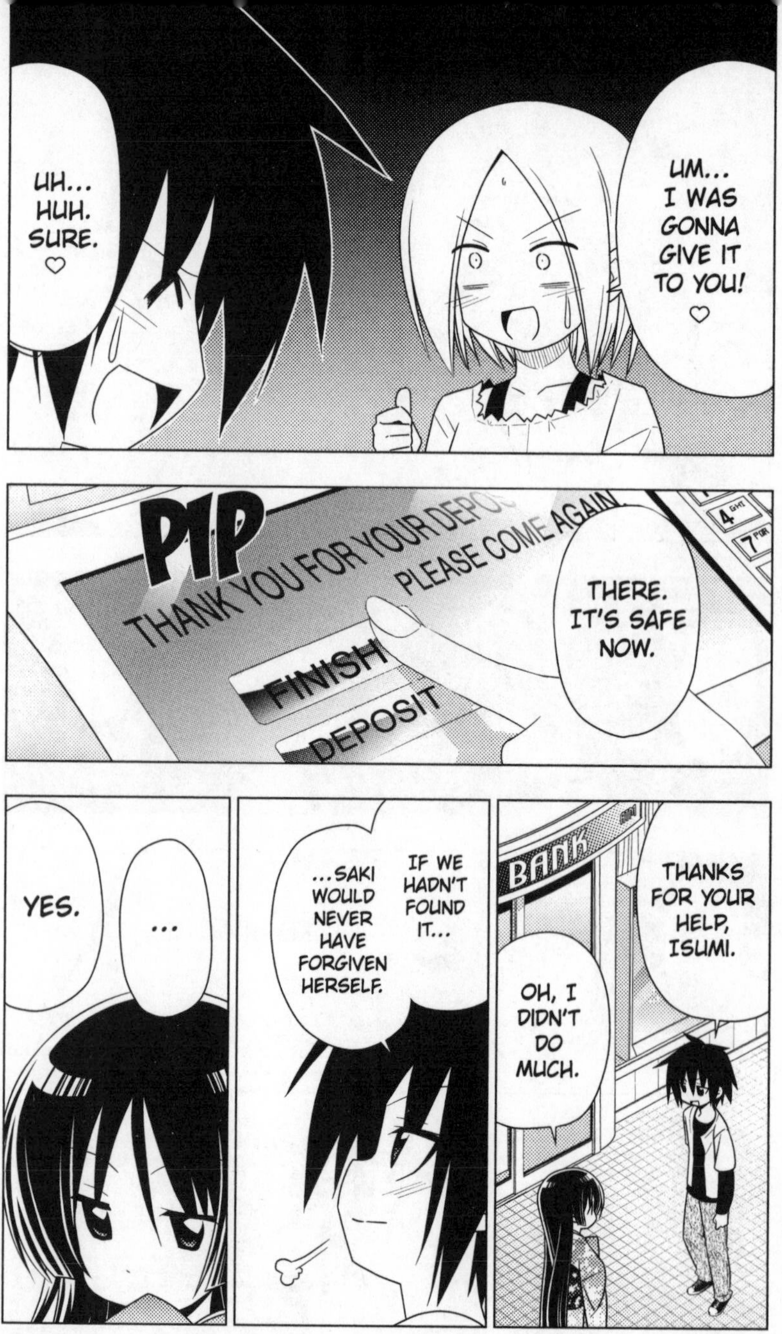
UM... I WAS GONNA GIVE IT TO YOU! ♡
UH... HUH. SURE. ♡
PIP
THANK YOU FOR YOUR DEPOS
PLEASE COME AGAIN.
THERE. IT'S SAFE NOW.
FINISH
DEPOSIT
BANK
THANKS FOR YOUR HELP, ISUMI.
OH, I DIDN'T DO MUCH.
IF WE HADN'T FOUND IT...
...SAKI WOULD NEVER HAVE FORGIVEN HERSELF.
...
YES.

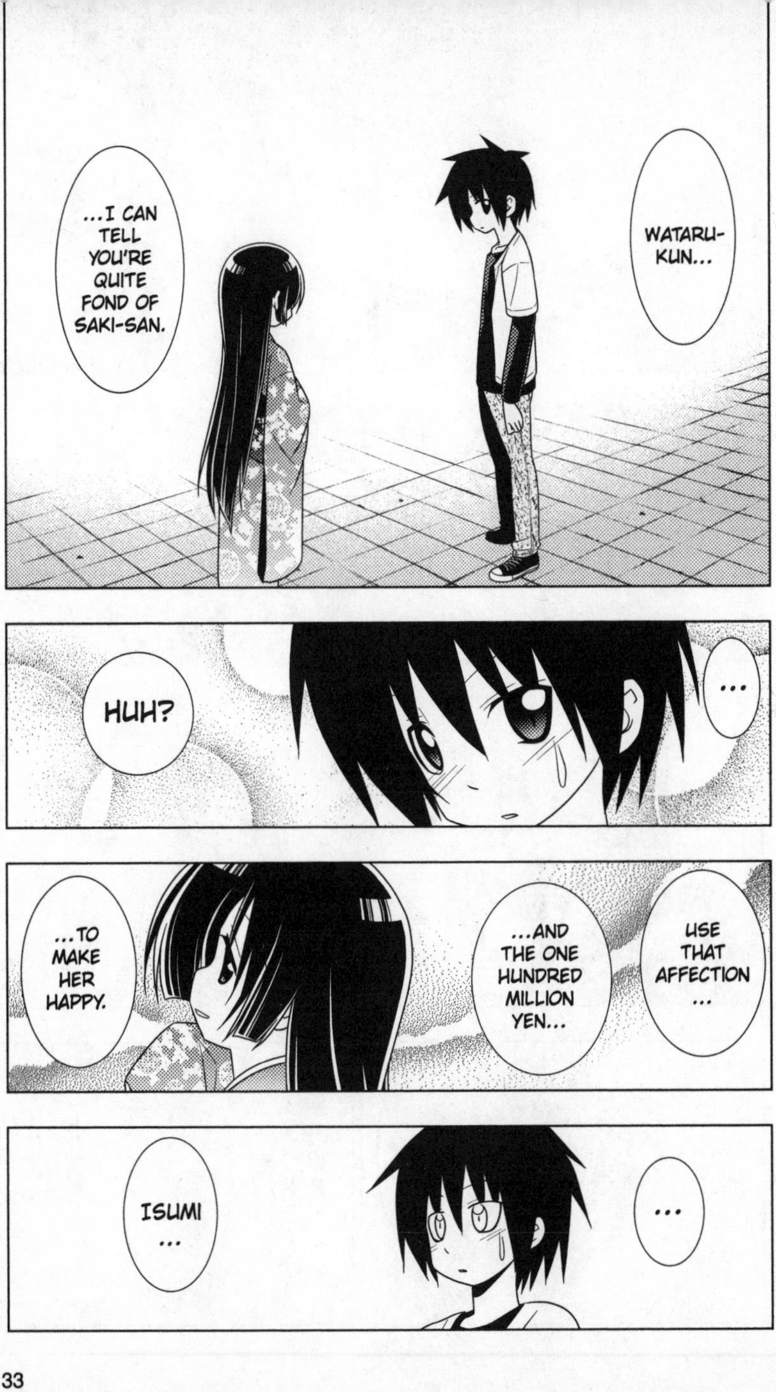
WATARU-KUN...
...I CAN TELL YOU'RE QUITE FOND OF SAKI-SAN.
...
HUH?
USE THAT AFFECTION ...
...AND THE ONE HUNDRED MILLION YEN...
...TO MAKE HER HAPPY.
...
ISUMI ...

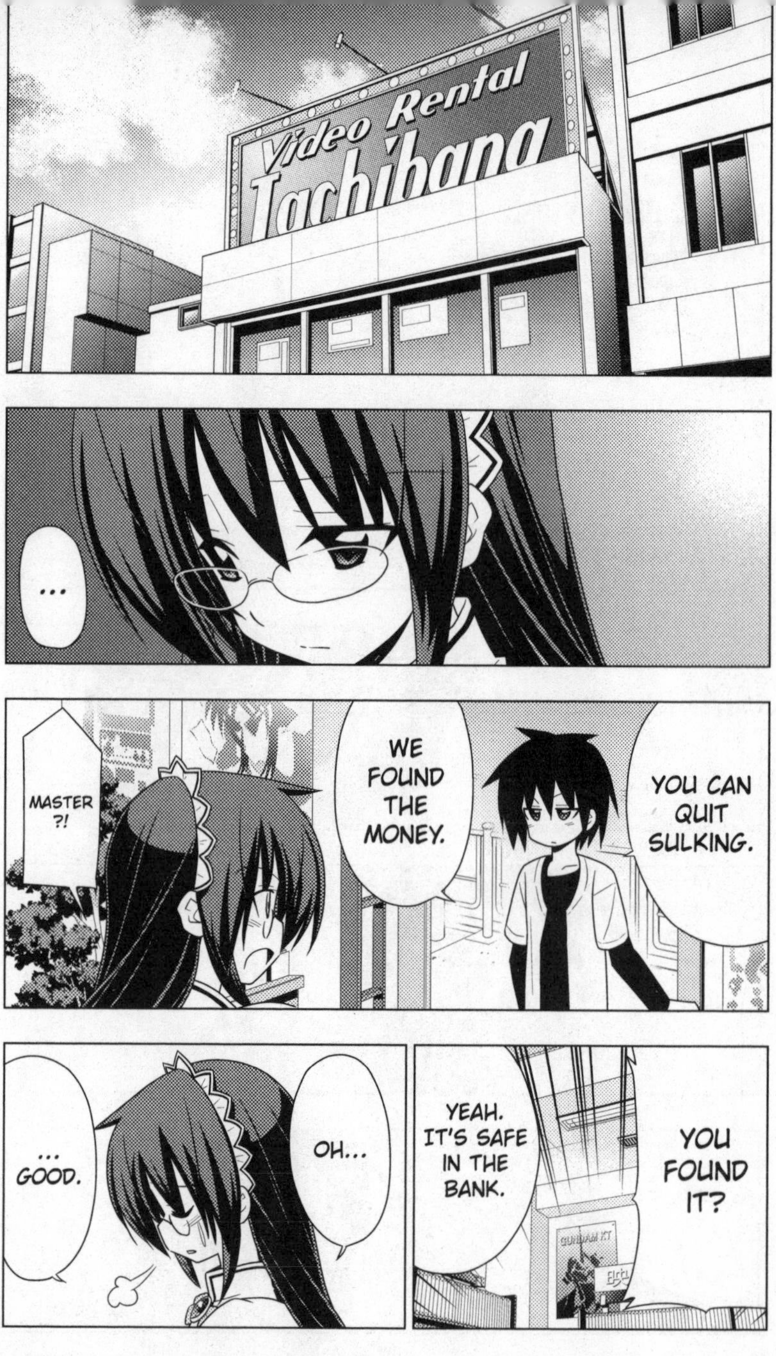
Video Rental
Tachibana
...
YOU CAN QUIT SULKING.
WE FOUND THE MONEY.
MASTER ?!
YOU FOUND IT?
YEAH. IT'S SAFE IN THE BANK.
OH...
... GOOD.

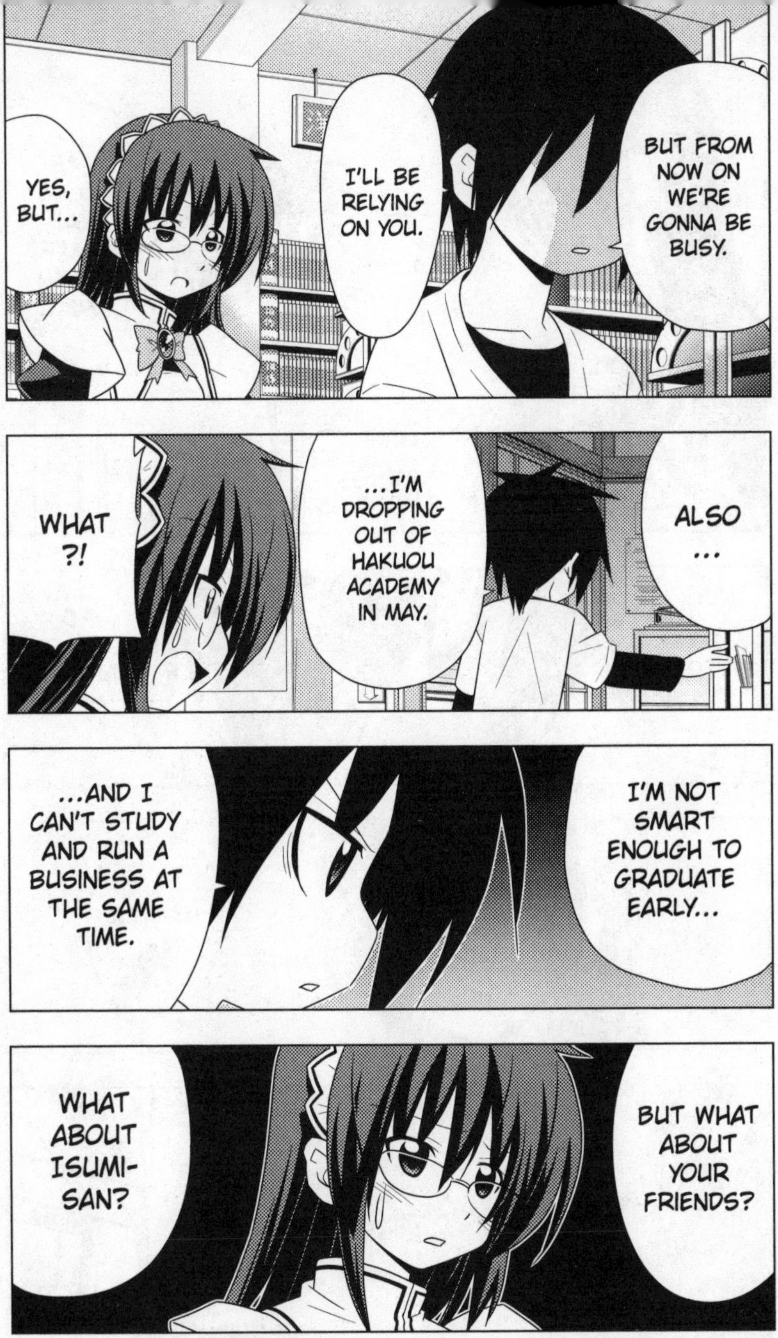
BUT FROM NOW ON WE'RE GONNA BE BUSY.
I'LL BE RELYING ON YOU.
YES, BUT...
ALSO ...
...I'M DROPPING OUT OF HAKUOU ACADEMY IN MAY.
WHAT ?!
I'M NOT SMART ENOUGH TO GRADUATE EARLY...
...AND I CAN'T STUDY AND RUN A BUSINESS AT THE SAME TIME.
BUT WHAT ABOUT YOUR FRIENDS?
WHAT ABOUT ISUMI-SAN?

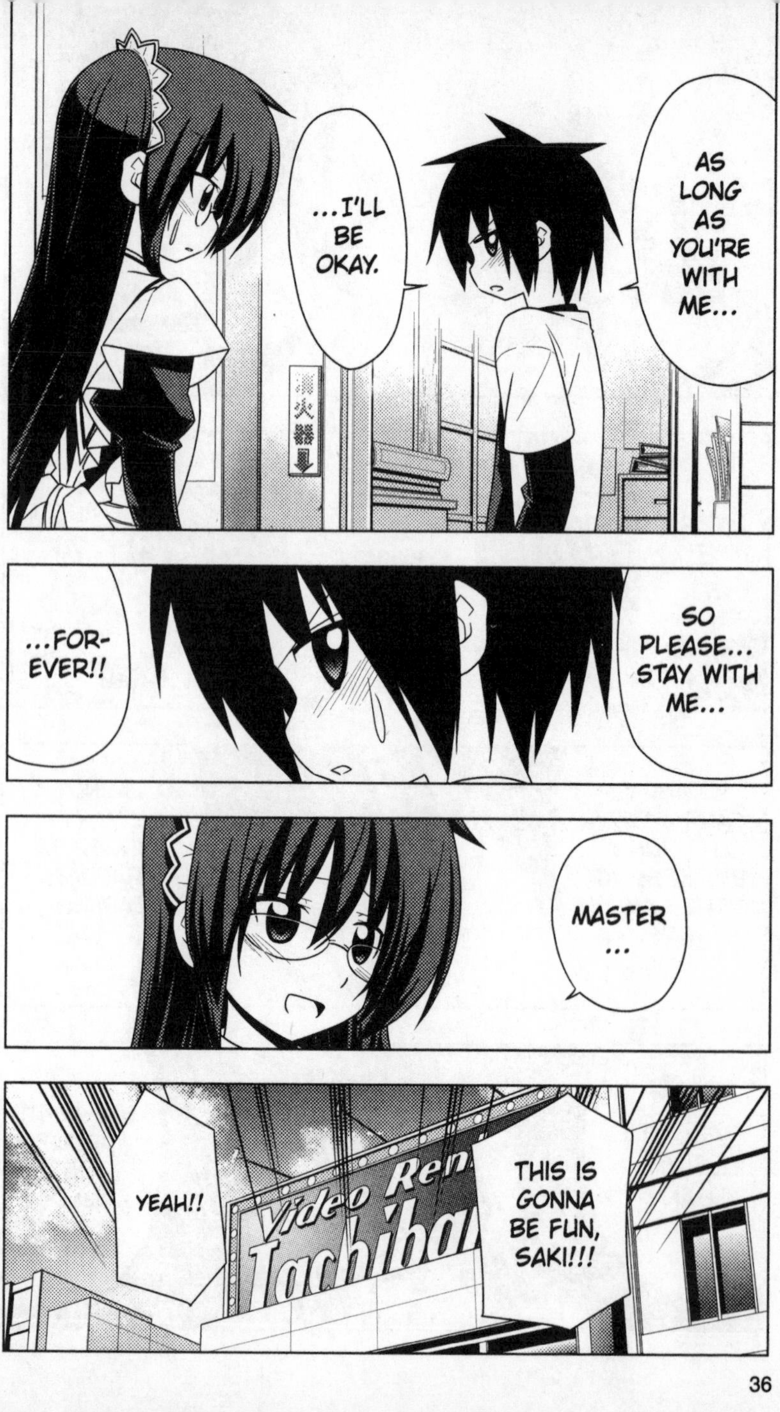
AS LONG AS YOU'RE WITH ME...
...I'LL BE OKAY.
SO PLEASE... STAY WITH ME...
...FOR-EVER!!
MASTER ...
THIS IS GONNA BE FUN, SAKI!!!
YEAH!!

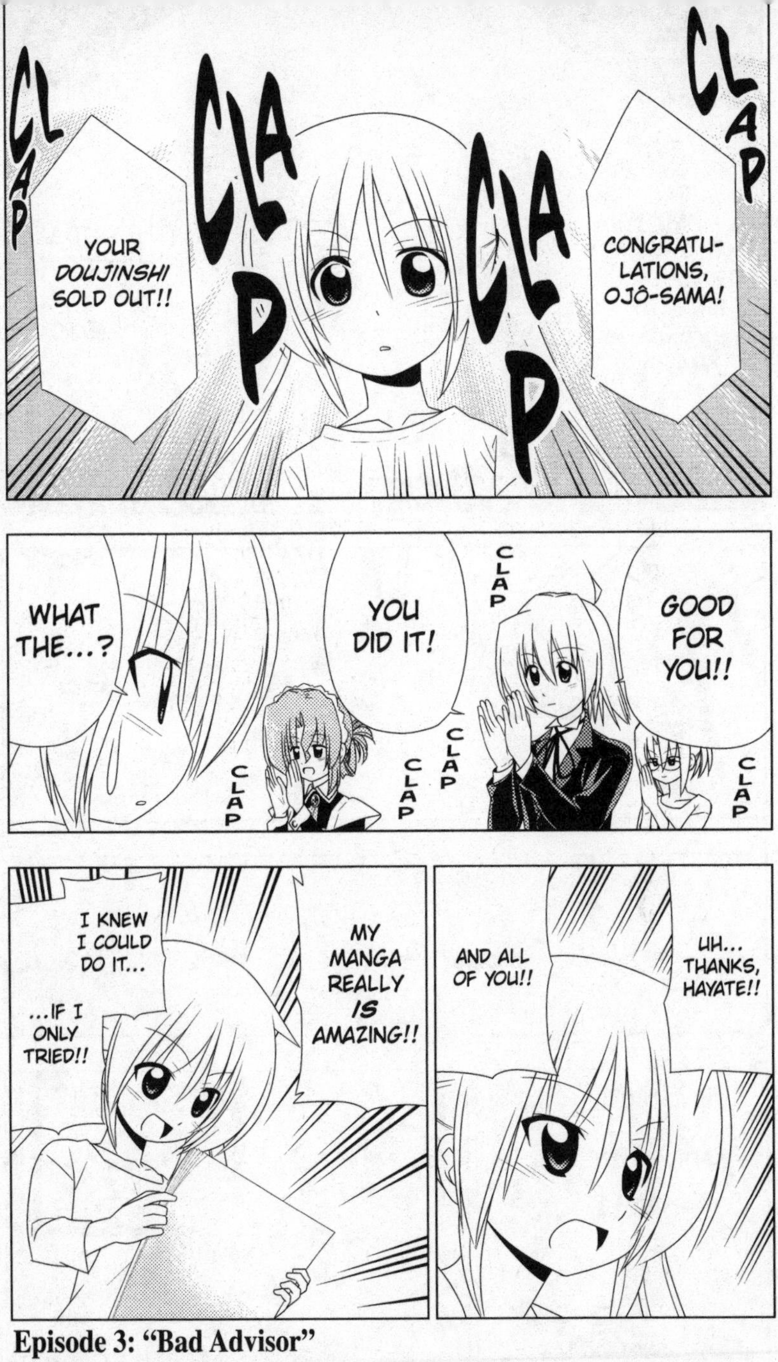
CLAP
CONGRATU-LATIONS, OJÔ-SAMA!
CLAP
CLAP
YOUR DOUJINSHI SOLD OUT!!
CLAP
GOOD FOR YOU!!
CLAP
CLAP
CLAP
YOU DID IT!
CLAP
CLAP
WHAT THE...?
UH... THANKS, HAYATE!!
AND ALL OF YOU!!
MY MANGA REALLY *IS* AMAZING!!
I KNEW I COULD DO IT...
...IF I ONLY TRIED!!

Episode 3: "Bad Advisor"

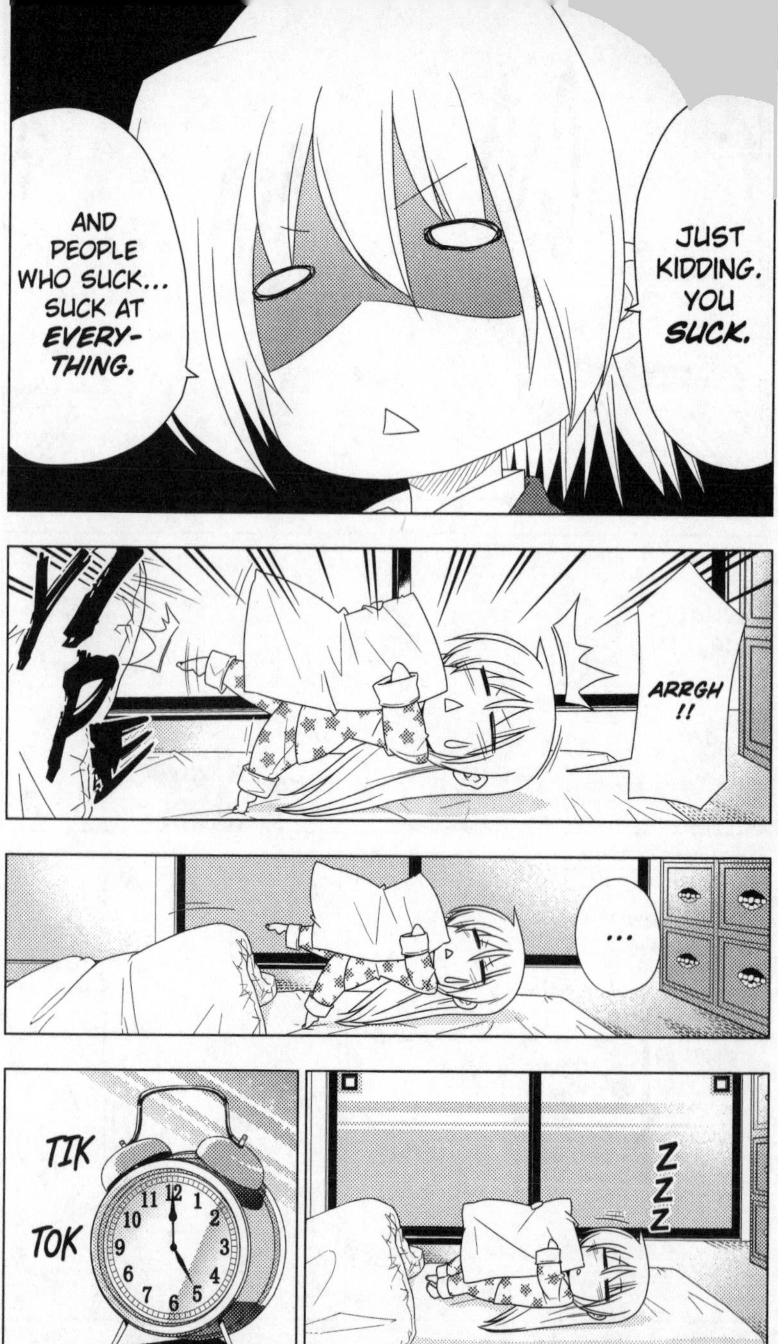
JUST KIDDING. YOU SUCK.
AND PEOPLE WHO SUCK... SUCK AT EVERYTHING.
ARRGH !!
YIPE
...
ZZZ
TIK
TOK

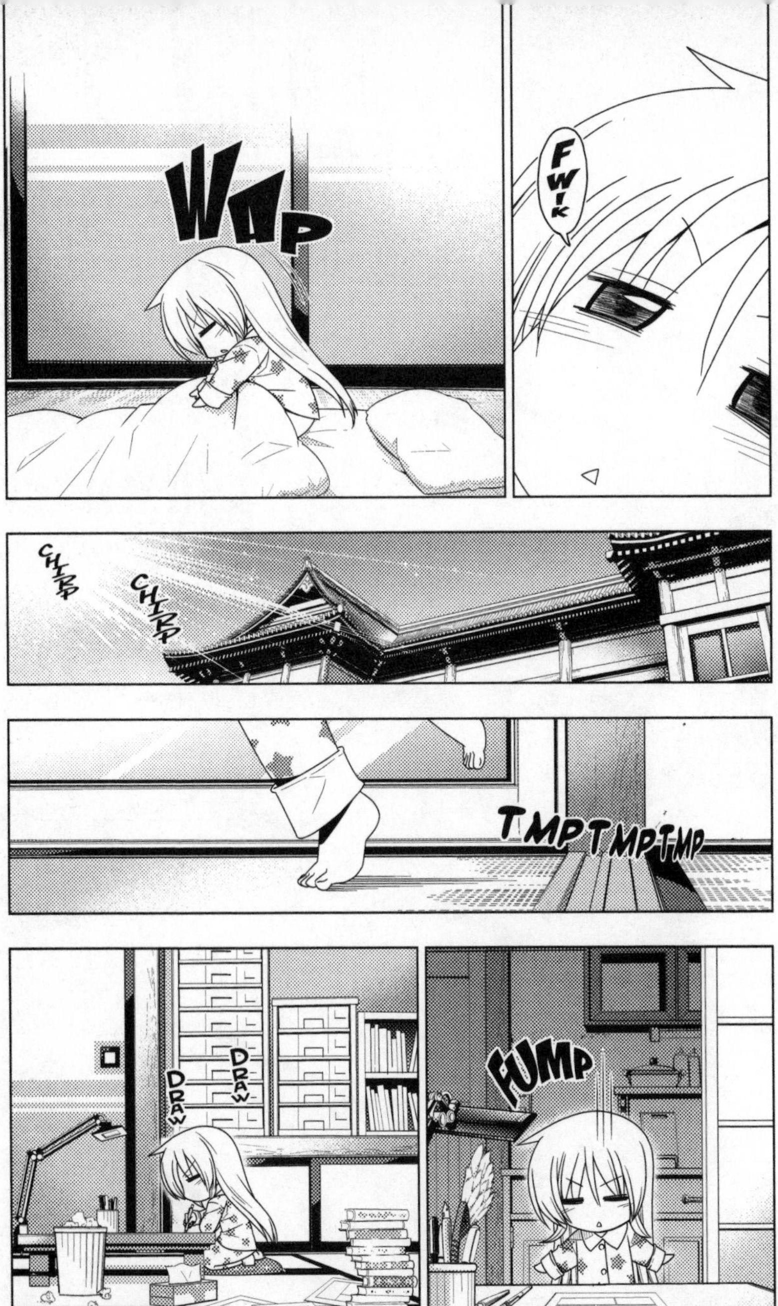
FWIK
WAP
CHIRP
CHIRP
TMP TMP TMP
FUMP
DRAW
DRAW

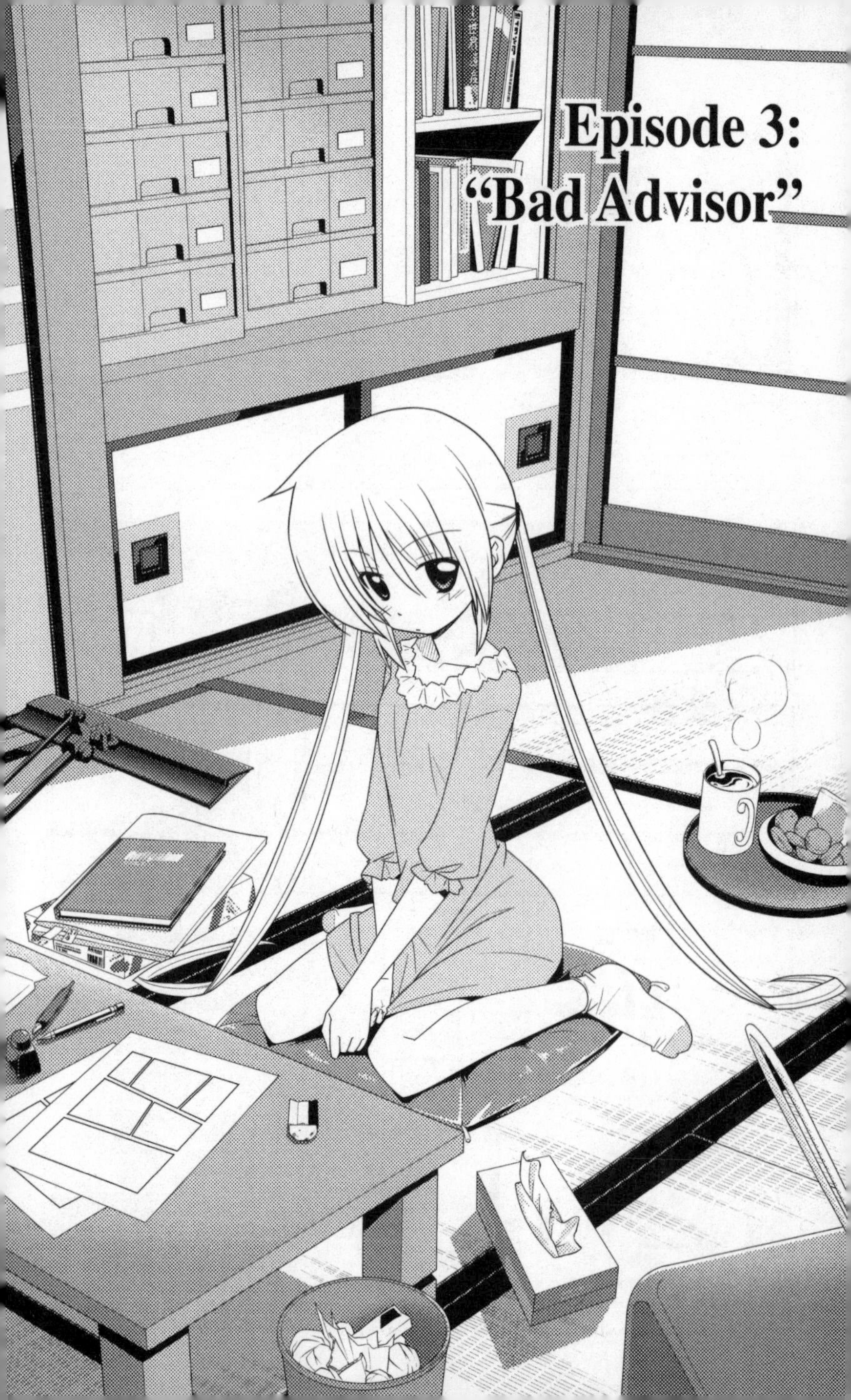
Episode 3:
"Bad Advisor"

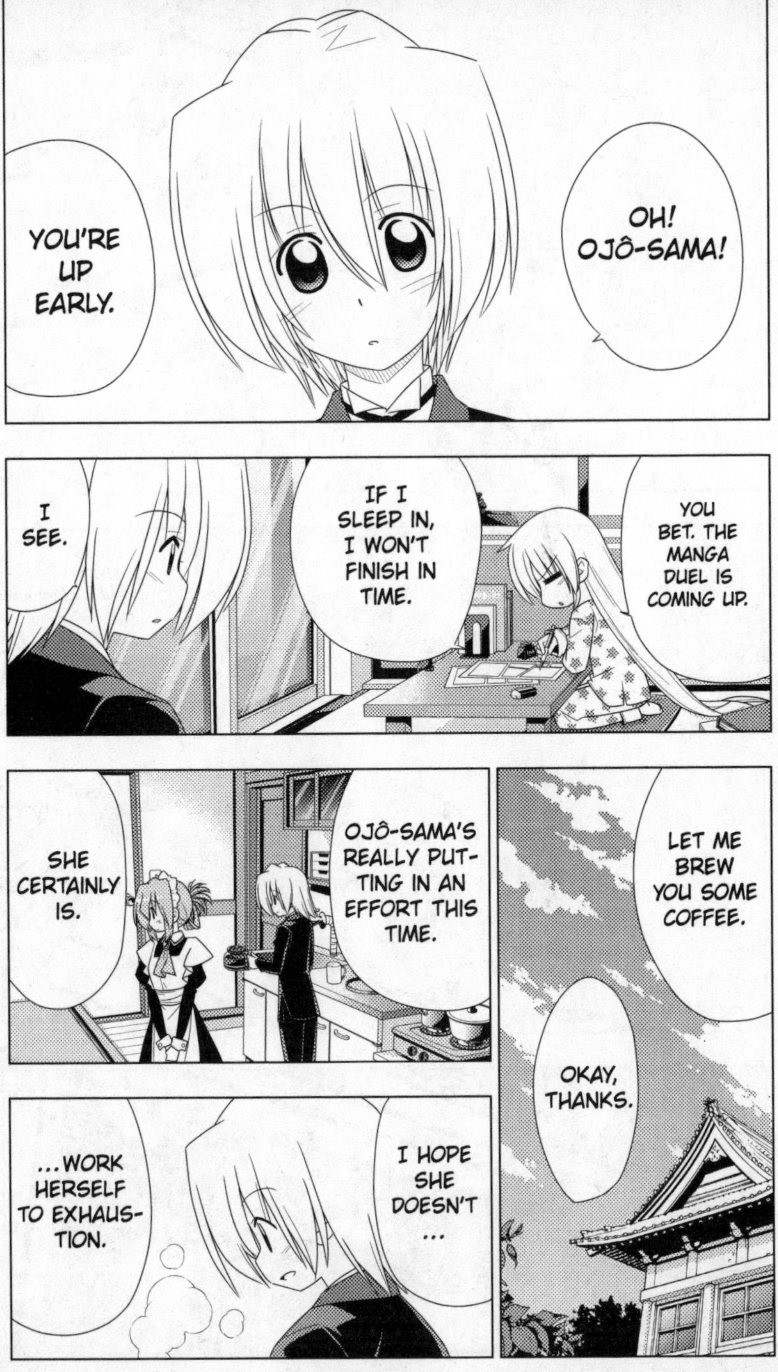
OH! OJÔ-SAMA!
YOU'RE UP EARLY.
YOU BET. THE MANGA DUEL IS COMING UP.
IF I SLEEP IN, I WON'T FINISH IN TIME.
I SEE.
LET ME BREW YOU SOME COFFEE.
OKAY, THANKS.
OJÔ-SAMA'S REALLY PUT-TING IN AN EFFORT THIS TIME.
SHE CERTAINLY IS.
I HOPE SHE DOESN'T ...
...WORK HERSELF TO EXHAUS-TION.

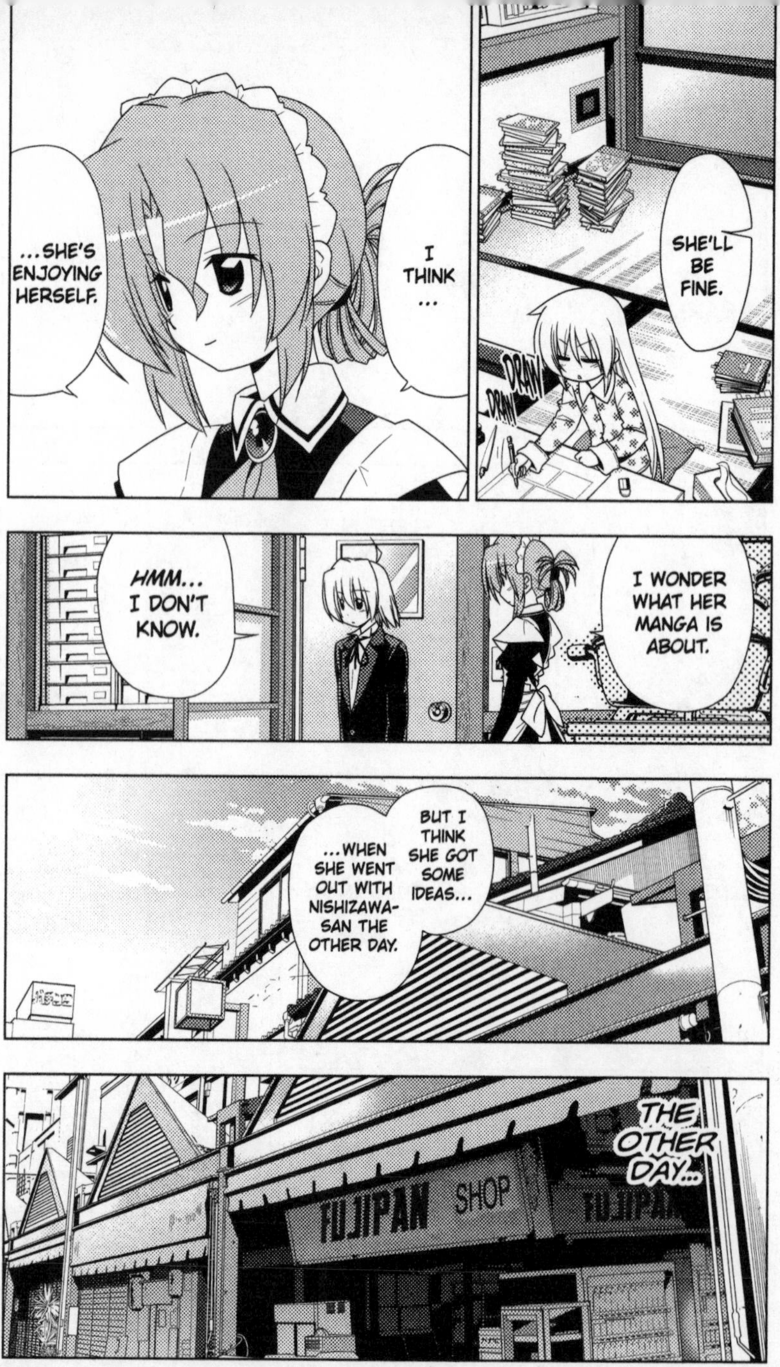
SHE'LL BE FINE.
DRAW
DRAW
I THINK ...
...SHE'S ENJOYING HERSELF.
I WONDER WHAT HER MANGA IS ABOUT.
HMM... I DON'T KNOW.
BUT I THINK SHE GOT SOME IDEAS...
...WHEN SHE WENT OUT WITH NISHIZAWA-SAN THE OTHER DAY.
THE OTHER DAY...
FUJIPAN
SHOP
FUJIPAN

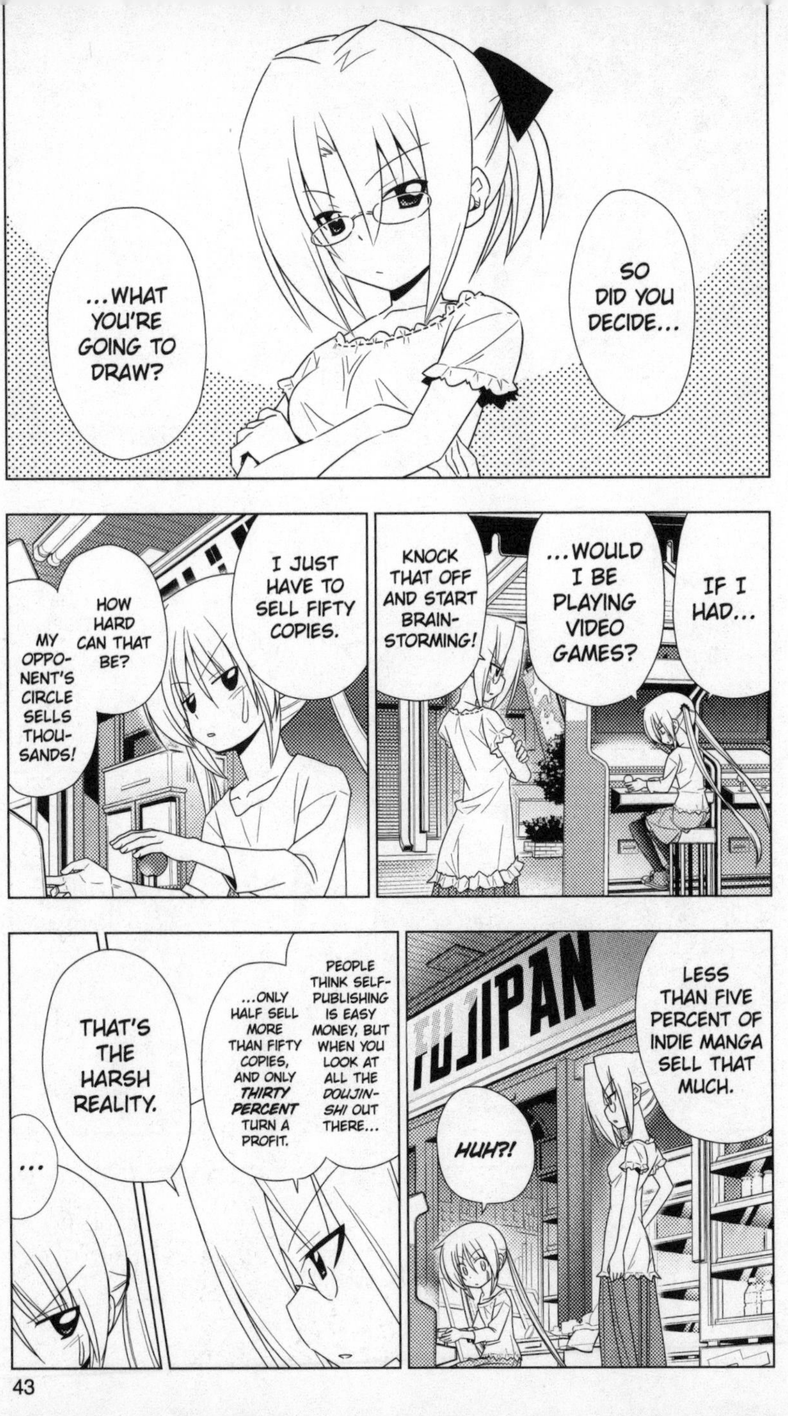
SO DID YOU DECIDE...
...WHAT YOU'RE GOING TO DRAW?
IF I HAD...
...WOULD I BE PLAYING VIDEO GAMES?
KNOCK THAT OFF AND START BRAIN-STORMING!
I JUST HAVE TO SELL FIFTY COPIES.
HOW HARD CAN THAT BE?
MY OPPO-NENT'S CIRCLE SELLS THOU-SANDS!
LESS THAN FIVE PERCENT OF INDIE MANGA SELL THAT MUCH.
HUH?!
PEOPLE THINK SELF-PUBLISHING IS EASY MONEY, BUT WHEN YOU LOOK AT ALL THE DOUJIN-SHI OUT THERE...
...ONLY HALF SELL MORE THAN FIFTY COPIES, AND ONLY THIRTY PERCENT TURN A PROFIT.
THAT'S THE HARSH REALITY.
...

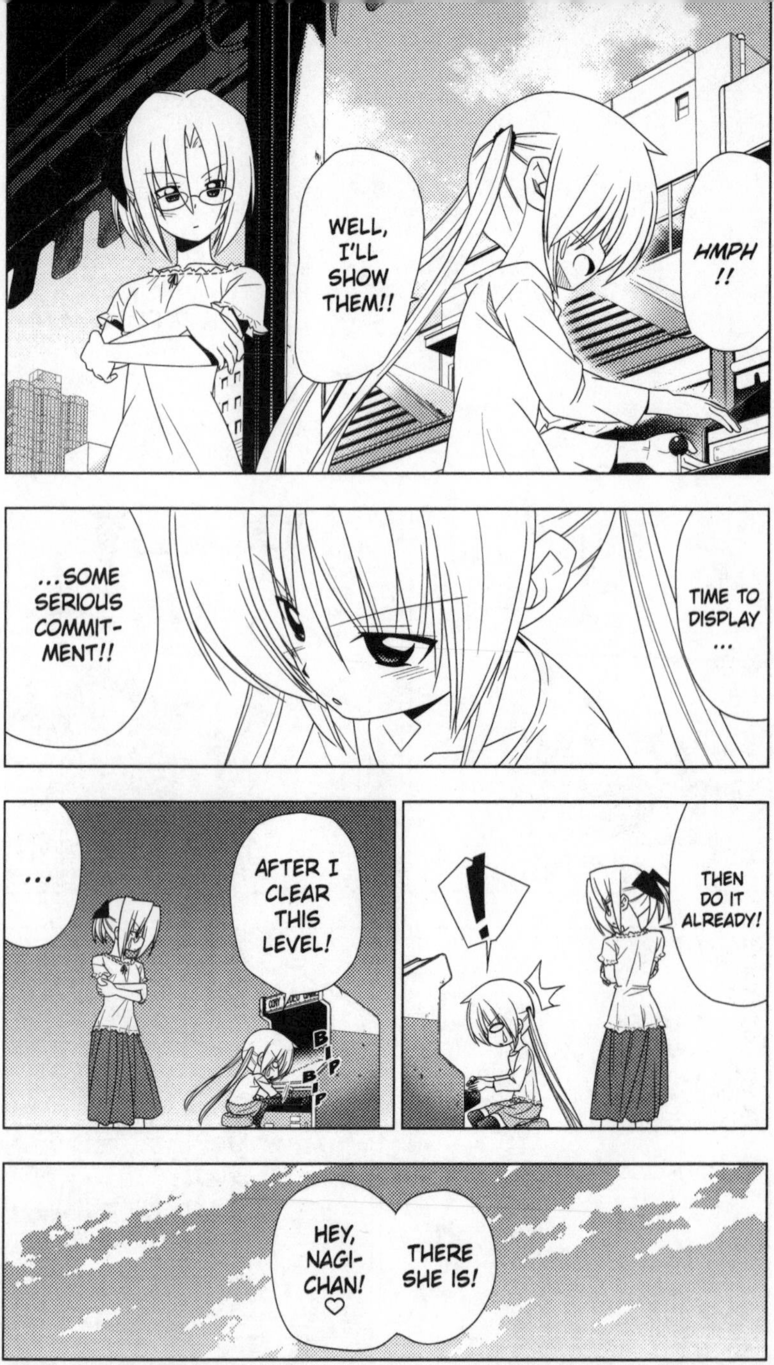
HMPH!!
WELL, I'LL SHOW THEM!!
TIME TO DISPLAY...
...SOME SERIOUS COMMIT-MENT!!
THEN DO IT ALREADY!
!
AFTER I CLEAR THIS LEVEL!
...
BIP BIP
THERE SHE IS!
HEY, NAGI-CHAN! ♡

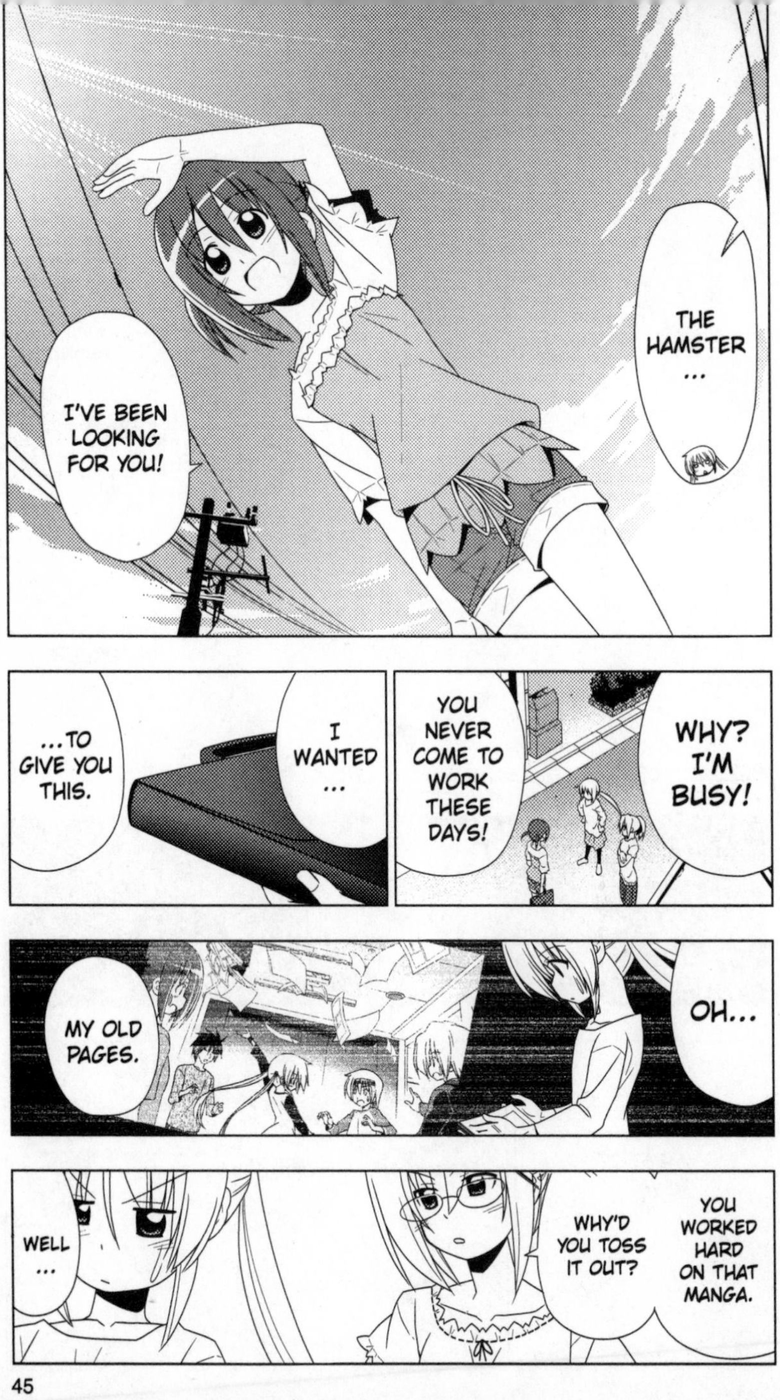
THE HAMSTER ...
I'VE BEEN LOOKING FOR YOU!
WHY? I'M BUSY!
YOU NEVER COME TO WORK THESE DAYS!
I WANTED ...
...TO GIVE YOU THIS.
OH...
MY OLD PAGES.
YOU WORKED HARD ON THAT MANGA.
WHY'D YOU TOSS IT OUT?
WELL ...

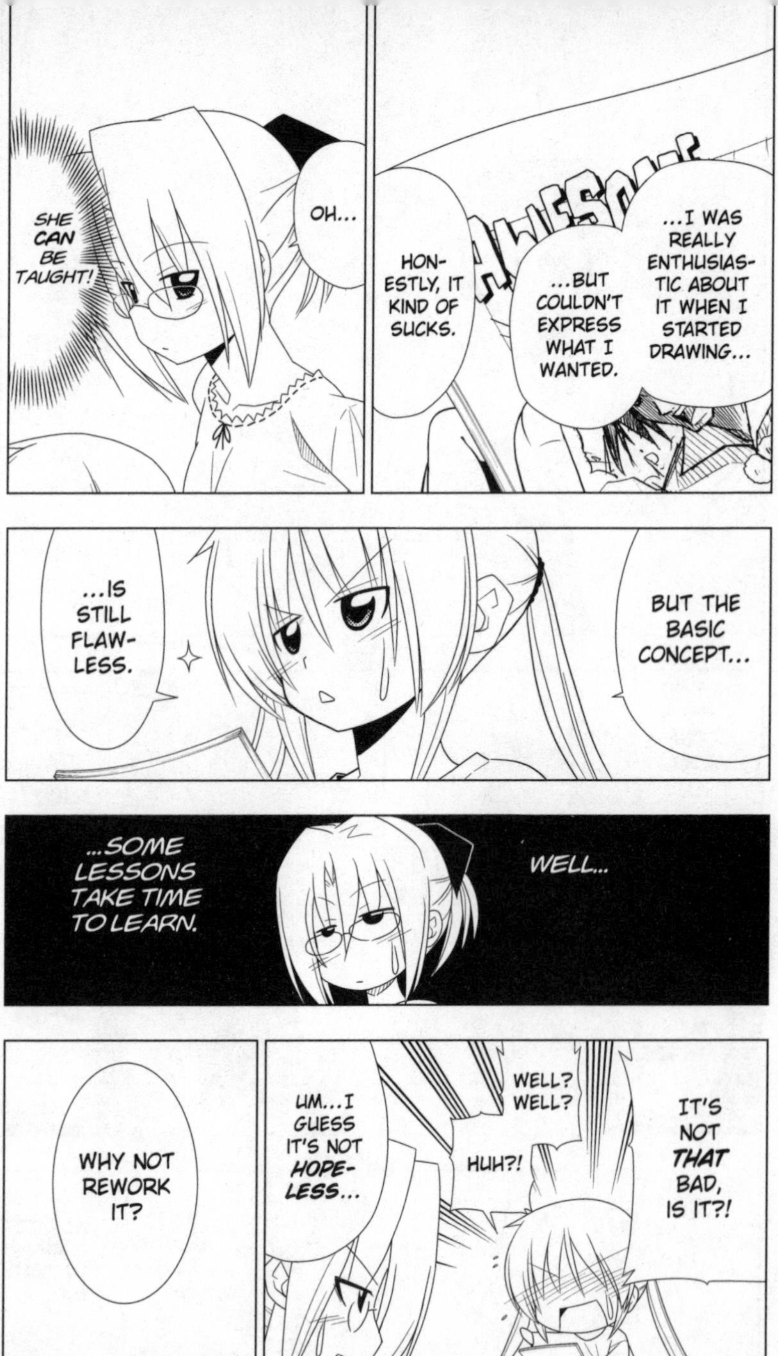
...I WAS REALLY ENTHUSIASTIC ABOUT IT WHEN I STARTED DRAWING...
...BUT COULDN'T EXPRESS WHAT I WANTED.
HONESTLY, IT KIND OF SUCKS.
OH...
SHE CAN BE TAUGHT!
BUT THE BASIC CONCEPT...
...IS STILL FLAWLESS.
WELL...
...SOME LESSONS TAKE TIME TO LEARN.
IT'S NOT *THAT* BAD, IS IT?!
WELL? WELL?
HUH?!
UM...I GUESS IT'S NOT *HOPELESS*...
WHY NOT REWORK IT?

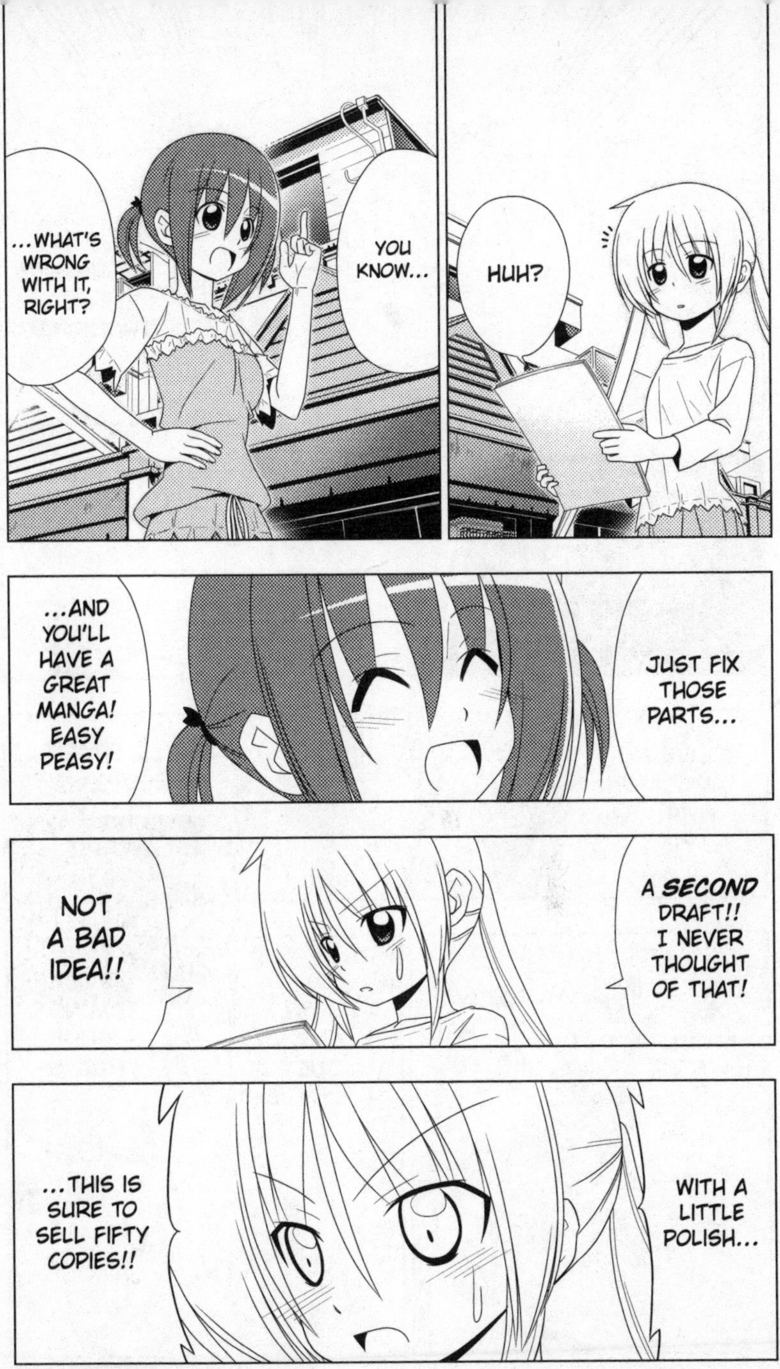
HUH?
YOU KNOW...
...WHAT'S WRONG WITH IT, RIGHT?
JUST FIX THOSE PARTS...
...AND YOU'LL HAVE A GREAT MANGA! EASY PEASY!
A *SECOND* DRAFT!! I NEVER THOUGHT OF THAT!
NOT A BAD IDEA!!
WITH A LITTLE POLISH...
...THIS IS SURE TO SELL FIFTY COPIES!!

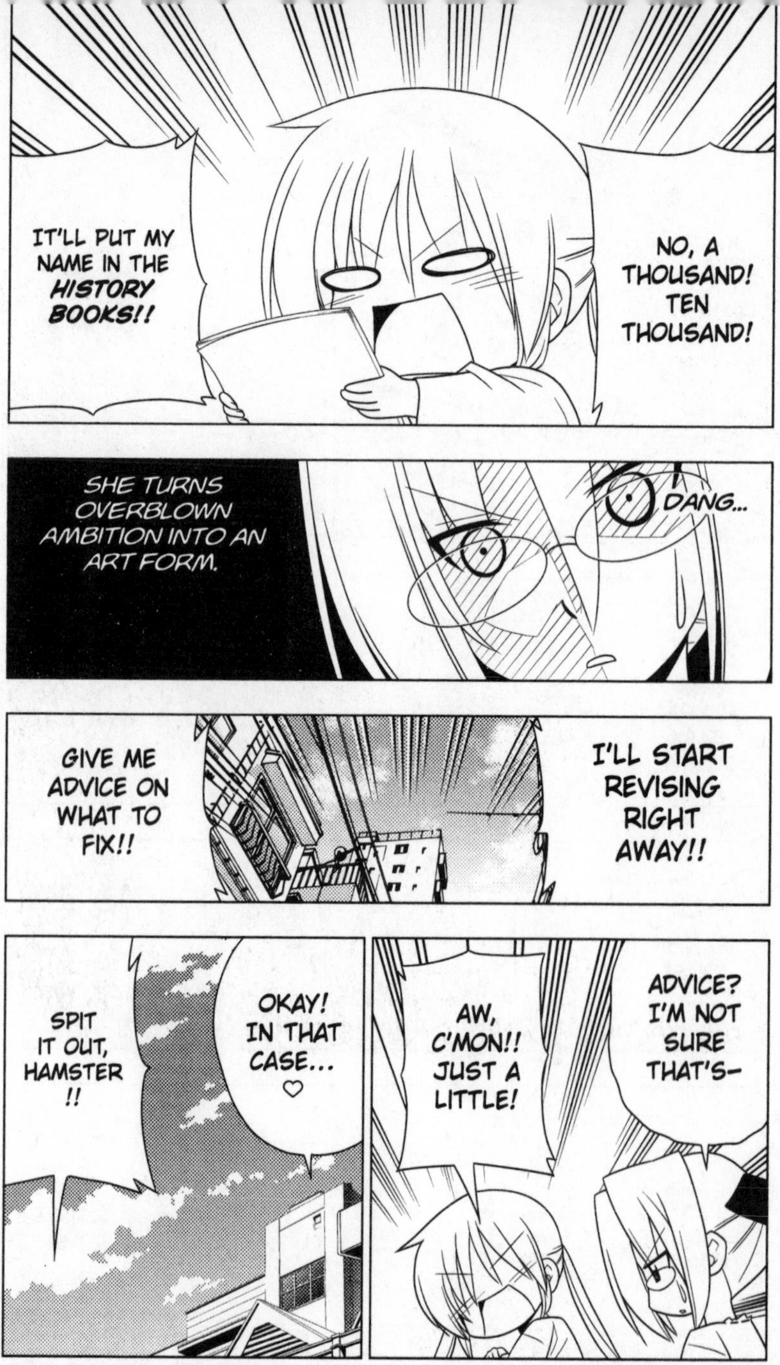
NO, A THOUSAND! TEN THOUSAND!
IT'LL PUT MY NAME IN THE HISTORY BOOKS!!
DANG...
SHE TURNS OVERBLOWN AMBITION INTO AN ART FORM.
I'LL START REVISING RIGHT AWAY!!
GIVE ME ADVICE ON WHAT TO FIX!!
ADVICE? I'M NOT SURE THAT'S-
AW, C'MON!! JUST A LITTLE!
OKAY! IN THAT CASE... ♡
SPIT IT OUT, HAMSTER!!

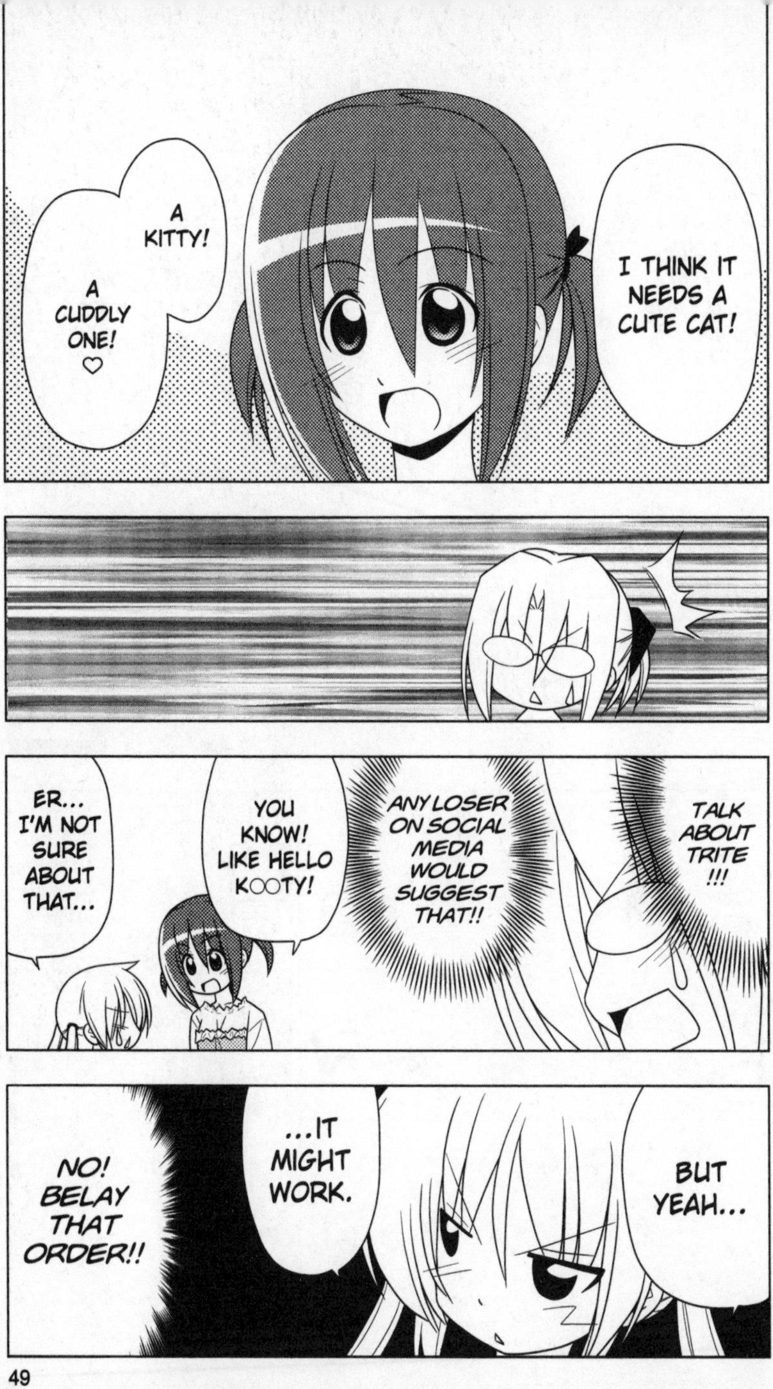
I THINK IT NEEDS A CUTE CAT!
A KITTY!
A CUDDLY ONE! ♡
TALK ABOUT TRITE!!!
ANY LOSER ON SOCIAL MEDIA WOULD SUGGEST THAT!!
YOU KNOW! LIKE HELLO K○○TY!
ER... I'M NOT SURE ABOUT THAT...
BUT YEAH...
...IT MIGHT WORK.
NO! BELAY THAT ORDER!!

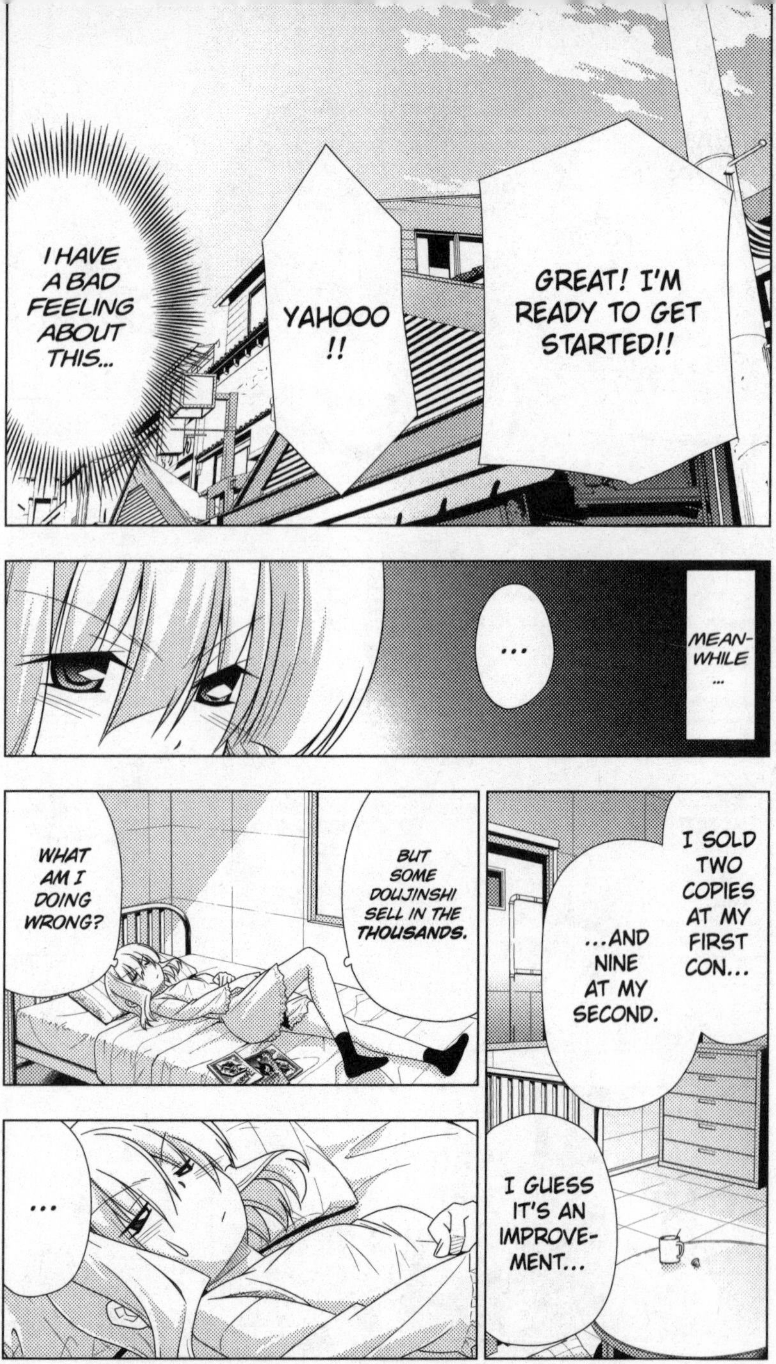
GREAT! I'M READY TO GET STARTED!!
YAHOOO !!
I HAVE A BAD FEELING ABOUT THIS...
MEAN-WHILE ...
...
I SOLD TWO COPIES AT MY FIRST CON...
...AND NINE AT MY SECOND.
I GUESS IT'S AN IMPROVEMENT...
BUT SOME DOUJINSHI SELL IN THE THOUSANDS.
WHAT AM I DOING WRONG?
...

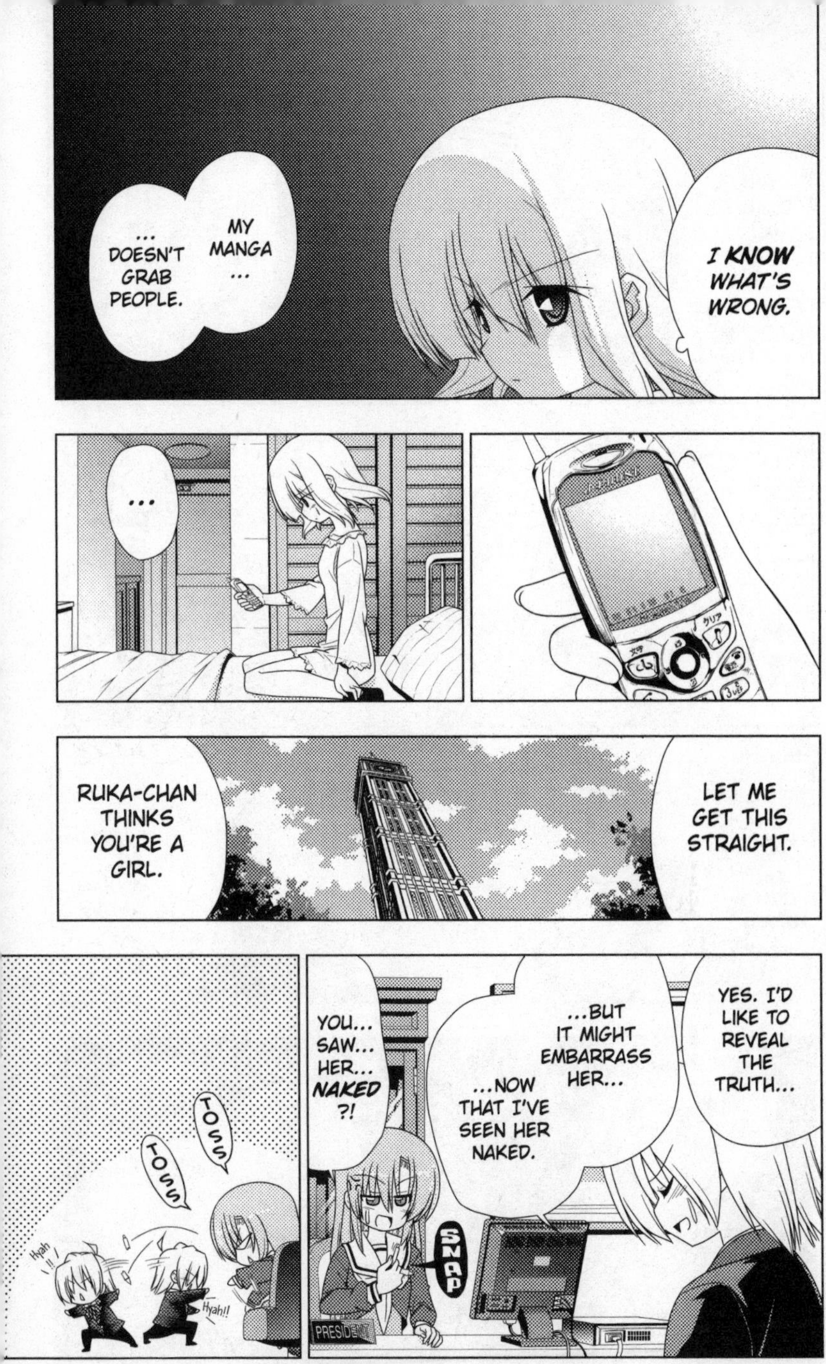
I KNOW WHAT'S WRONG.
MY MANGA ...
... DOESN'T GRAB PEOPLE.
...
LET ME GET THIS STRAIGHT.
RUKA-CHAN THINKS YOU'RE A GIRL.
YES. I'D LIKE TO REVEAL THE TRUTH...
...BUT IT MIGHT EMBARRASS HER...
...NOW THAT I'VE SEEN HER NAKED.
YOU... SAW... HER... NAKED ?!
SNAP
PRESIDENT
TOSS
TOSS
Hyah!!
Hyah!!

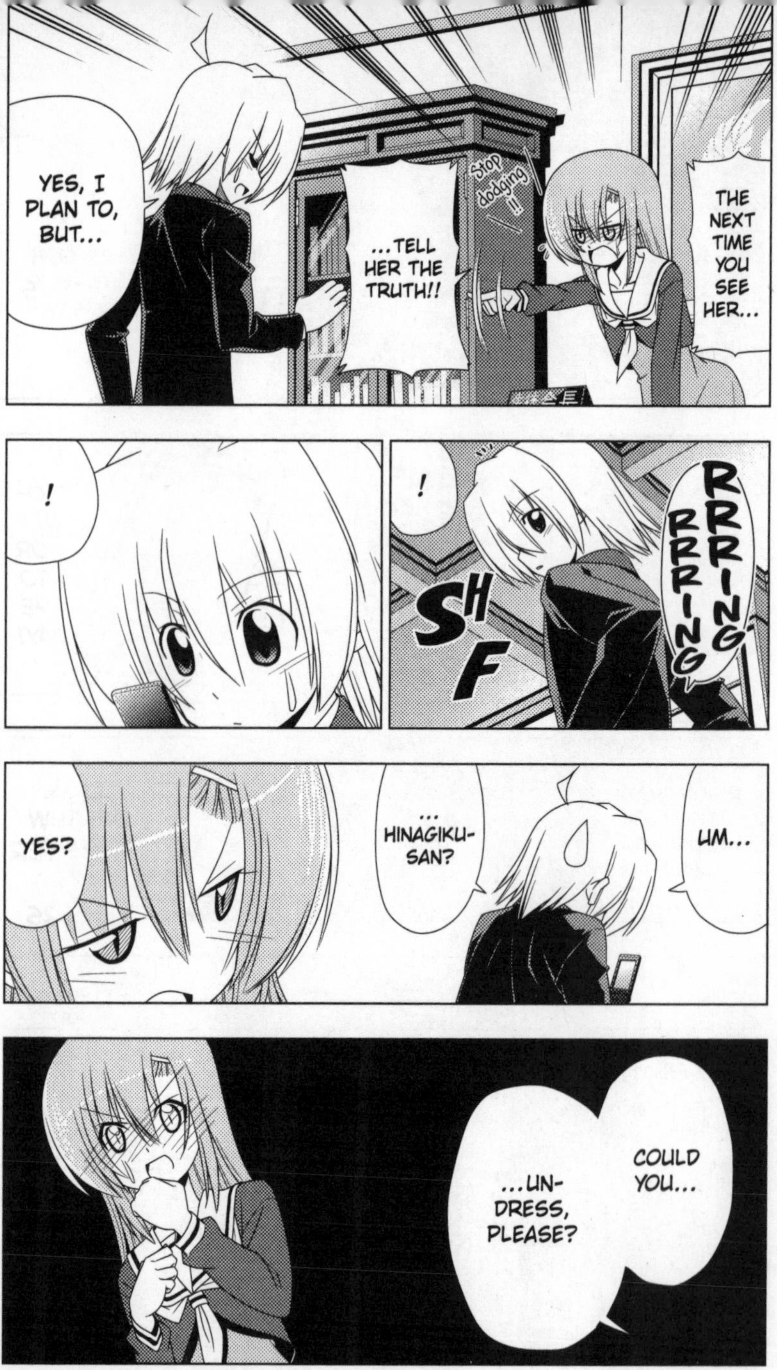
THE NEXT TIME YOU SEE HER...
Stop dodging!!
...TELL HER THE TRUTH!!
YES, I PLAN TO, BUT...
RRRING RRRING
SHF
!
!
UM...
...HINAGIKU-SAN?
YES?
COULD YOU...
...UN-DRESS, PLEASE?

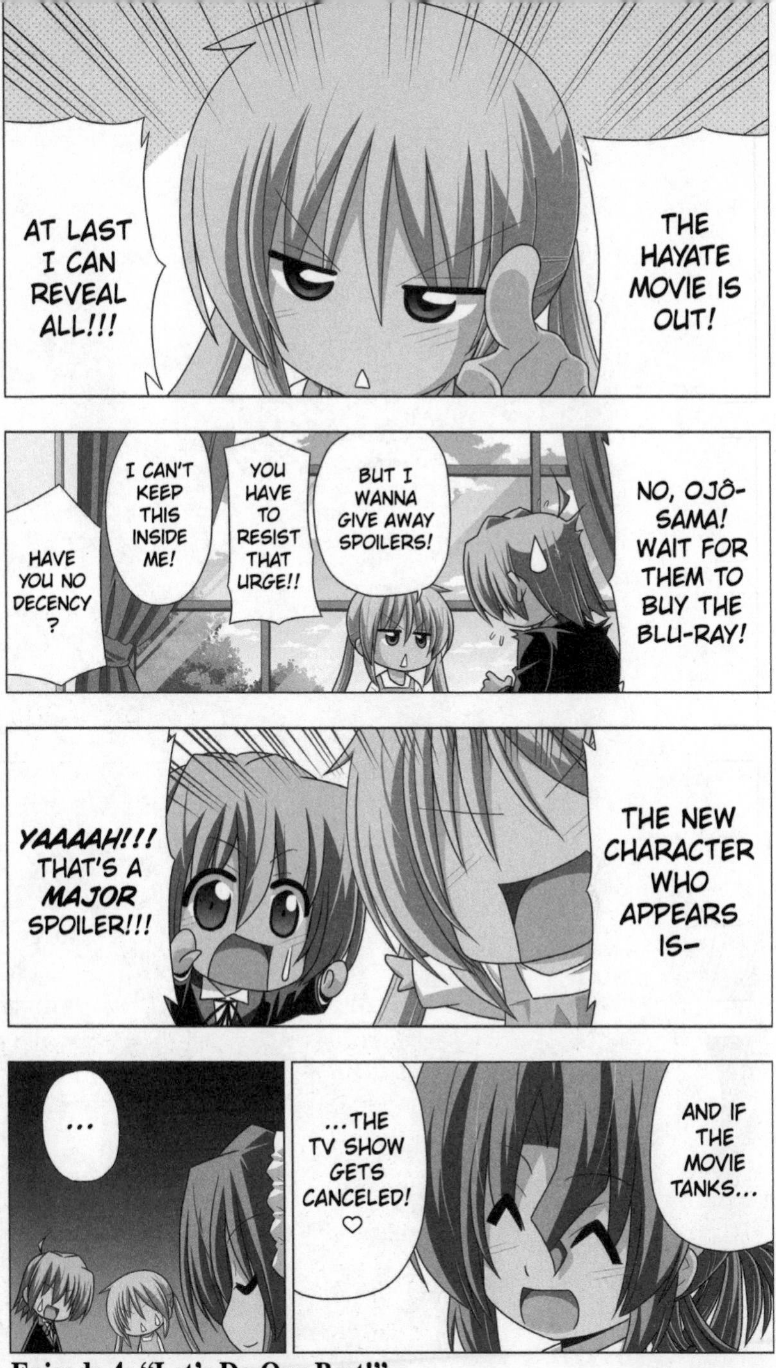

THE HAYATE MOVIE IS OUT!
AT LAST I CAN REVEAL ALL!!!
NO, OJÔ-SAMA! WAIT FOR THEM TO BUY THE BLU-RAY!
BUT I WANNA GIVE AWAY SPOILERS!
YOU HAVE TO RESIST THAT URGE!!
I CAN'T KEEP THIS INSIDE ME!
HAVE YOU NO DECENCY?
THE NEW CHARACTER WHO APPEARS IS–
YAAAAH!!! THAT'S A MAJOR SPOILER!!!
AND IF THE MOVIE TANKS...
...THE TV SHOW GETS CANCELED! ♡
...

Episode 4: "Let's Do Our Best!"

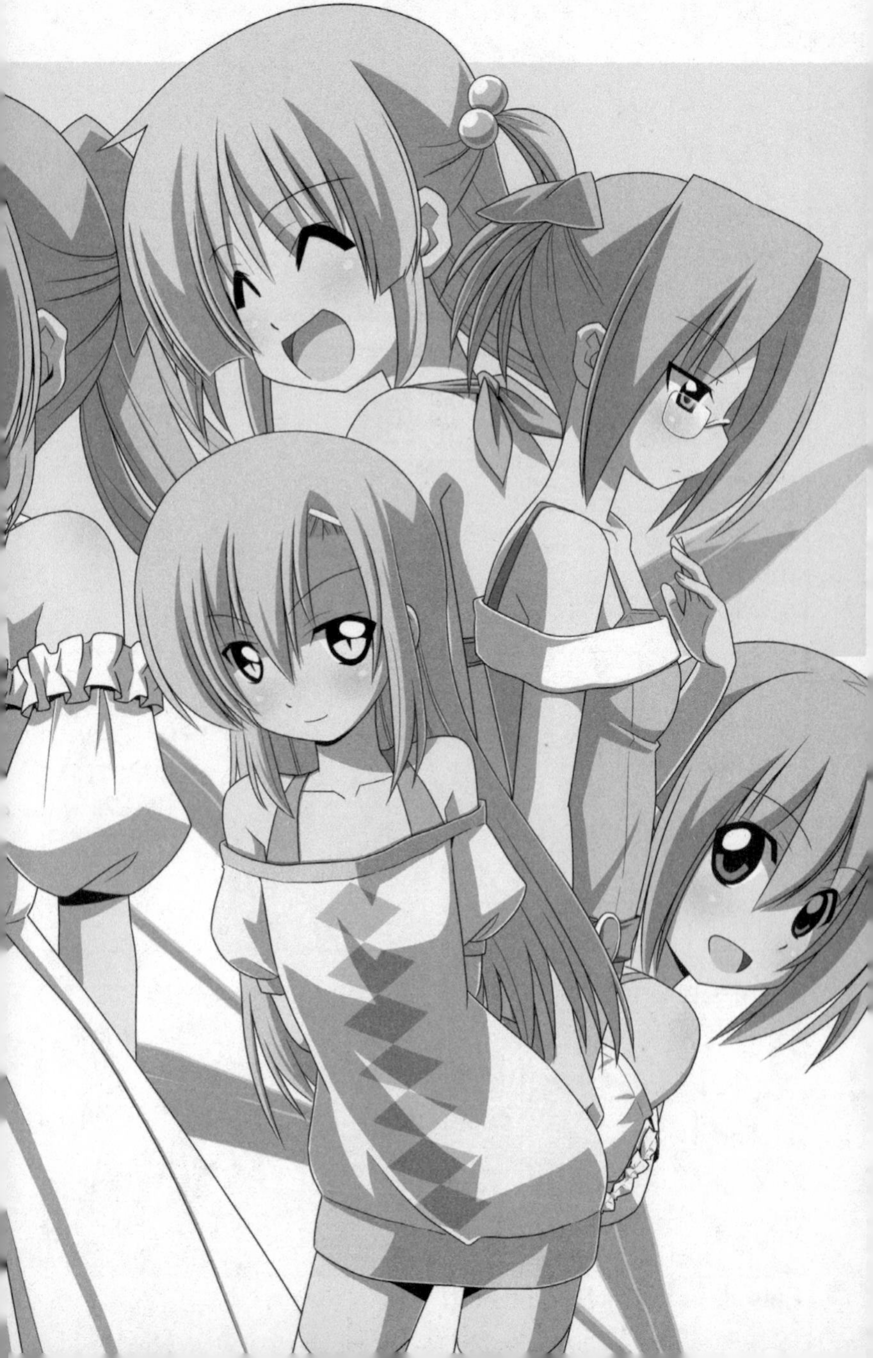

Episode 4:
"Let's Do Our Best!"

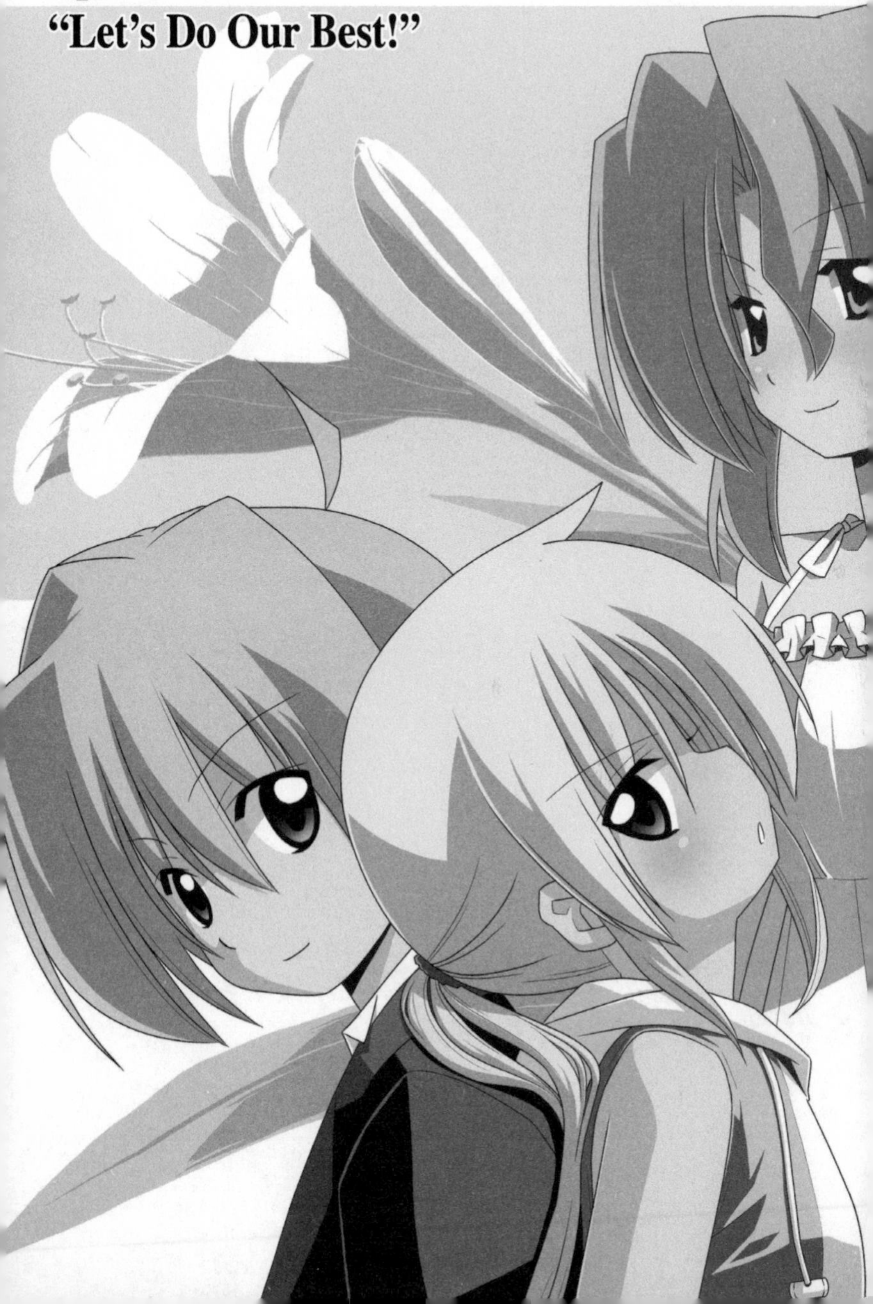

ハヤテのごとく!
Hayate the combat butler

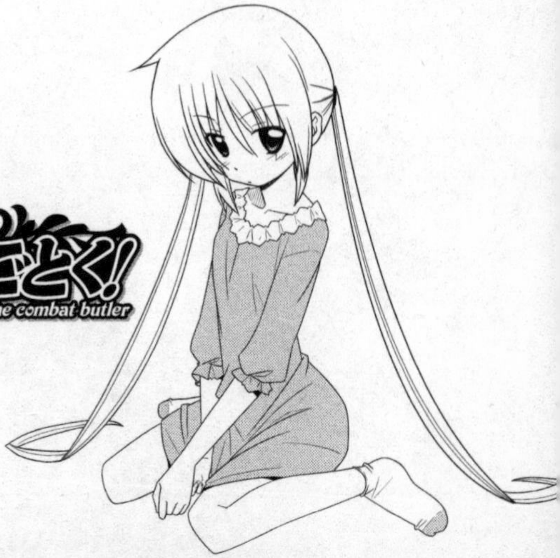

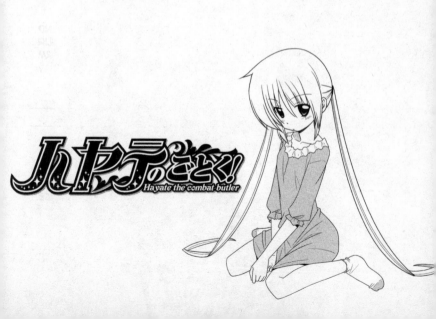

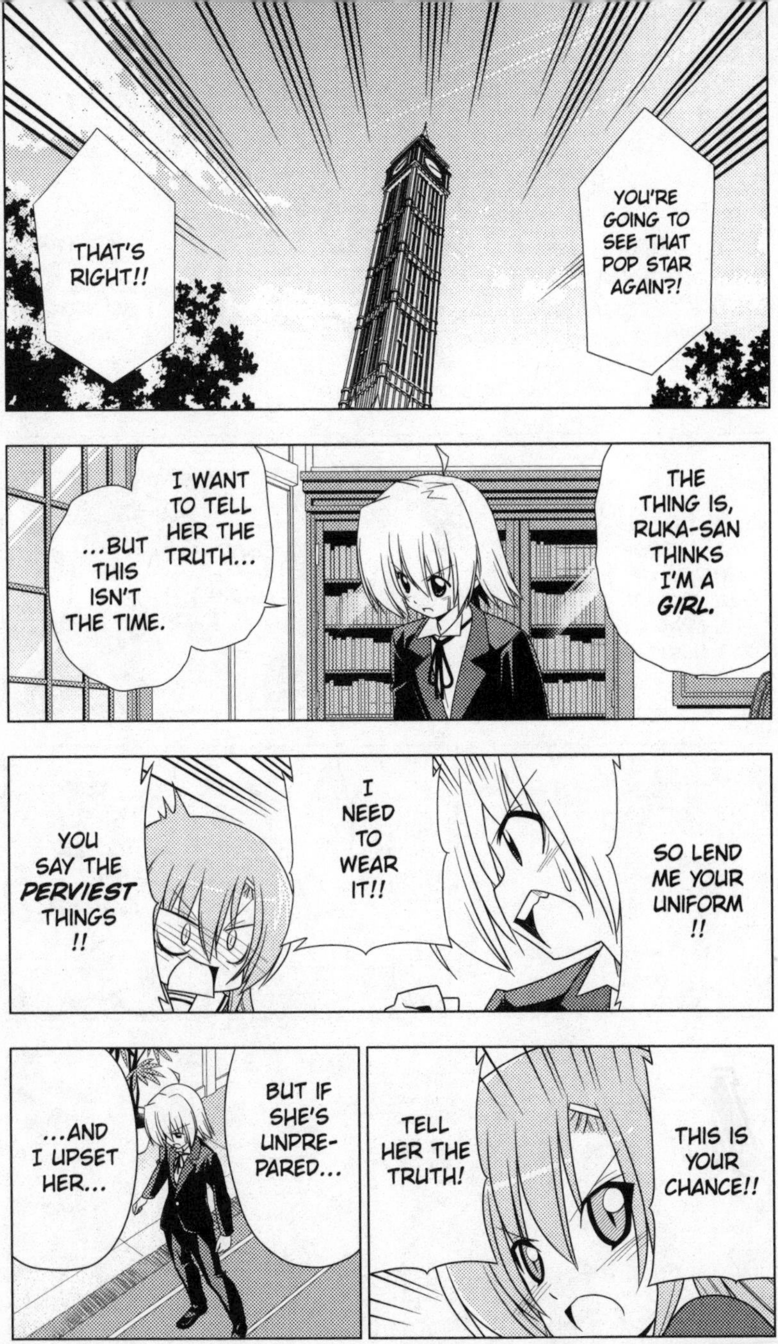
YOU'RE GOING TO SEE THAT POP STAR AGAIN?!
THAT'S RIGHT!!
THE THING IS, RUKA-SAN THINKS I'M A *GIRL.*
I WANT TO TELL HER THE TRUTH...
...BUT THIS ISN'T THE TIME.
SO LEND ME YOUR UNIFORM!!
I NEED TO WEAR IT!!
YOU SAY THE *PERVIEST* THINGS!!
THIS IS YOUR CHANCE!!
TELL HER THE TRUTH!
BUT IF SHE'S UNPRE-PARED...
...AND I UPSET HER...

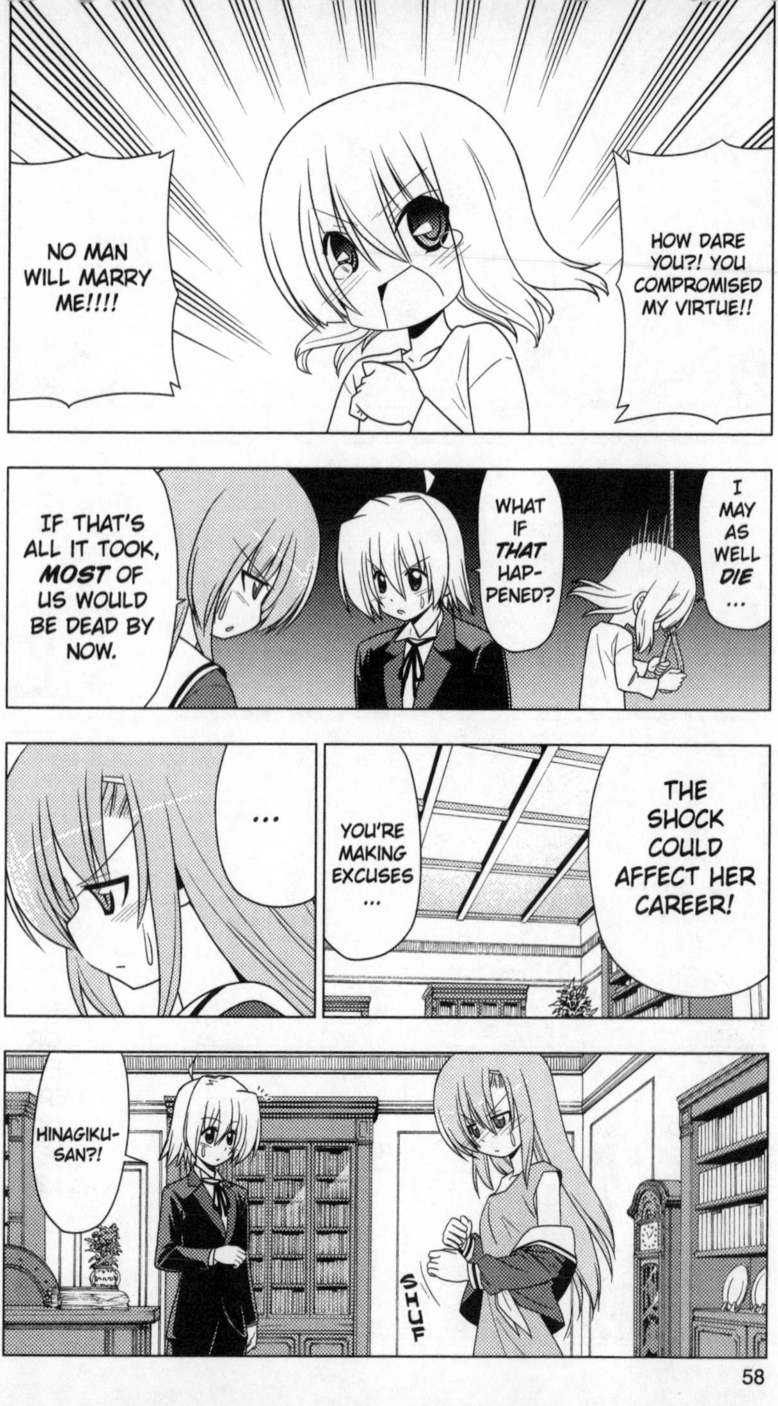
HOW DARE YOU?! YOU COMPROMISED MY VIRTUE!!
NO MAN WILL MARRY ME!!!!
I MAY AS WELL DIE ...
WHAT IF THAT HAPPENED?
IF THAT'S ALL IT TOOK, MOST OF US WOULD BE DEAD BY NOW.
THE SHOCK COULD AFFECT HER CAREER!
YOU'RE MAKING EXCUSES ...
...
HINAGIKU-SAN?!
SHUF

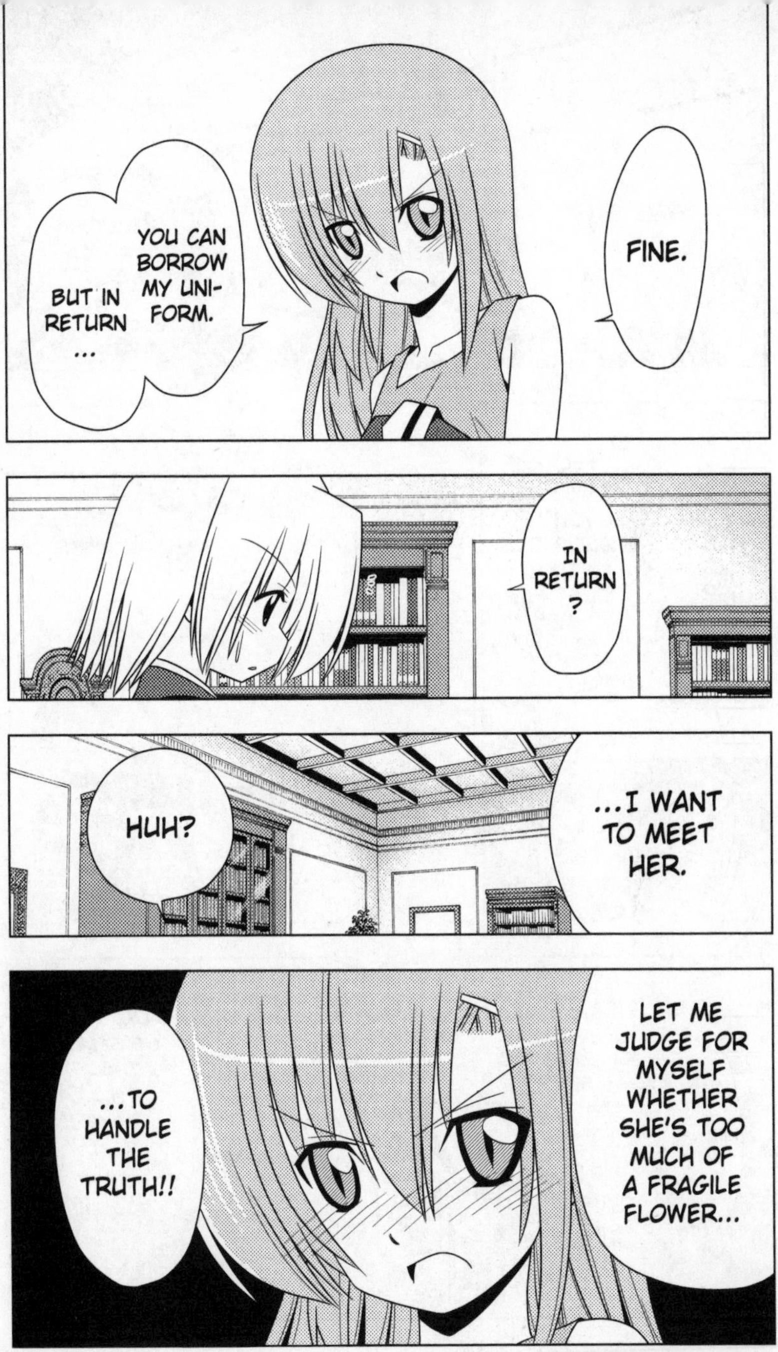
FINE.
YOU CAN BORROW MY UNI-FORM.
BUT IN RETURN ...
IN RETURN?
...I WANT TO MEET HER.
HUH?
LET ME JUDGE FOR MYSELF WHETHER SHE'S TOO MUCH OF A FRAGILE FLOWER...
...TO HANDLE THE TRUTH!!

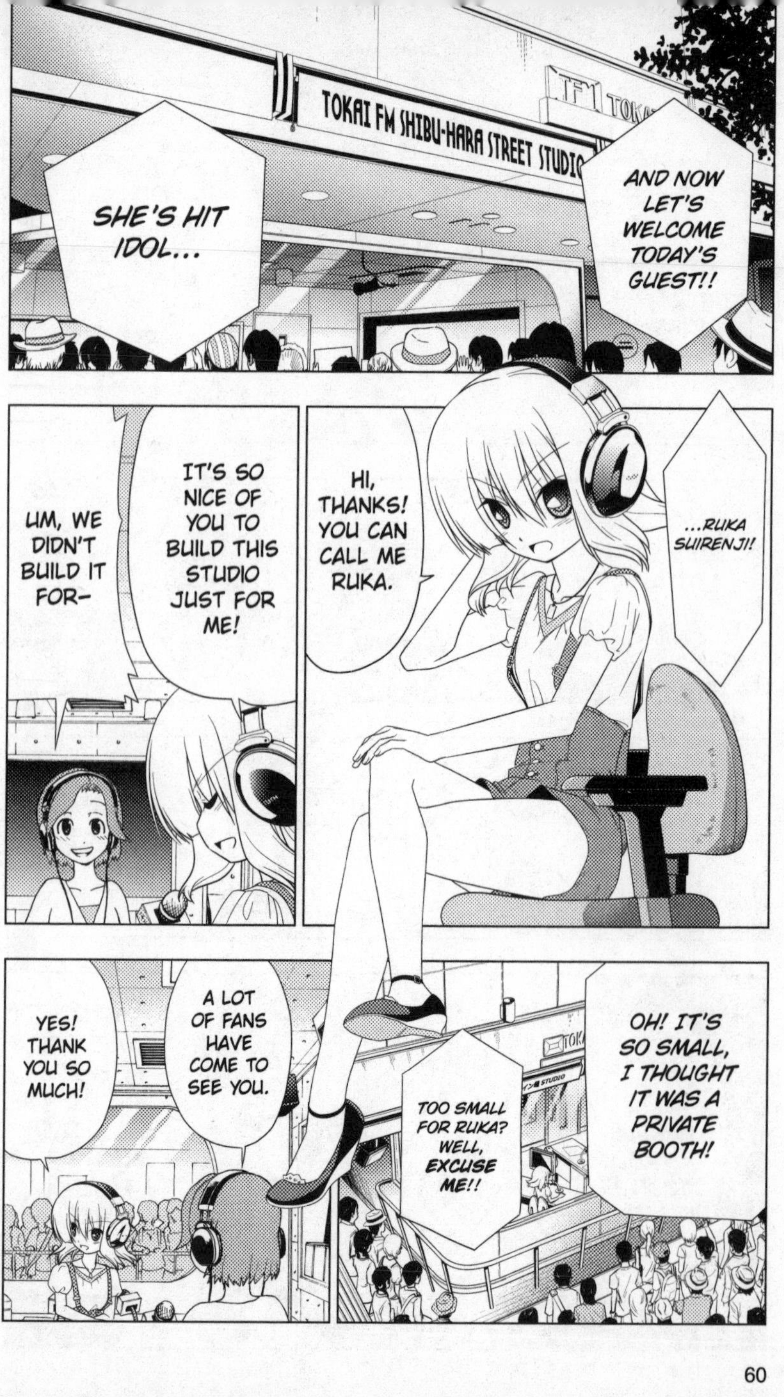
TOKAI FM SHIBU-HARA STREET STUDIO
AND NOW LET'S WELCOME TODAY'S GUEST!!
SHE'S HIT IDOL...
...RUKA SUIRENJI!
HI, THANKS! YOU CAN CALL ME RUKA.
IT'S SO NICE OF YOU TO BUILD THIS STUDIO JUST FOR ME!
UM, WE DIDN'T BUILD IT FOR—
OH! IT'S SO SMALL, I THOUGHT IT WAS A PRIVATE BOOTH!
TOO SMALL FOR RUKA? WELL, EXCUSE ME!!
A LOT OF FANS HAVE COME TO SEE YOU.
YES! THANK YOU SO MUCH!

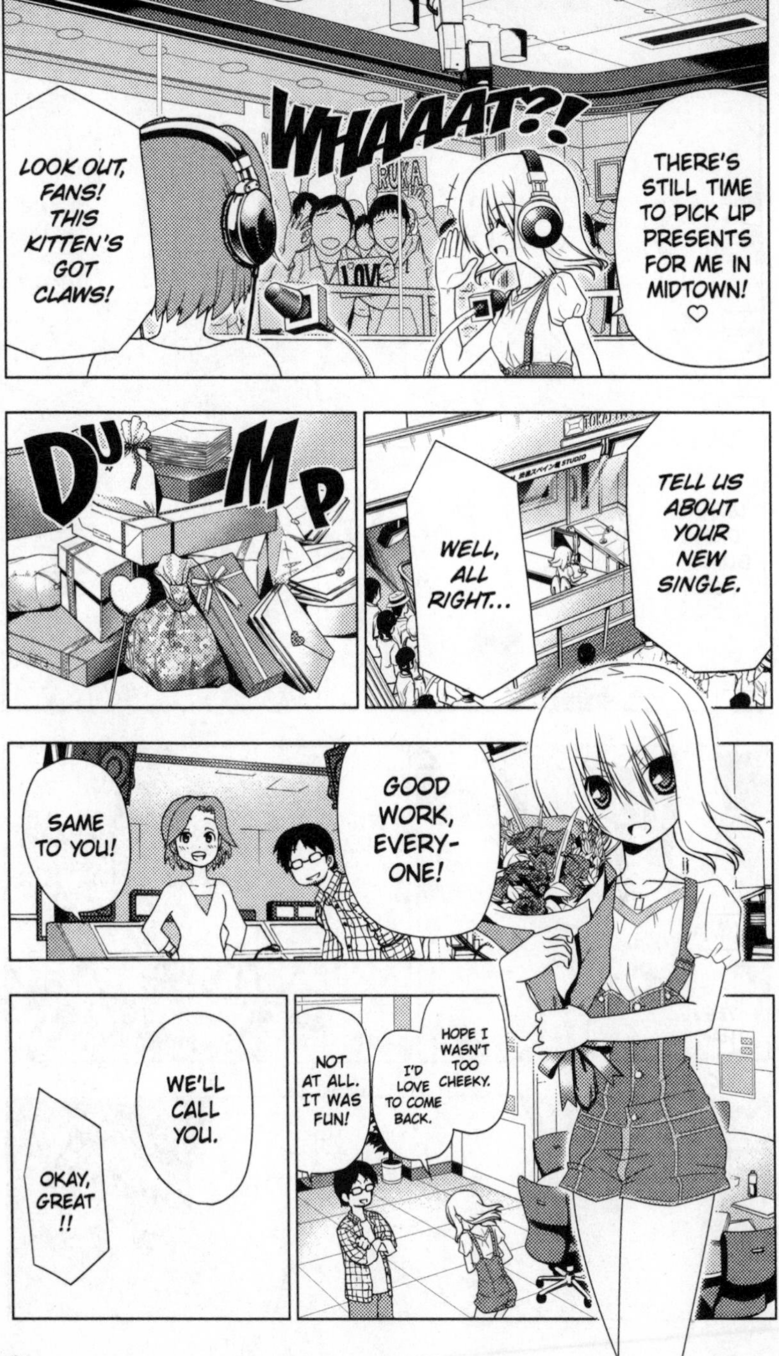
THERE'S STILL TIME TO PICK UP PRESENTS FOR ME IN MIDTOWN! ♡
WHAAAT?!
RUKA
LOOK OUT, FANS! THIS KITTEN'S GOT CLAWS!
TELL US ABOUT YOUR NEW SINGLE.
WELL, ALL RIGHT...
DUMP
GOOD WORK, EVERY-ONE!
SAME TO YOU!
HOPE I WASN'T TOO CHEEKY.
I'D LOVE TO COME BACK.
NOT AT ALL. IT WAS FUN!
WE'LL CALL YOU.
OKAY, GREAT !!

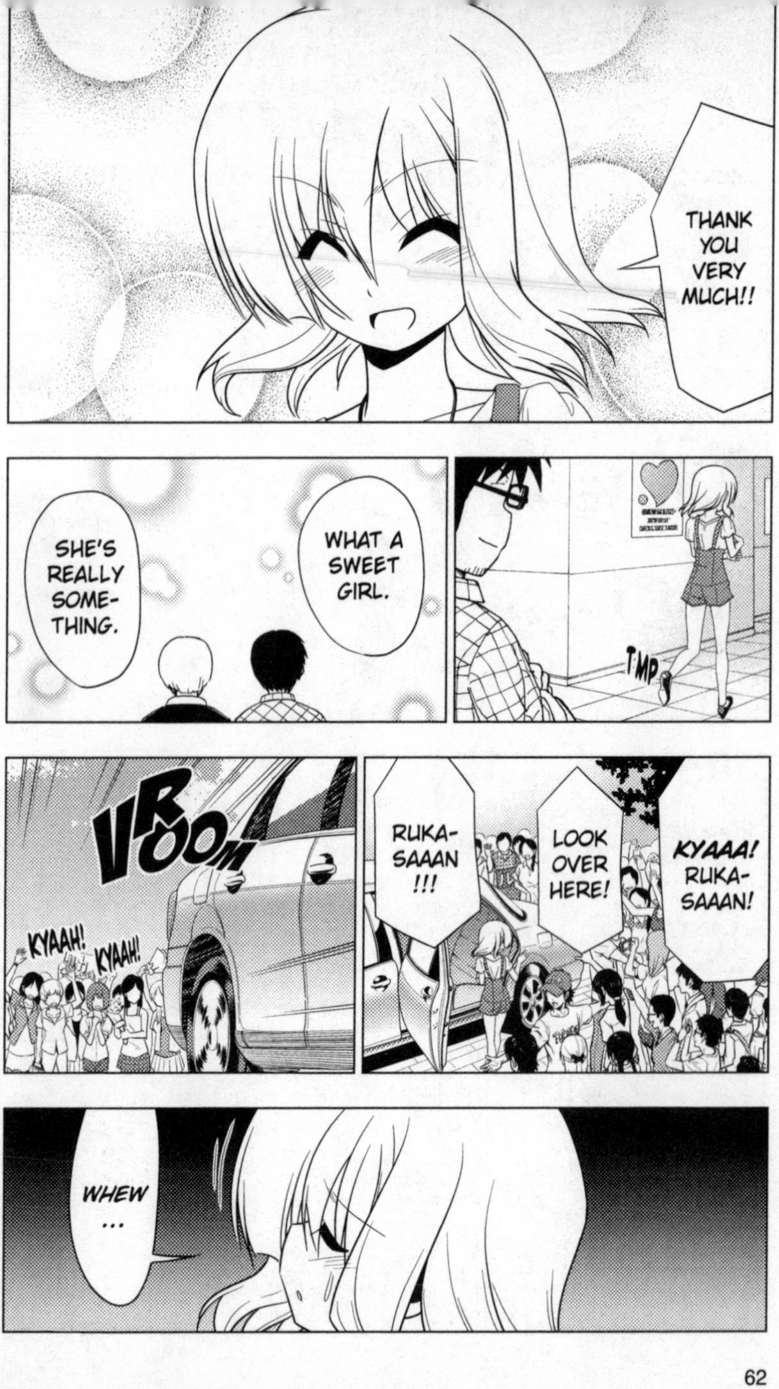
THANK YOU VERY MUCH!!
TMP
WHAT A SWEET GIRL.
SHE'S REALLY SOME-THING.
KYAAA! RUKA-SAAAN!
LOOK OVER HERE!
RUKA-SAAAN!!!
VROOM
KYAAH!
KYAAH!
WHEW...

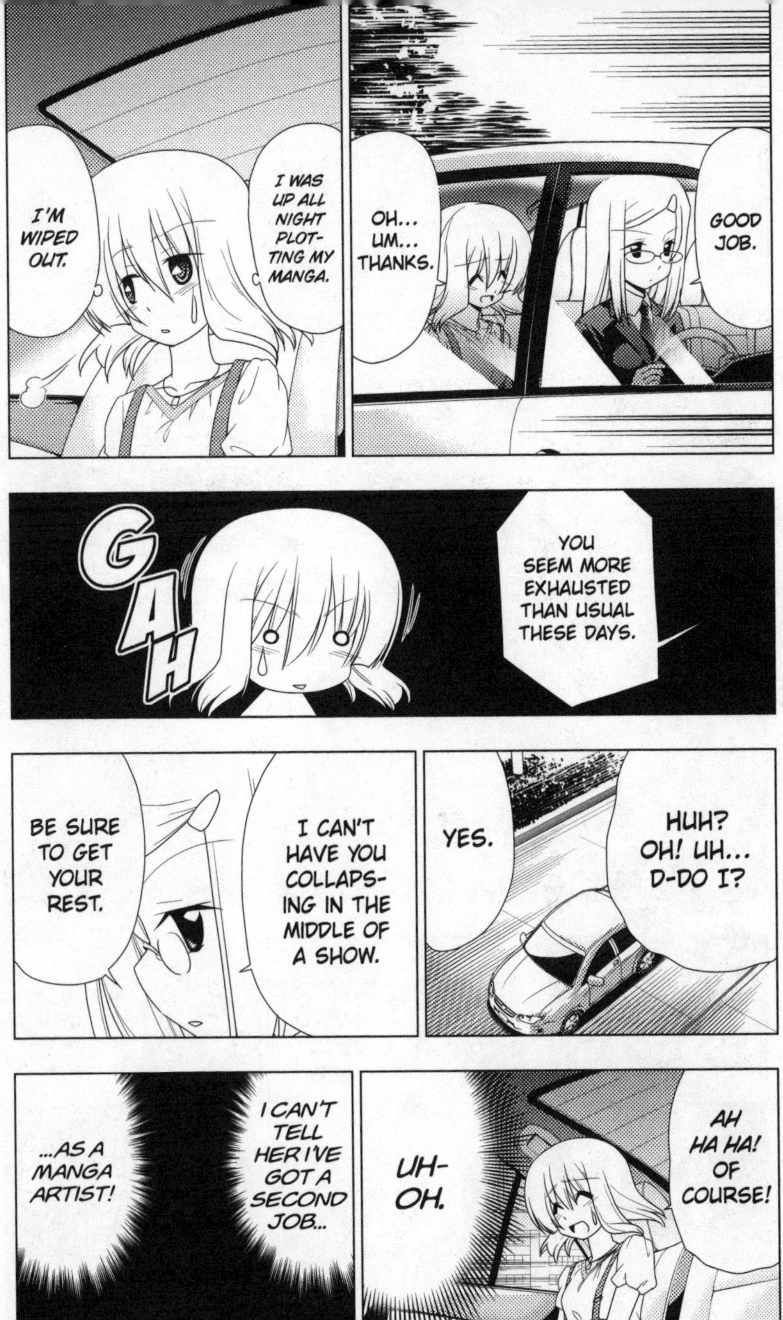
GOOD JOB.
OH... UM... THANKS.
I WAS UP ALL NIGHT PLOTTING MY MANGA.
I'M WIPED OUT.
YOU SEEM MORE EXHAUSTED THAN USUAL THESE DAYS.
GAH
HUH? OH! UH... D-DO I?
YES.
I CAN'T HAVE YOU COLLAPSING IN THE MIDDLE OF A SHOW.
BE SURE TO GET YOUR REST.
AH HA HA! OF COURSE!
UH-OH.
I CAN'T TELL HER I'VE GOT A SECOND JOB...
...AS A MANGA ARTIST!

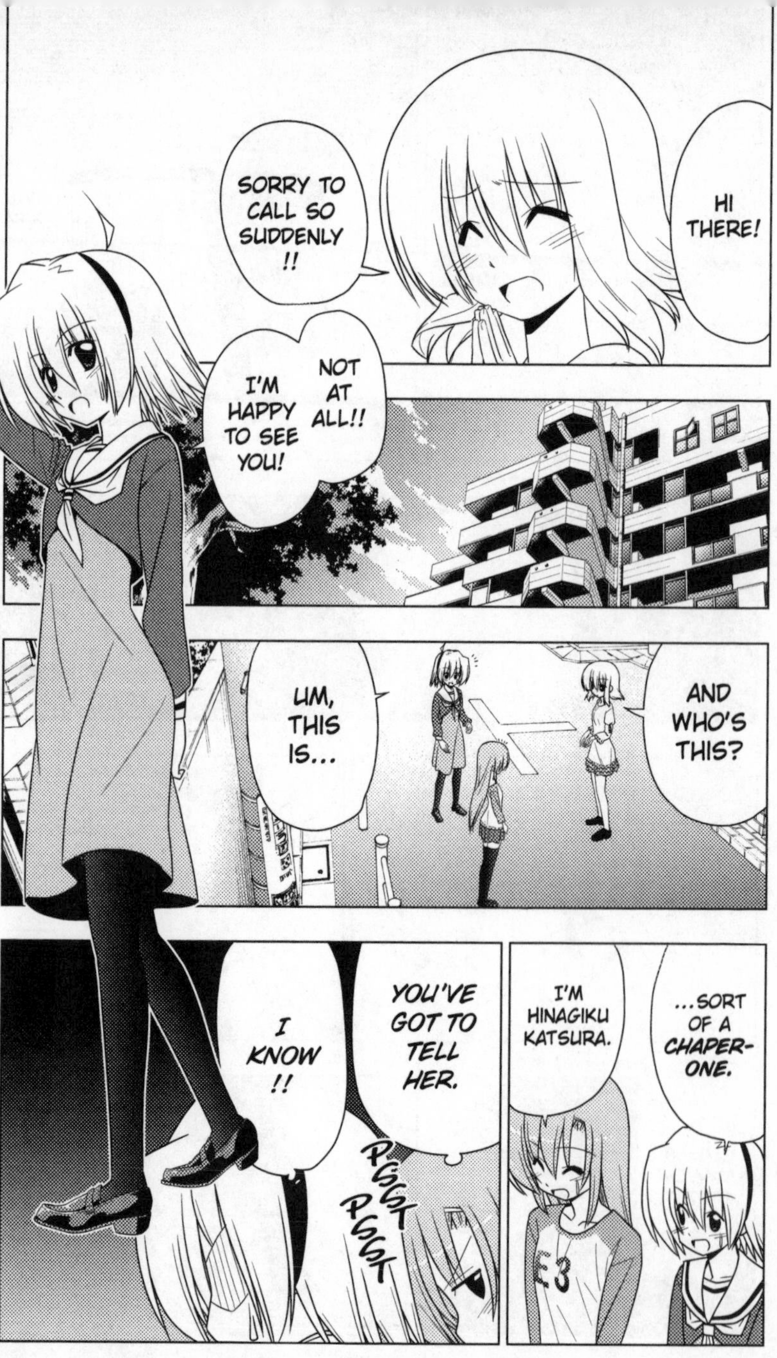
HI THERE!
SORRY TO CALL SO SUDDENLY !!
NOT AT ALL!!
I'M HAPPY TO SEE YOU!
AND WHO'S THIS?
UM, THIS IS...
...SORT OF A CHAPER-ONE.
I'M HINAGIKU KATSURA.
YOU'VE GOT TO TELL HER.
I KNOW !!
PSSST PSSST

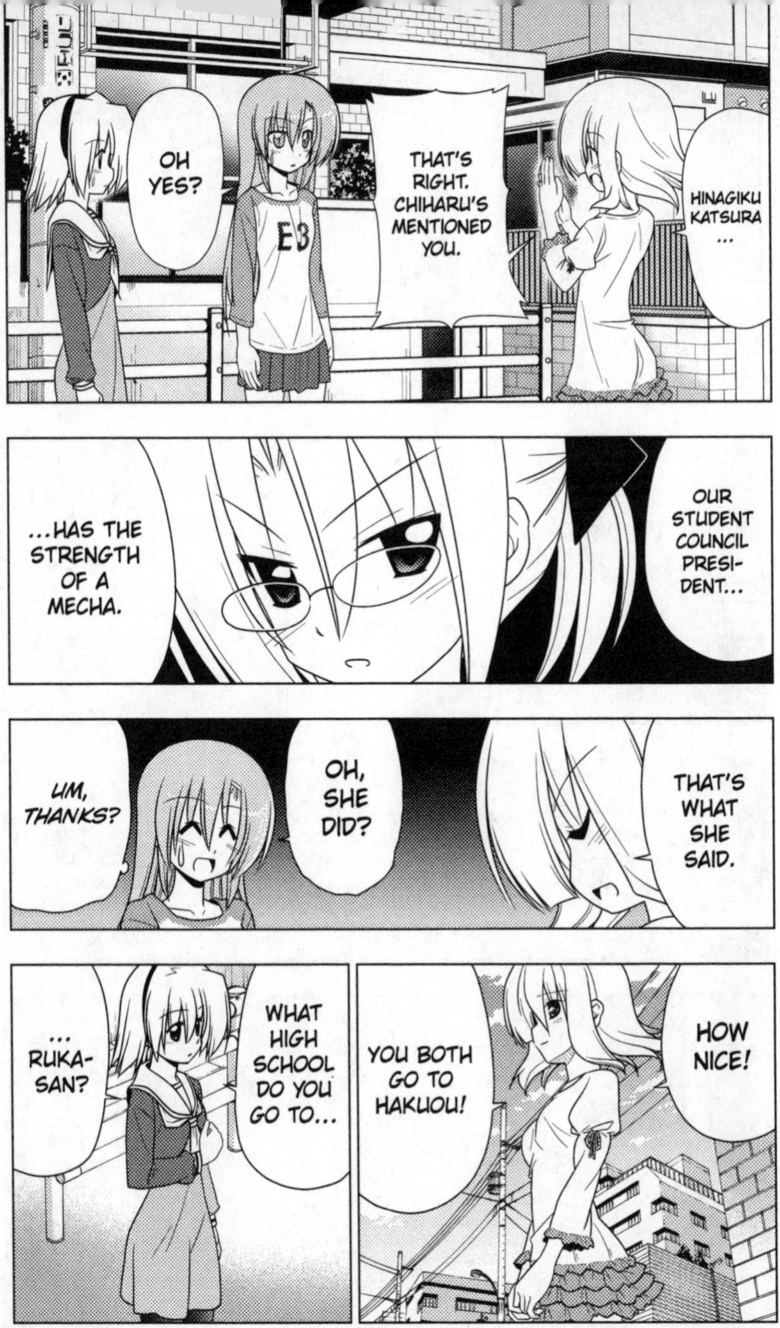
HINAGIKU KATSURA...
THAT'S RIGHT. CHIHARU'S MENTIONED YOU.
OH YES?
OUR STUDENT COUNCIL PRESI-DENT...
...HAS THE STRENGTH OF A MECHA.
THAT'S WHAT SHE SAID.
OH, SHE DID?
UM, THANKS?
HOW NICE!
YOU BOTH GO TO HAKUOU!
WHAT HIGH SCHOOL DO YOU GO TO...
...RUKA-SAN?

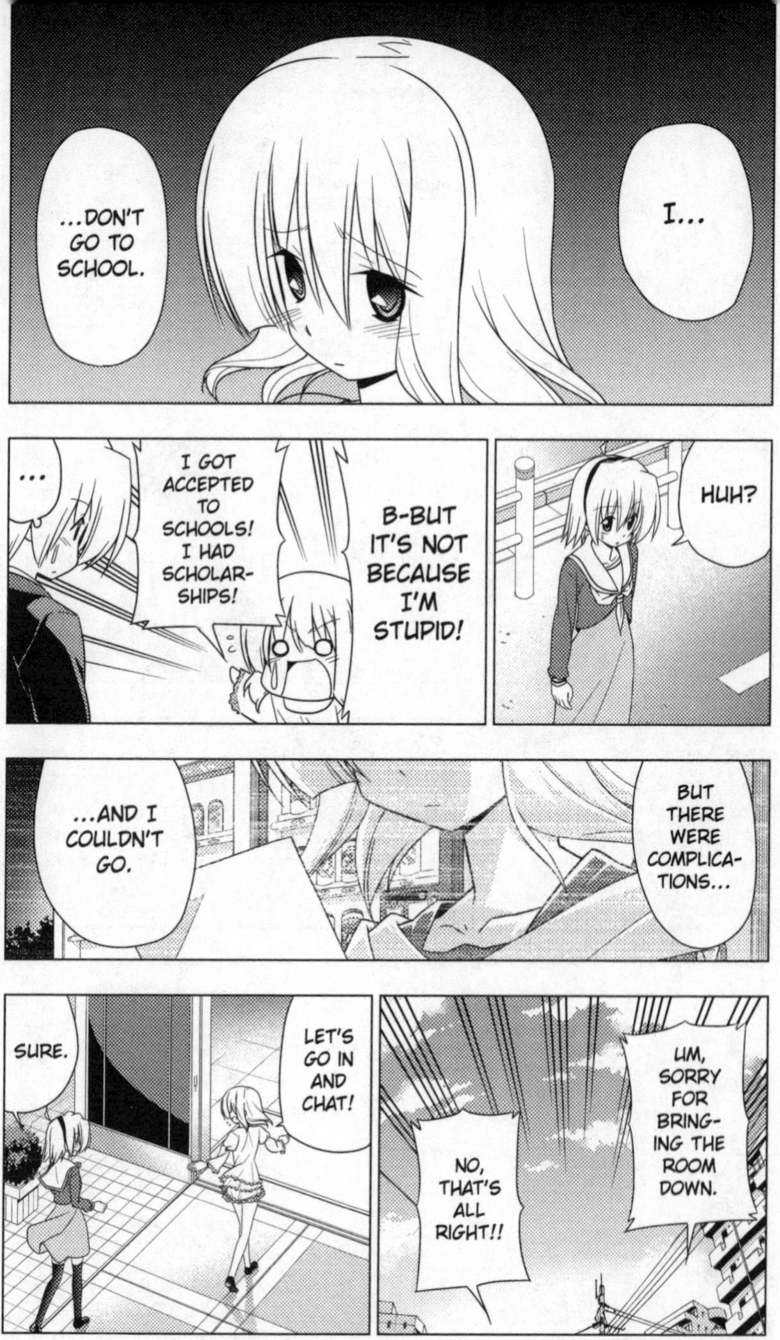
I...
...DON'T GO TO SCHOOL.
HUH?
B-BUT IT'S NOT BECAUSE I'M STUPID!
I GOT ACCEPTED TO SCHOOLS! I HAD SCHOLAR-SHIPS!
...
BUT THERE WERE COMPLICA-TIONS...
...AND I COULDN'T GO.
UM, SORRY FOR BRING-ING THE ROOM DOWN.
NO, THAT'S ALL RIGHT!!
LET'S GO IN AND CHAT!
SURE.

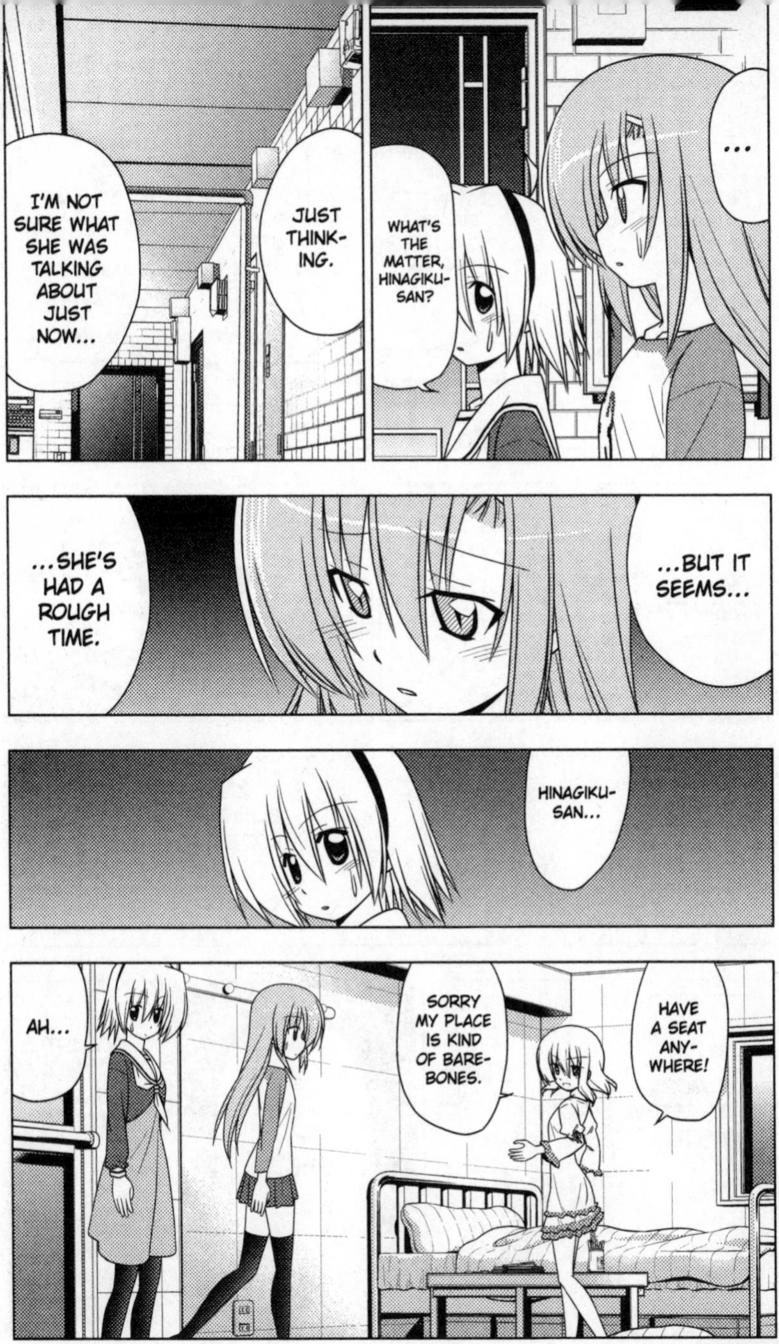
...
WHAT'S THE MATTER, HINAGIKU-SAN?
JUST THINKING.
I'M NOT SURE WHAT SHE WAS TALKING ABOUT JUST NOW...
...BUT IT SEEMS...
...SHE'S HAD A ROUGH TIME.
HINAGIKU-SAN...
HAVE A SEAT ANYWHERE!
SORRY MY PLACE IS KIND OF BARE-BONES.
AH...

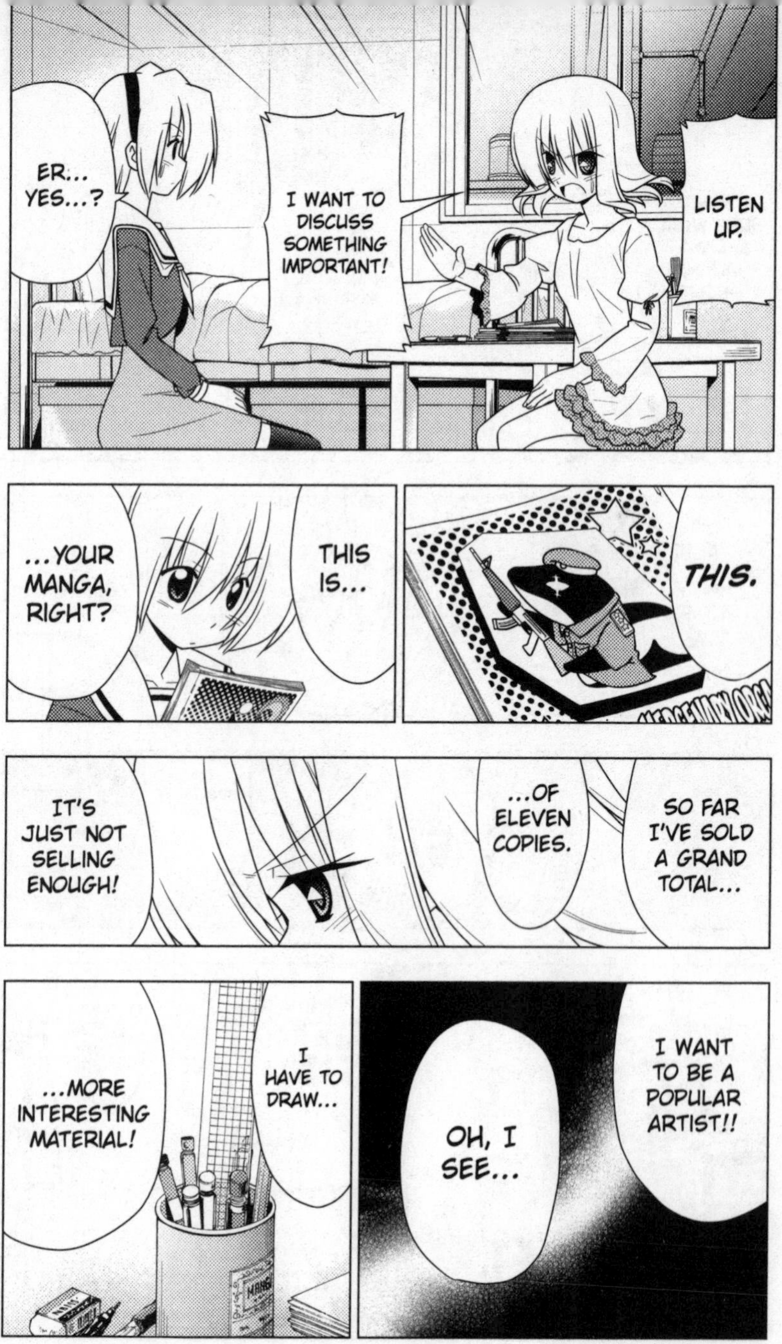
LISTEN UP.
I WANT TO DISCUSS SOMETHING IMPORTANT!
ER... YES...?
THIS.
THIS IS...
...YOUR MANGA, RIGHT?
SO FAR I'VE SOLD A GRAND TOTAL...
...OF ELEVEN COPIES.
IT'S JUST NOT SELLING ENOUGH!
I WANT TO BE A POPULAR ARTIST!!
OH, I SEE...
I HAVE TO DRAW...
...MORE INTERESTING MATERIAL!

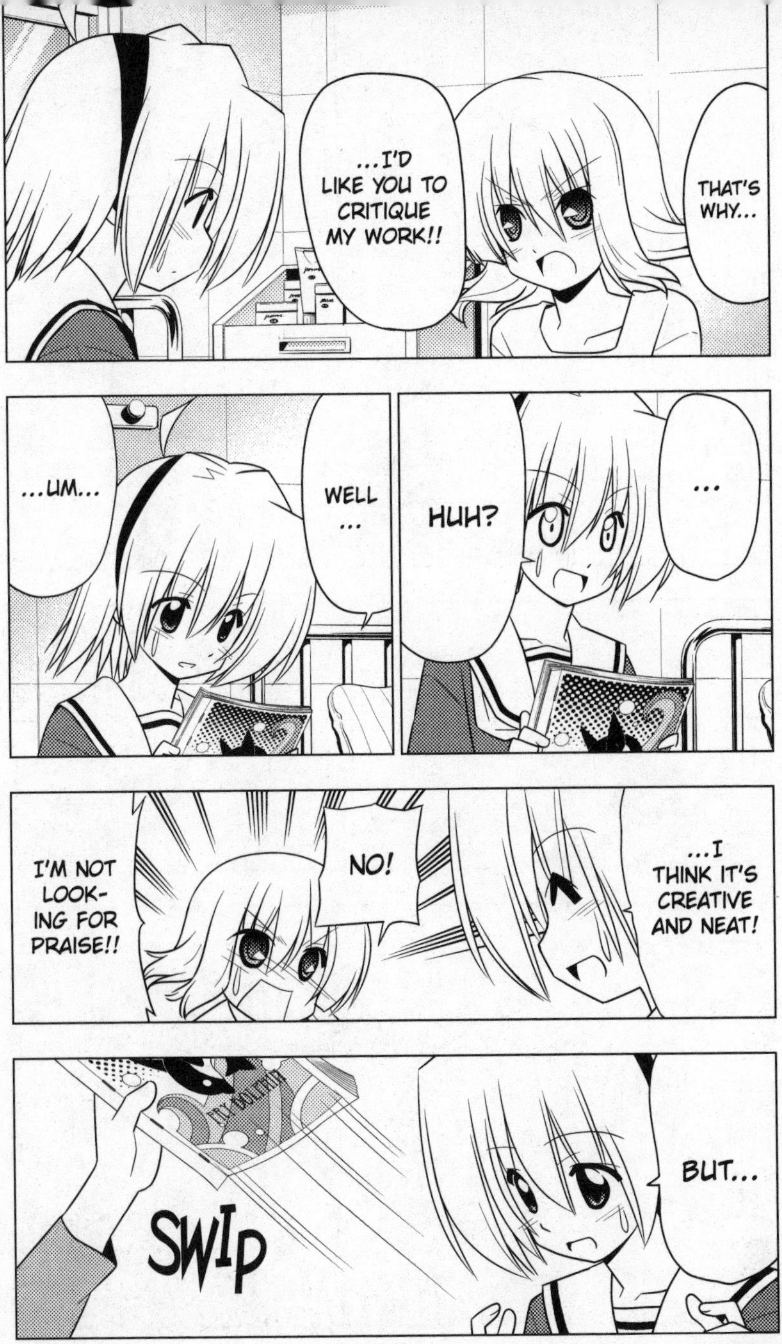
THAT'S WHY...
...I'D LIKE YOU TO CRITIQUE MY WORK!!
...
HUH?
WELL ...
...UM...
...I THINK IT'S CREATIVE AND NEAT!
NO!
I'M NOT LOOKING-ING FOR PRAISE!!
BUT...
SWIP

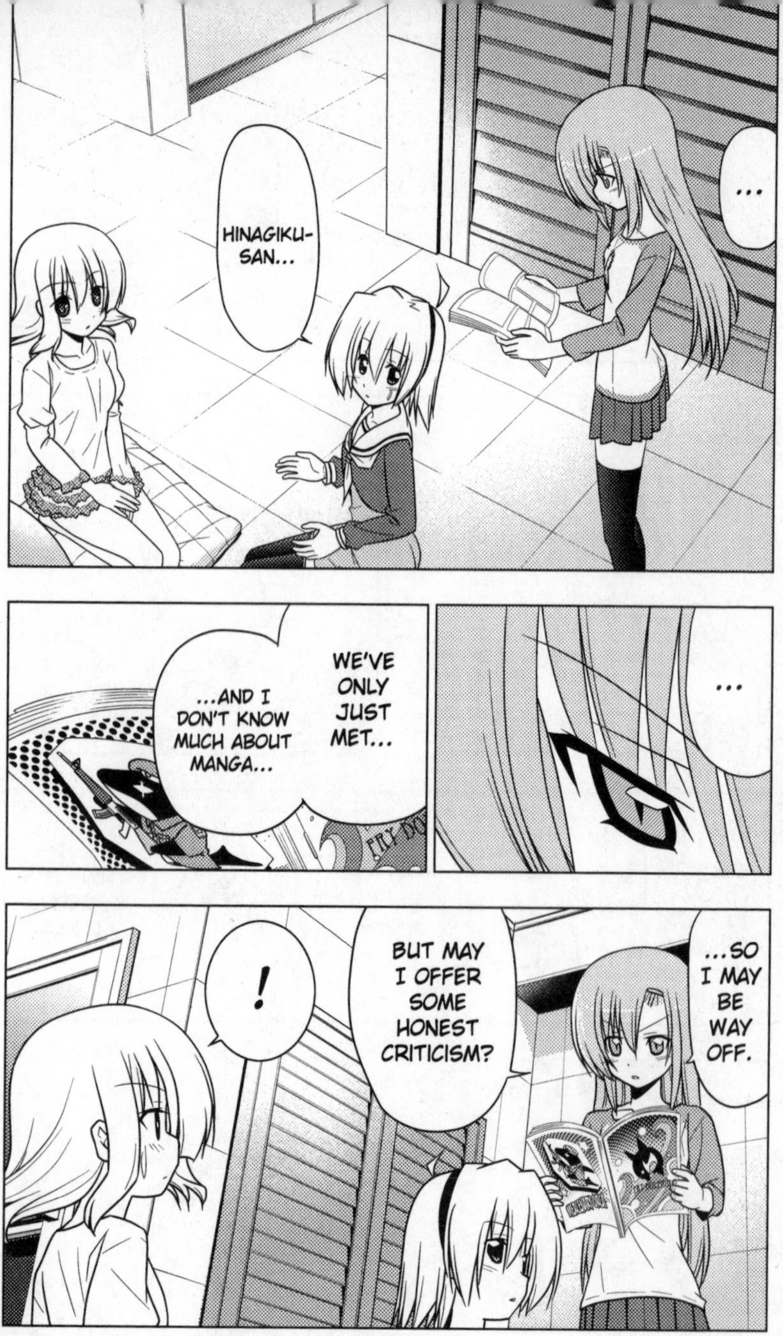
...
HINAGIKU-SAN...
...
WE'VE ONLY JUST MET...
...AND I DON'T KNOW MUCH ABOUT MANGA...
...SO I MAY BE WAY OFF.
BUT MAY I OFFER SOME HONEST CRITICISM?
!

Episode 5: "High-Spec Advisor"

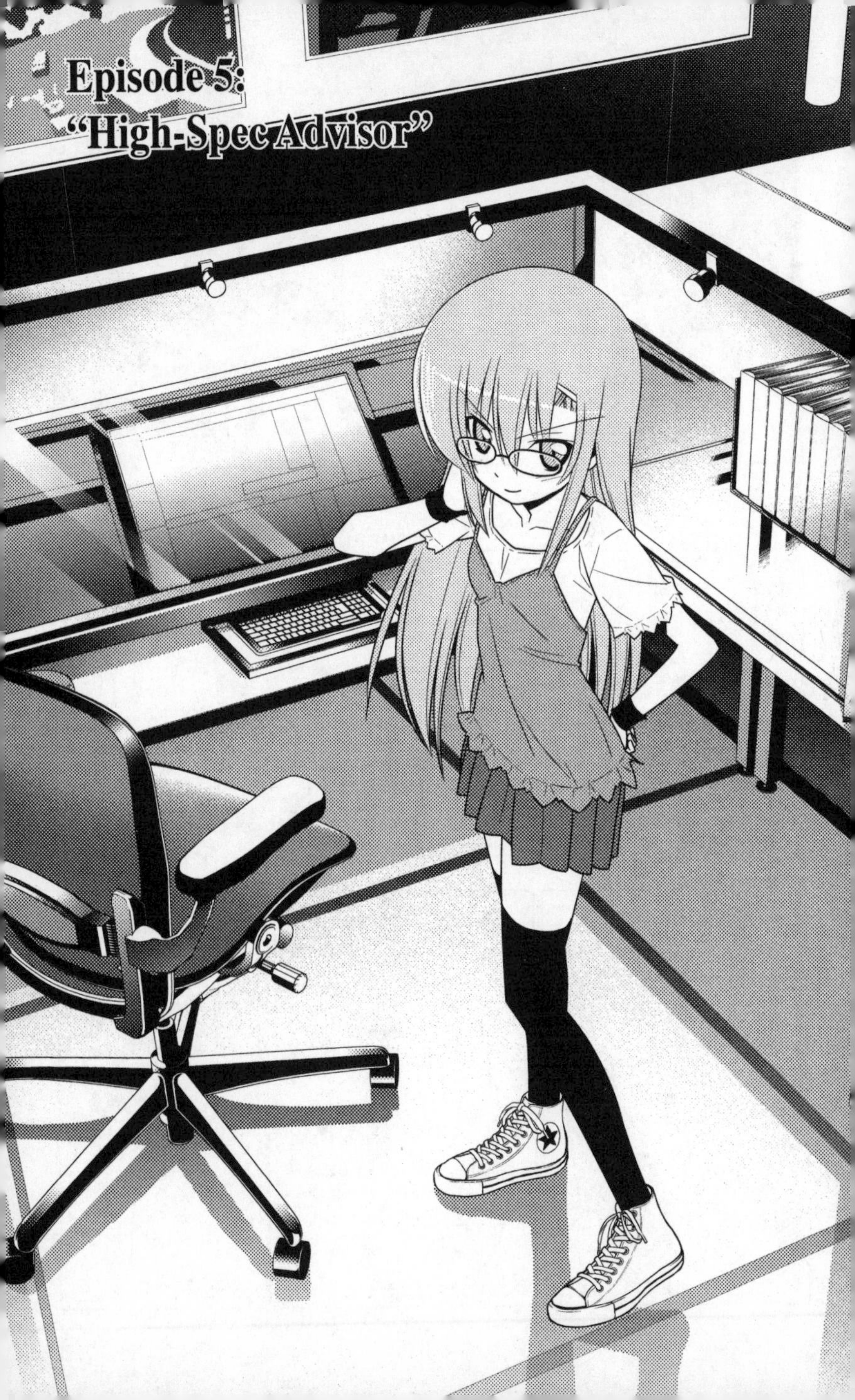

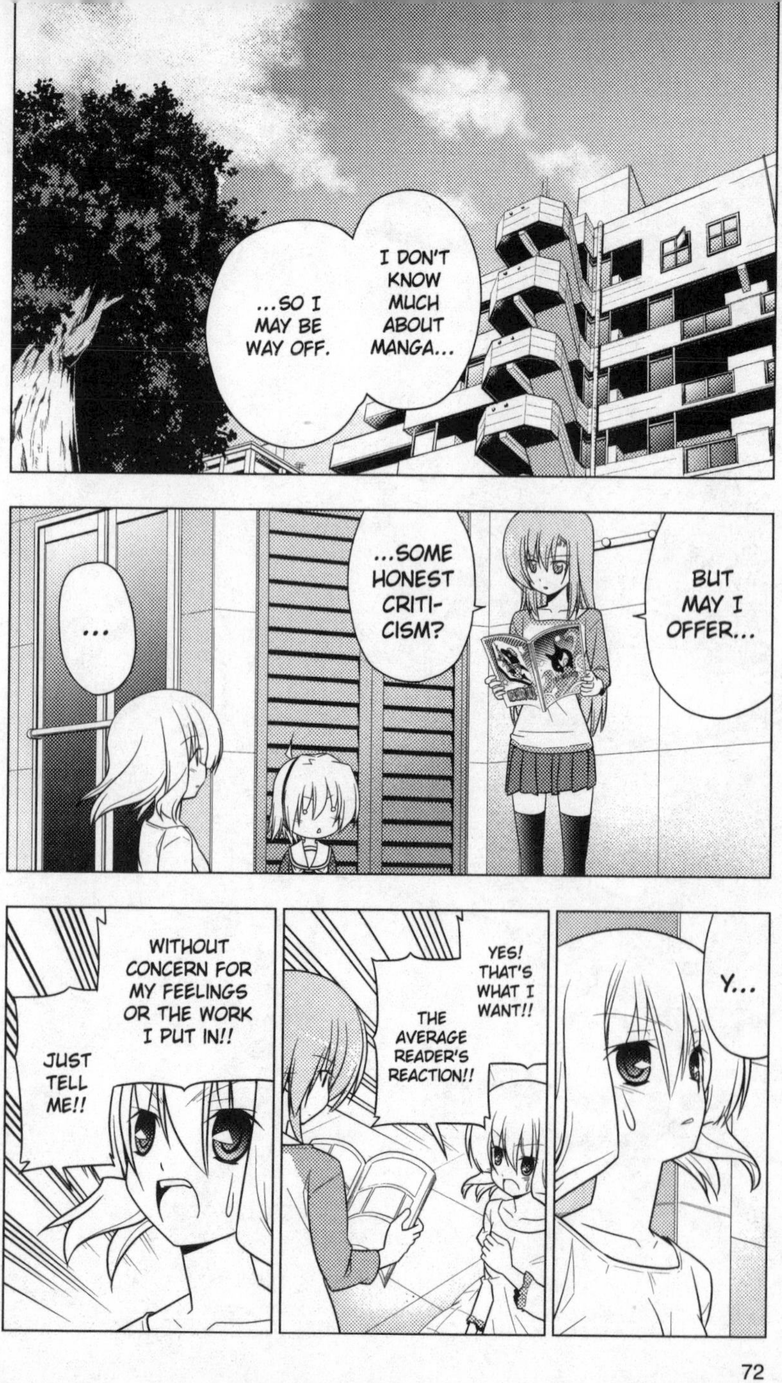
I DON'T KNOW MUCH ABOUT MANGA...
...SO I MAY BE WAY OFF.
BUT MAY I OFFER...
...SOME HONEST CRITI-CISM?
...
Y...
YES! THAT'S WHAT I WANT!!
THE AVERAGE READER'S REACTION!!
WITHOUT CONCERN FOR MY FEELINGS OR THE WORK I PUT IN!!
JUST TELL ME!!

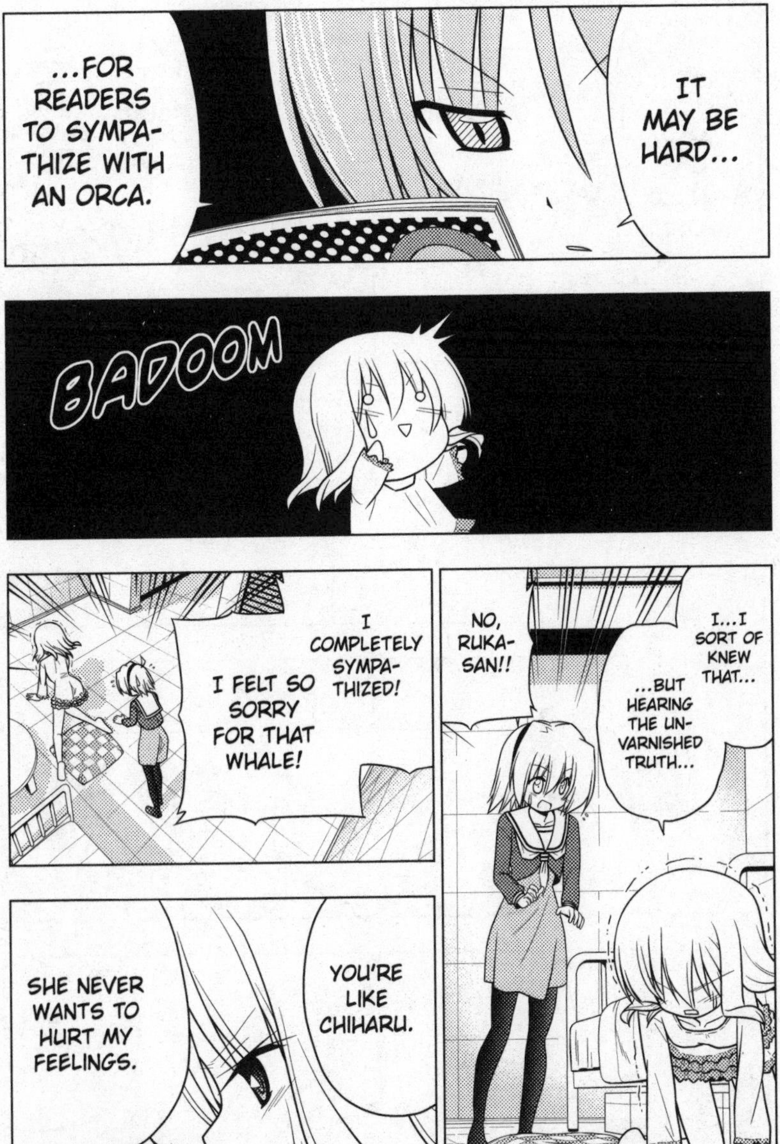
IT MAY BE HARD...
...FOR READERS TO SYMPA-THIZE WITH AN ORCA.
BADOOM
I...I SORT OF KNEW THAT...
...BUT HEARING THE UN-VARNISHED TRUTH...
NO, RUKA-SAN!!
I COMPLETELY SYMPA-THIZED!
I FELT SO SORRY FOR THAT WHALE!
YOU'RE LIKE CHIHARU.
SHE NEVER WANTS TO HURT MY FEELINGS.

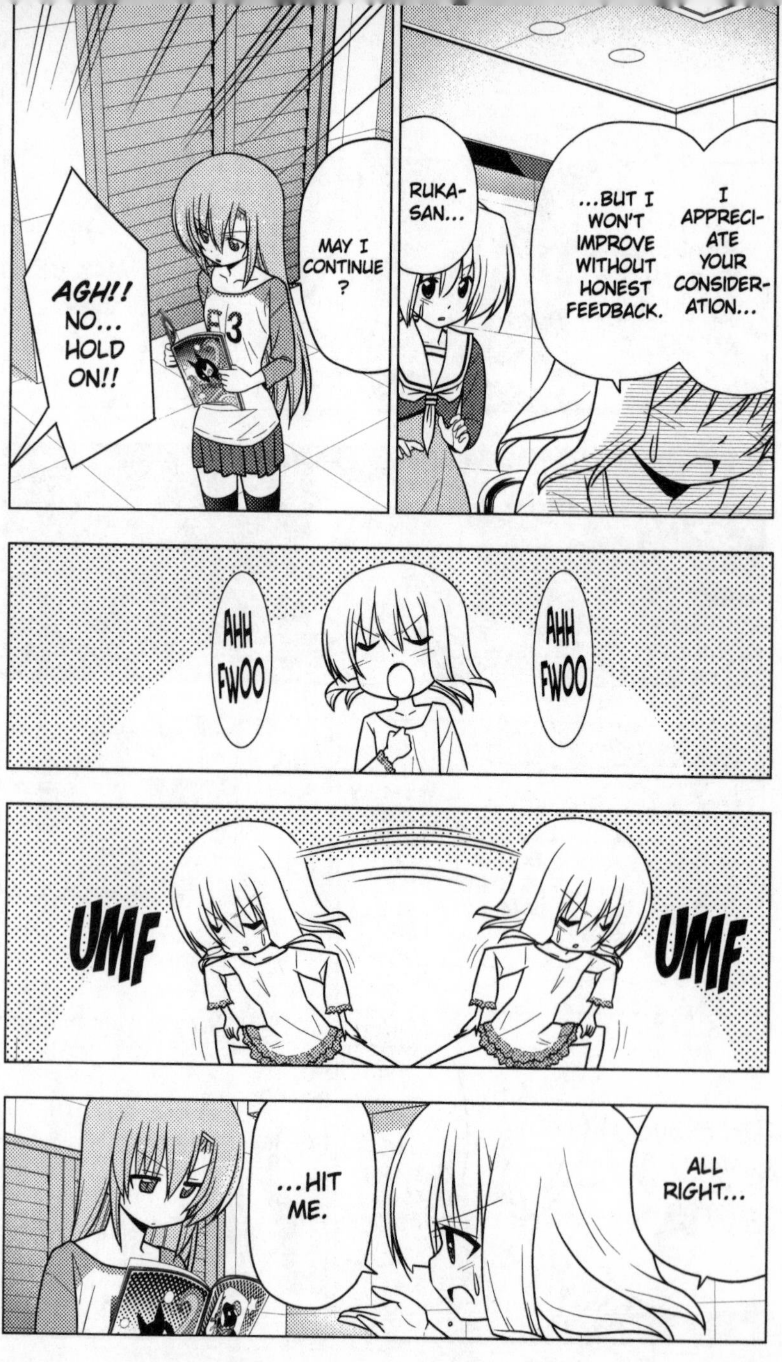
I APPRECIATE YOUR CONSIDERATION...
...BUT I WON'T IMPROVE WITHOUT HONEST FEEDBACK.
RUKA-SAN...
MAY I CONTINUE?
AGH!! NO... HOLD ON!!
AHH FWOO
AHH FWOO
UMF
UMF
ALL RIGHT...
...HIT ME.

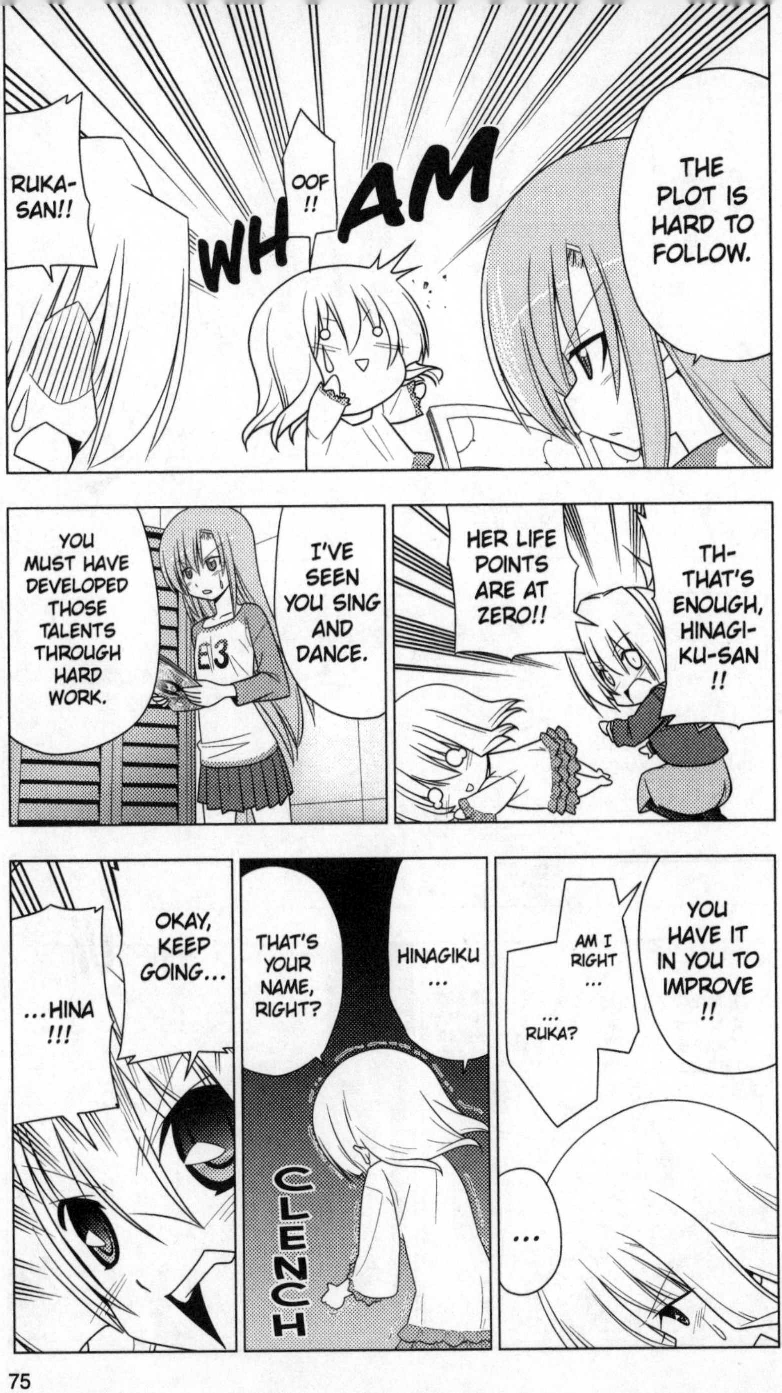
THE PLOT IS HARD TO FOLLOW.
OOF!!
WHAM
RUKA-SAN!!
TH-THAT'S ENOUGH, HINAGIKU-SAN!!
HER LIFE POINTS ARE AT ZERO!!
I'VE SEEN YOU SING AND DANCE.
YOU MUST HAVE DEVELOPED THOSE TALENTS THROUGH HARD WORK.
YOU HAVE IT IN YOU TO IMPROVE!!
AM I RIGHT...
...RUKA?
...
HINAGIKU...
THAT'S YOUR NAME, RIGHT?
CLENCH
OKAY, KEEP GOING...
...HINA!!!

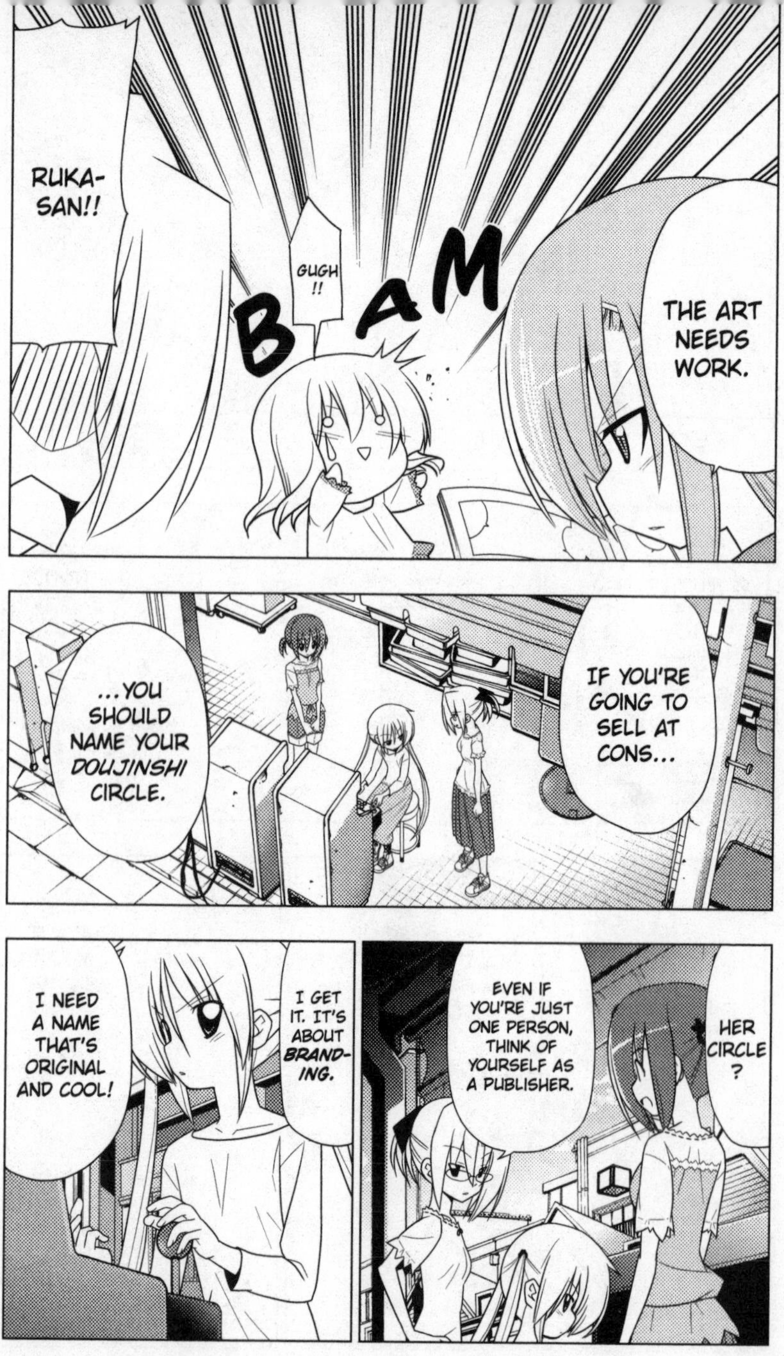
THE ART NEEDS WORK.
BAM
GUGH!!
RUKA-SAN!!
IF YOU'RE GOING TO SELL AT CONS...
...YOU SHOULD NAME YOUR *DOUJINSHI* CIRCLE.
HER CIRCLE?
EVEN IF YOU'RE JUST ONE PERSON, THINK OF YOURSELF AS A PUBLISHER.
I GET IT. IT'S ABOUT *BRANDING.*
I NEED A NAME THAT'S ORIGINAL AND COOL!

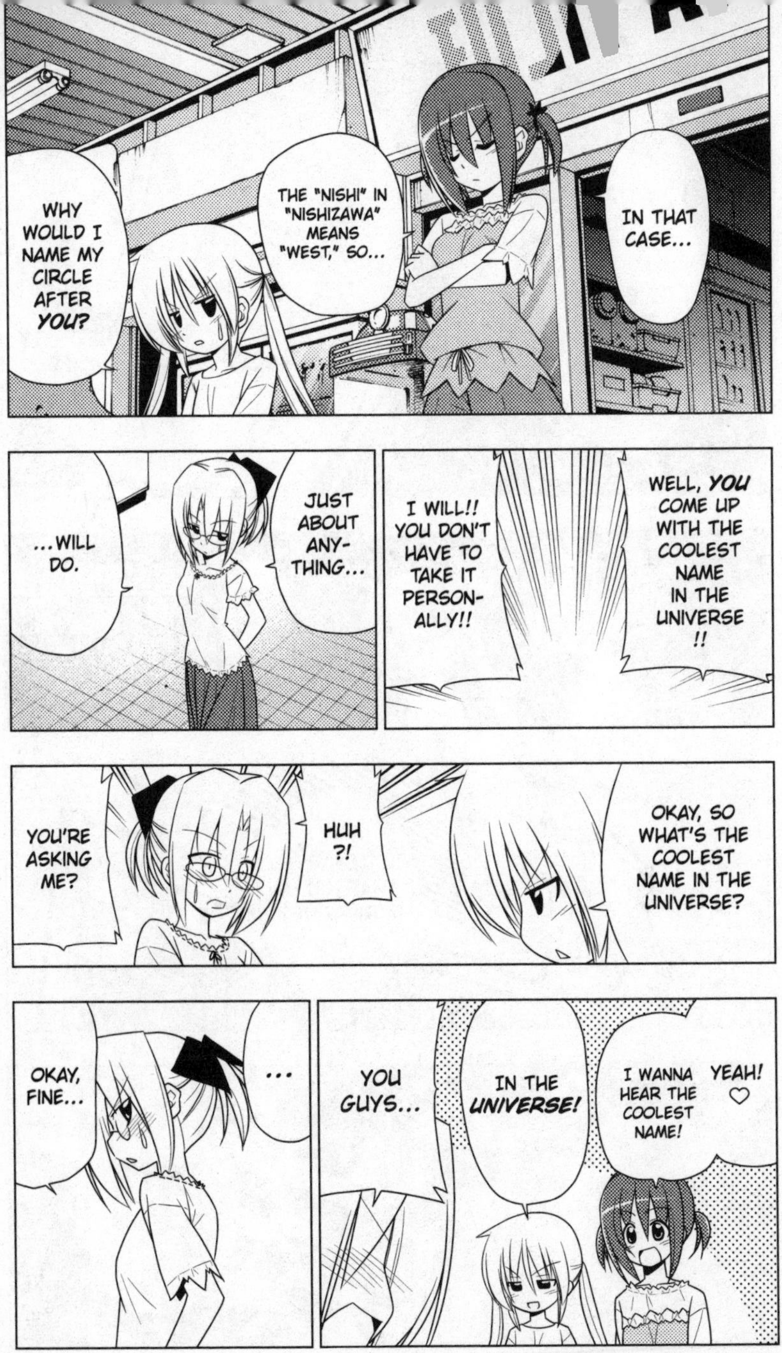
IN THAT CASE...
THE "NISHI" IN "NISHIZAWA" MEANS "WEST," SO...
WHY WOULD I NAME MY CIRCLE AFTER *YOU*?
WELL, *YOU* COME UP WITH THE COOLEST NAME IN THE UNIVERSE!!
I WILL!! YOU DON'T HAVE TO TAKE IT PERSONALLY!!
JUST ABOUT ANYTHING...
...WILL DO.
OKAY, SO WHAT'S THE COOLEST NAME IN THE UNIVERSE?
HUH?!
YOU'RE ASKING ME?
YEAH! ♡
I WANNA HEAR THE COOLEST NAME!
IN THE *UNIVERSE!*
YOU GUYS...
...
OKAY, FINE...

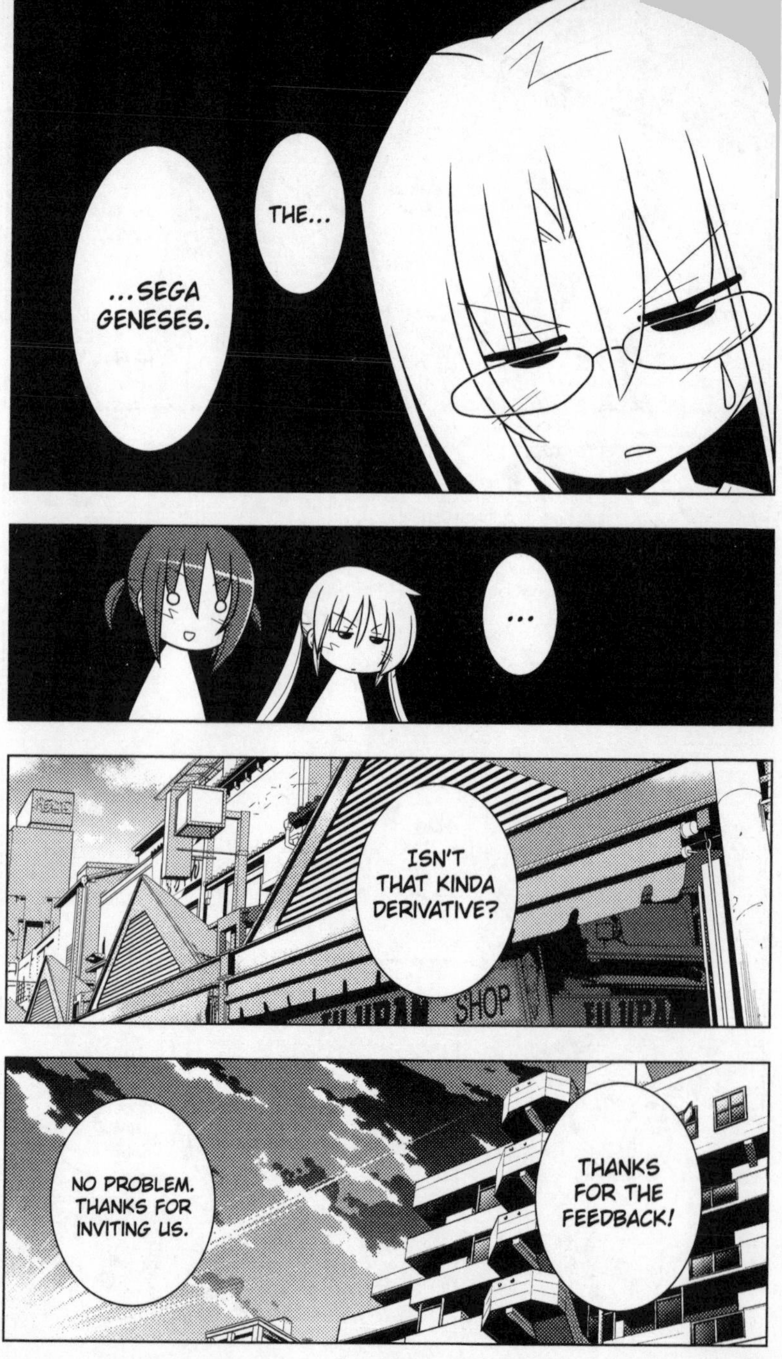
THE...
...SEGA GENESES.
...
ISN'T THAT KINDA DERIVATIVE?
SHOP
THANKS FOR THE FEEDBACK!
NO PROBLEM. THANKS FOR INVITING US.

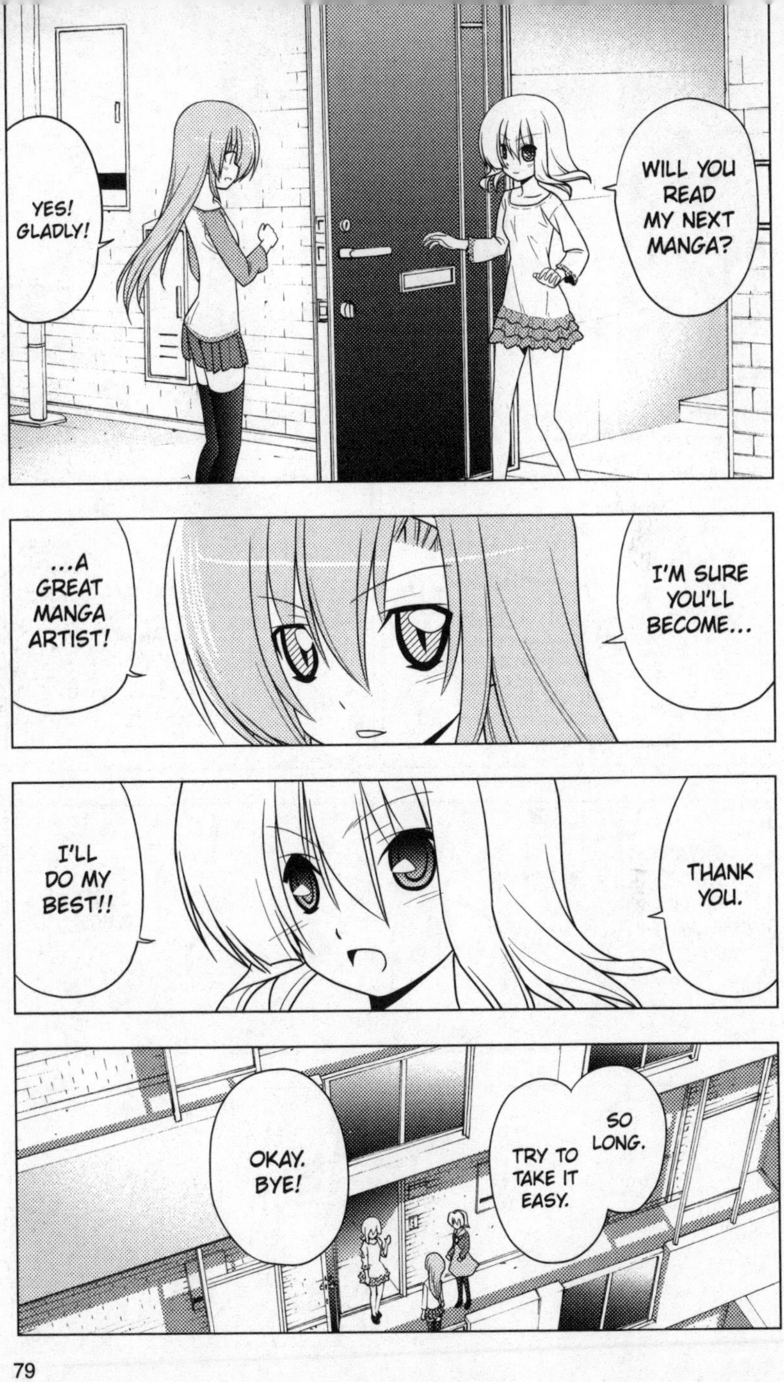
WILL YOU READ MY NEXT MANGA?
YES! GLADLY!
I'M SURE YOU'LL BECOME...
...A GREAT MANGA ARTIST!
THANK YOU.
I'LL DO MY BEST!!
SO LONG.
TRY TO TAKE IT EASY.
OKAY. BYE!

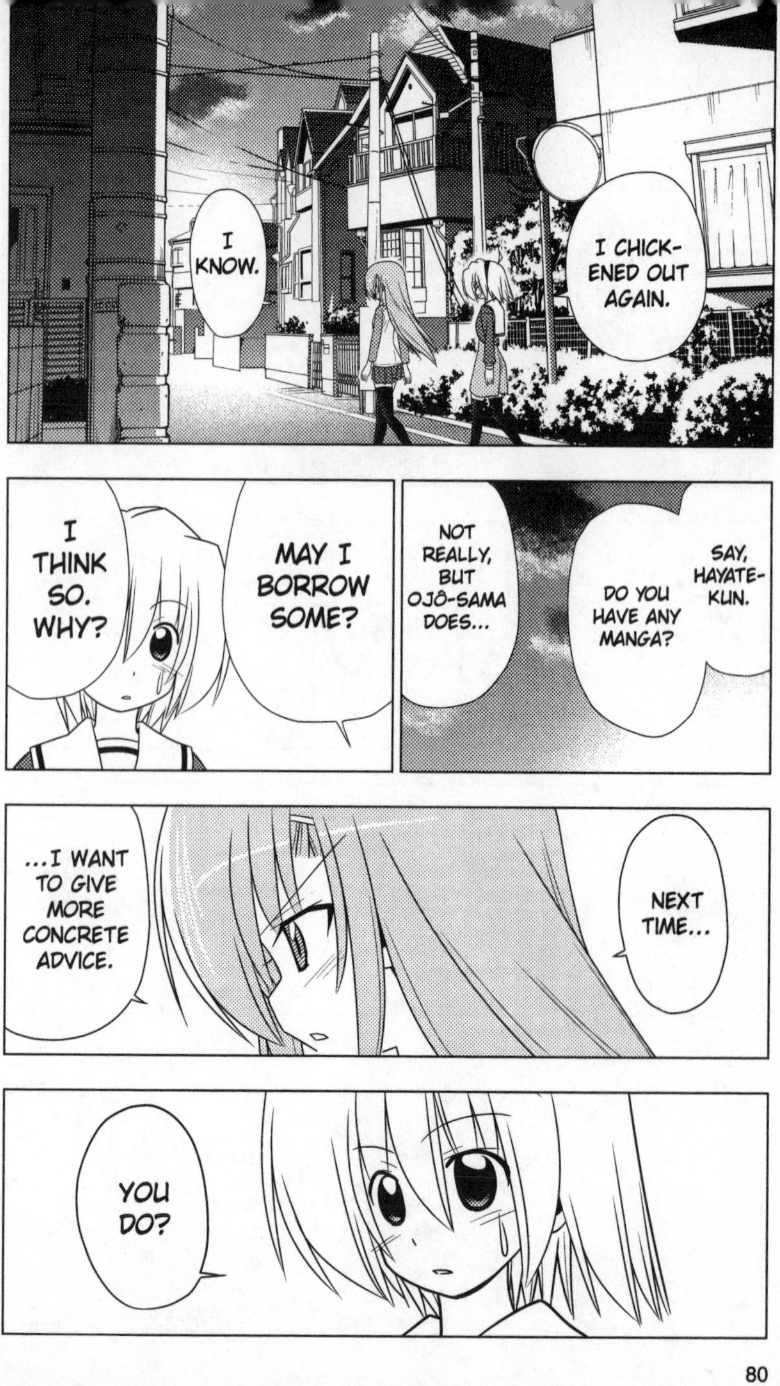
I CHICK-ENED OUT AGAIN.
I KNOW.
SAY, HAYATE-KUN.
DO YOU HAVE ANY MANGA?
NOT REALLY, BUT OJÔ-SAMA DOES...
MAY I BORROW SOME?
I THINK SO. WHY?
NEXT TIME...
...I WANT TO GIVE MORE CONCRETE ADVICE.
YOU DO?

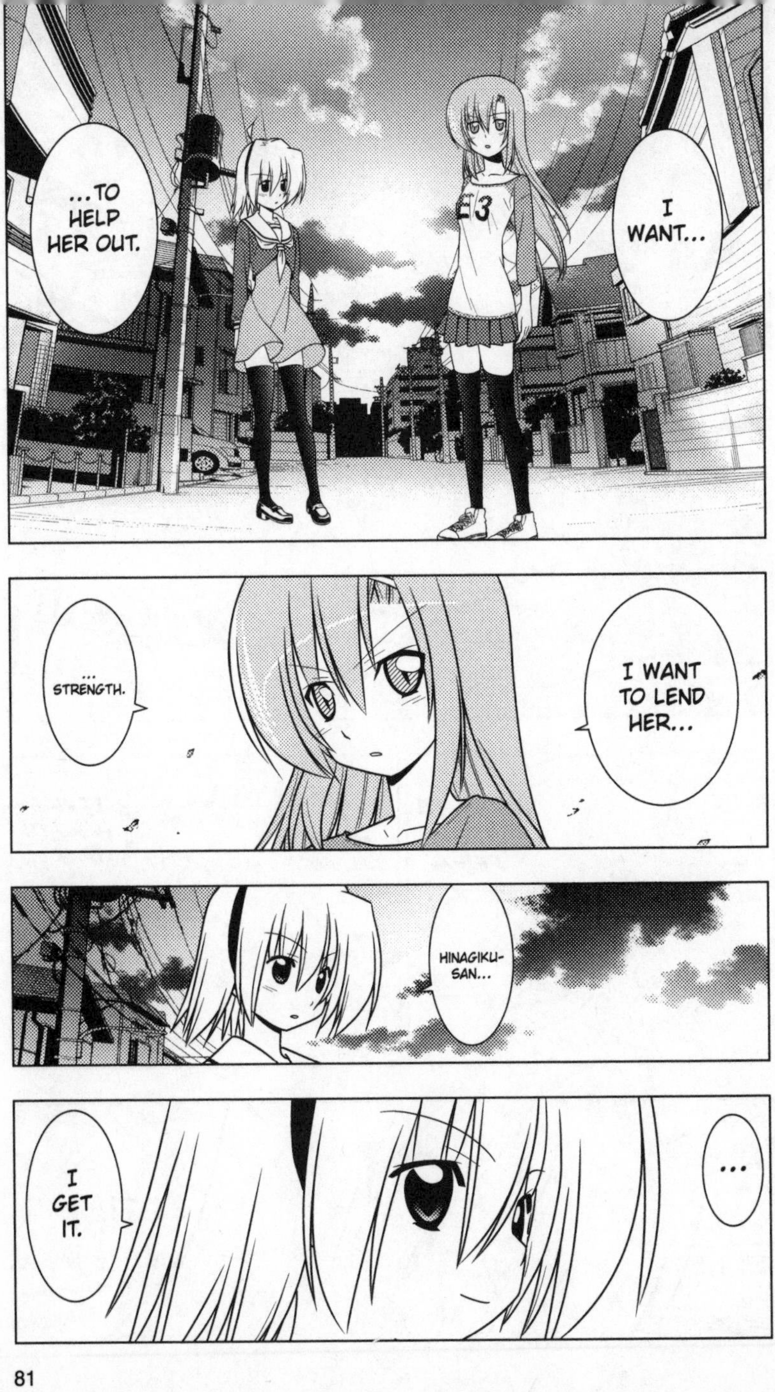
I WANT...
...TO HELP HER OUT.
I WANT TO LEND HER...
...STRENGTH.
HINAGIKU-SAN...
...
I GET IT.

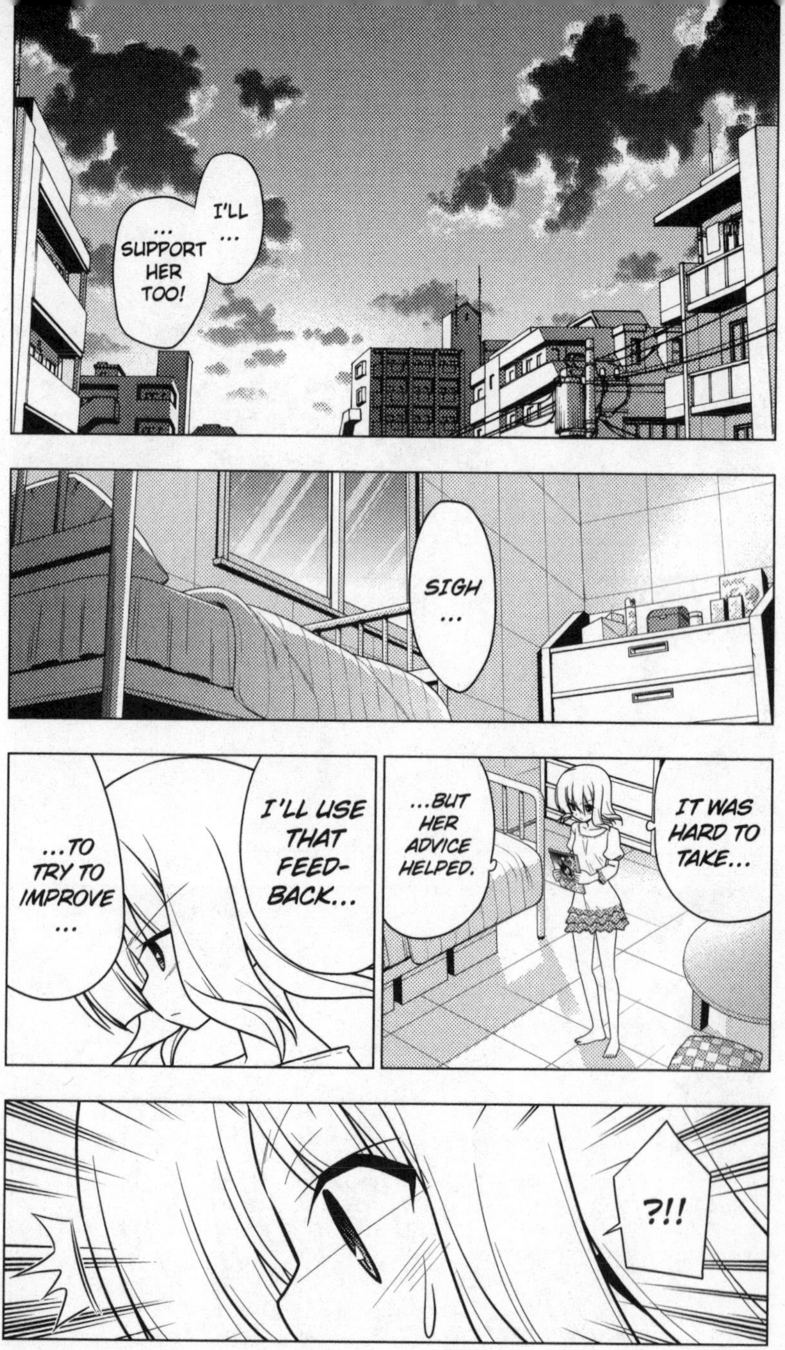
I'LL ... ... SUPPORT HER TOO!
SIGH ...
IT WAS HARD TO TAKE...
...BUT HER ADVICE HELPED.
I'LL USE THAT FEED-BACK...
...TO TRY TO IMPROVE ...
?!!

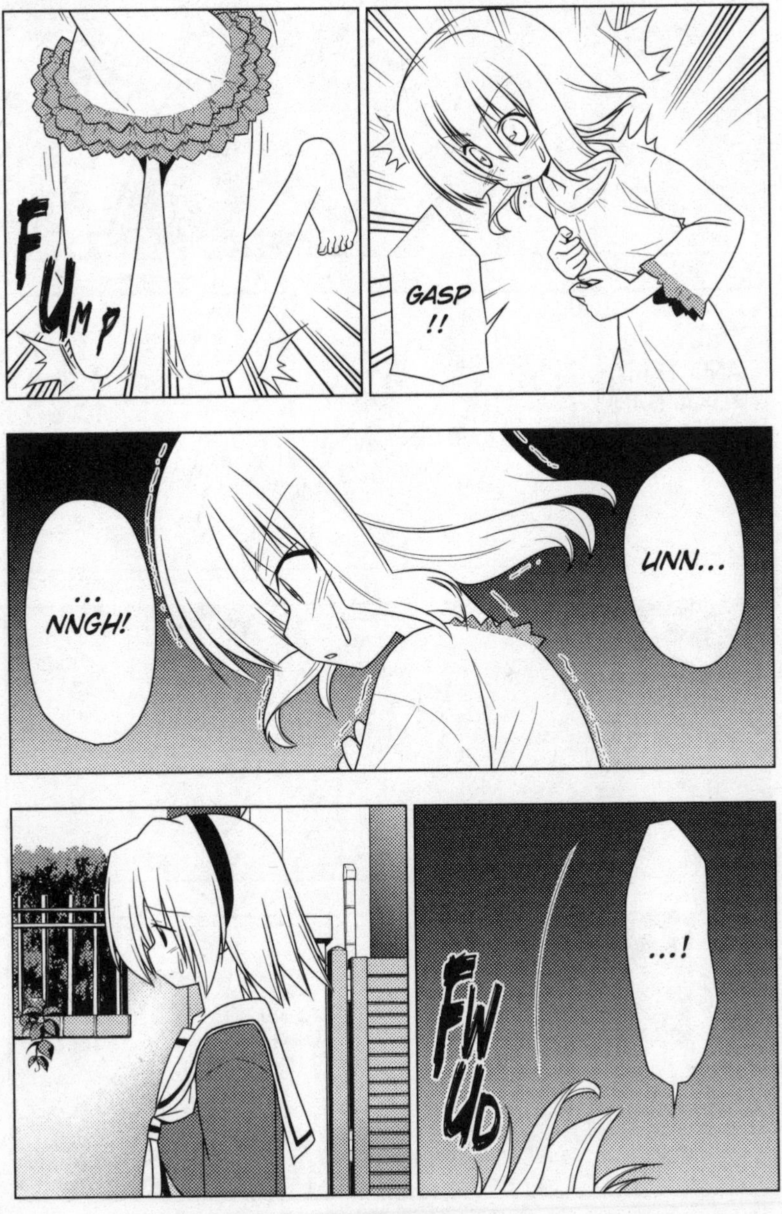
GASP !!
FUMP
UNN...
... NNGH!
...!
FWUD

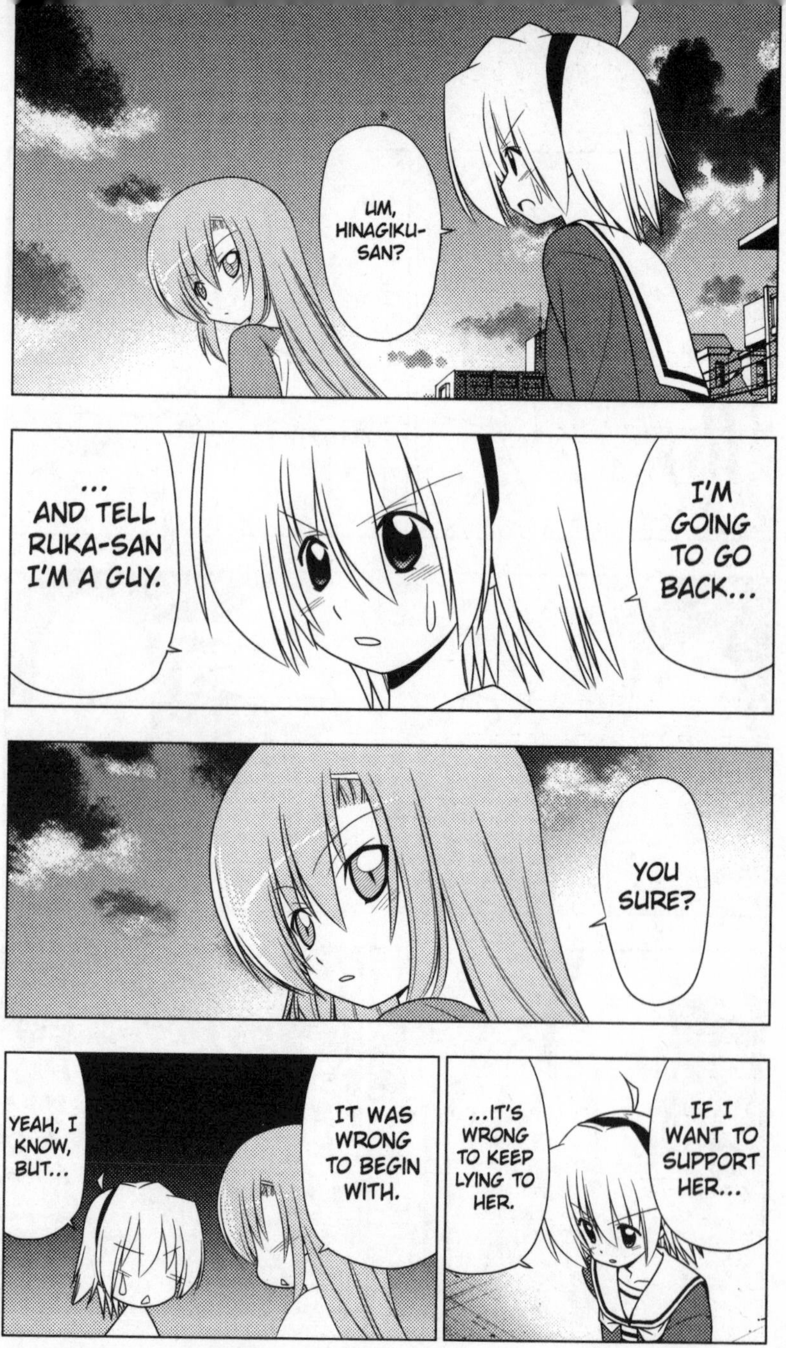
UM, HINAGIKU-SAN?
I'M GOING TO GO BACK...
... AND TELL RUKA-SAN I'M A GUY.
YOU SURE?
IF I WANT TO SUPPORT HER...
...IT'S WRONG TO KEEP LYING TO HER.
IT WAS WRONG TO BEGIN WITH.
YEAH, I KNOW, BUT...

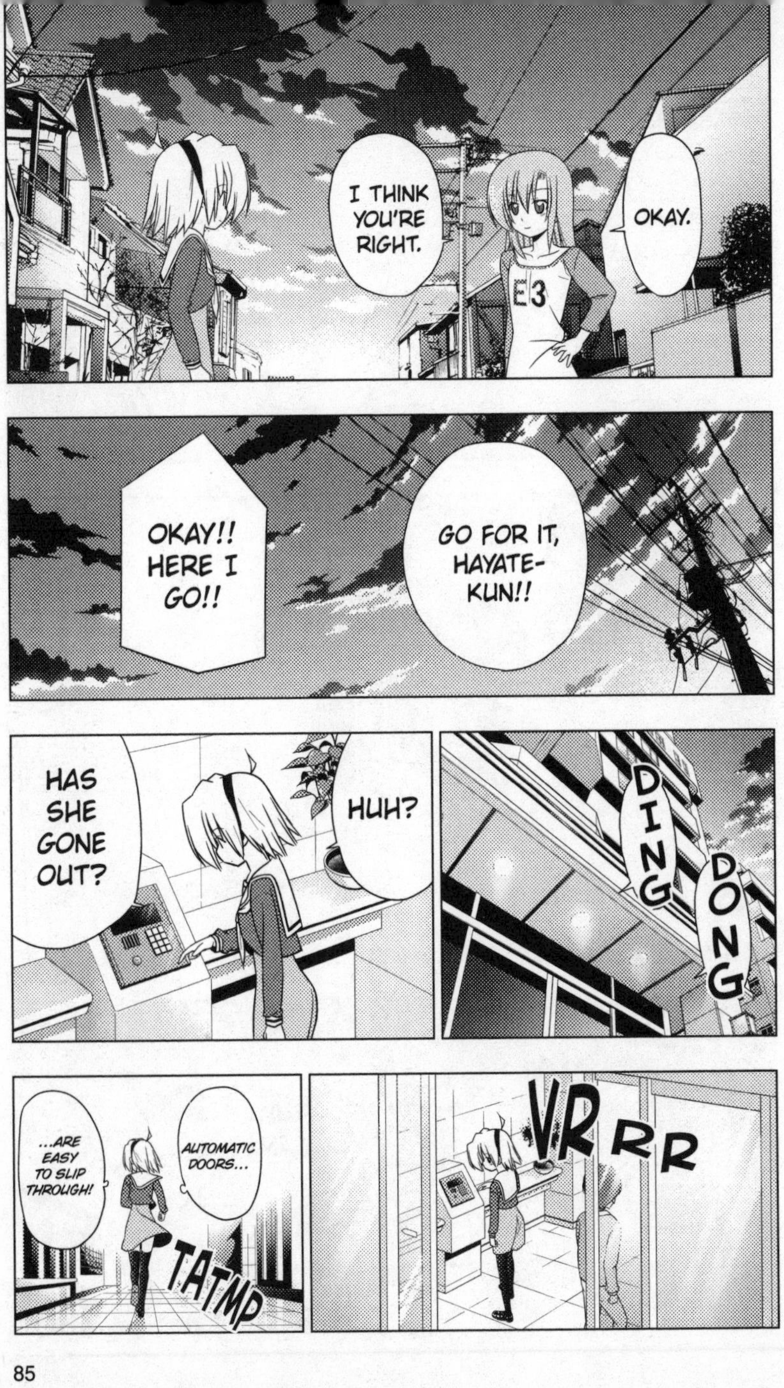
OKAY.
I THINK YOU'RE RIGHT.
GO FOR IT, HAYATE-KUN!!
OKAY!! HERE I GO!!
DING DONG
HUH?
HAS SHE GONE OUT?
VRRR
AUTOMATIC DOORS...
...ARE EASY TO SLIP THROUGH!
TATMP

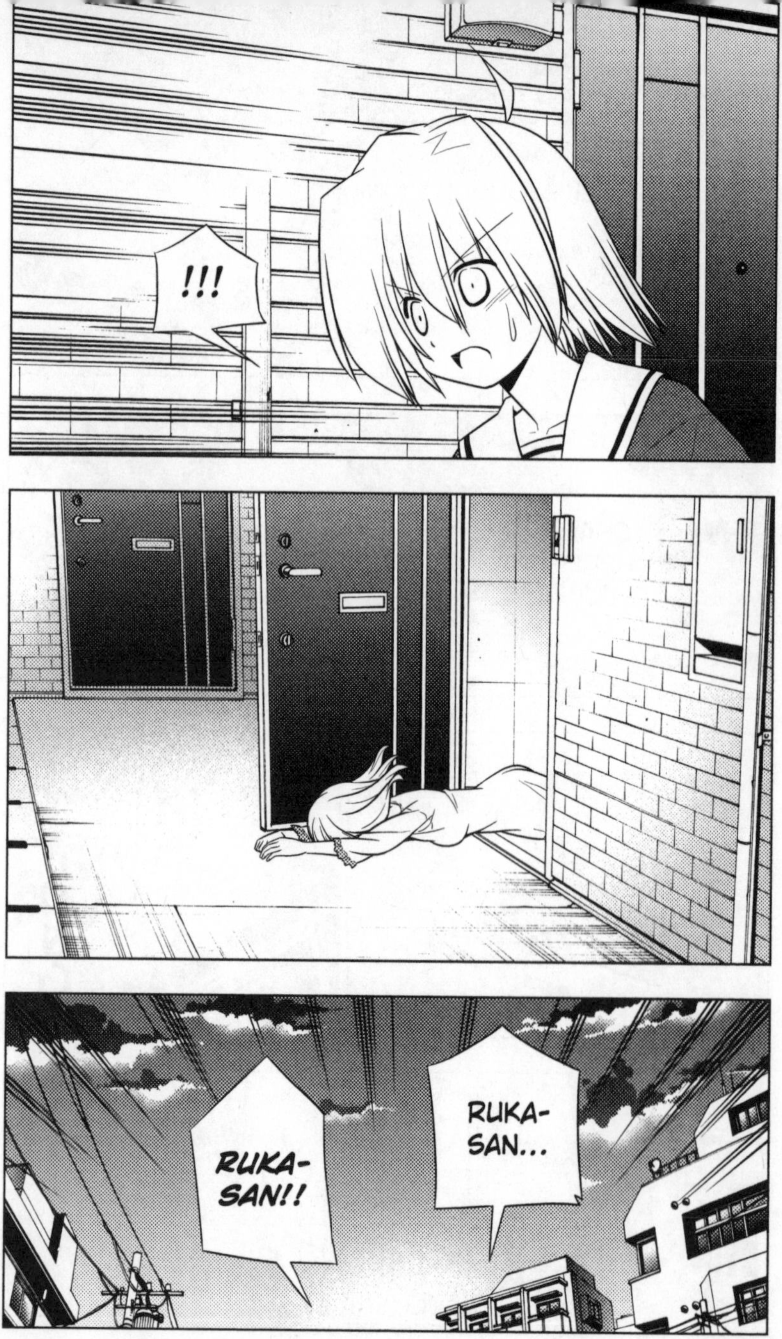
!!!
RUKA-SAN...
RUKA-SAN!!

Episode 6:
"Before I Knew It, I Was in Mud up to My Waist"

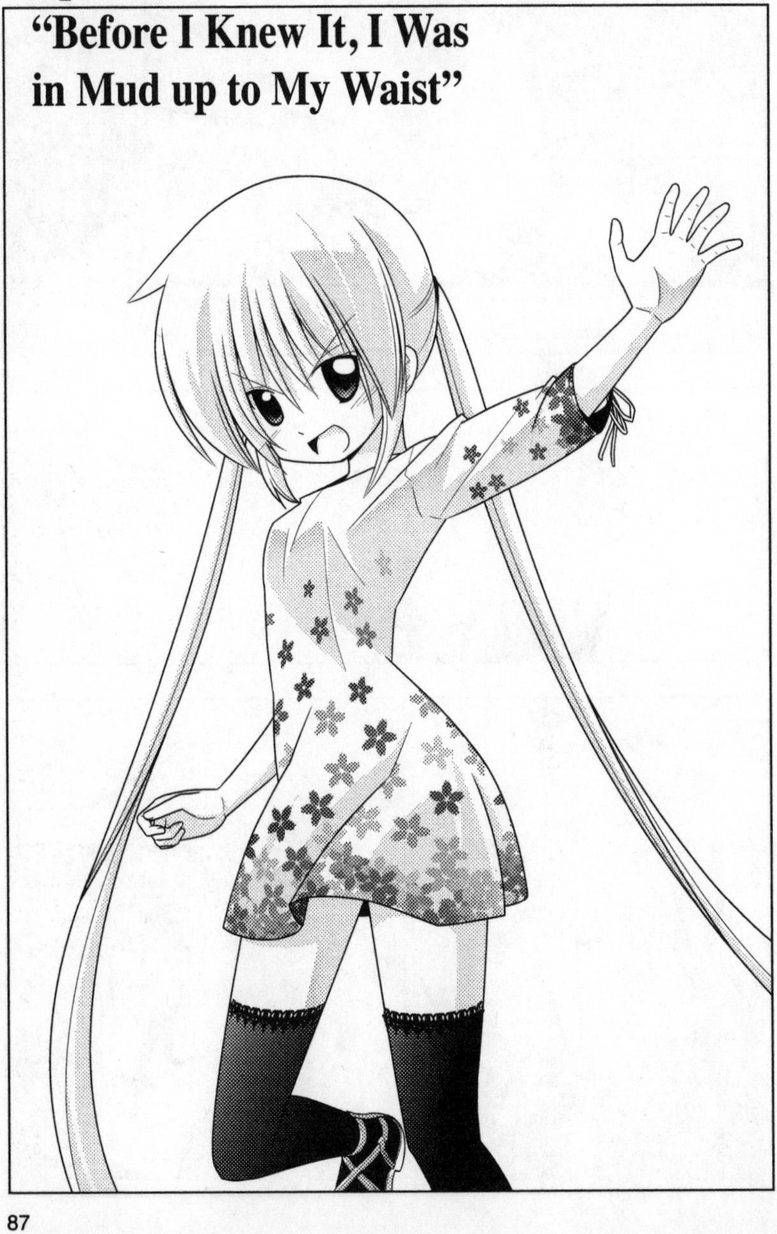

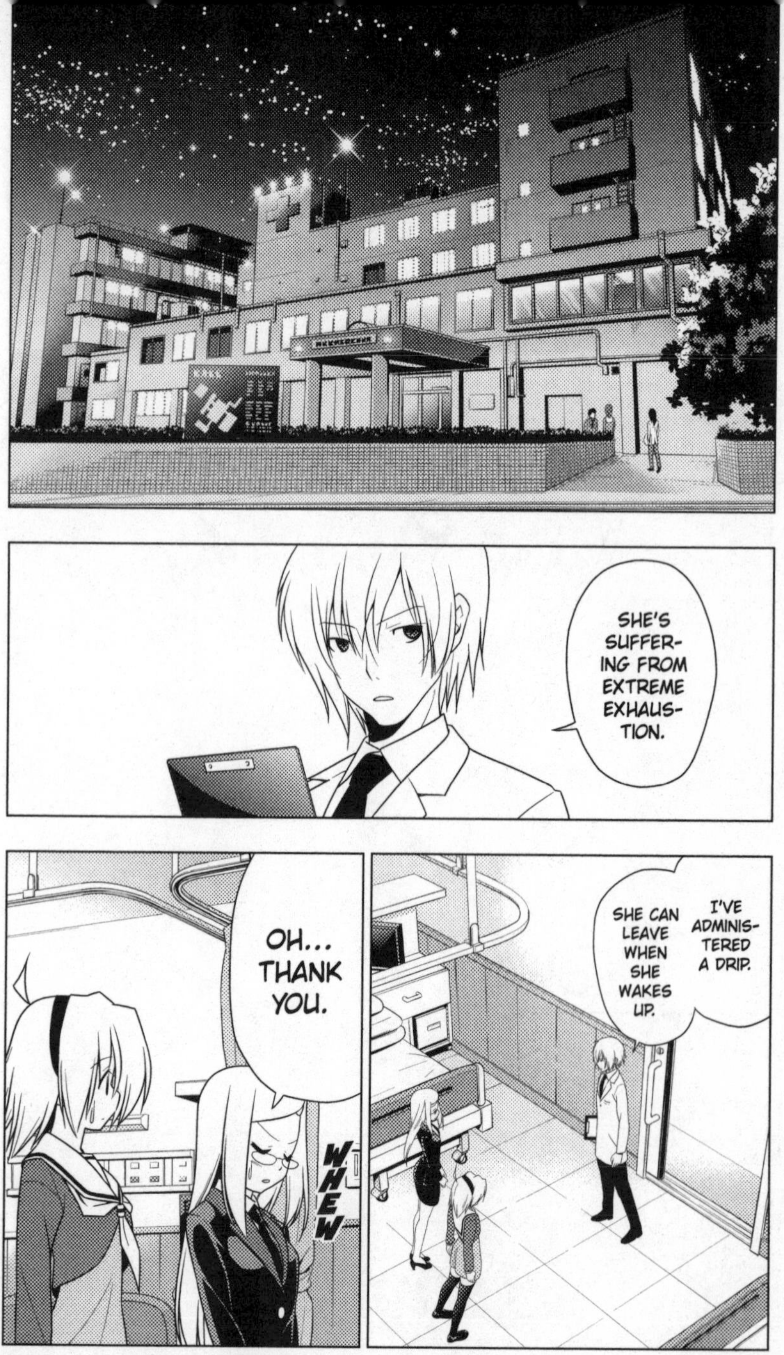
SHE'S SUFFERING FROM EXTREME EXHAUSTION.
I'VE ADMINISTERED A DRIP.
SHE CAN LEAVE WHEN SHE WAKES UP.
OH... THANK YOU.
WHEW

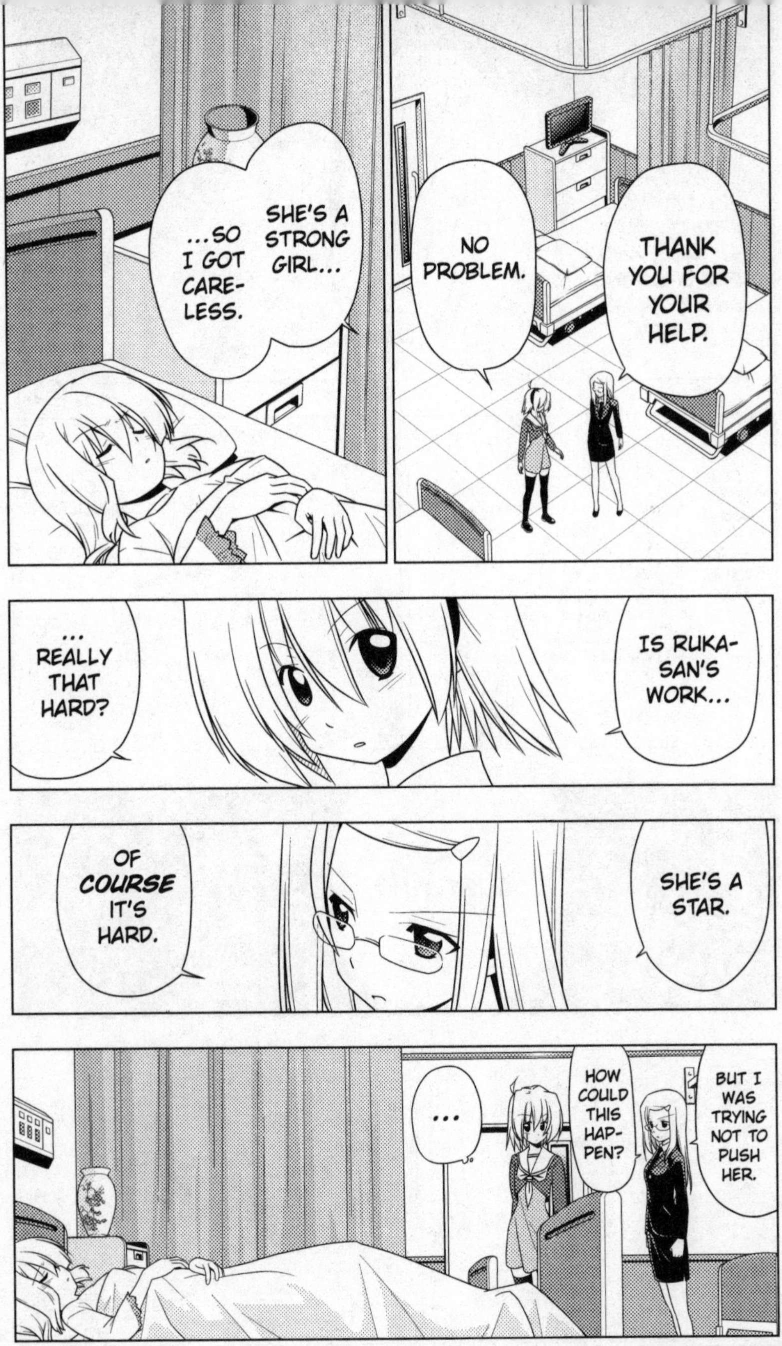
THANK YOU FOR YOUR HELP.
NO PROBLEM.
SHE'S A STRONG GIRL...
...SO I GOT CARELESS.
IS RUKA-SAN'S WORK...
...REALLY THAT HARD?
SHE'S A STAR.
OF COURSE IT'S HARD.
BUT I WAS TRYING NOT TO PUSH HER.
HOW COULD THIS HAPPEN?
...

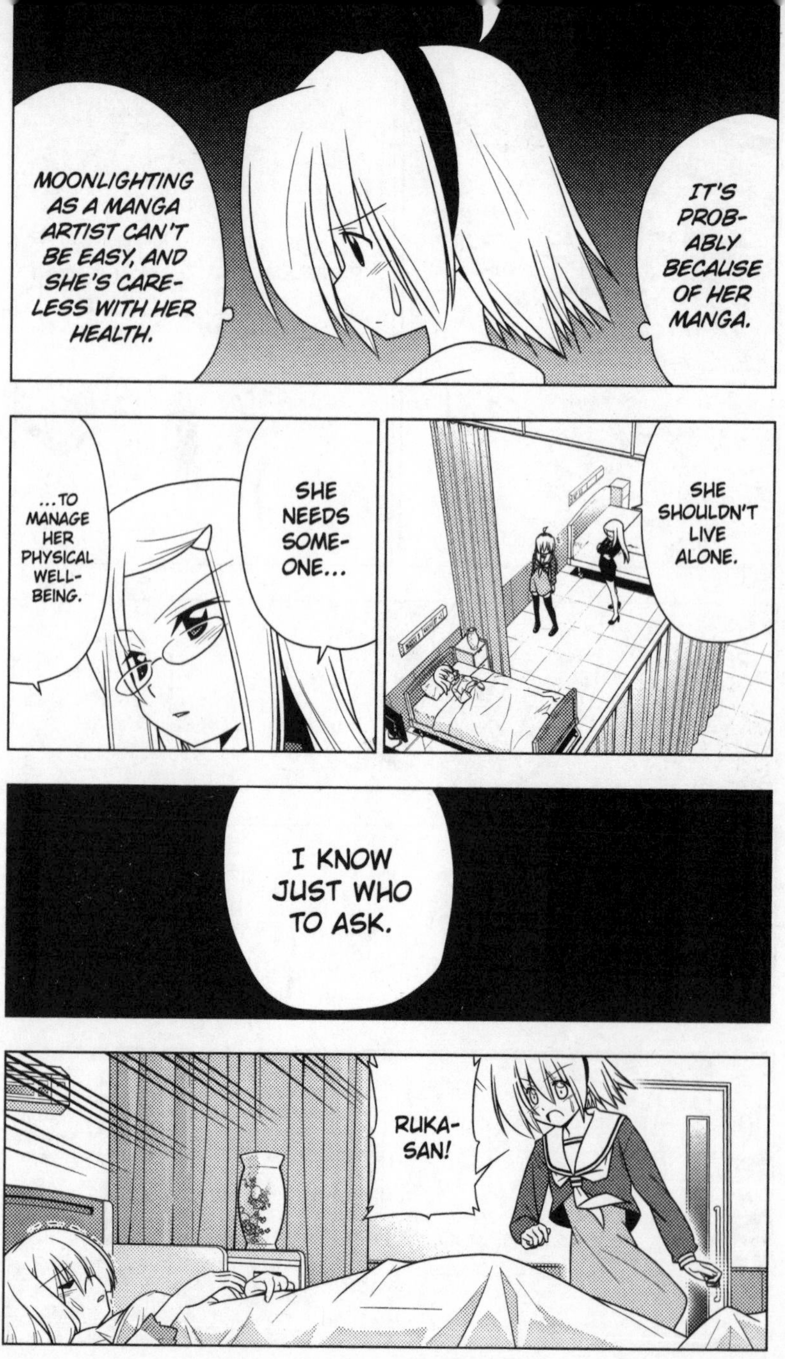
IT'S PROBABLY BECAUSE OF HER MANGA.
MOONLIGHTING AS A MANGA ARTIST CAN'T BE EASY, AND SHE'S CARELESS WITH HER HEALTH.
SHE SHOULDN'T LIVE ALONE.
SHE NEEDS SOMEONE...
...TO MANAGE HER PHYSICAL WELL-BEING.
I KNOW JUST WHO TO ASK.
RUKA-SAN!

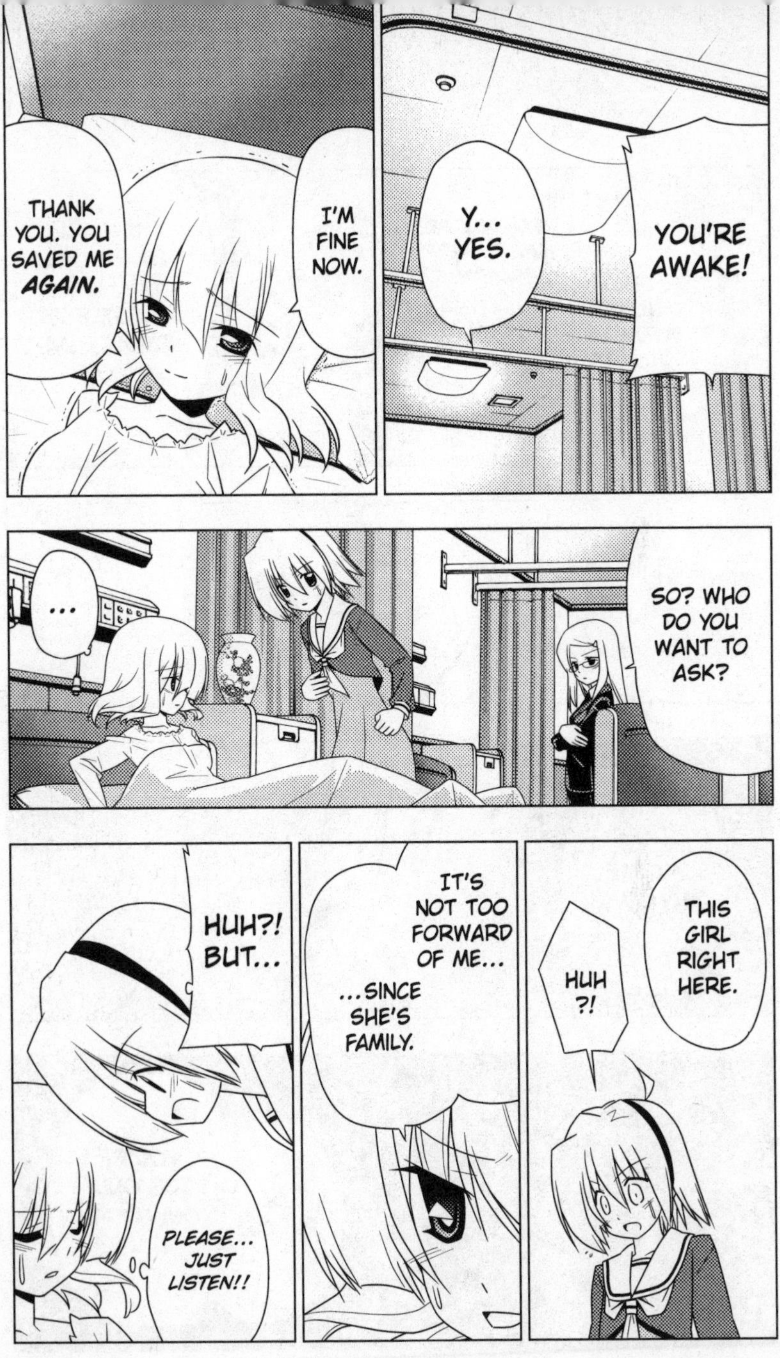
YOU'RE AWAKE!
Y... YES.
I'M FINE NOW.
THANK YOU. YOU SAVED ME AGAIN.
SO? WHO DO YOU WANT TO ASK?
...
THIS GIRL RIGHT HERE.
HUH ?!
IT'S NOT TOO FORWARD OF ME...
...SINCE SHE'S FAMILY.
HUH?! BUT...
PLEASE... JUST LISTEN!!

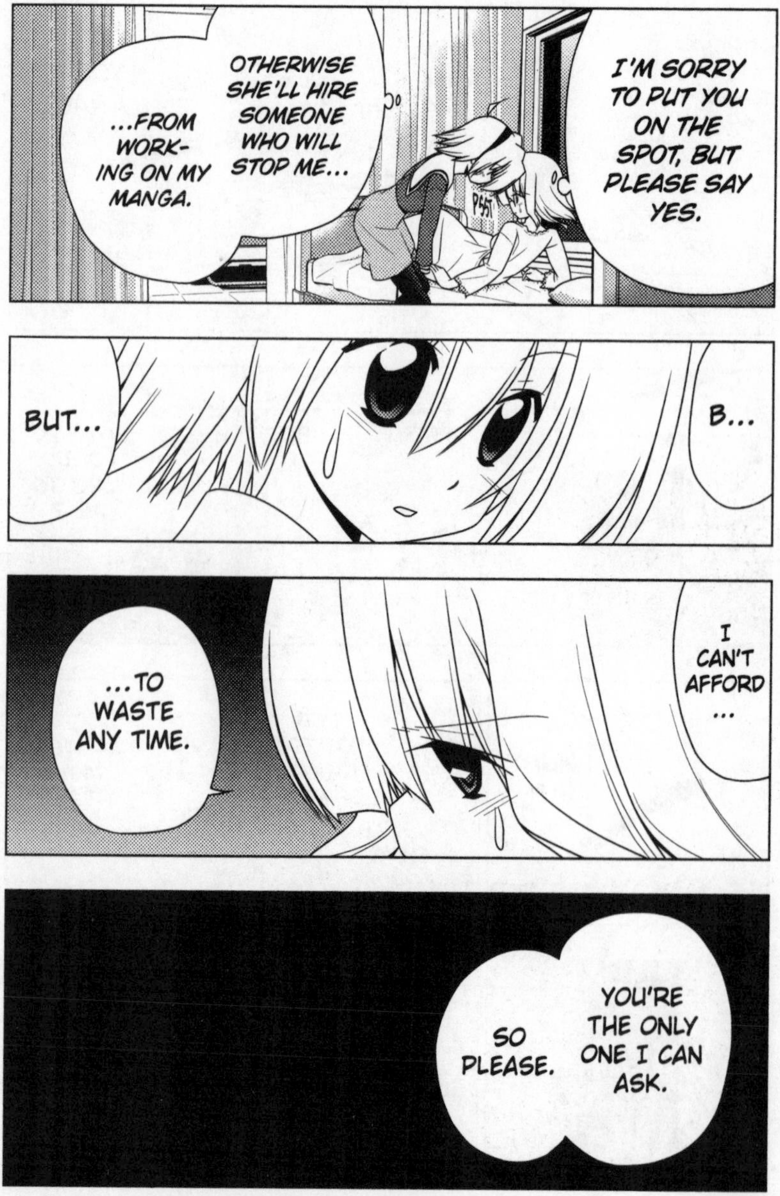
I'M SORRY TO PUT YOU ON THE SPOT, BUT PLEASE SAY YES.
PSST
OTHERWISE SHE'LL HIRE SOMEONE WHO WILL STOP ME...
...FROM WORKING ON MY MANGA.
B...
BUT...
I CAN'T AFFORD...
...TO WASTE ANY TIME.
YOU'RE THE ONLY ONE I CAN ASK.
SO PLEASE.

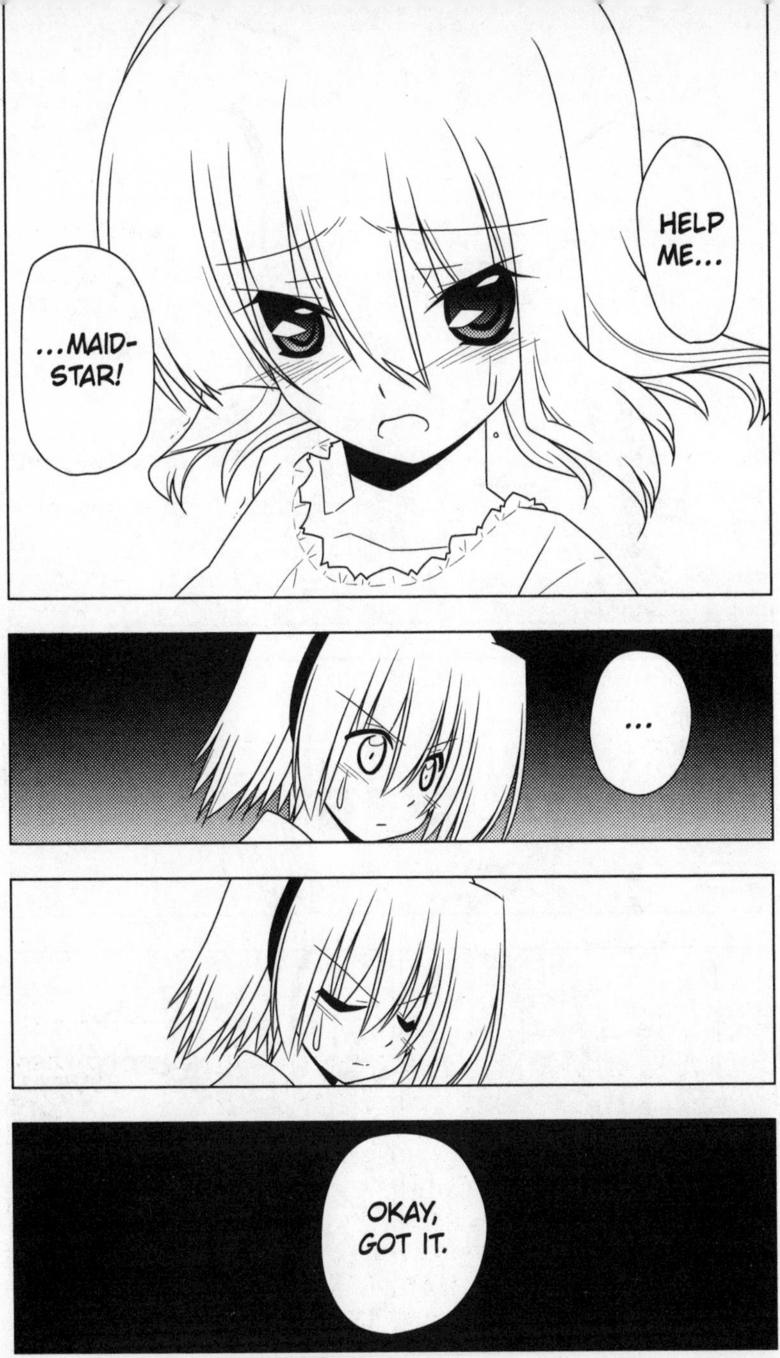
HELP ME...
...MAID-STAR!
...
OKAY, GOT IT.

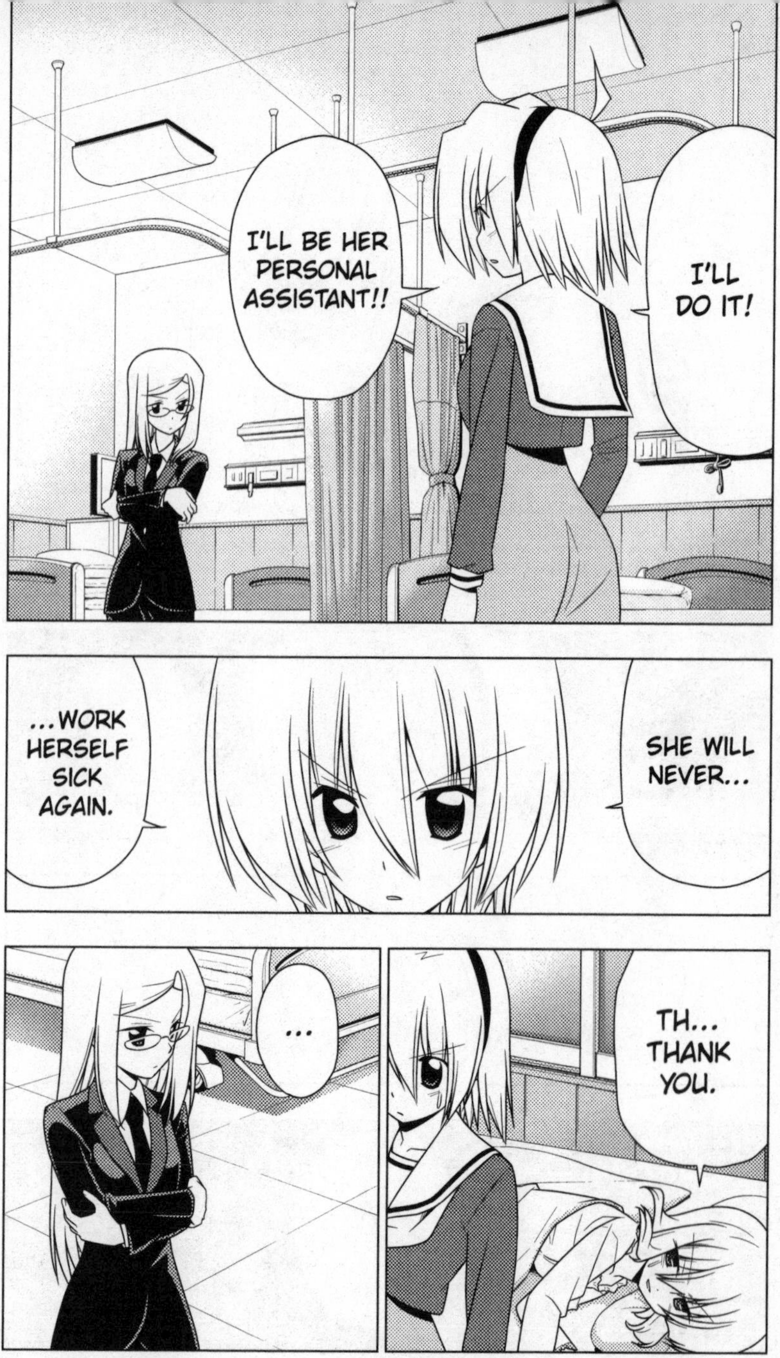
I'LL DO IT!
I'LL BE HER PERSONAL ASSISTANT!!
SHE WILL NEVER...
...WORK HERSELF SICK AGAIN.
TH... THANK YOU.
...

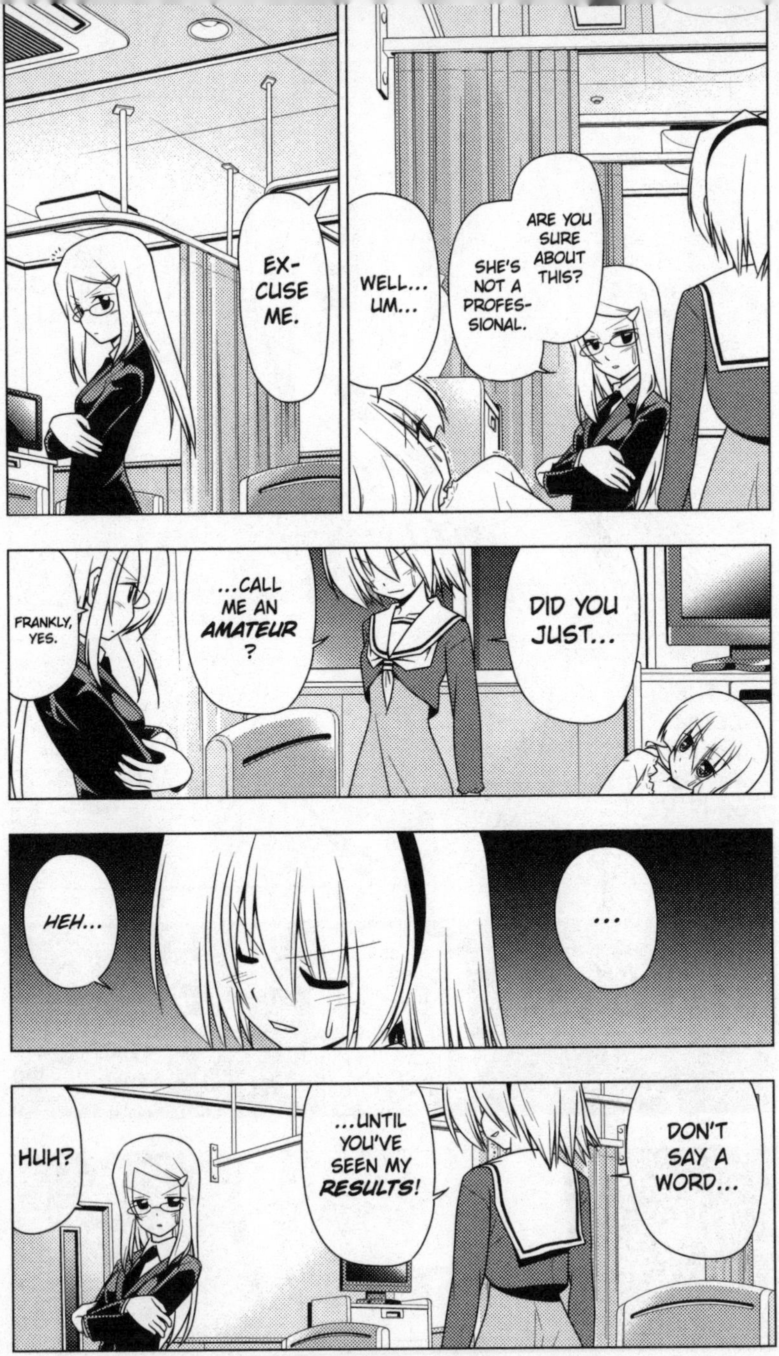
ARE YOU SURE ABOUT THIS?
SHE'S NOT A PROFESSIONAL.
WELL... UM...
EX-CUSE ME.
DID YOU JUST...
...CALL ME AN *AMATEUR*?
FRANKLY, YES.
...
HEH...
DON'T SAY A WORD...
...UNTIL YOU'VE SEEN MY *RESULTS*!
HUH?

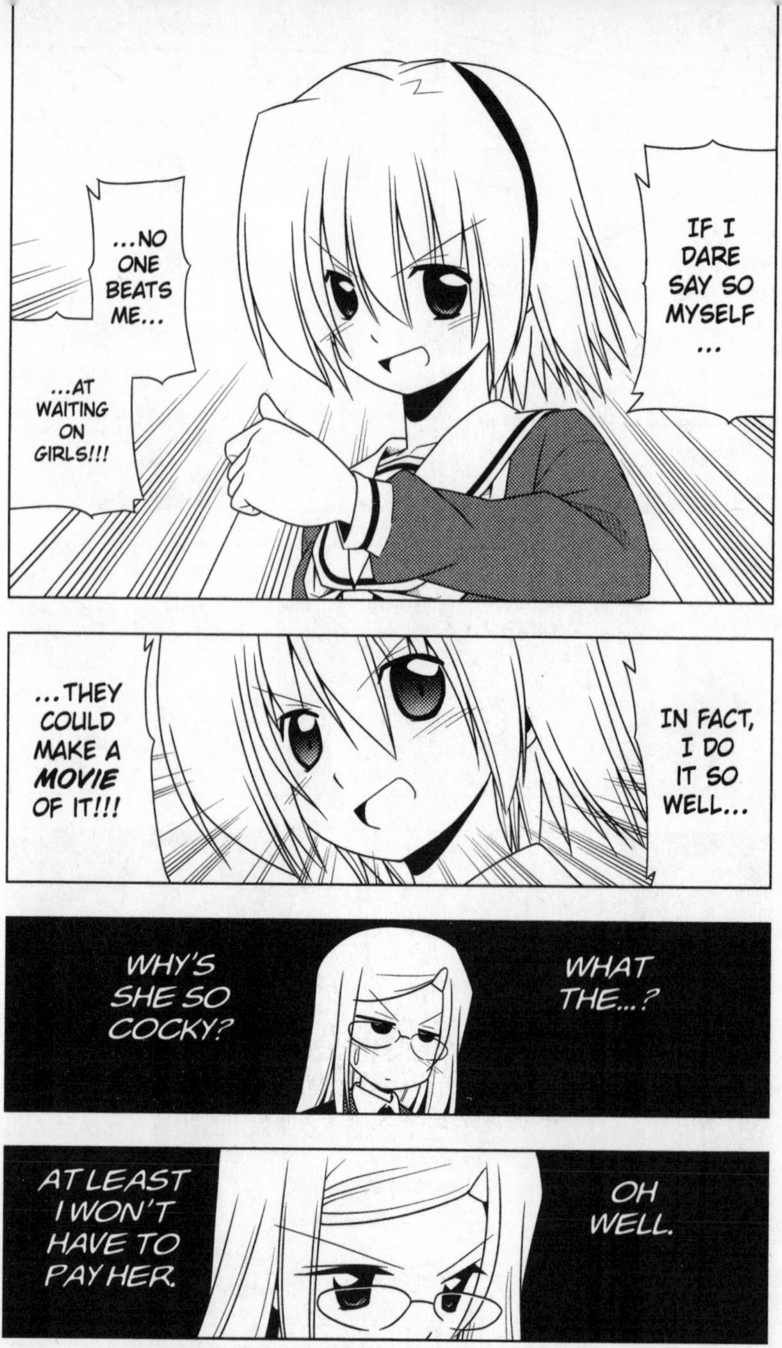
IF I DARE SAY SO MYSELF...
...NO ONE BEATS ME...
...AT WAITING ON GIRLS!!!
IN FACT, I DO IT SO WELL...
...THEY COULD MAKE A MOVIE OF IT!!!
WHAT THE...?
WHY'S SHE SO COCKY?
OH WELL.
AT LEAST I WON'T HAVE TO PAY HER.

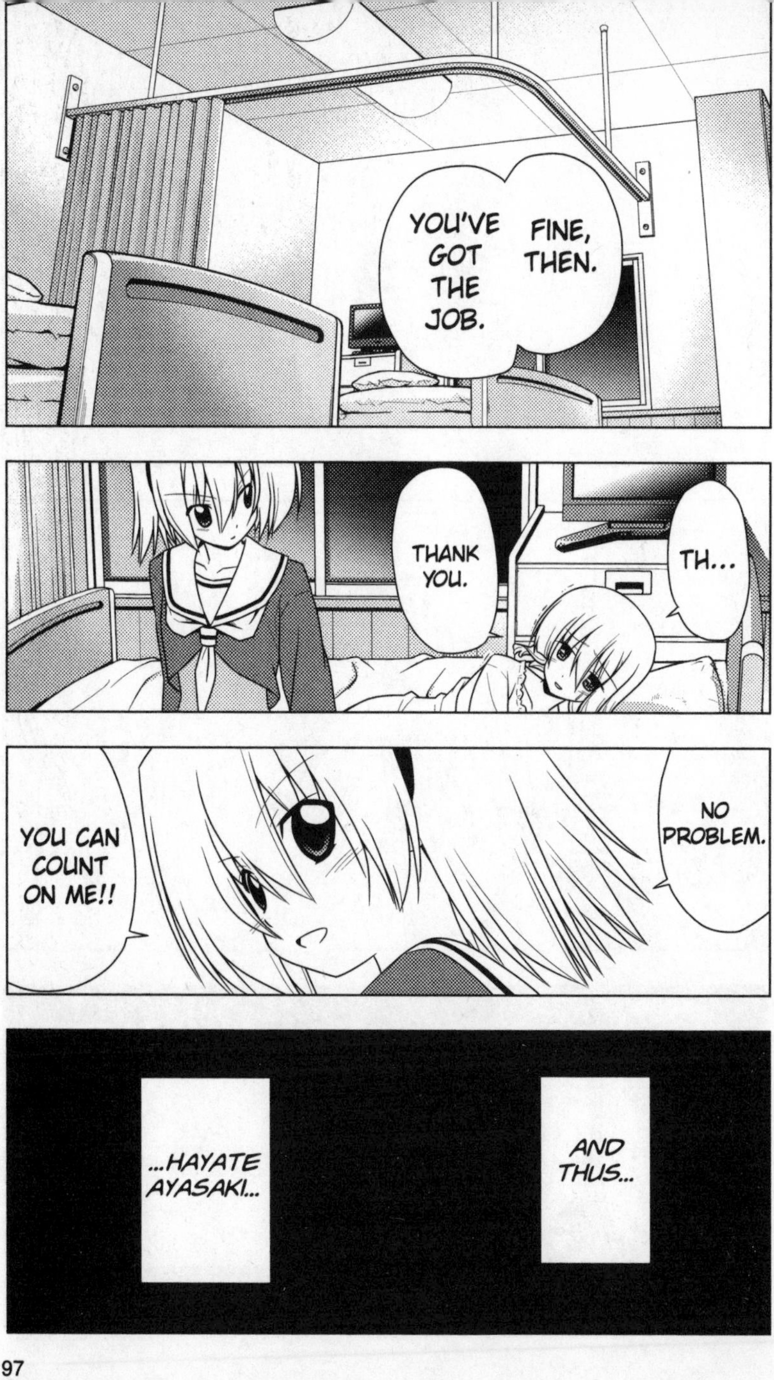
FINE, THEN.
YOU'VE GOT THE JOB.
TH...
THANK YOU.
NO PROBLEM.
YOU CAN COUNT ON ME!!
AND THUS...
...HAYATE AYASAKI...

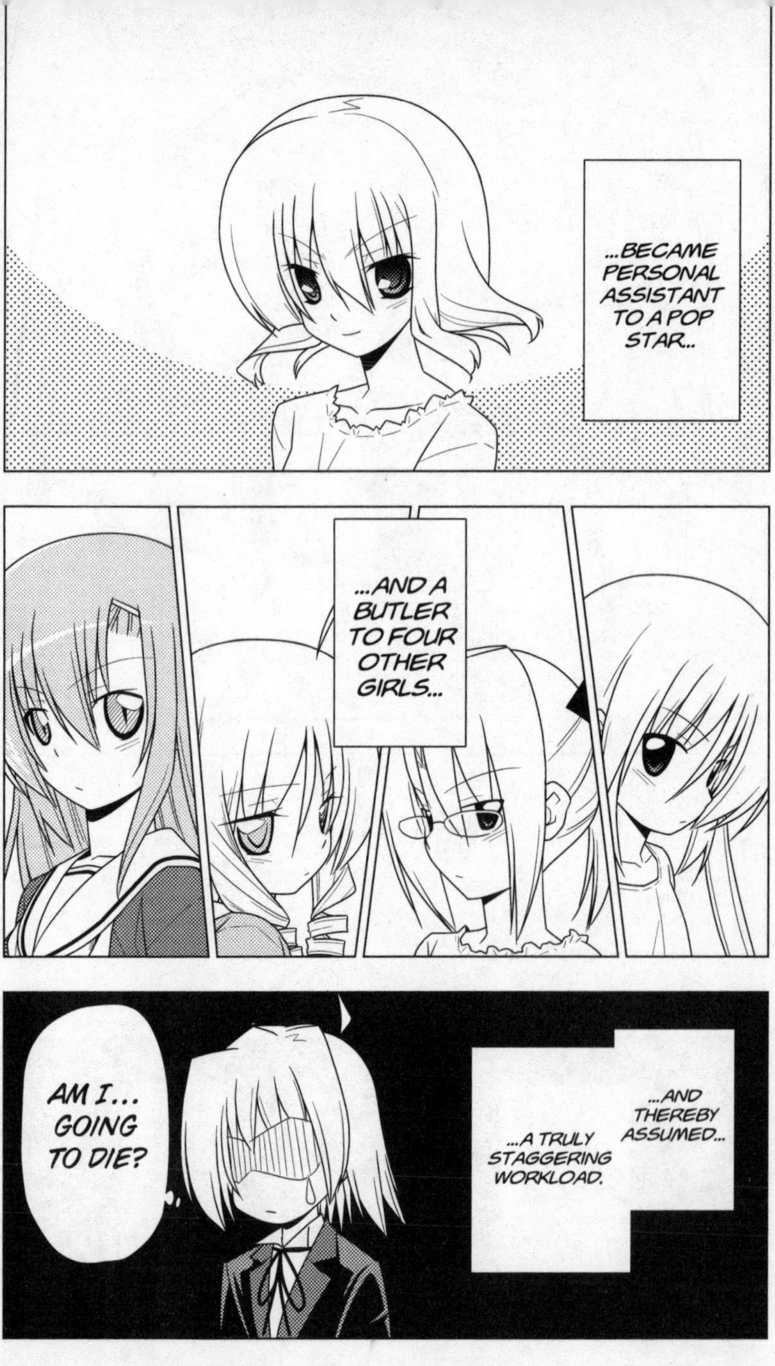
...BECAME PERSONAL ASSISTANT TO A POP STAR...
...AND A BUTLER TO FOUR OTHER GIRLS...
...AND THEREBY ASSUMED...
...A TRULY STAGGERING WORKLOAD.
AM I... GOING TO DIE?

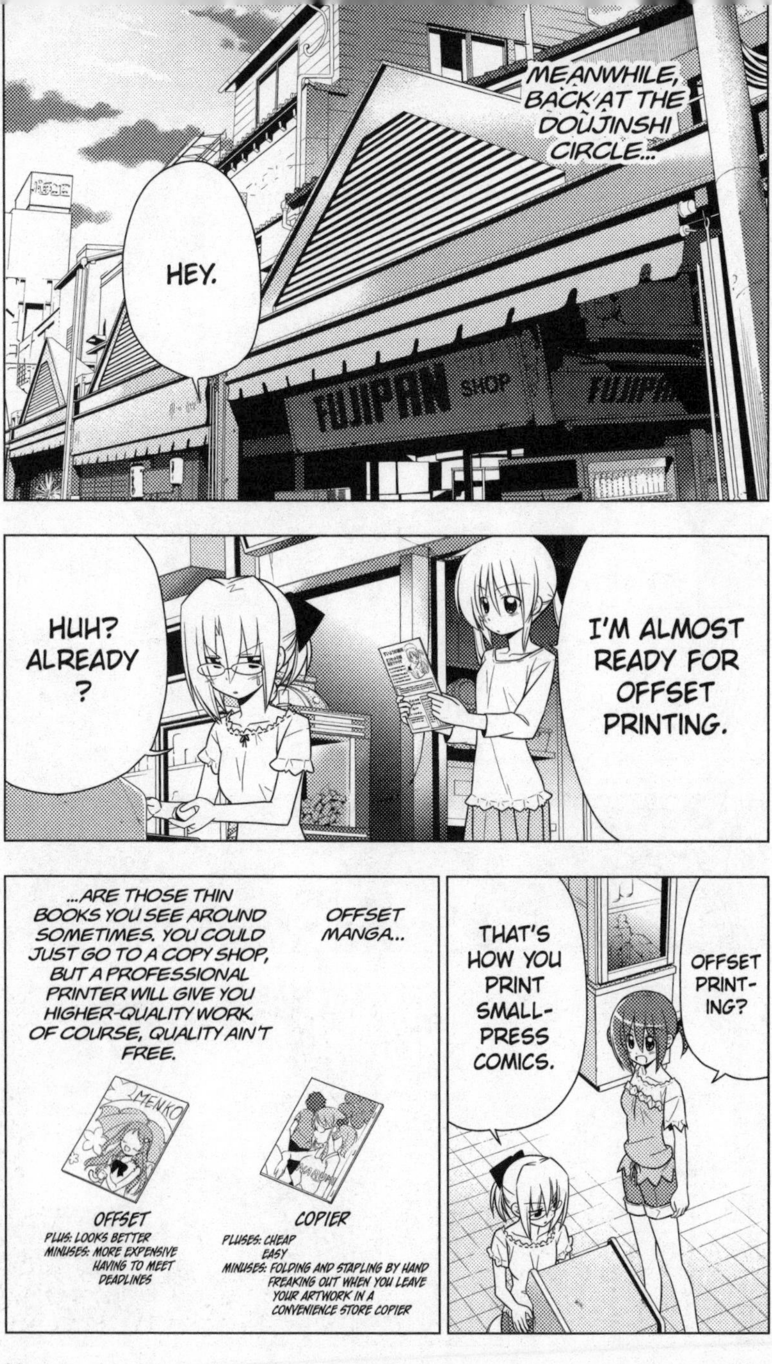
MEANWHILE, BACK AT THE DOUJINSHI CIRCLE...
HEY.
FUJIPAN SHOP
FUJIPAN
I'M ALMOST READY FOR OFFSET PRINTING.
HUH? ALREADY?
OFFSET PRINTING?
THAT'S HOW YOU PRINT SMALL-PRESS COMICS.
OFFSET MANGA...
...ARE THOSE THIN BOOKS YOU SEE AROUND SOMETIMES. YOU COULD JUST GO TO A COPY SHOP, BUT A PROFESSIONAL PRINTER WILL GIVE YOU HIGHER-QUALITY WORK. OF COURSE, QUALITY AIN'T FREE.
MENKO
OFFSET
PLUS: LOOKS BETTER
MINUSES: MORE EXPENSIVE
HAVING TO MEET DEADLINES
COPIER
PLUSES: CHEAP
EASY
MINUSES: FOLDING AND STAPLING BY HAND
FREAKING OUT WHEN YOU LEAVE YOUR ARTWORK IN A CONVENIENCE STORE COPIER

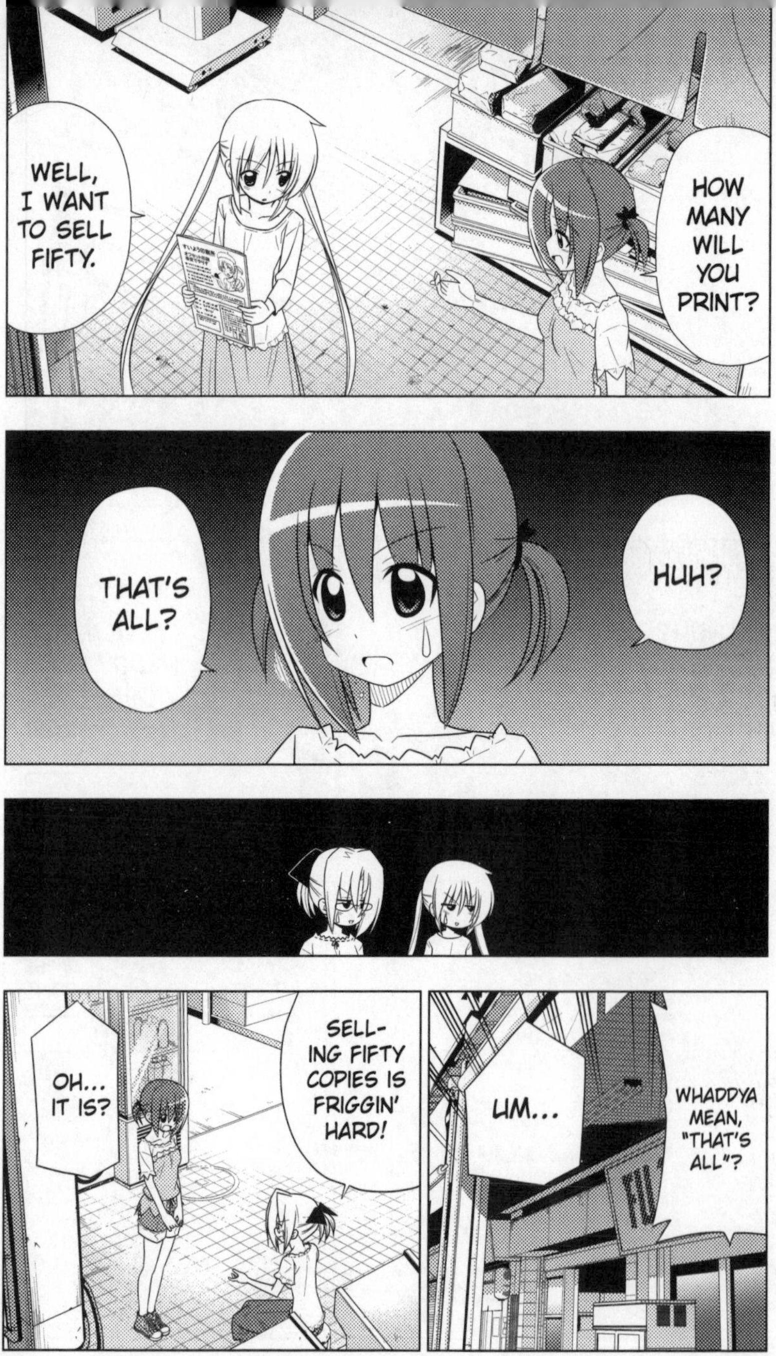
HOW MANY WILL YOU PRINT?
WELL, I WANT TO SELL FIFTY.
HUH?
THAT'S ALL?
WHADDYA MEAN, "THAT'S ALL"?
UM...
SELL-ING FIFTY COPIES IS FRIGGIN' HARD!
OH... IT IS?

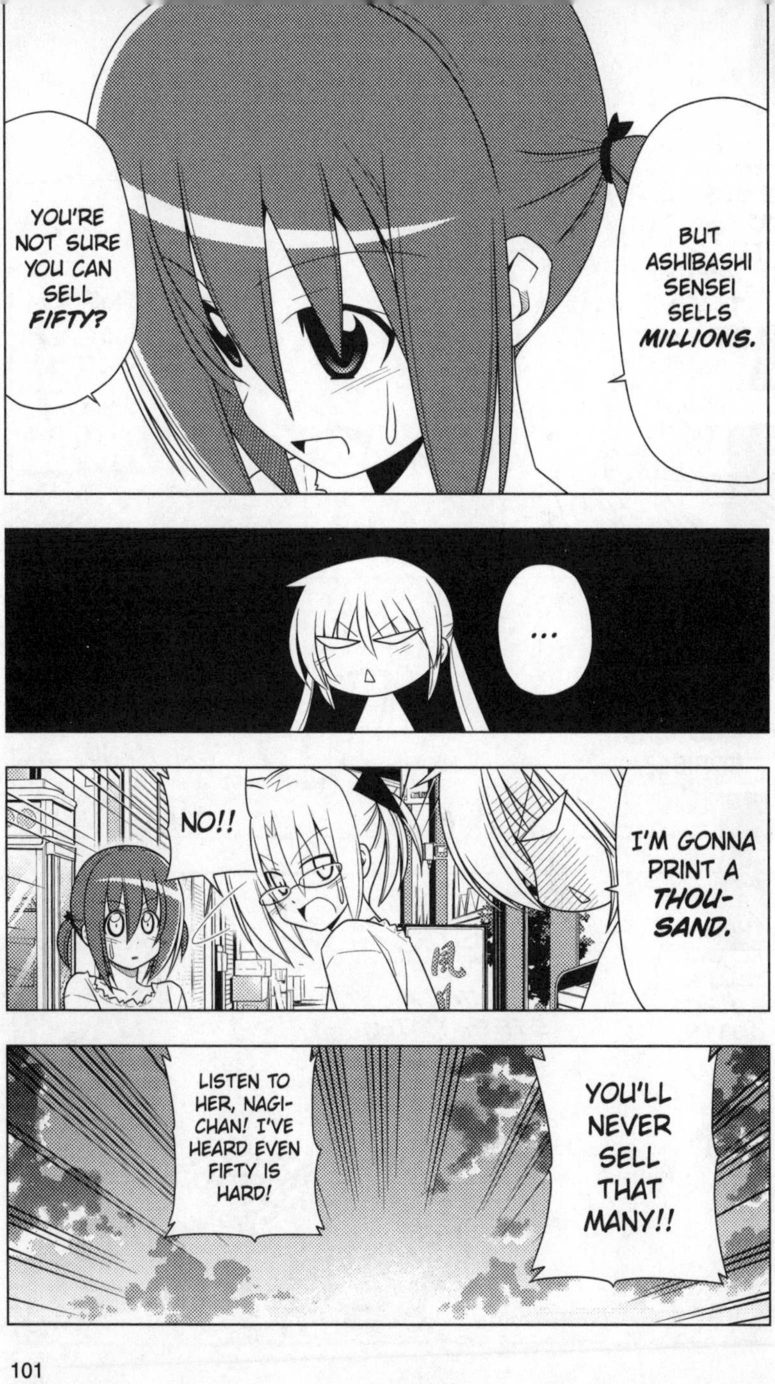
BUT ASHIBASHI SENSEI SELLS *MILLIONS.*
YOU'RE NOT SURE YOU CAN SELL *FIFTY?*
...
I'M GONNA PRINT A *THOU-SAND.*
NO!!
YOU'LL NEVER SELL THAT MANY!!
LISTEN TO HER, NAGI-CHAN! I'VE HEARD EVEN FIFTY IS HARD!

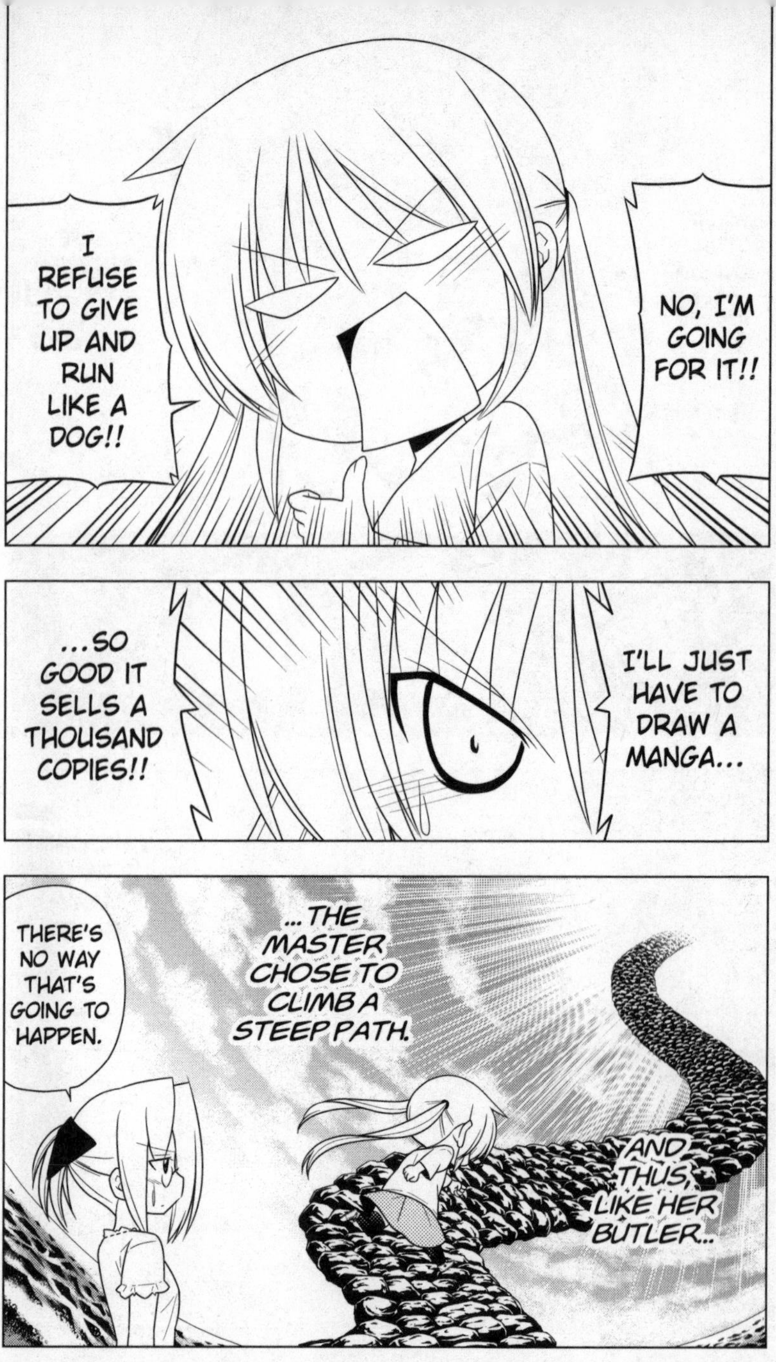
NO, I'M GOING FOR IT!!
I REFUSE TO GIVE UP AND RUN LIKE A DOG!!
I'LL JUST HAVE TO DRAW A MANGA...
...SO GOOD IT SELLS A THOUSAND COPIES!!
AND THUS, LIKE HER BUTLER...
...THE MASTER CHOSE TO CLIMB A STEEP PATH.
THERE'S NO WAY THAT'S GOING TO HAPPEN.

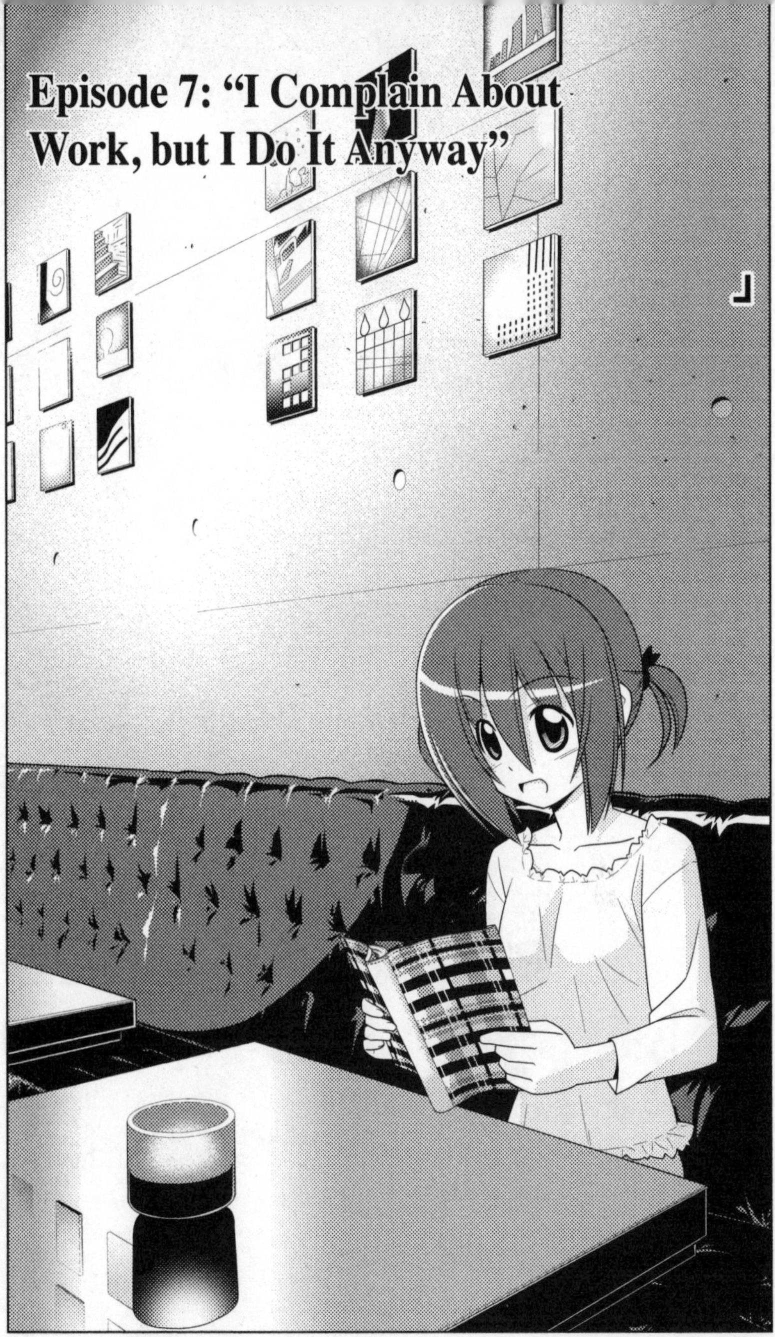
Episode 7: "I Complain About Work, but I Do It Anyway"

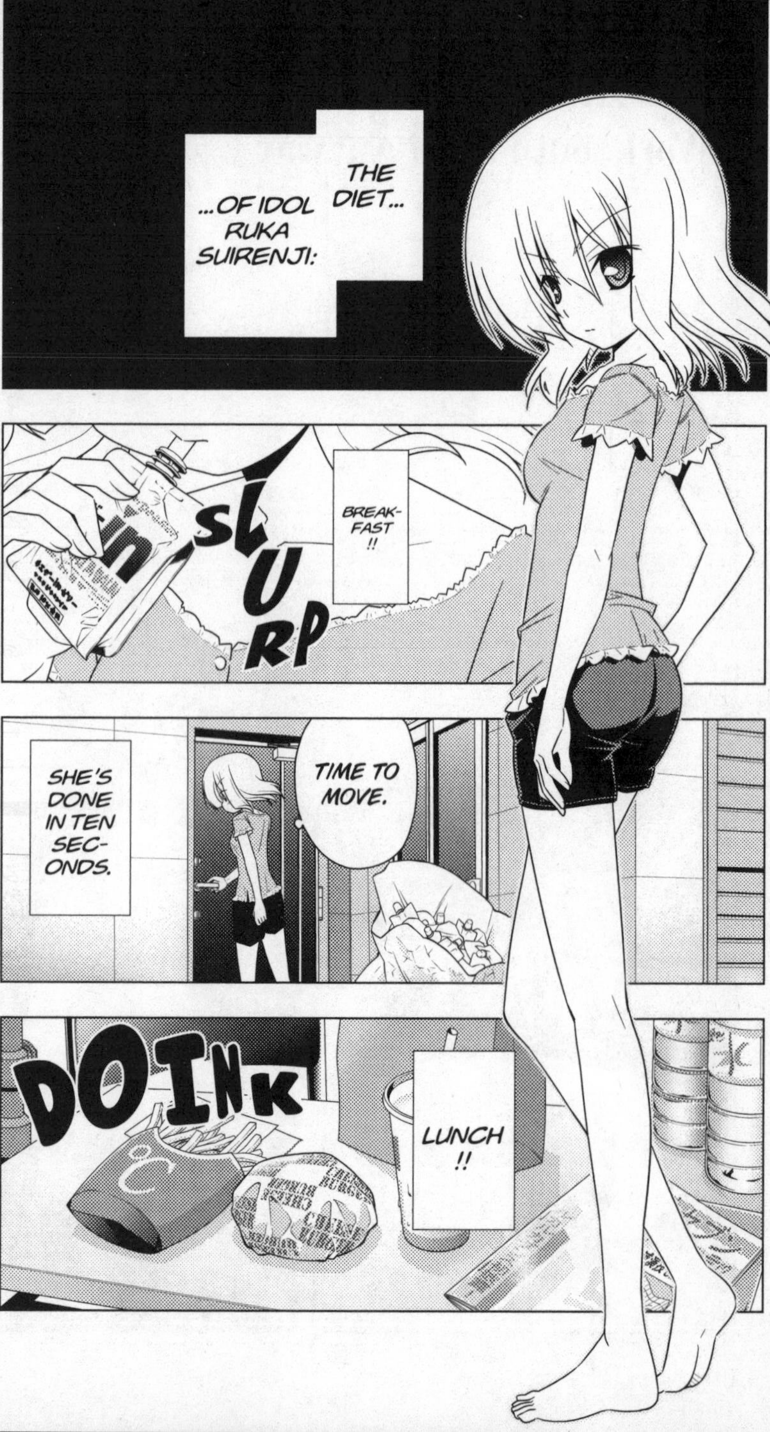
THE DIET...
...OF IDOL RUKA SUIRENJI:
BREAKFAST!!
SLURP
TIME TO MOVE.
SHE'S DONE IN TEN SECONDS.
LUNCH!!
DOINK

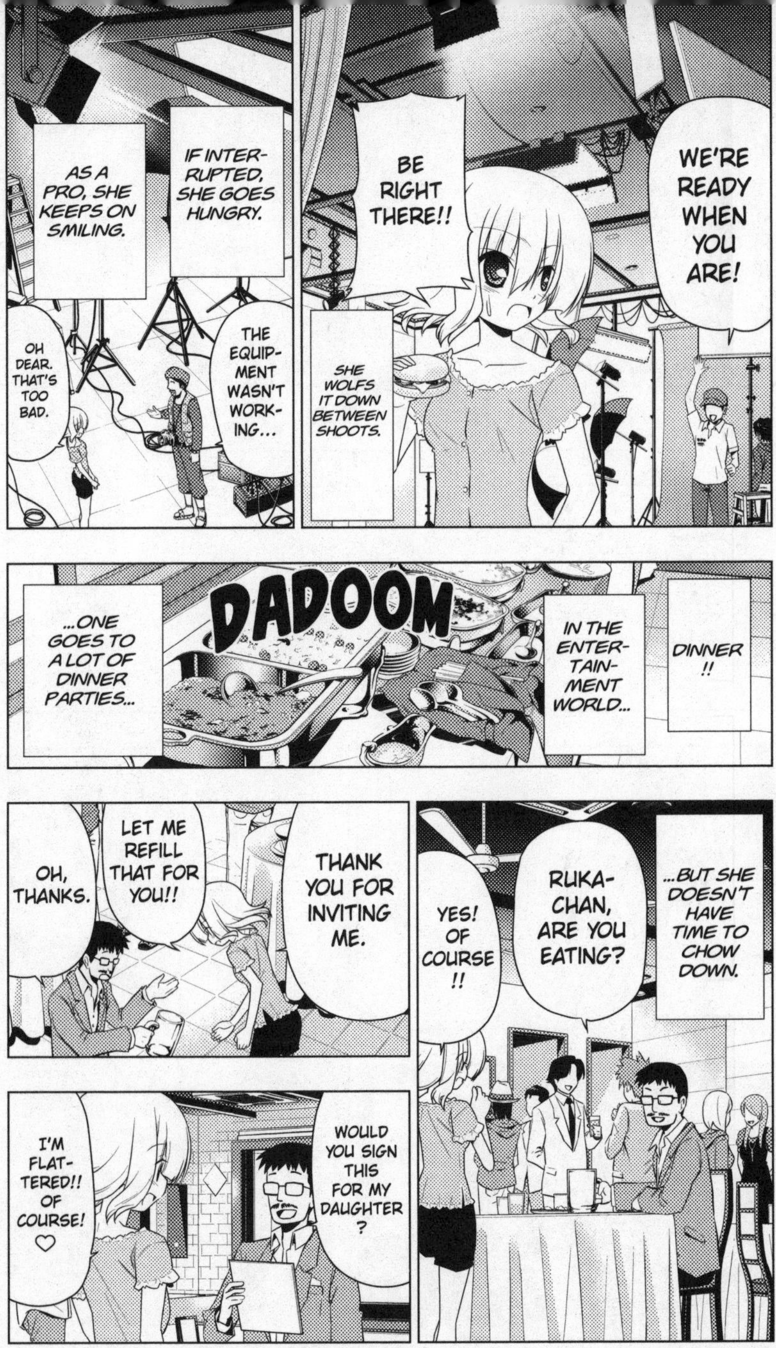
WE'RE READY WHEN YOU ARE!
BE RIGHT THERE!!
SHE WOLFS IT DOWN BETWEEN SHOOTS.
IF INTERRUPTED, SHE GOES HUNGRY.
AS A PRO, SHE KEEPS ON SMILING.
THE EQUIPMENT WASN'T WORKING...
OH DEAR. THAT'S TOO BAD.
DINNER!!
IN THE ENTERTAINMENT WORLD...
DADOOM
...ONE GOES TO A LOT OF DINNER PARTIES...
...BUT SHE DOESN'T HAVE TIME TO CHOW DOWN.
RUKA-CHAN, ARE YOU EATING?
YES! OF COURSE!!
THANK YOU FOR INVITING ME.
LET ME REFILL THAT FOR YOU!!
OH, THANKS.
WOULD YOU SIGN THIS FOR MY DAUGHTER?
I'M FLATTERED!! OF COURSE! ♡

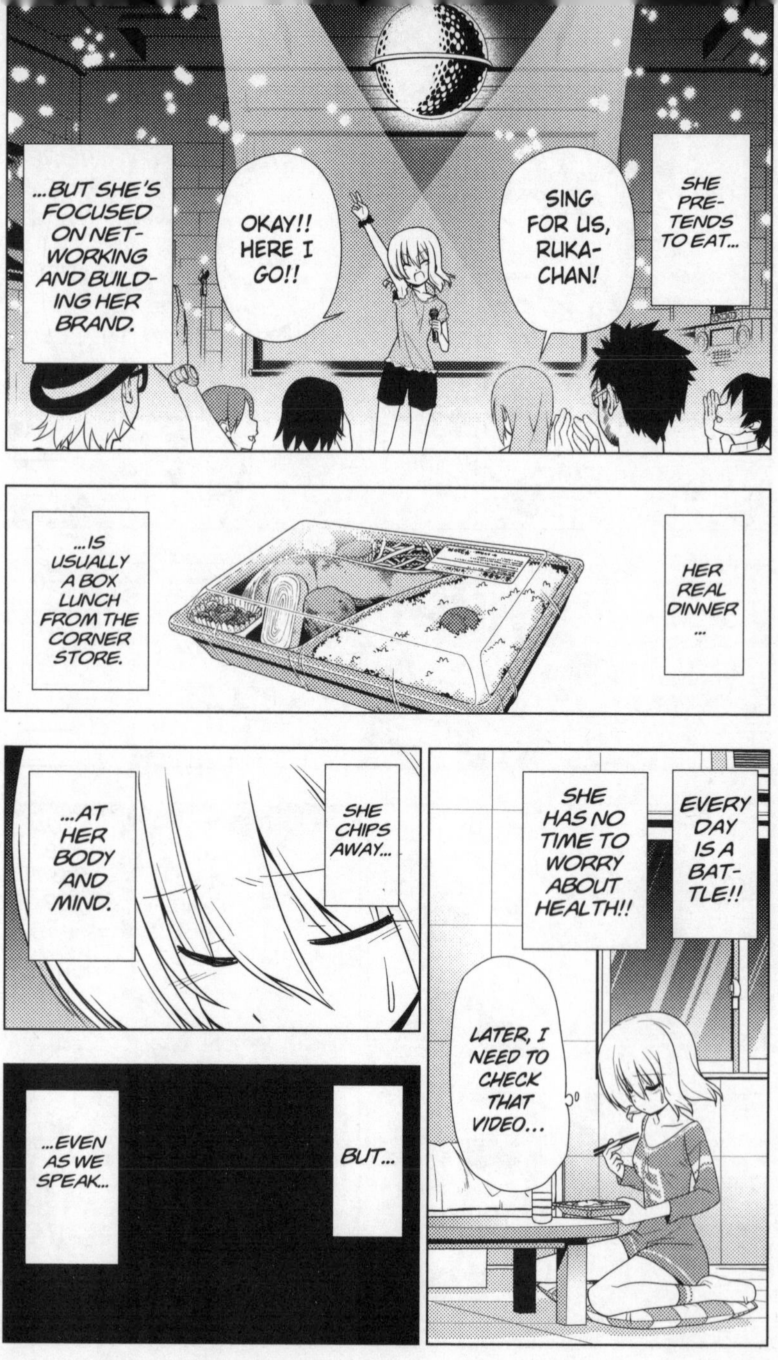
SHE PRETENDS TO EAT...
SING FOR US, RUKA-CHAN!
OKAY!! HERE I GO!!
...BUT SHE'S FOCUSED ON NETWORKING AND BUILDING HER BRAND.
HER REAL DINNER ...
...IS USUALLY A BOX LUNCH FROM THE CORNER STORE.
EVERY DAY IS A BATTLE!!
SHE HAS NO TIME TO WORRY ABOUT HEALTH!!
LATER, I NEED TO CHECK THAT VIDEO...
SHE CHIPS AWAY...
...AT HER BODY AND MIND.
BUT...
...EVEN AS WE SPEAK...

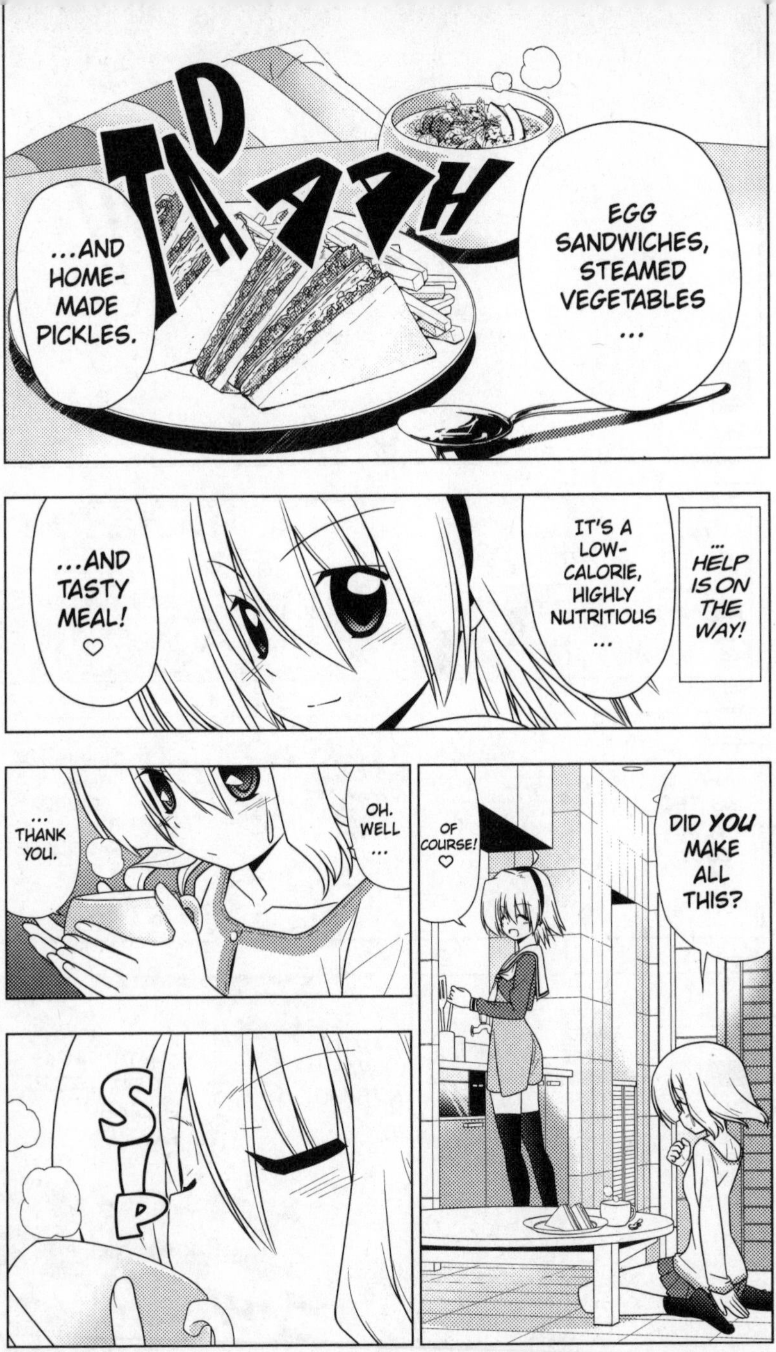
EGG SANDWICHES, STEAMED VEGETABLES ...
TADAAAH
...AND HOME-MADE PICKLES.
... HELP IS ON THE WAY!
IT'S A LOW-CALORIE, HIGHLY NUTRITIOUS ...
...AND TASTY MEAL! ♡
DID YOU MAKE ALL THIS?
OF COURSE! ♡
OH. WELL ...
... THANK YOU.
SIP

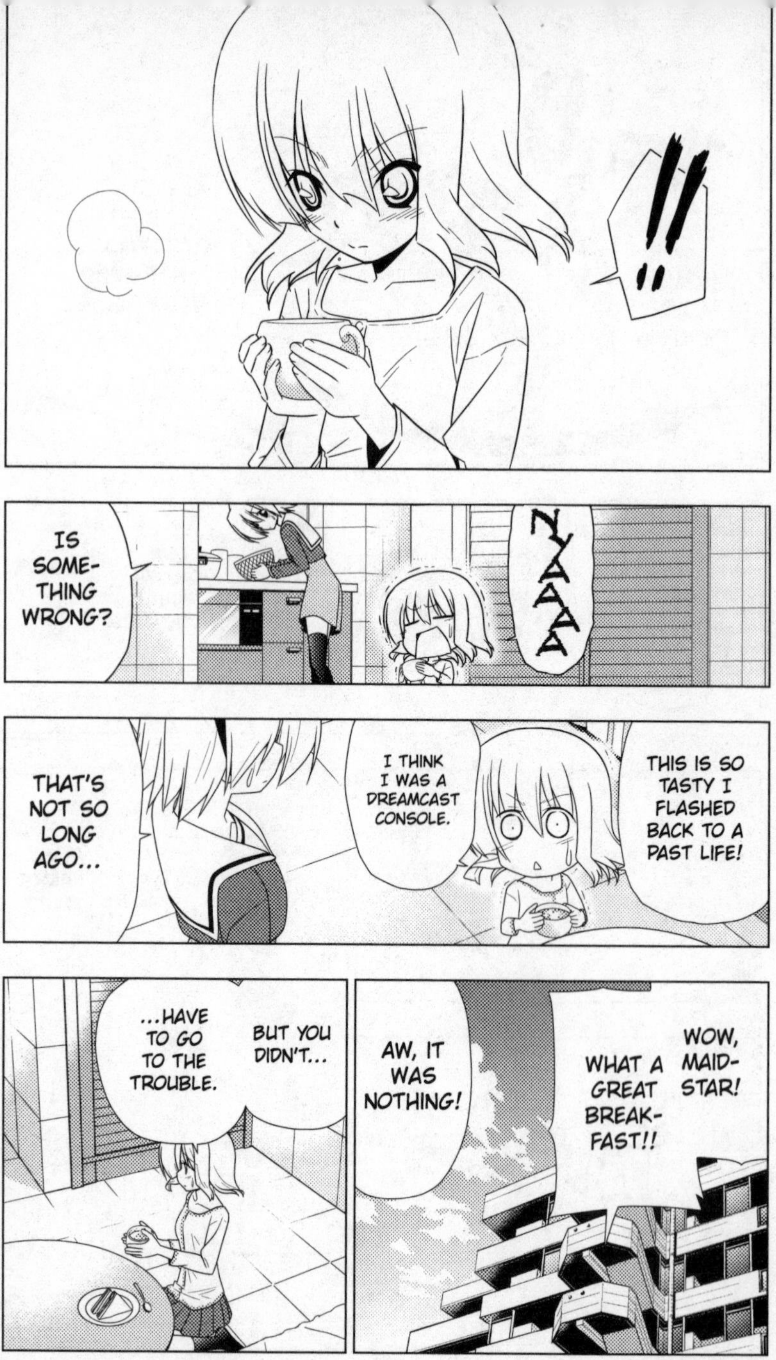
!!
NYAAAA
IS SOMETHING WRONG?
THIS IS SO TASTY I FLASHED BACK TO A PAST LIFE!
I THINK I WAS A DREAMCAST CONSOLE.
THAT'S NOT SO LONG AGO...
WOW, MAID-STAR!
WHAT A GREAT BREAKFAST!!
AW, IT WAS NOTHING!
BUT YOU DIDN'T...
...HAVE TO GO TO THE TROUBLE.

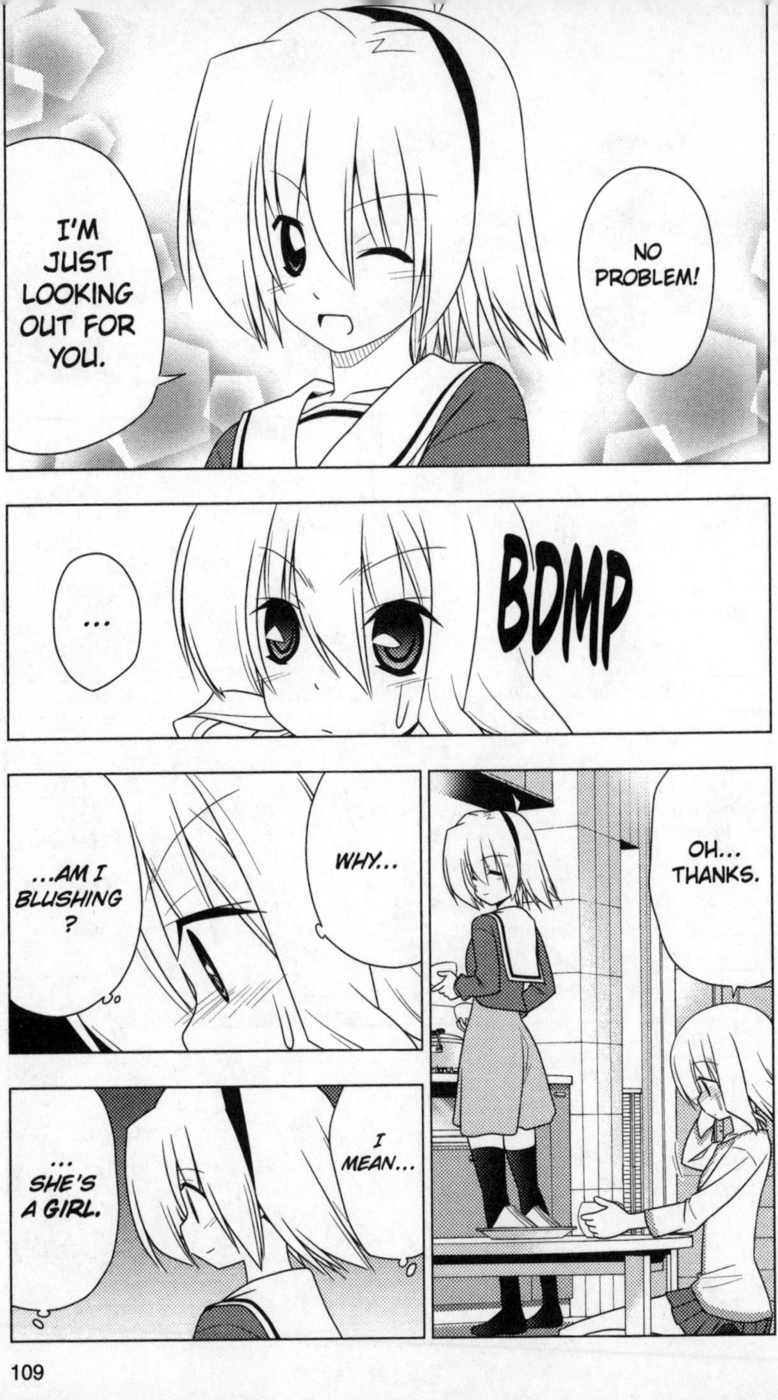
NO PROBLEM!
I'M JUST LOOKING OUT FOR YOU.
BDMP
...
OH... THANKS.
WHY...
...AM I BLUSHING?
I MEAN...
...SHE'S A GIRL.

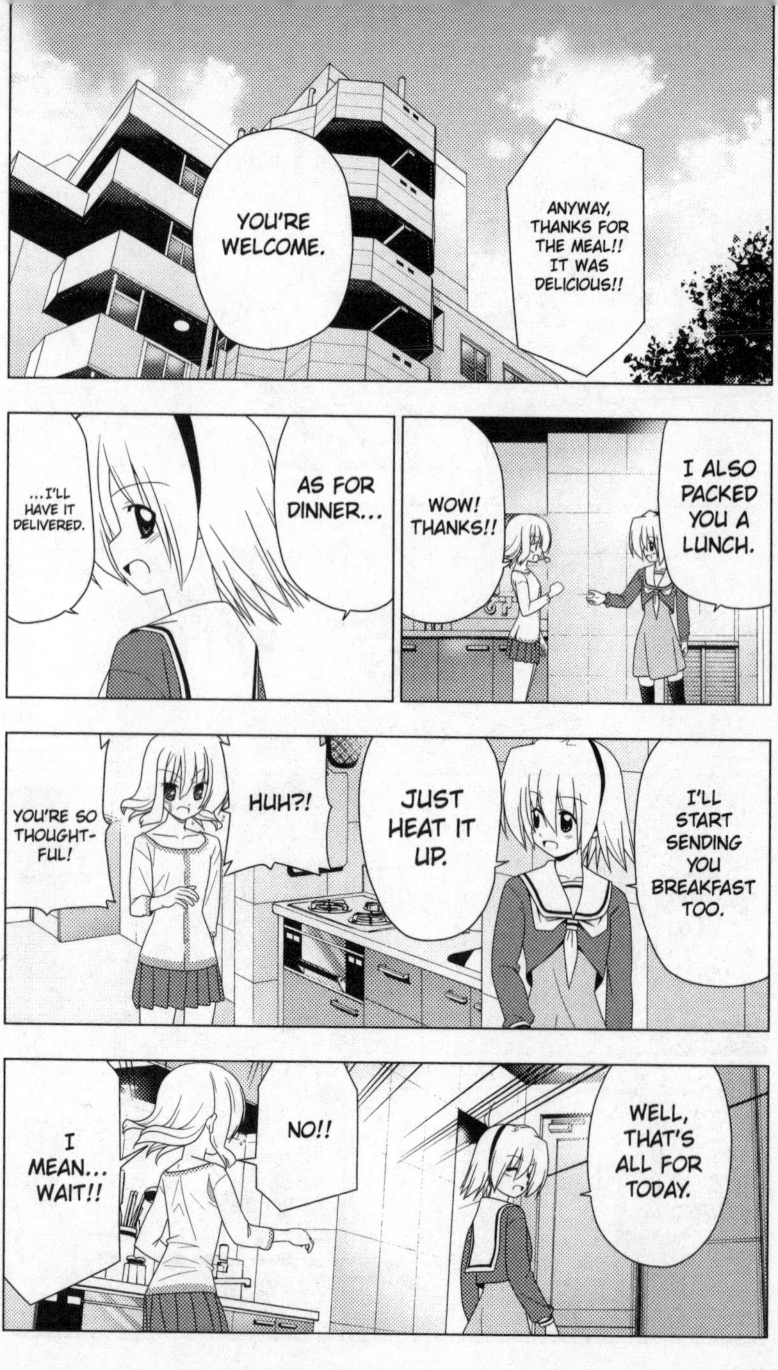
ANYWAY, THANKS FOR THE MEAL!! IT WAS DELICIOUS!!
YOU'RE WELCOME.
I ALSO PACKED YOU A LUNCH.
WOW! THANKS!!
AS FOR DINNER...
...I'LL HAVE IT DELIVERED.
I'LL START SENDING YOU BREAKFAST TOO.
JUST HEAT IT UP.
HUH?!
YOU'RE SO THOUGHT-FUL!
WELL, THAT'S ALL FOR TODAY.
NO!!
I MEAN... WAIT!!

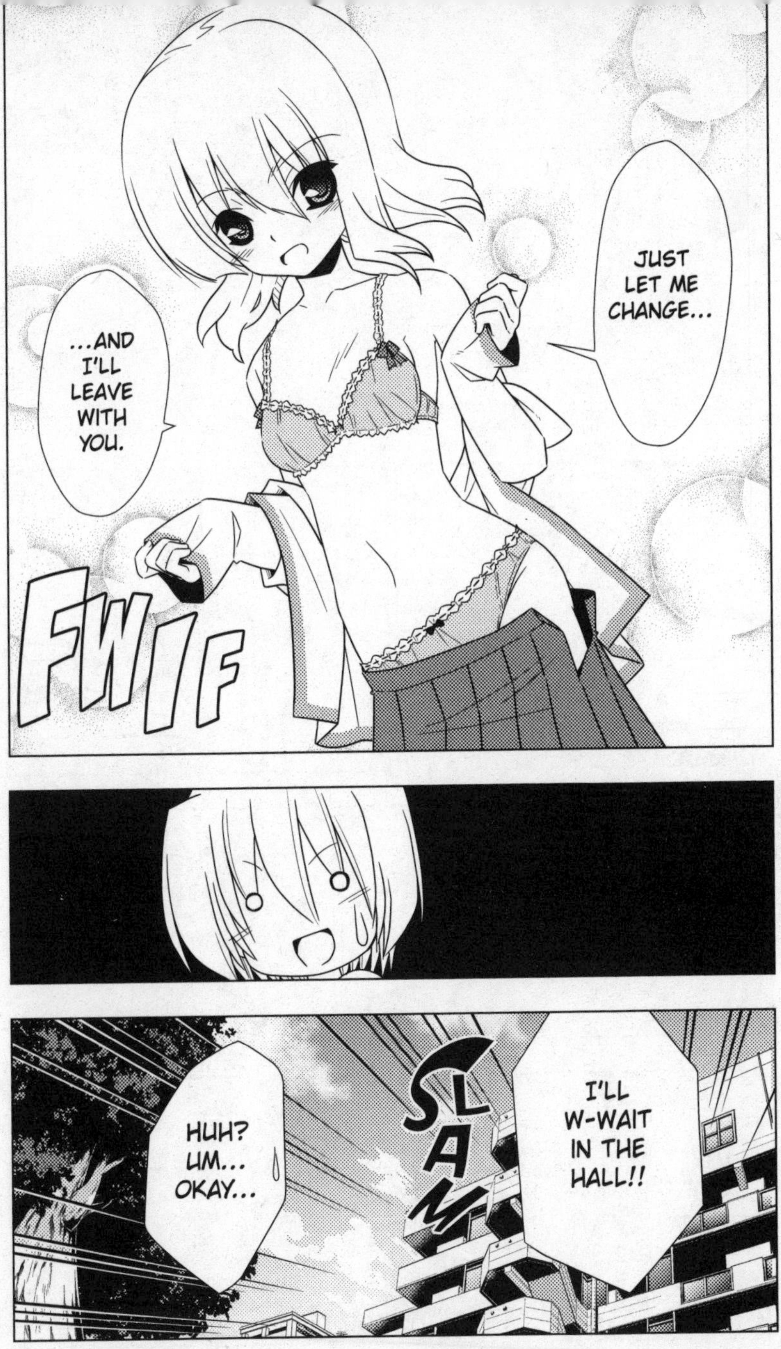
JUST LET ME CHANGE...
...AND I'LL LEAVE WITH YOU.
FWIF
I'LL W-WAIT IN THE HALL!!
SLAM
HUH? UM... OKAY...

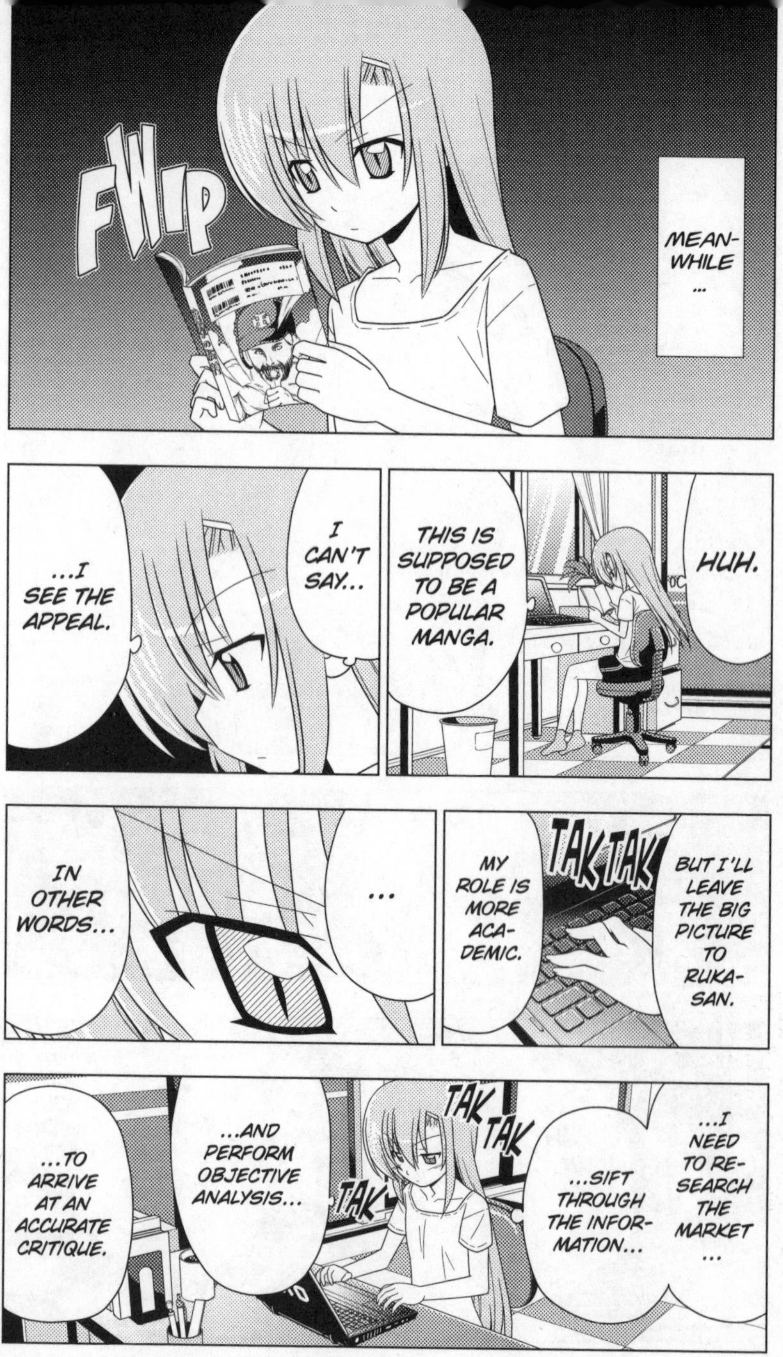
MEAN-WHILE ...
FWIP
HUH.
THIS IS SUPPOSED TO BE A POPULAR MANGA.
I CAN'T SAY...
...I SEE THE APPEAL.
BUT I'LL LEAVE THE BIG PICTURE TO RUKA-SAN.
TAK TAK
MY ROLE IS MORE ACA-DEMIC.
...
IN OTHER WORDS...
...I NEED TO RE-SEARCH THE MARKET ...
TAK TAK
...SIFT THROUGH THE INFOR-MATION...
TAK
...AND PERFORM OBJECTIVE ANALYSIS...
...TO ARRIVE AT AN ACCURATE CRITIQUE.

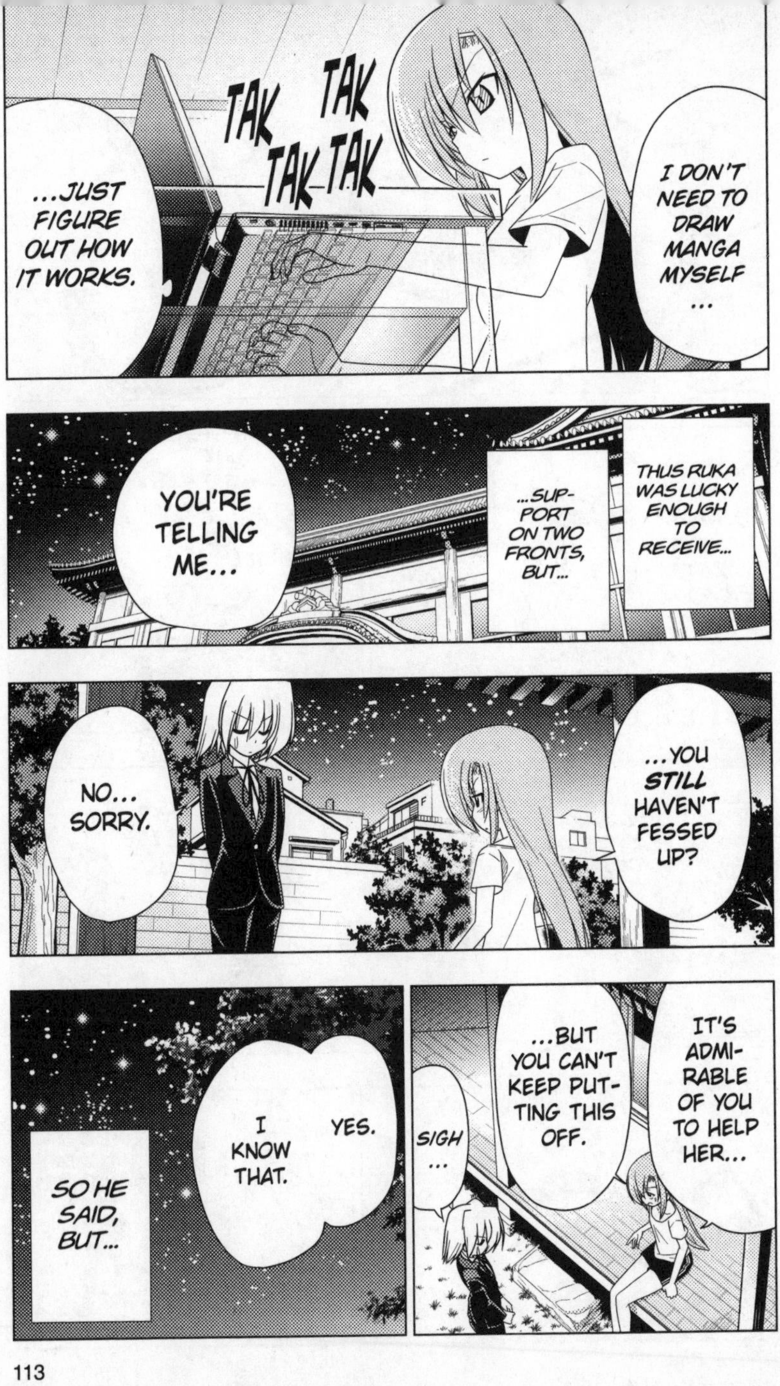
I DON'T NEED TO DRAW MANGA MYSELF ...
TAK TAK TAK TAK
...JUST FIGURE OUT HOW IT WORKS.
THUS RUKA WAS LUCKY ENOUGH TO RECEIVE...
...SUP-PORT ON TWO FRONTS, BUT...
YOU'RE TELLING ME...
...YOU STILL HAVEN'T FESSED UP?
NO... SORRY.
IT'S ADMI-RABLE OF YOU TO HELP HER...
...BUT YOU CAN'T KEEP PUT-TING THIS OFF.
SIGH ...
YES. I KNOW THAT.
SO HE SAID, BUT...

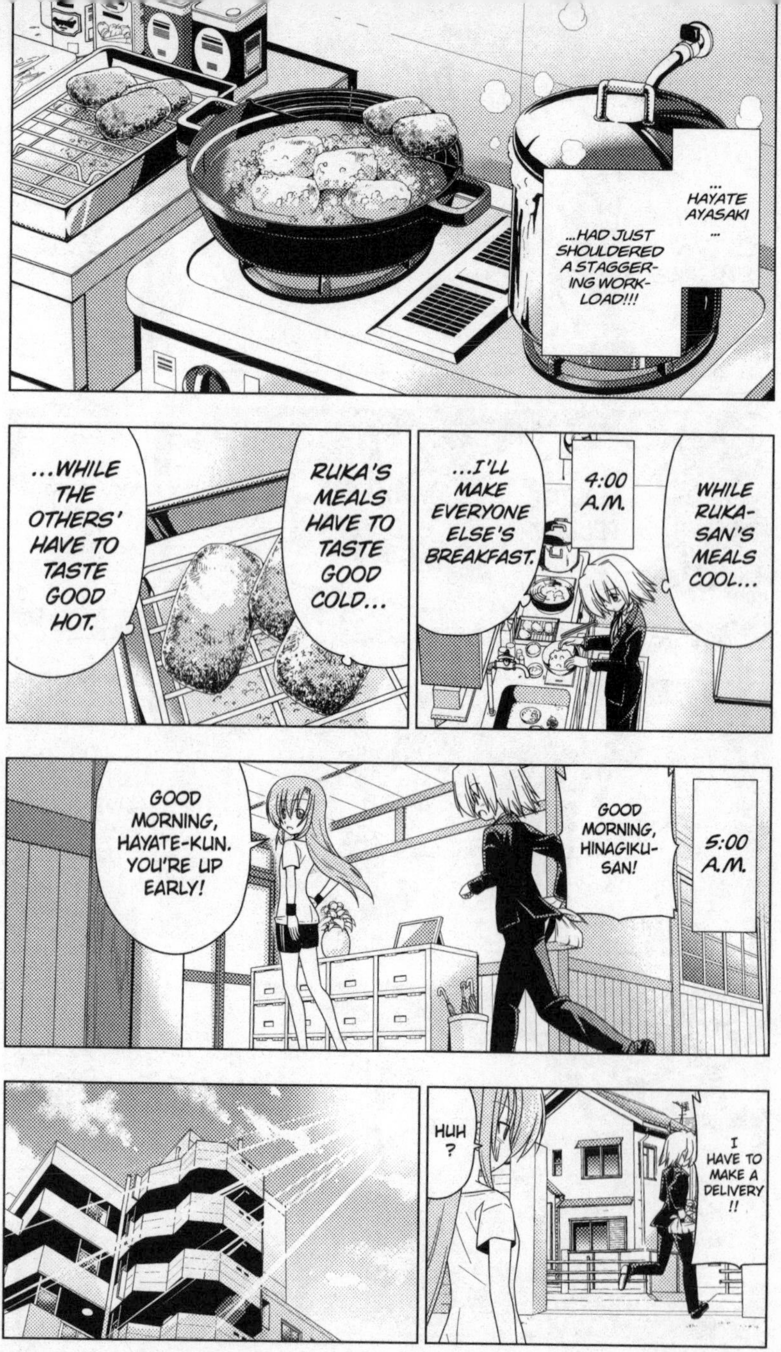
... HAYATE AYASAKI ...
...HAD JUST SHOULDERED A STAGGERING WORKLOAD!!!
4:00 A.M.
WHILE RUKA-SAN'S MEALS COOL...
...I'LL MAKE EVERYONE ELSE'S BREAKFAST.
RUKA'S MEALS HAVE TO TASTE GOOD COLD...
...WHILE THE OTHERS' HAVE TO TASTE GOOD HOT.
5:00 A.M.
GOOD MORNING, HINAGIKU-SAN!
GOOD MORNING, HAYATE-KUN. YOU'RE UP EARLY!
I HAVE TO MAKE A DELIVERY!!
HUH?

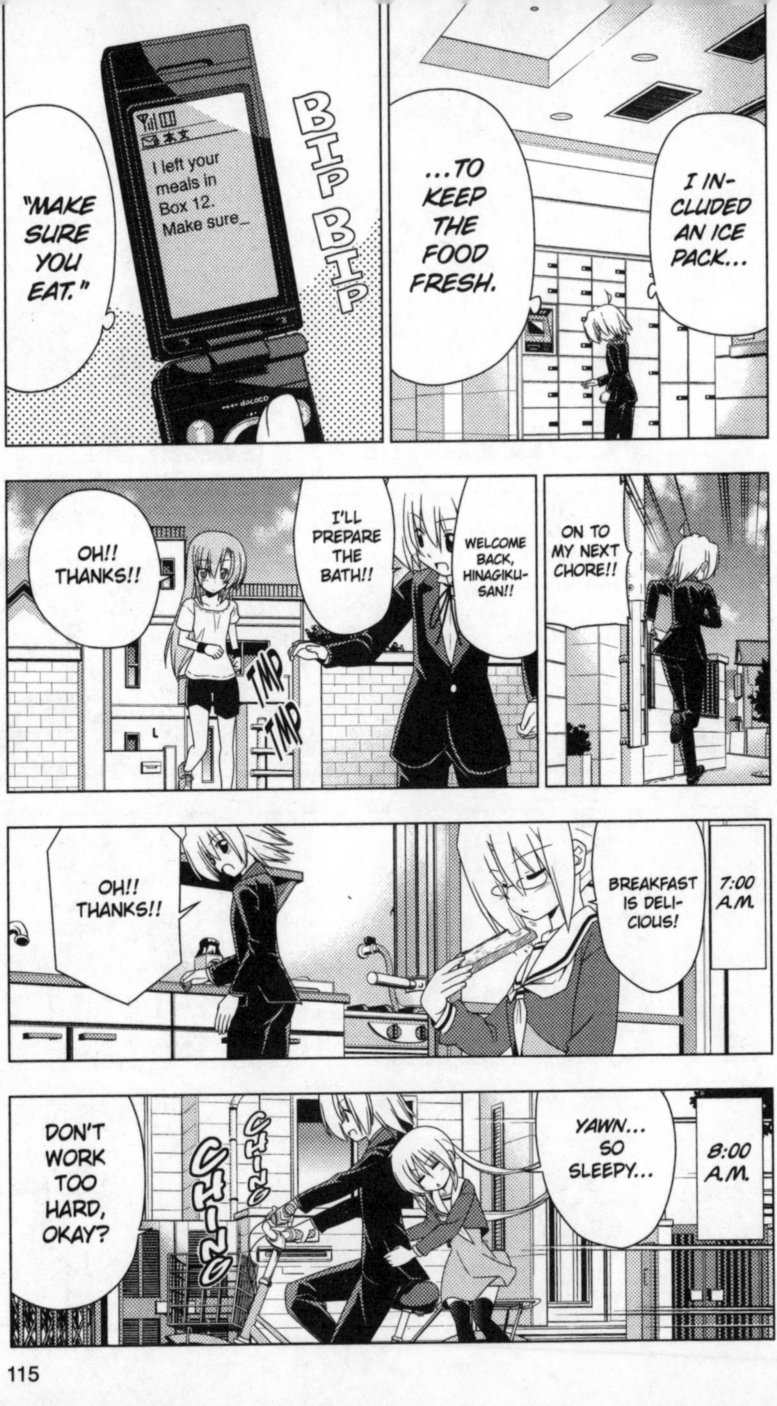
I IN-CLUDED AN ICE PACK...
...TO KEEP THE FOOD FRESH.
I left your meals in Box 12. Make sure_
BIP BIP
"MAKE SURE YOU EAT."
ON TO MY NEXT CHORE!!
WELCOME BACK, HINAGIKU-SAN!!
I'LL PREPARE THE BATH!!
TMP TMP
OH!! THANKS!!
7:00 A.M.
BREAKFAST IS DELI-CIOUS!
OH!! THANKS!!
8:00 A.M.
YAWN... SO SLEEPY...
CHING CHING
DON'T WORK TOO HARD, OKAY?

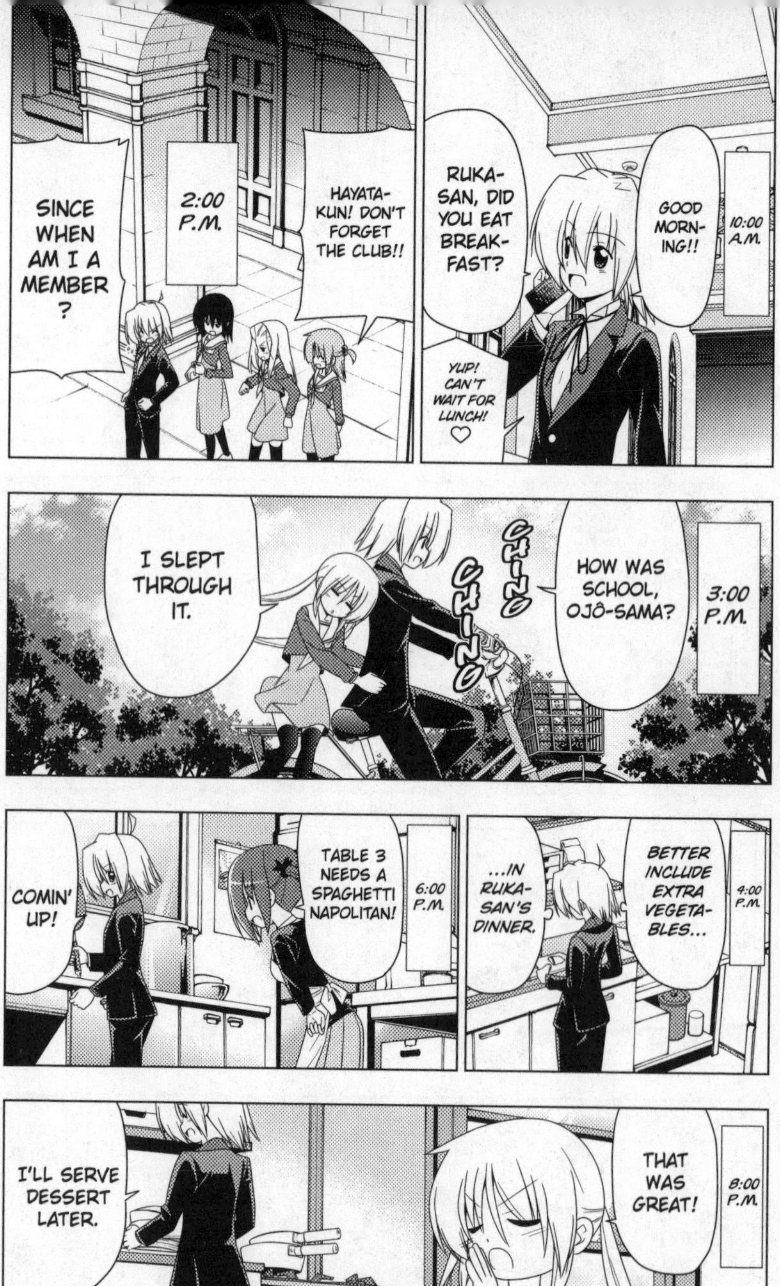
10:00 A.M.
GOOD MORNING!!
RUKA-SAN, DID YOU EAT BREAKFAST?
YUP! CAN'T WAIT FOR LUNCH! ♥
2:00 P.M.
HAYATA-KUN! DON'T FORGET THE CLUB!!
SINCE WHEN AM I A MEMBER?
3:00 P.M.
HOW WAS SCHOOL, OJÔ-SAMA?
CHING
CHING
I SLEPT THROUGH IT.
4:00 P.M.
BETTER INCLUDE EXTRA VEGETABLES...
...IN RUKA-SAN'S DINNER.
6:00 P.M.
TABLE 3 NEEDS A SPAGHETTI NAPOLITAN!
COMIN' UP!
8:00 P.M.
THAT WAS GREAT!
I'LL SERVE DESSERT LATER.

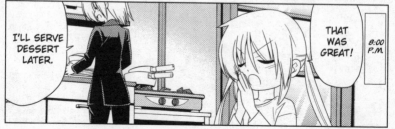

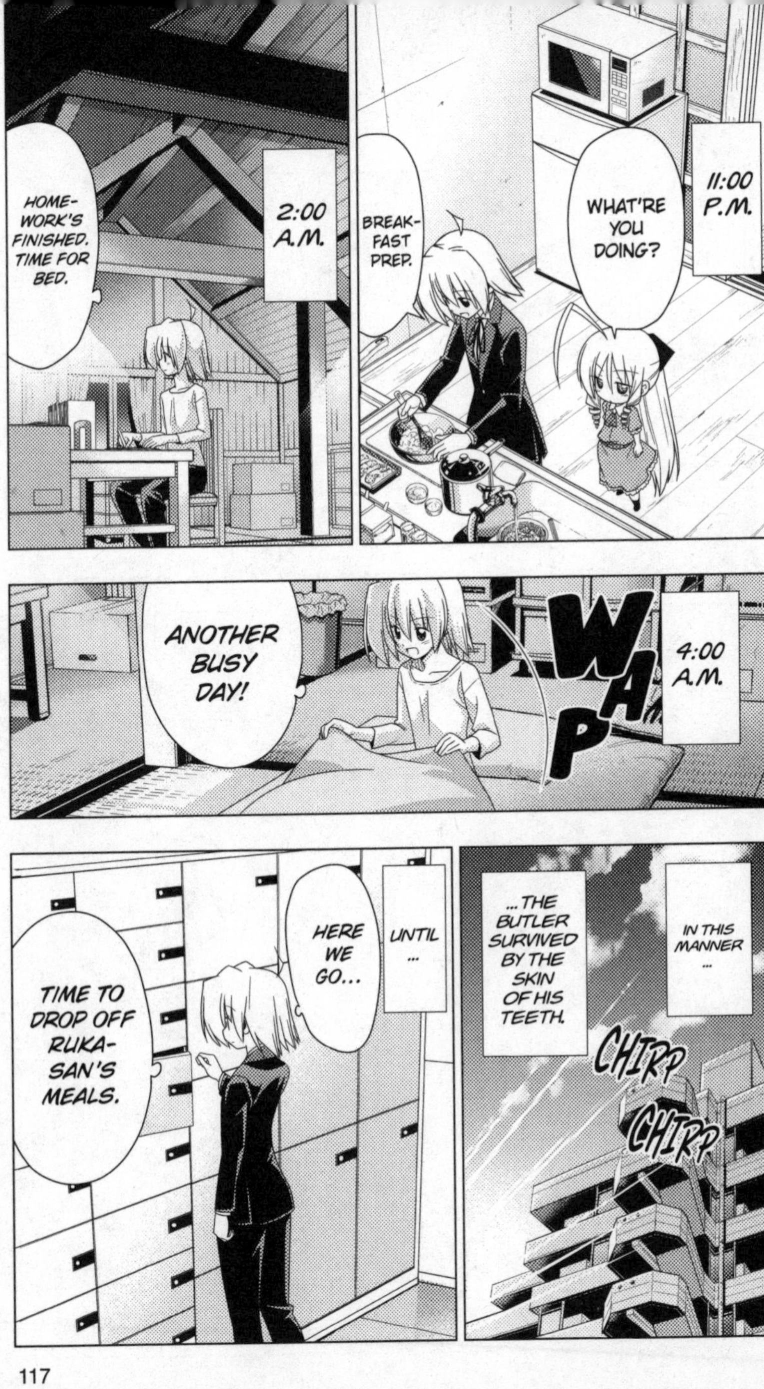
11:00 P.M.
WHAT'RE YOU DOING?
BREAK-FAST PREP.
2:00 A.M.
HOME-WORK'S FINISHED. TIME FOR BED.
4:00 A.M.
WAP
ANOTHER BUSY DAY!
IN THIS MANNER ...
...THE BUTLER SURVIVED BY THE SKIN OF HIS TEETH.
CHIRP
CHIRP
UNTIL ...
HERE WE GO...
TIME TO DROP OFF RUKA-SAN'S MEALS.

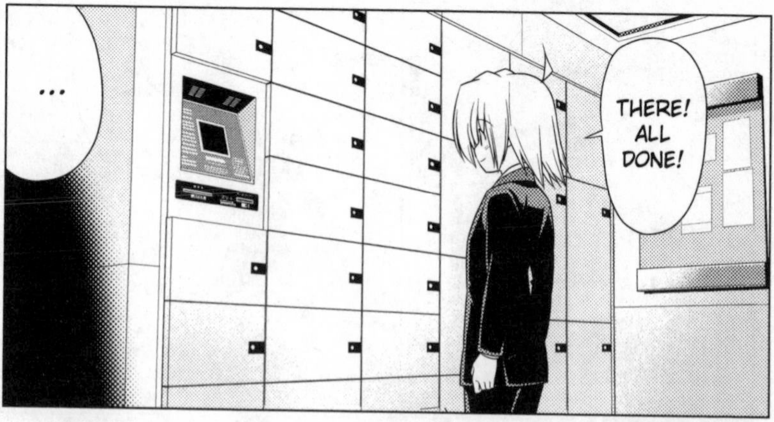
THERE! ALL DONE!
...
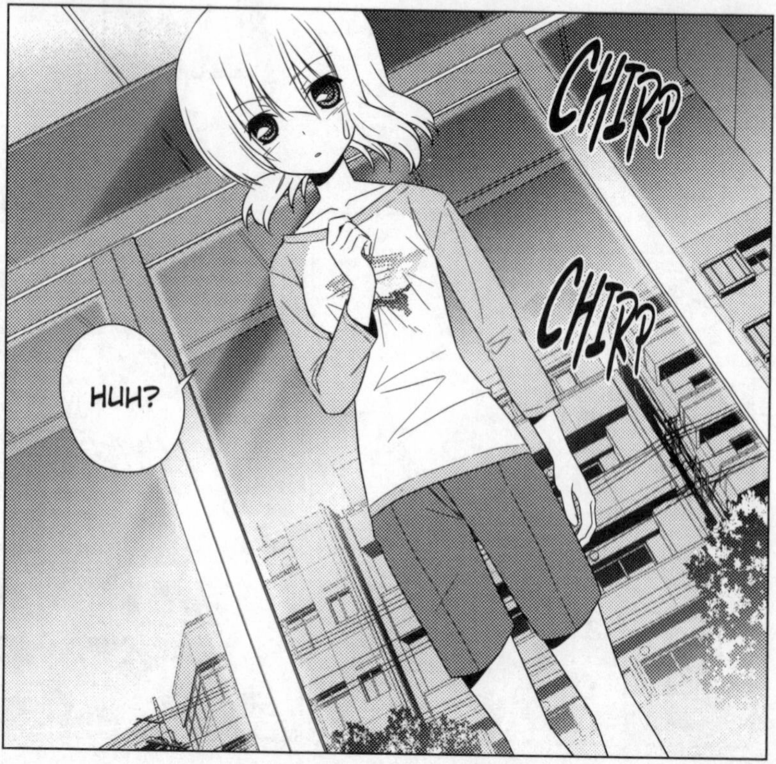
CHIRP
CHIRP
HUH?

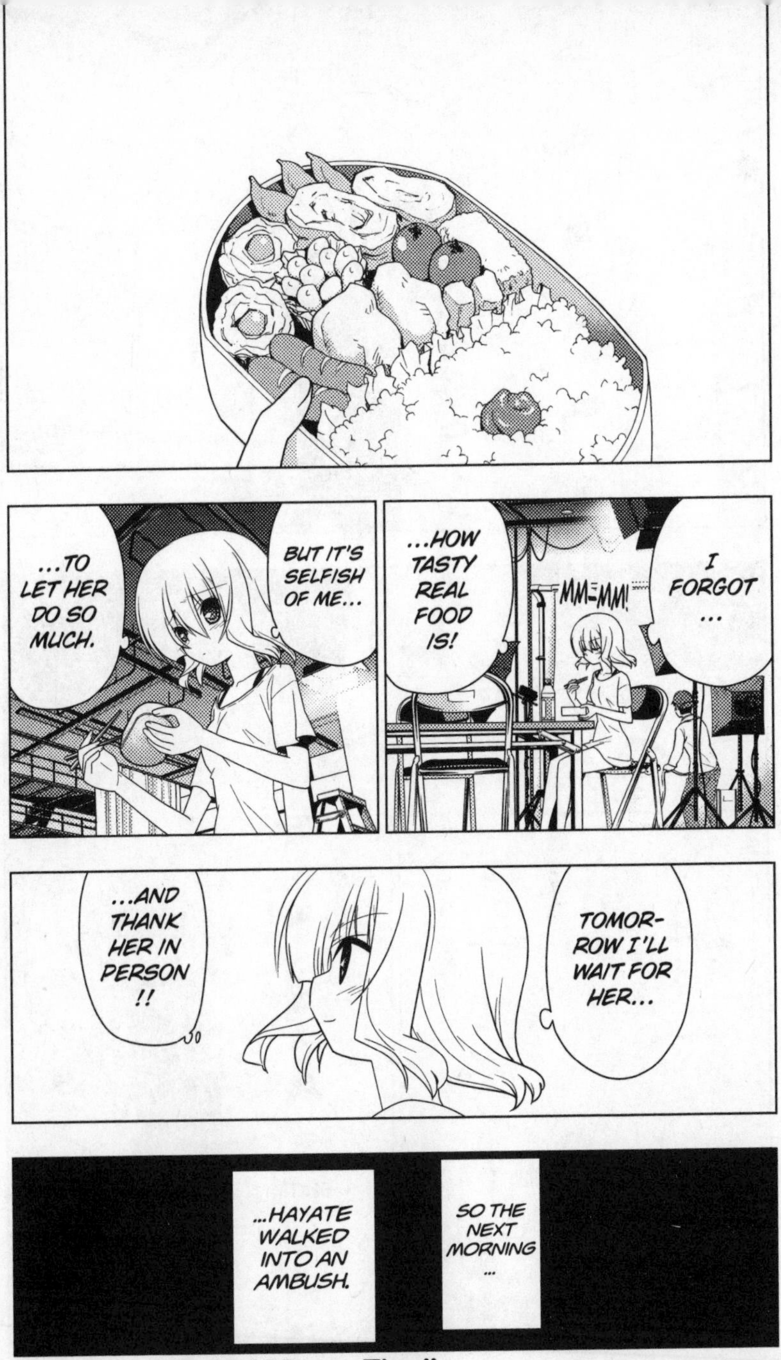
I FORGOT ...
...HOW TASTY REAL FOOD IS!
MM-MM!
BUT IT'S SELFISH OF ME...
...TO LET HER DO SO MUCH.
TOMOR-ROW I'LL WAIT FOR HER...
...AND THANK HER IN PERSON !!
SO THE NEXT MORNING ...
...HAYATE WALKED INTO AN AMBUSH.

Episode 8: "The Maid Passes Time"

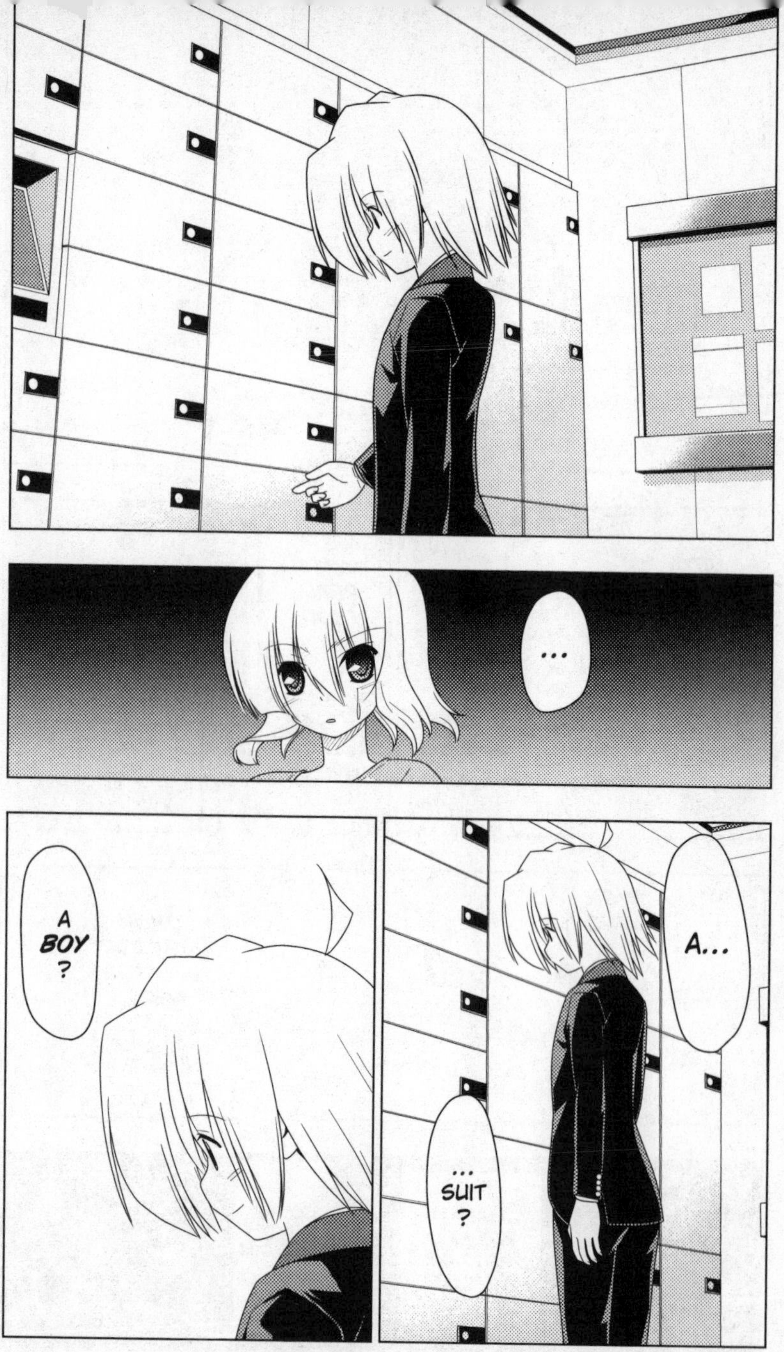
...
A...
... SUIT ?
A BOY ?

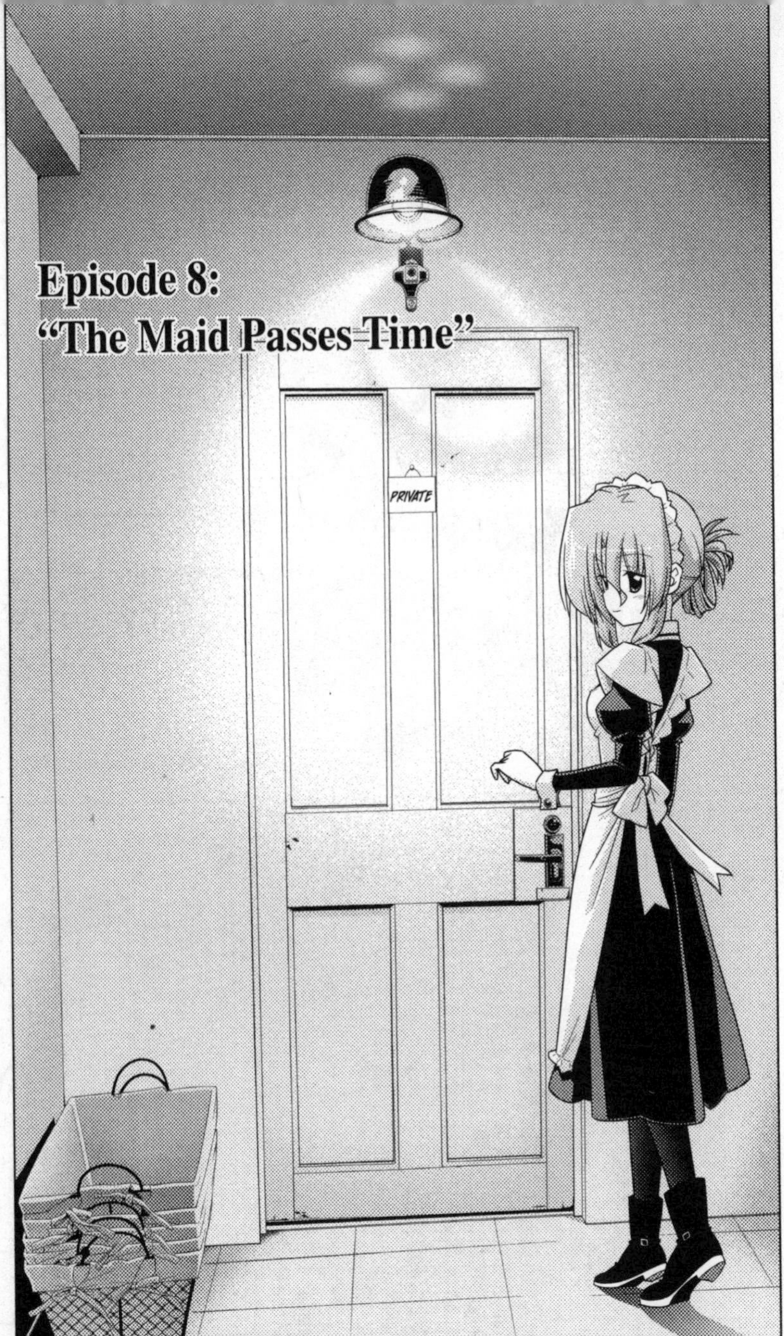
Episode 8:
"The Maid Passes Time"
PRIVATE

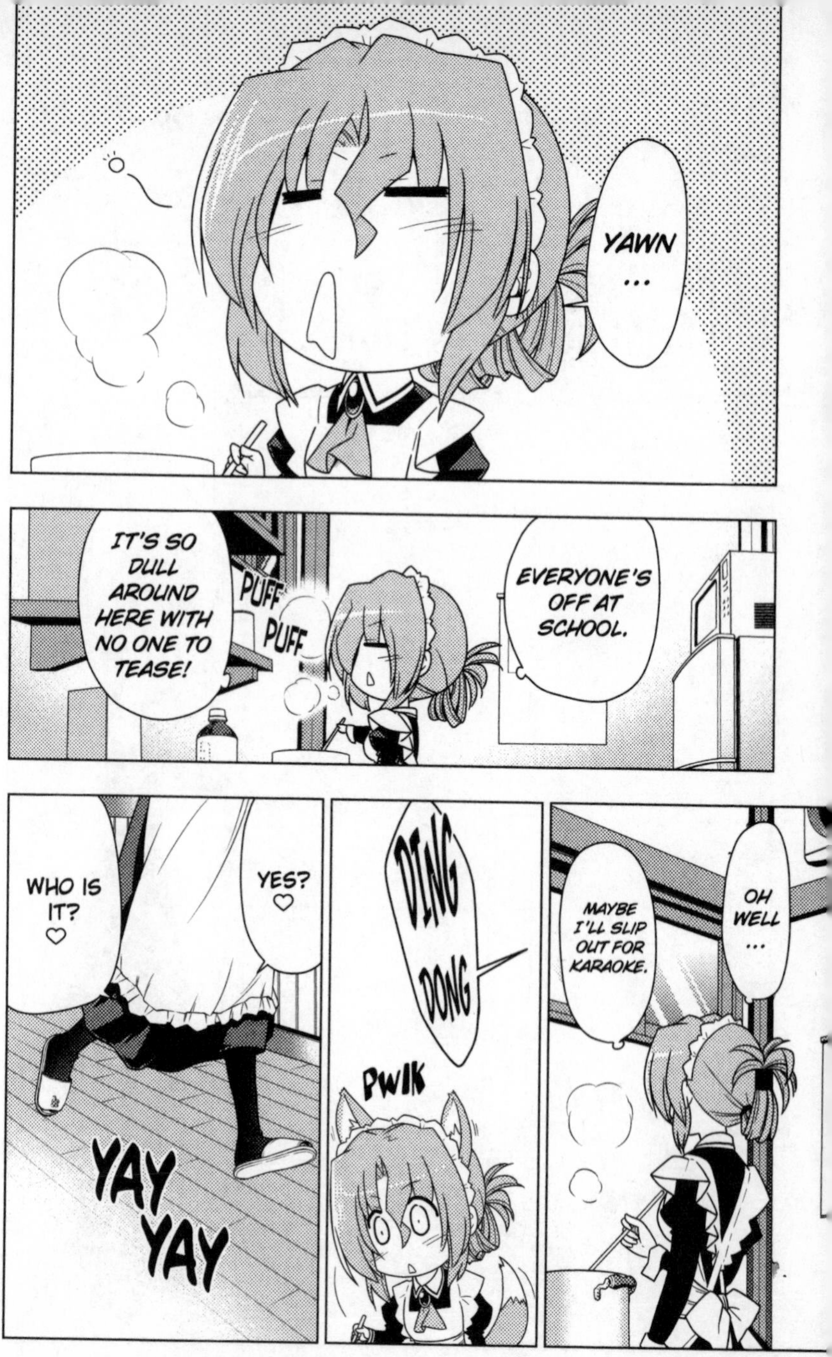
YAWN ...
EVERYONE'S OFF AT SCHOOL.
PUFF PUFF
IT'S SO DULL AROUND HERE WITH NO ONE TO TEASE!
OH WELL ...
MAYBE I'LL SLIP OUT FOR KARAOKE.
DING DONG
PWIK
YES? ♡
WHO IS IT? ♡
YAY YAY

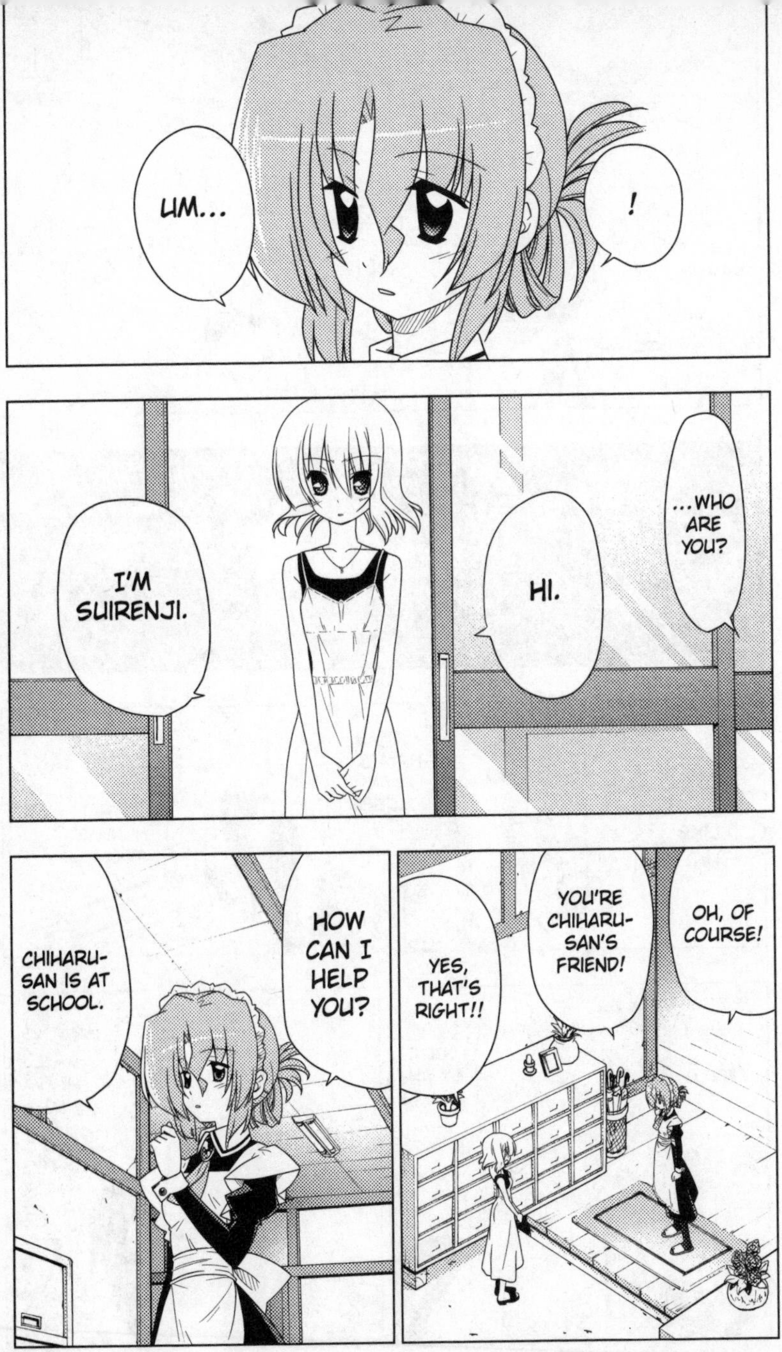
!
UM...
...WHO ARE YOU?
HI.
I'M SUIRENJI.
OH, OF COURSE!
YOU'RE CHIHARU-SAN'S FRIEND!
YES, THAT'S RIGHT!!
HOW CAN I HELP YOU?
CHIHARU-SAN IS AT SCHOOL.

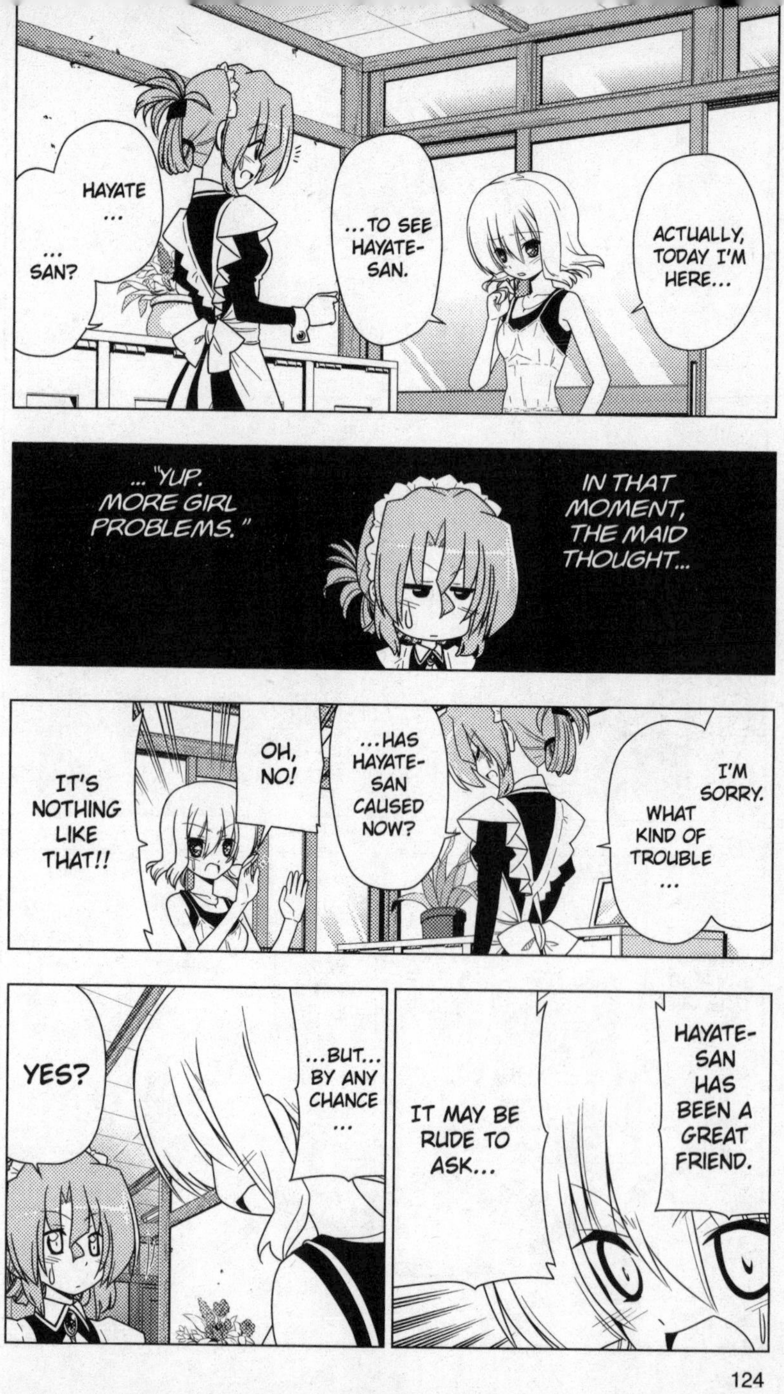
ACTUALLY, TODAY I'M HERE...
...TO SEE HAYATE-SAN.
HAYATE... ...SAN?
IN THAT MOMENT, THE MAID THOUGHT...
..."YUP. MORE GIRL PROBLEMS."
I'M SORRY. WHAT KIND OF TROUBLE...
...HAS HAYATE-SAN CAUSED NOW?
OH, NO!
IT'S NOTHING LIKE THAT!!
HAYATE-SAN HAS BEEN A GREAT FRIEND.
IT MAY BE RUDE TO ASK...
...BUT... BY ANY CHANCE...
YES?

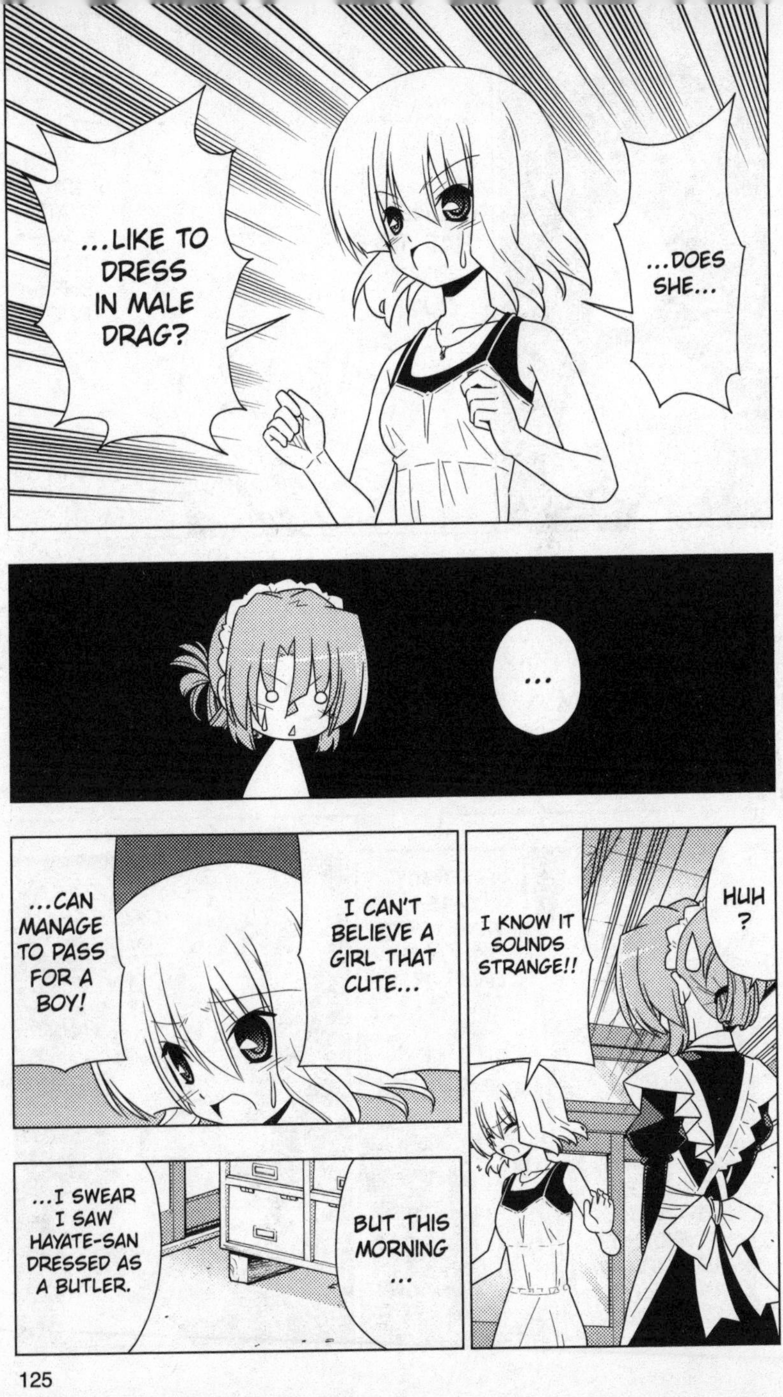
...DOES SHE...
...LIKE TO DRESS IN MALE DRAG?
...
HUH?
I KNOW IT SOUNDS STRANGE!!
I CAN'T BELIEVE A GIRL THAT CUTE...
...CAN MANAGE TO PASS FOR A BOY!
BUT THIS MORNING...
...I SWEAR I SAW HAYATE-SAN DRESSED AS A BUTLER.

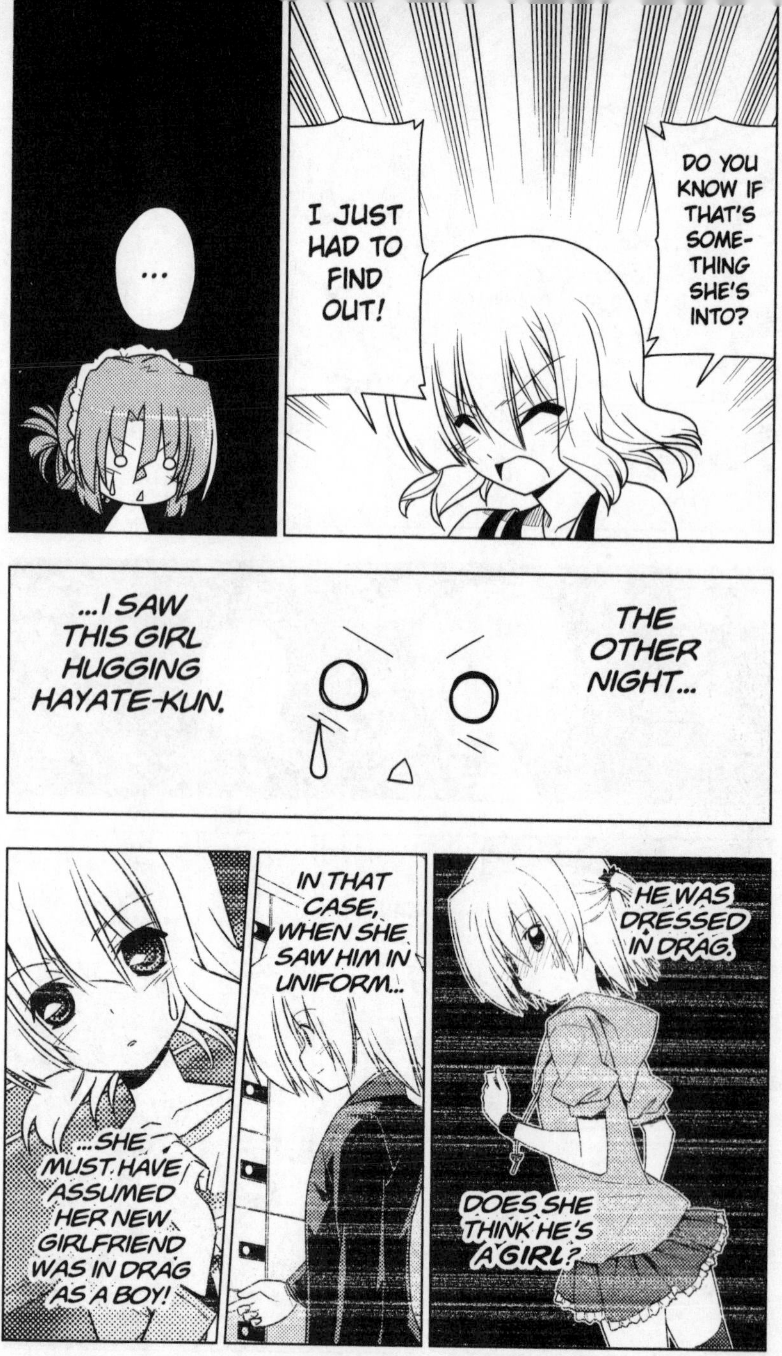
DO YOU KNOW IF THAT'S SOME-THING SHE'S INTO?
I JUST HAD TO FIND OUT!
...
THE OTHER NIGHT...
...I SAW THIS GIRL HUGGING HAYATE-KUN.
HE WAS DRESSED IN DRAG.
DOES SHE THINK HE'S A GIRL?
IN THAT CASE, WHEN SHE SAW HIM IN UNIFORM...
...SHE MUST HAVE ASSUMED HER NEW GIRLFRIEND WAS IN DRAG AS A BOY!

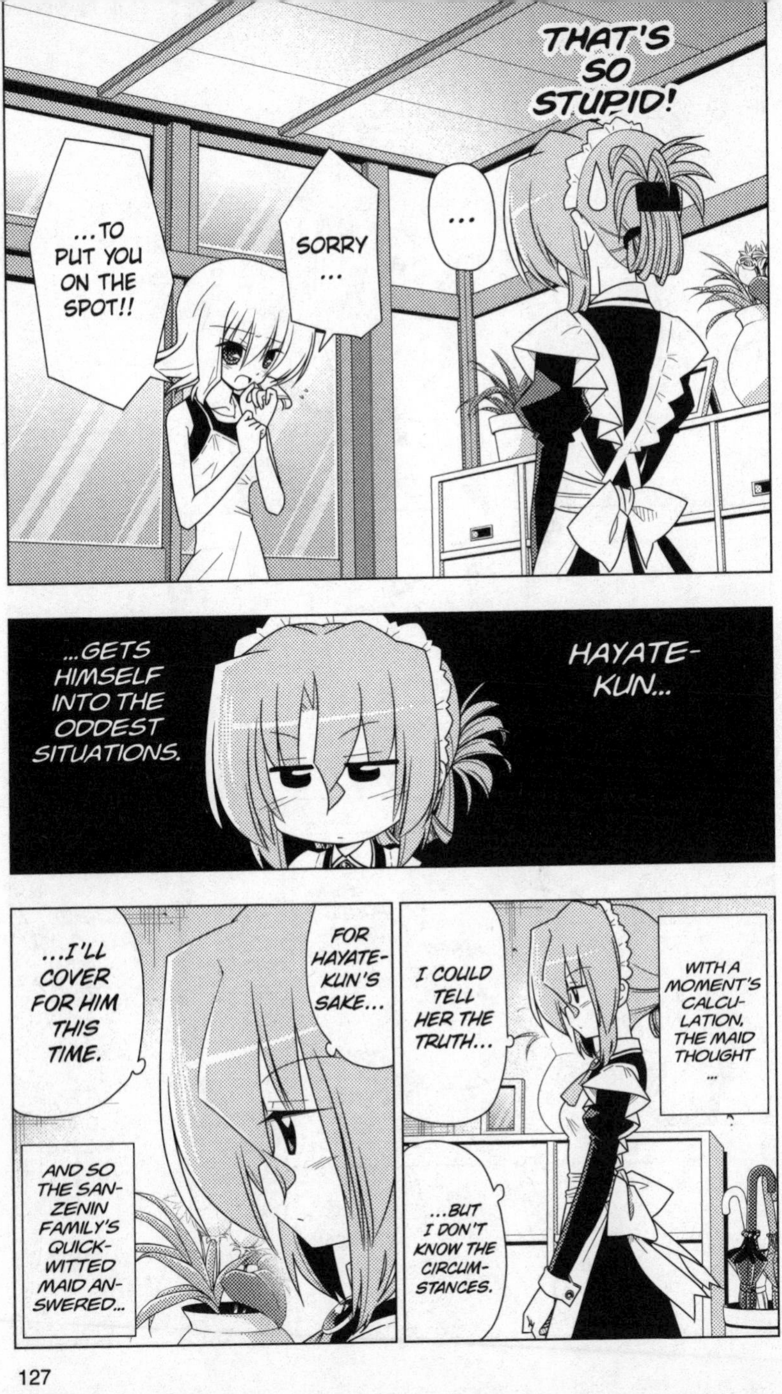
THAT'S SO STUPID!
...
SORRY ...
...TO PUT YOU ON THE SPOT!!
HAYATE-KUN...
...GETS HIMSELF INTO THE ODDEST SITUATIONS.
WITH A MOMENT'S CALCULATION, THE MAID THOUGHT ...
I COULD TELL HER THE TRUTH...
...BUT I DON'T KNOW THE CIRCUMSTANCES.
FOR HAYATE-KUN'S SAKE...
...I'LL COVER FOR HIM THIS TIME.
AND SO THE SANZENIN FAMILY'S QUICK-WITTED MAID ANSWERED...

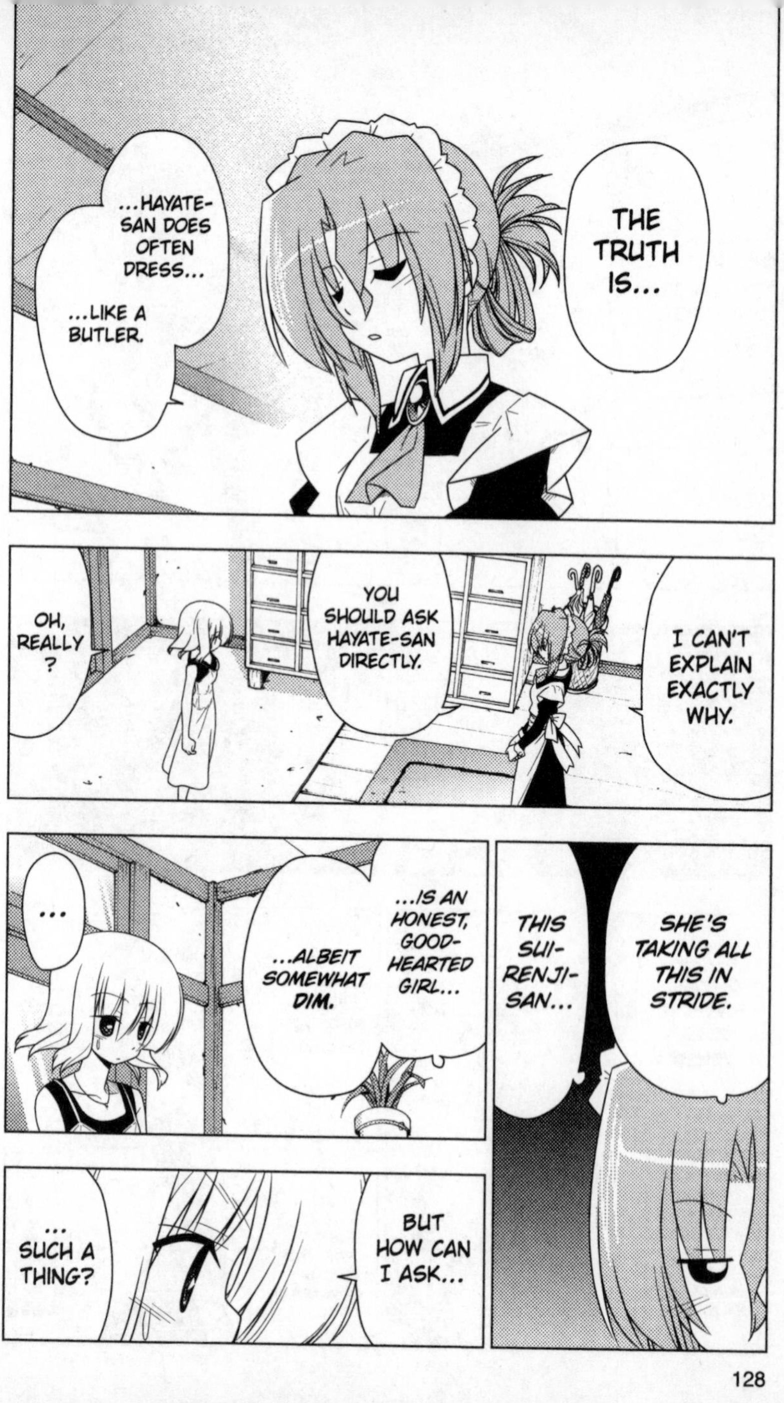
THE TRUTH IS...
...HAYATE-SAN DOES OFTEN DRESS...
...LIKE A BUTLER.
I CAN'T EXPLAIN EXACTLY WHY.
YOU SHOULD ASK HAYATE-SAN DIRECTLY.
OH, REALLY?
SHE'S TAKING ALL THIS IN STRIDE.
THIS SUI-RENJI-SAN...
...IS AN HONEST, GOOD-HEARTED GIRL...
...ALBEIT SOMEWHAT DIM.
...
BUT HOW CAN I ASK...
...SUCH A THING?

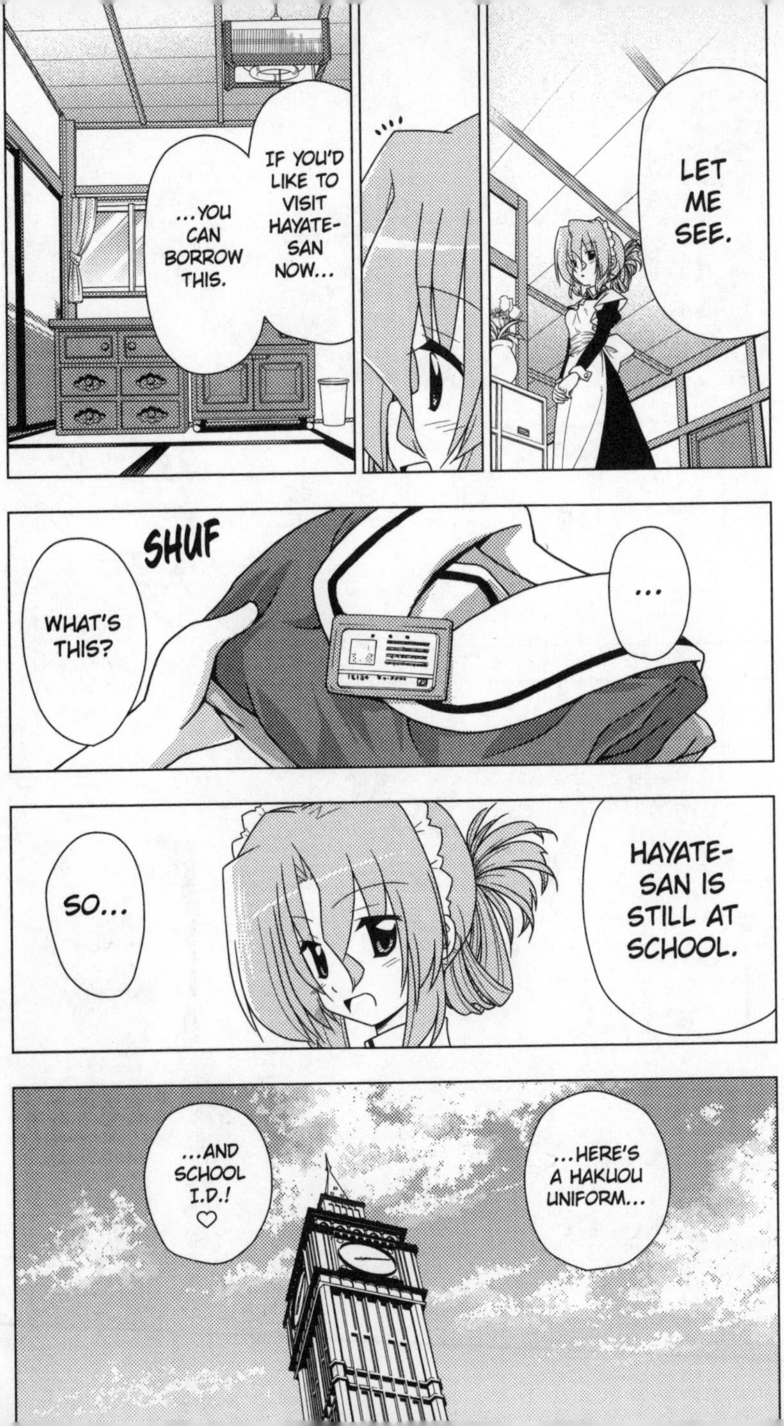
LET ME SEE.
...
IF YOU'D LIKE TO VISIT HAYATE-SAN NOW...
...YOU CAN BORROW THIS.
...
SHUF
WHAT'S THIS?
HAYATE-SAN IS STILL AT SCHOOL.
SO...
...HERE'S A HAKUOU UNIFORM...
...AND SCHOOL I.D.! ♡

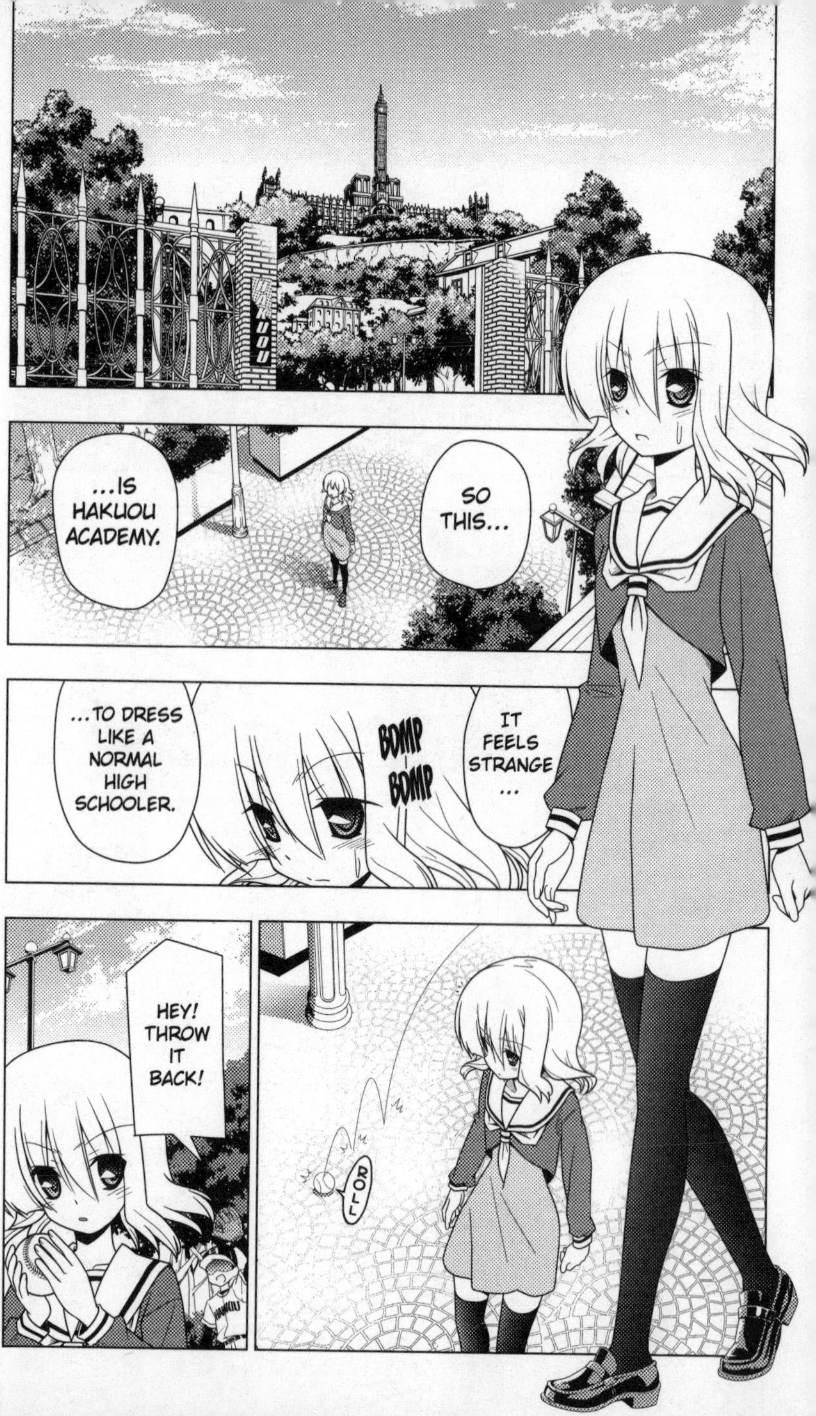
SO THIS...
...IS HAKUOU ACADEMY.
IT FEELS STRANGE ...
BDMP BDMP
...TO DRESS LIKE A NORMAL HIGH SCHOOLER.
ROLL
HEY! THROW IT BACK!

OKAY! ♡

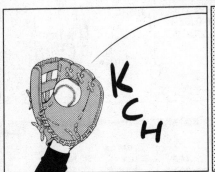

KCH

BWOOM

HAKUOU HAKUOU

WHEN DID WE GET THAT *BABE*?

MUST BE NEW...

UH...

WHUH...

...

BYE, NOW! ♡

131

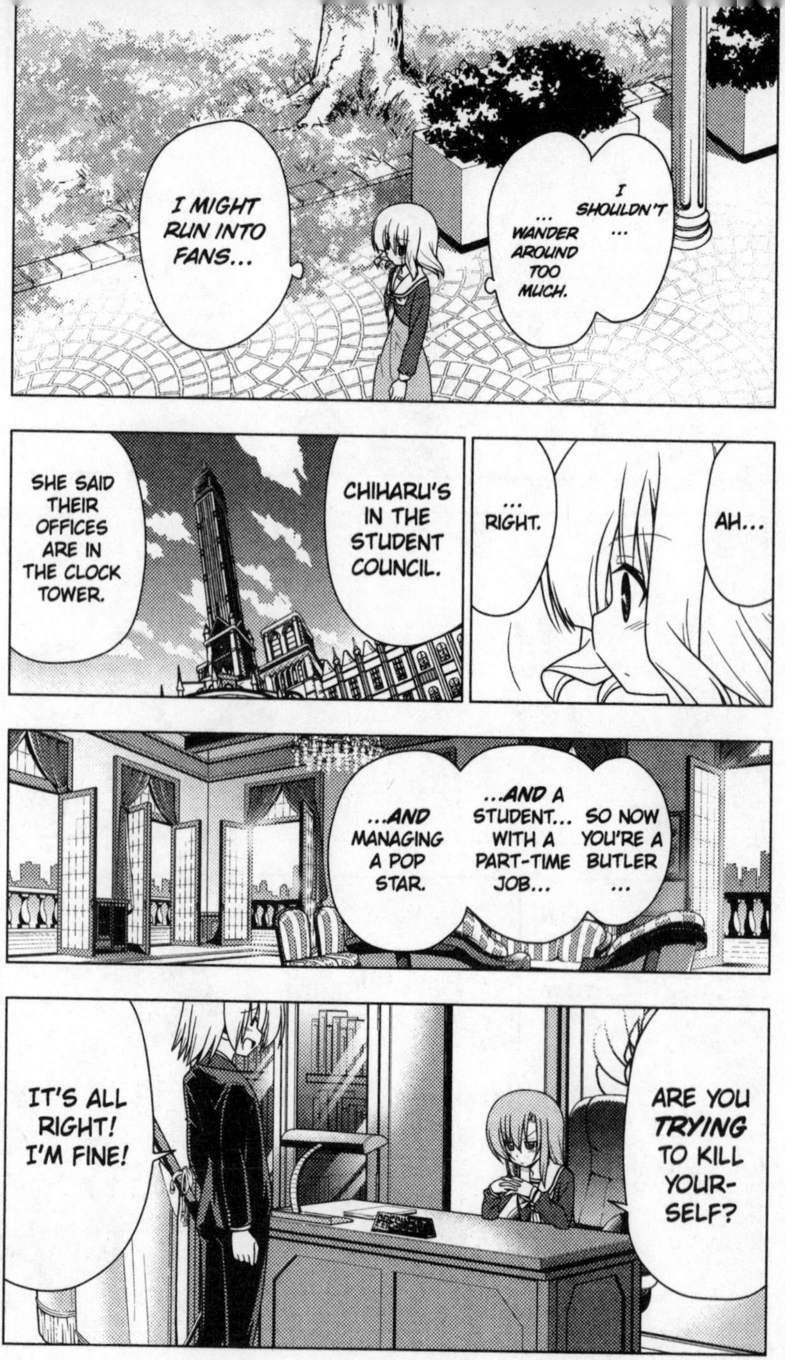
I SHOULDN'T ... ... WANDER AROUND TOO MUCH.
I MIGHT RUN INTO FANS...
AH...
... RIGHT.
CHIHARU'S IN THE STUDENT COUNCIL.
SHE SAID THEIR OFFICES ARE IN THE CLOCK TOWER.
SO NOW YOU'RE A BUTLER ...
...AND A STUDENT... WITH A PART-TIME JOB...
...AND MANAGING A POP STAR.
ARE YOU TRYING TO KILL YOUR-SELF?
IT'S ALL RIGHT! I'M FINE!

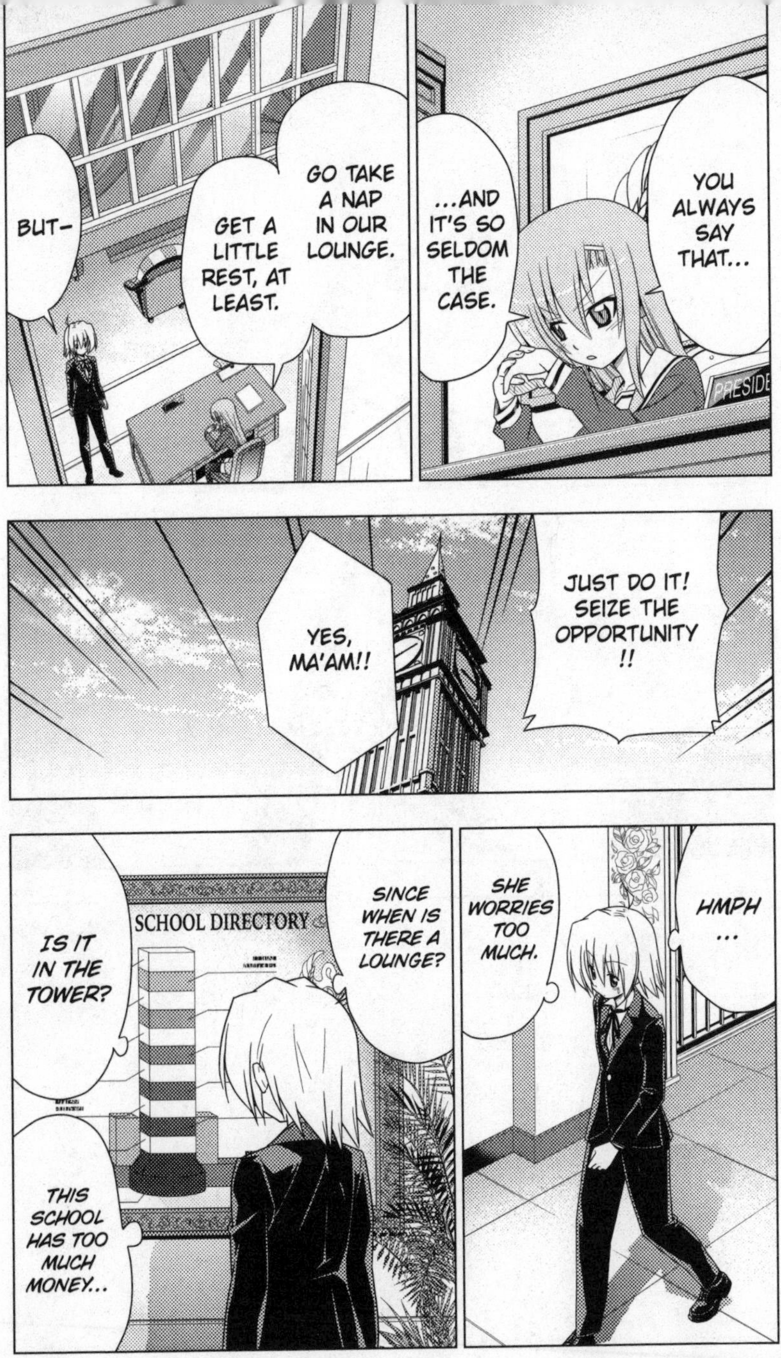
YOU ALWAYS SAY THAT...
...AND IT'S SO SELDOM THE CASE.
PRESIDE
GO TAKE A NAP IN OUR LOUNGE.
GET A LITTLE REST, AT LEAST.
BUT-
JUST DO IT! SEIZE THE OPPORTUNITY !!
YES, MA'AM!!
HMPH ...
SHE WORRIES TOO MUCH.
SINCE WHEN IS THERE A LOUNGE?
SCHOOL DIRECTORY
IS IT IN THE TOWER?
THIS SCHOOL HAS TOO MUCH MONEY...

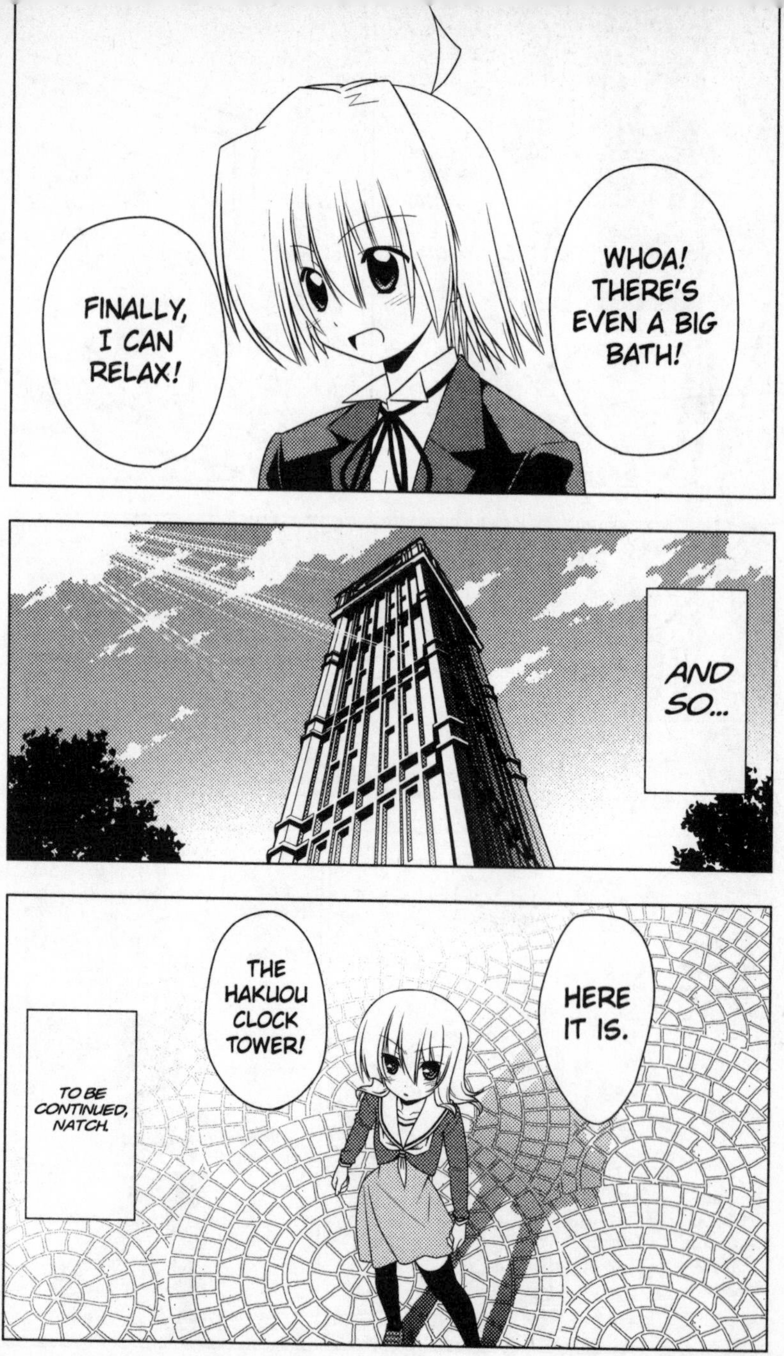
WHOA! THERE'S EVEN A BIG BATH!
FINALLY, I CAN RELAX!
AND SO...
HERE IT IS.
THE HAKUOU CLOCK TOWER!
TO BE CONTINUED, NATCH.

Episode 9: "The Secret Ingredient Is Salt"

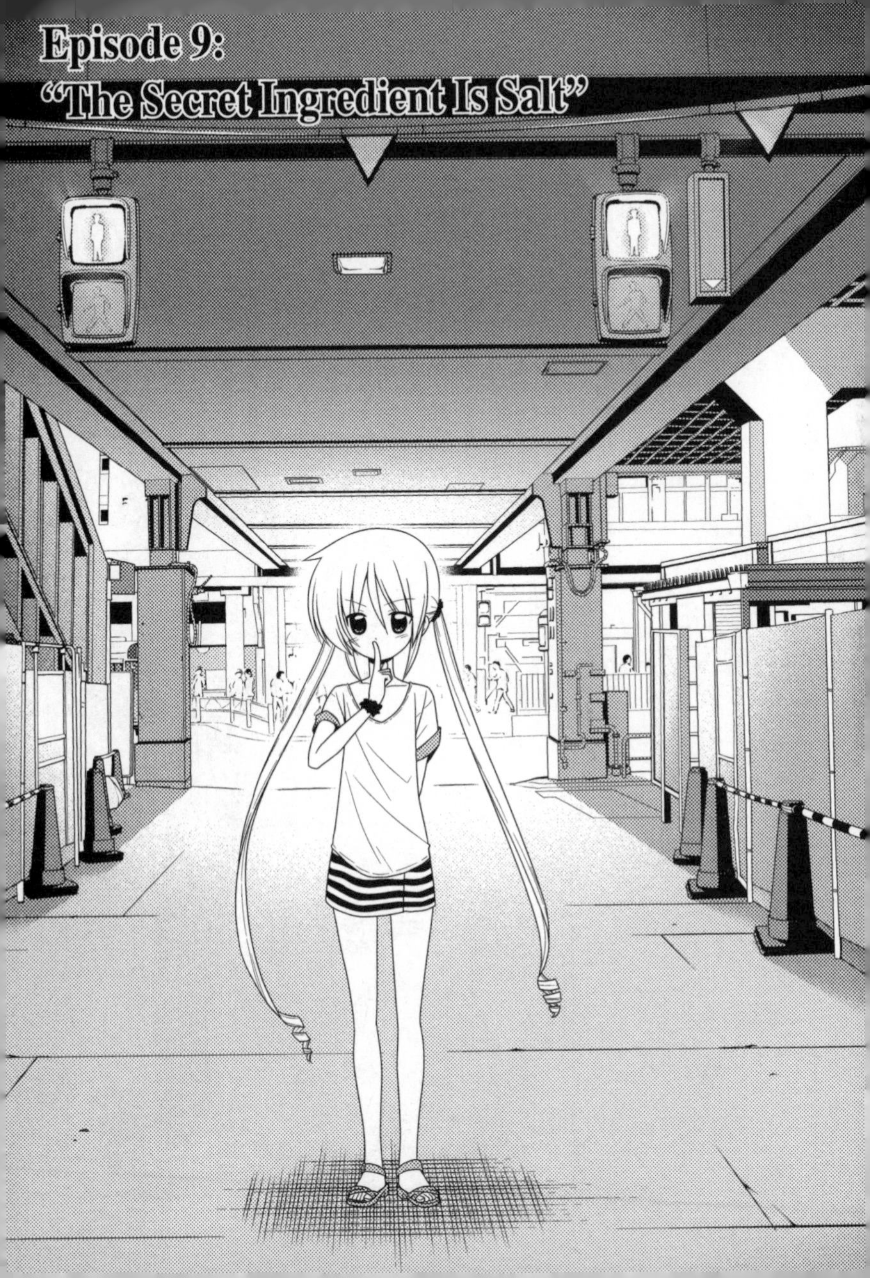

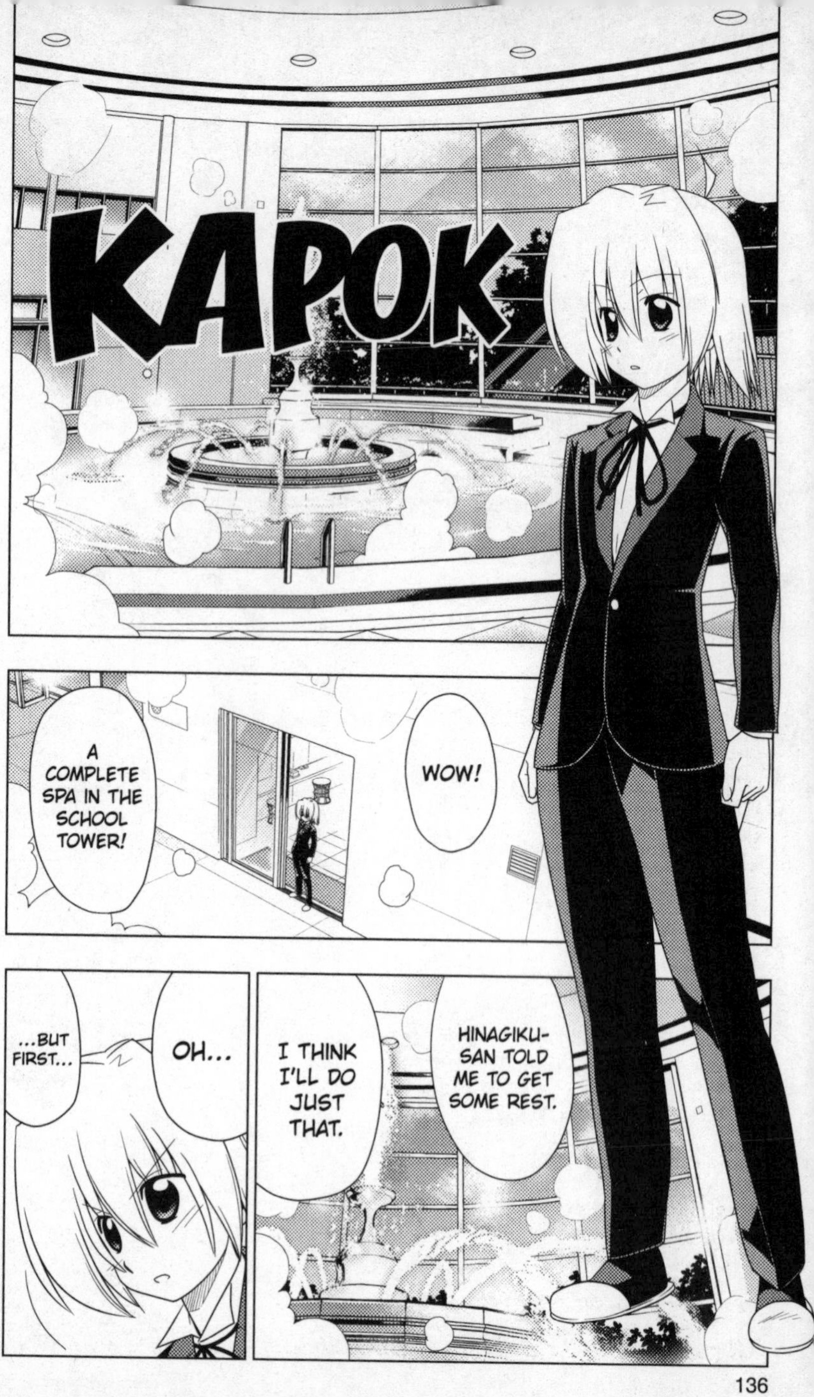
KAPOK
WOW!
A COMPLETE SPA IN THE SCHOOL TOWER!
HINAGIKU-SAN TOLD ME TO GET SOME REST.
I THINK I'LL DO JUST THAT.
OH...
...BUT FIRST...

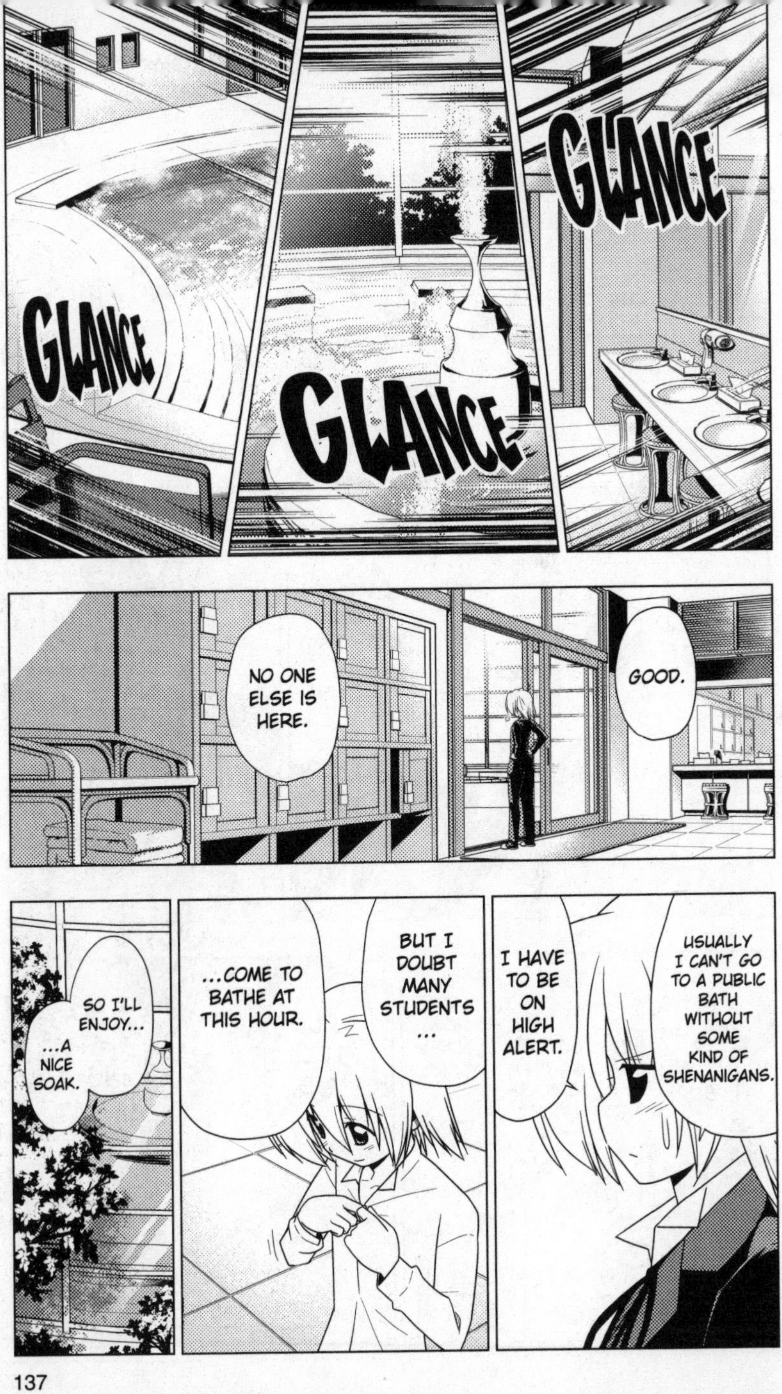
GLANCE
GLANCE
GLANCE
GOOD.
NO ONE ELSE IS HERE.
USUALLY I CAN'T GO TO A PUBLIC BATH WITHOUT SOME KIND OF SHENANIGANS.
I HAVE TO BE ON HIGH ALERT.
BUT I DOUBT MANY STUDENTS...
...COME TO BATHE AT THIS HOUR.
SO I'LL ENJOY...
...A NICE SOAK.

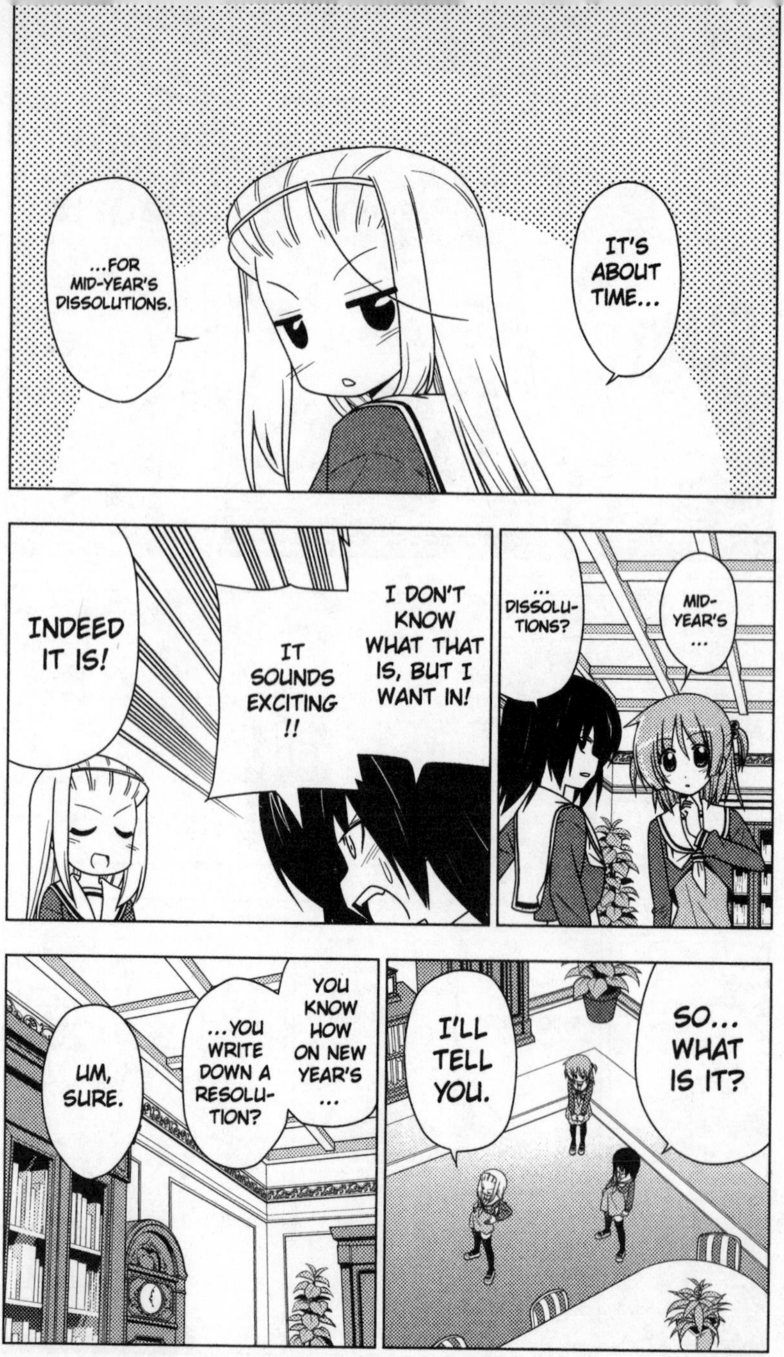
IT'S ABOUT TIME...
...FOR MID-YEAR'S DISSOLUTIONS.
MID-YEAR'S...
...DISSOLUTIONS?
I DON'T KNOW WHAT THAT IS, BUT I WANT IN!
IT SOUNDS EXCITING!!
INDEED IT IS!
SO... WHAT IS IT?
I'LL TELL YOU.
YOU KNOW HOW ON NEW YEAR'S...
...YOU WRITE DOWN A RESOLUTION?
UM, SURE.

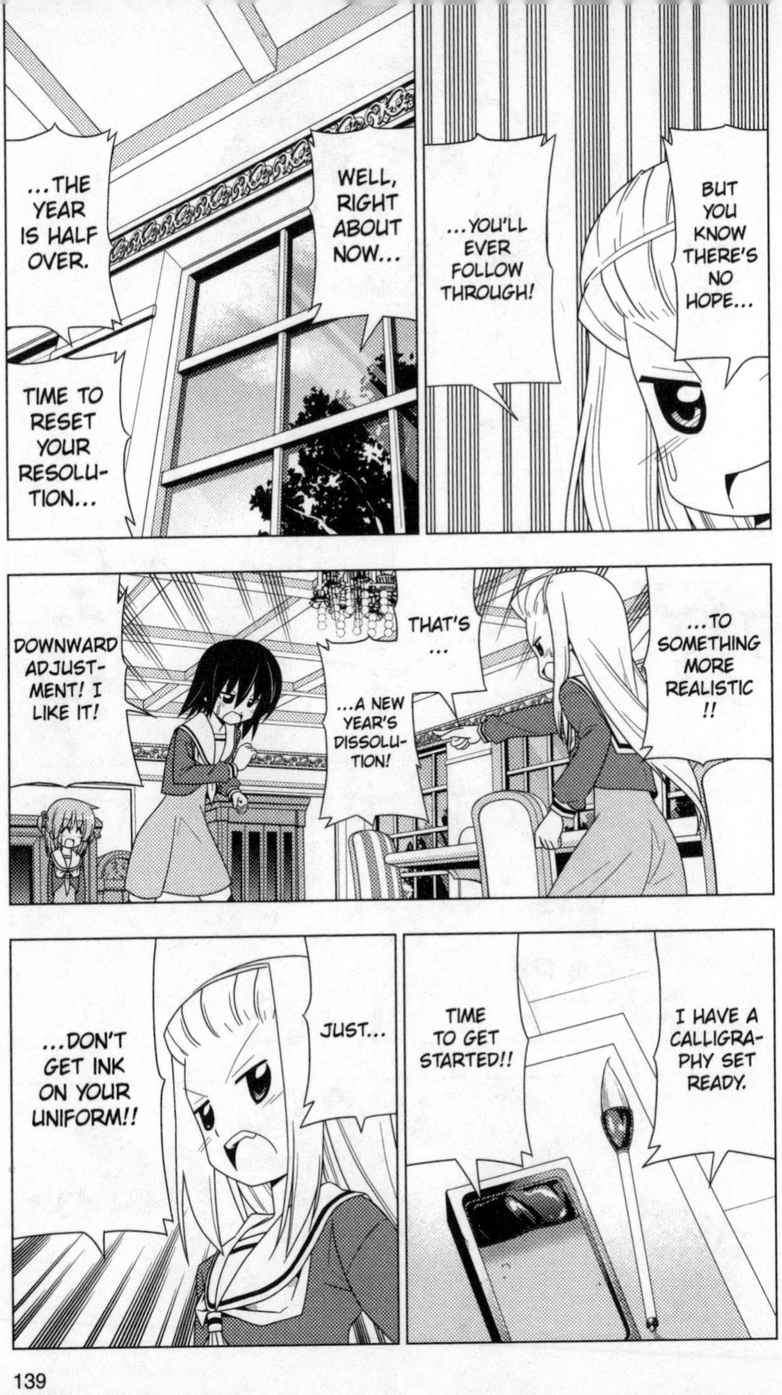
BUT YOU KNOW THERE'S NO HOPE...
...YOU'LL EVER FOLLOW THROUGH!
WELL, RIGHT ABOUT NOW...
...THE YEAR IS HALF OVER.
TIME TO RESET YOUR RESOLUTION...
...TO SOMETHING MORE REALISTIC!!
THAT'S ...
...A NEW YEAR'S DISSOLUTION!
DOWNWARD ADJUSTMENT! I LIKE IT!
I HAVE A CALLIGRAPHY SET READY.
TIME TO GET STARTED!!
JUST...
...DON'T GET INK ON YOUR UNIFORM!!

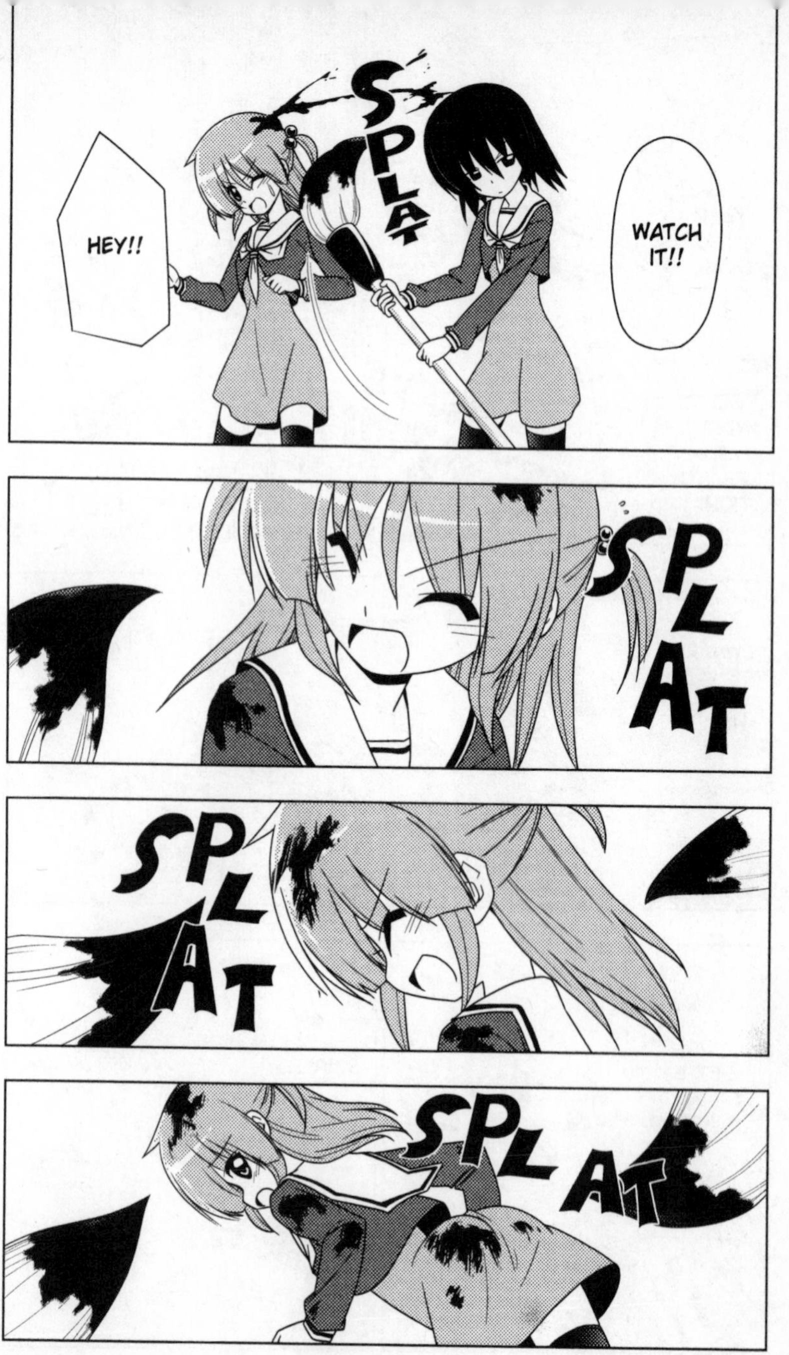
WATCH IT!!
SPLAT
HEY!!
SPLAT
SPLAT
SPLAT

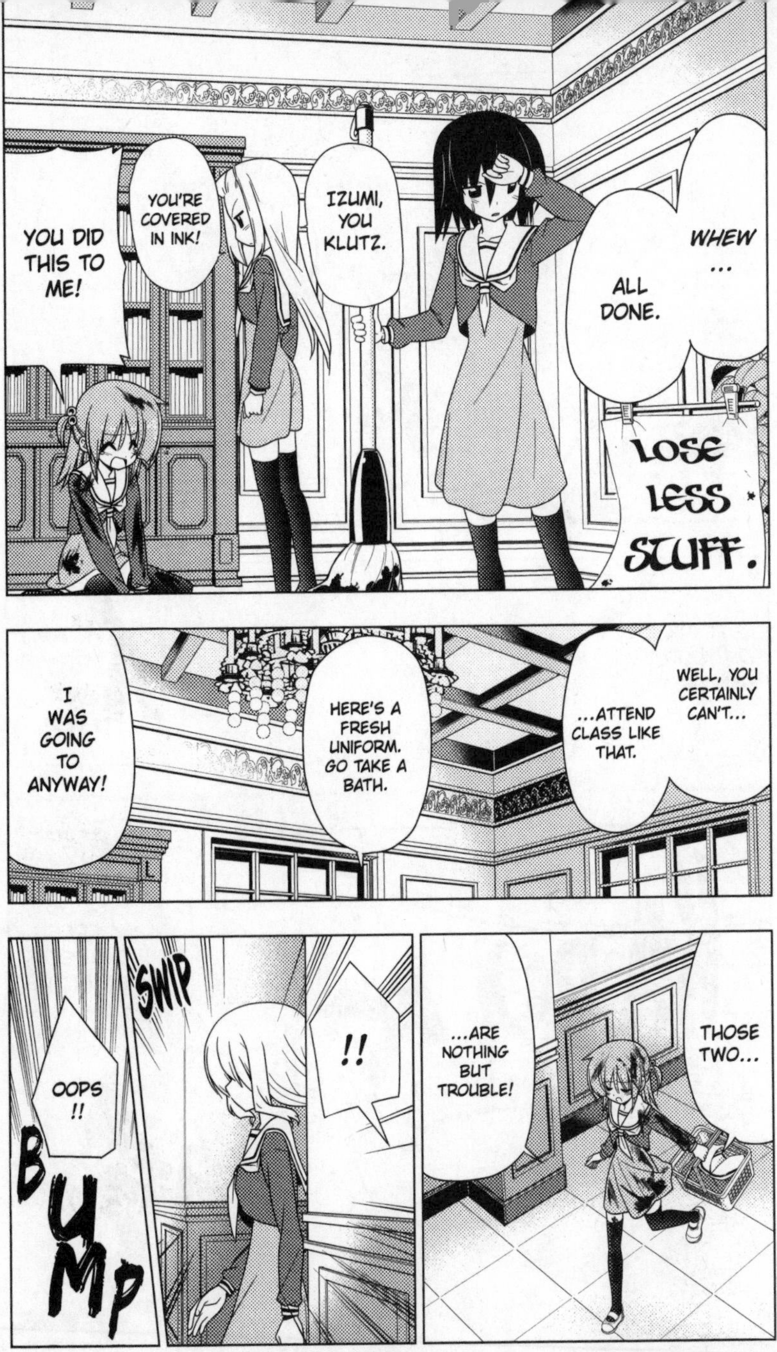
WHEW ...
ALL DONE.
LOSE LESS STUFF.
IZUMI, YOU KLUTZ.
YOU'RE COVERED IN INK!
YOU DID THIS TO ME!
WELL, YOU CERTAINLY CAN'T...
...ATTEND CLASS LIKE THAT.
HERE'S A FRESH UNIFORM. GO TAKE A BATH.
I WAS GOING TO ANYWAY!
THOSE TWO...
...ARE NOTHING BUT TROUBLE!
!!
SWIP
OOPS !!
BUMP

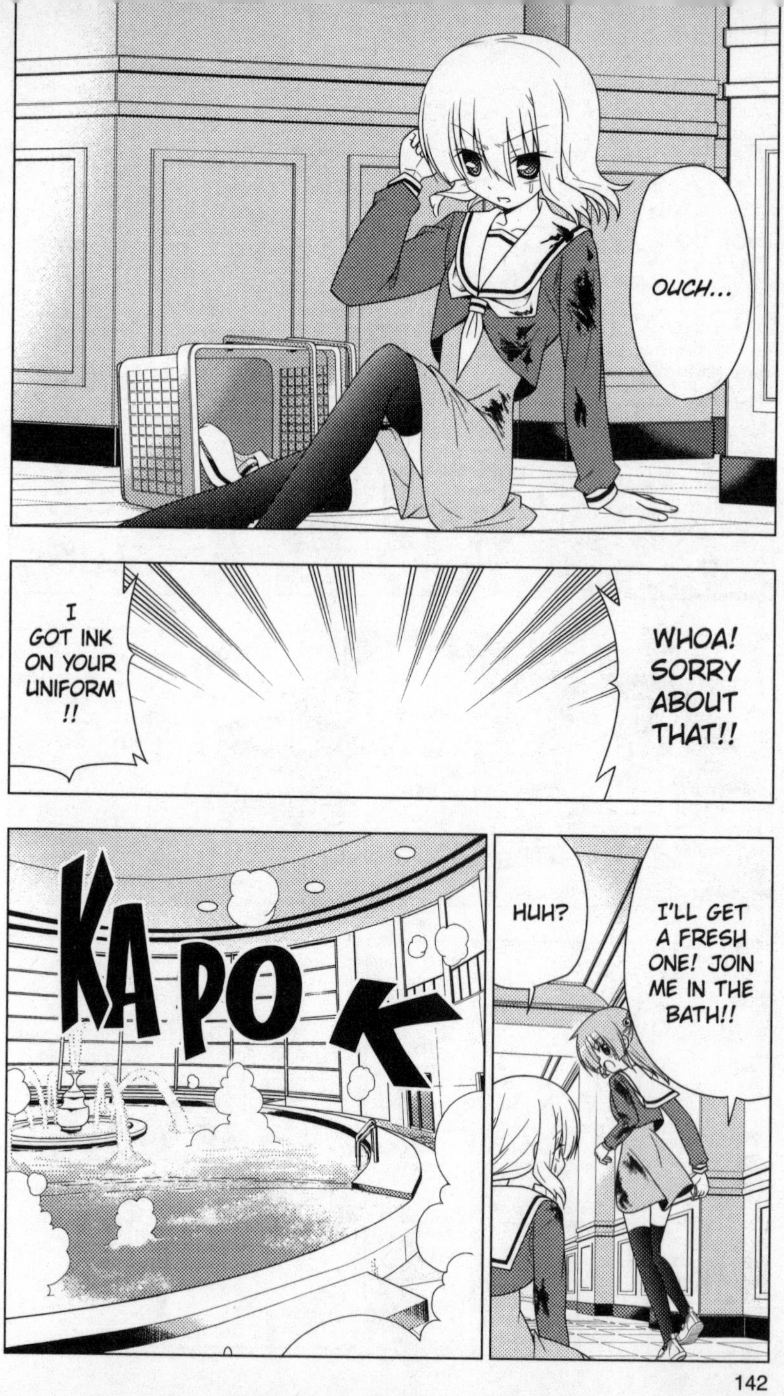
OUCH...
WHOA! SORRY ABOUT THAT!!
I GOT INK ON YOUR UNIFORM !!
I'LL GET A FRESH ONE! JOIN ME IN THE BATH!!
HUH?
KAPOK

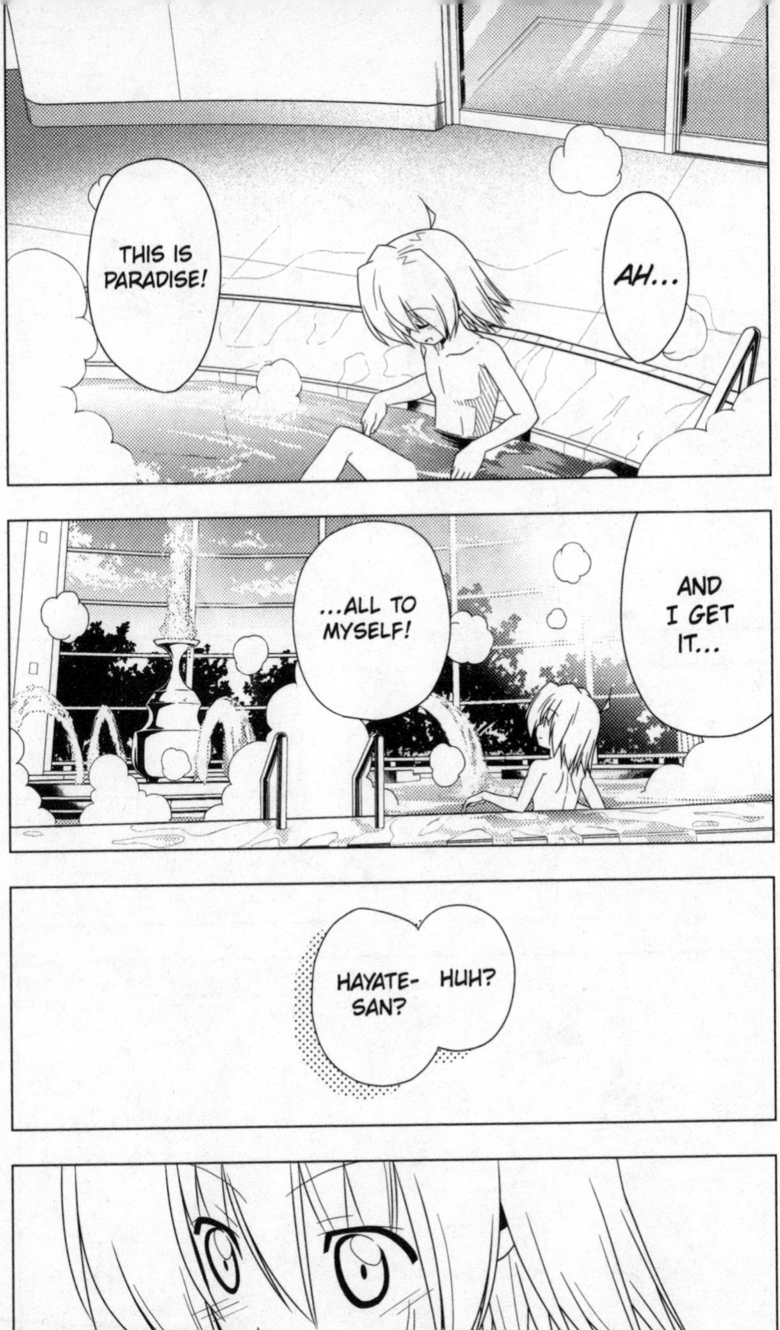
AH...
THIS IS PARADISE!
AND I GET IT...
...ALL TO MYSELF!
HUH?
HAYATE-SAN?

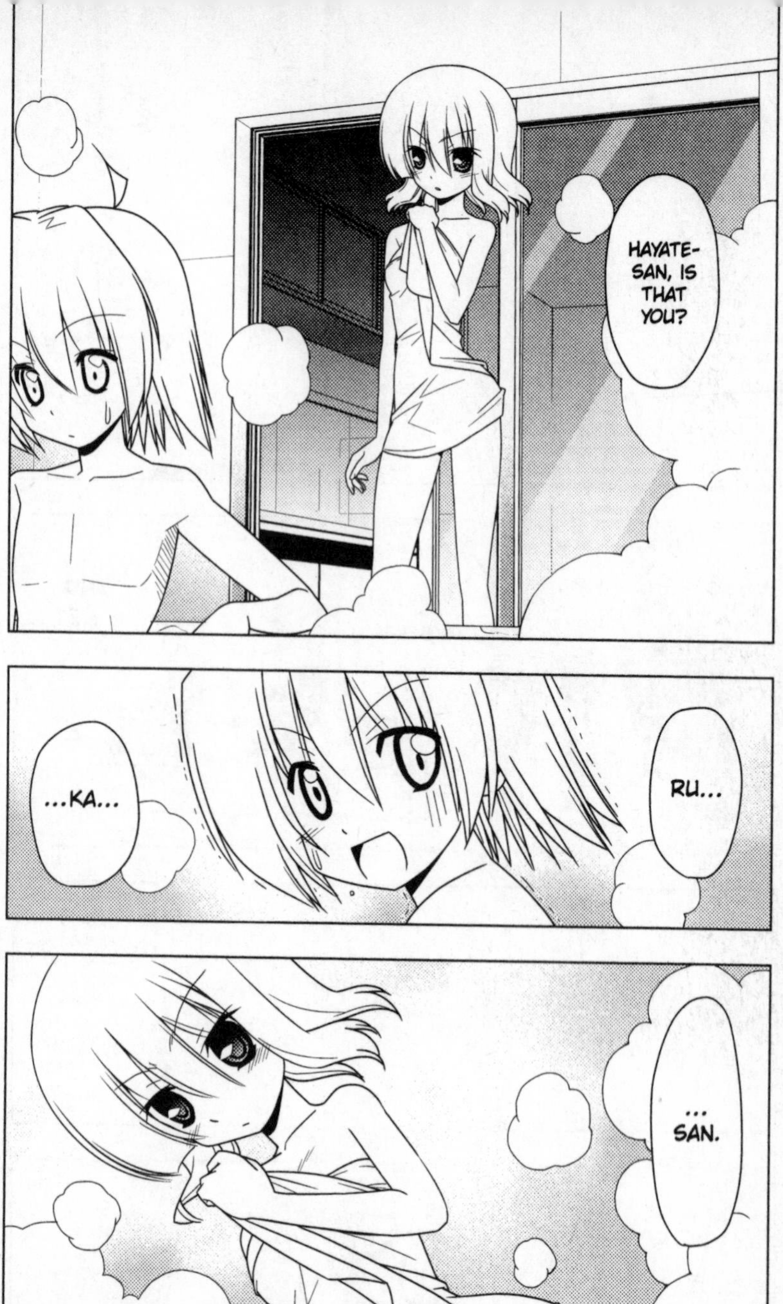
HAYATE-SAN, IS THAT YOU?
RU...
...KA...
...SAN.

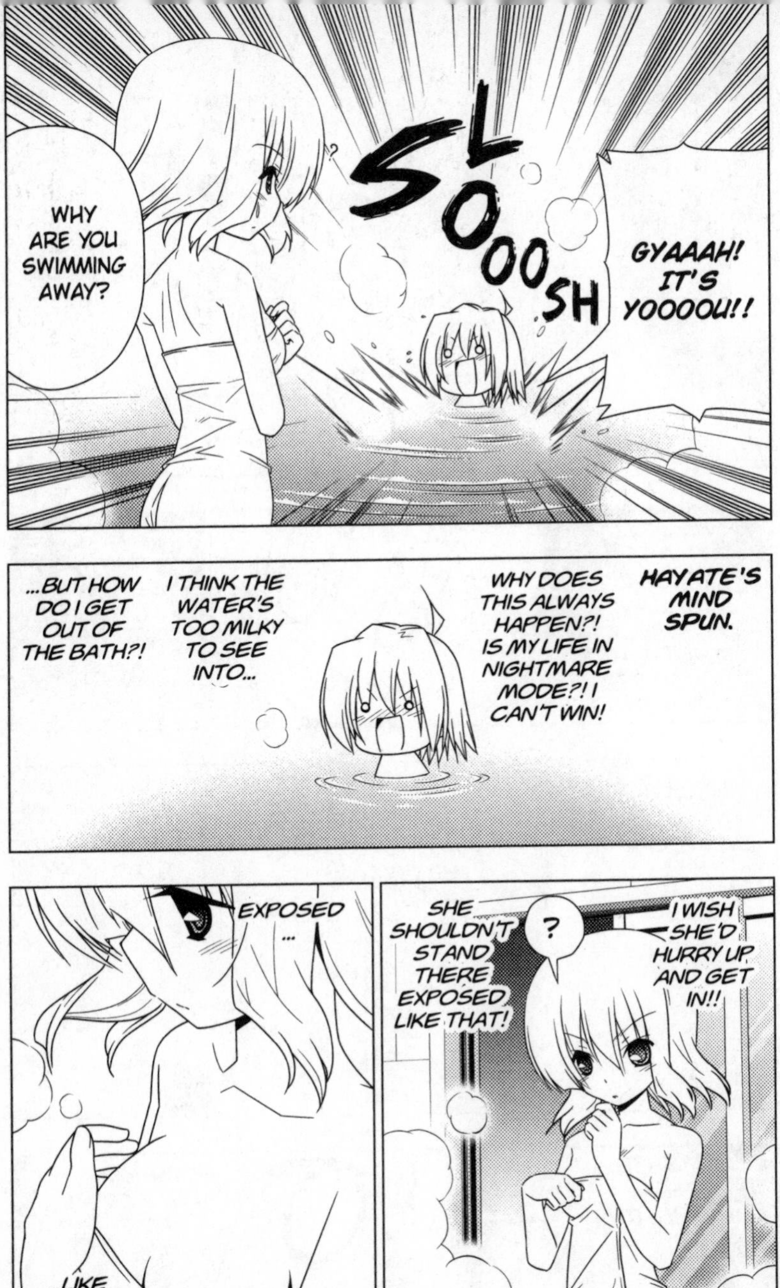
GYAAAH! IT'S YOOOOU!!
SLOOOSH
?
WHY ARE YOU SWIMMING AWAY?
HAYATE'S MIND SPUN.
WHY DOES THIS ALWAYS HAPPEN?! IS MY LIFE IN NIGHTMARE MODE?! I CAN'T WIN!
I THINK THE WATER'S TOO MILKY TO SEE INTO...
...BUT HOW DO I GET OUT OF THE BATH?!
I WISH SHE'D HURRY UP AND GET IN!!
?
SHE SHOULDN'T STAND THERE EXPOSED LIKE THAT!
EXPOSED ...
...LIKE THAT...

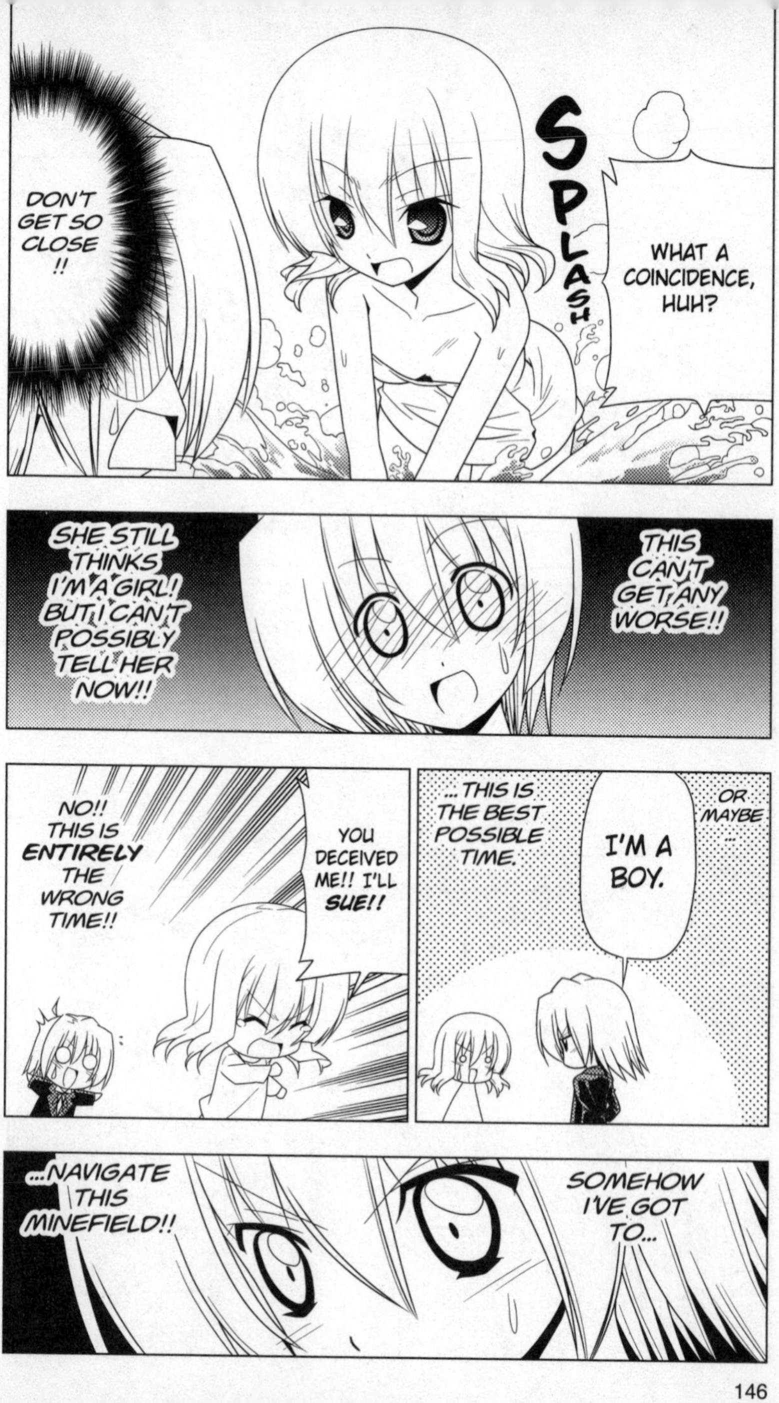
WHAT A COINCIDENCE, HUH?
SPLASH
DON'T GET SO CLOSE !!
THIS CAN'T GET ANY WORSE!!
SHE STILL THINKS I'M A GIRL! BUT I CAN'T POSSIBLY TELL HER NOW!!
OR MAYBE ...
...THIS IS THE BEST POSSIBLE TIME.
I'M A BOY.
YOU DECEIVED ME!! I'LL **SUE!!**
NO!! THIS IS **ENTIRELY** THE WRONG TIME!!
SOMEHOW I'VE GOT TO...
...NAVIGATE THIS MINEFIELD!!

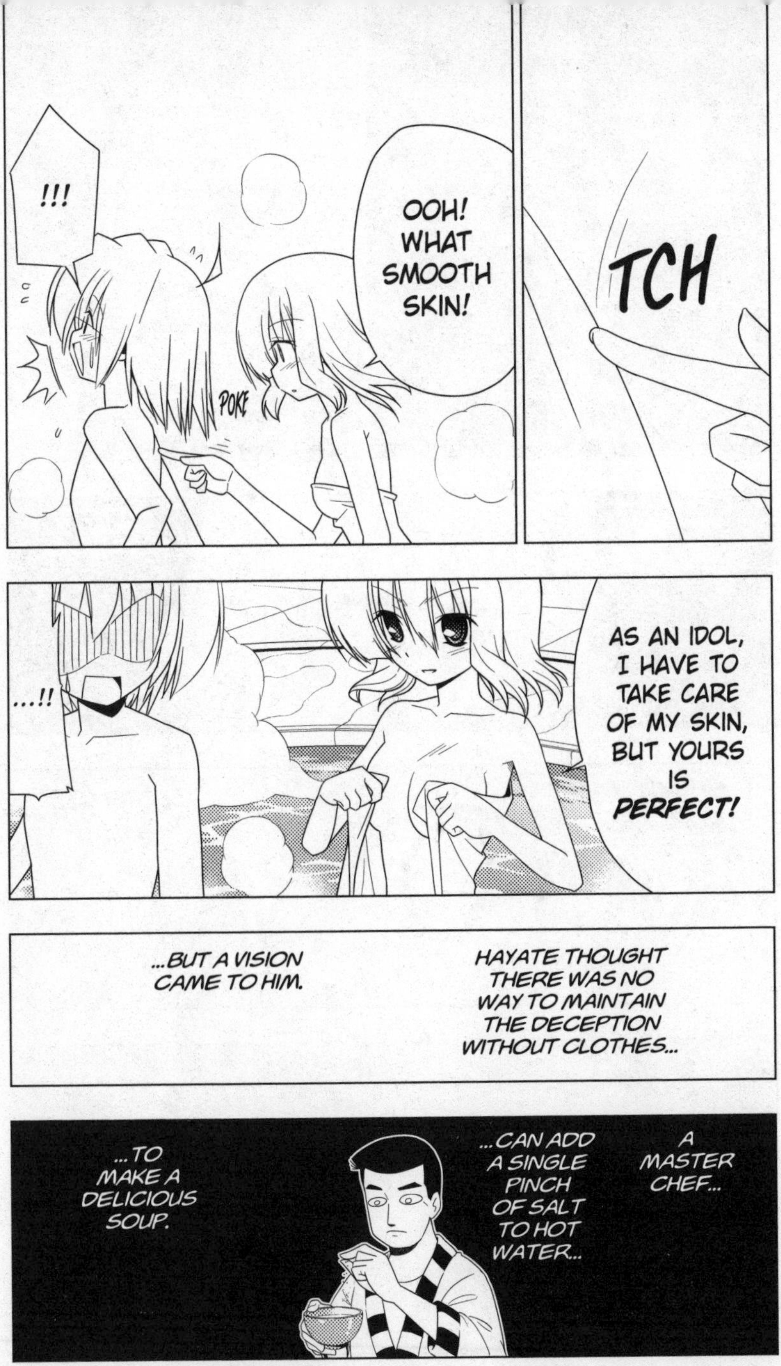
TCH
OOH! WHAT SMOOTH SKIN!
POKE
!!!
AS AN IDOL, I HAVE TO TAKE CARE OF MY SKIN, BUT YOURS IS PERFECT!
...!!
HAYATE THOUGHT THERE WAS NO WAY TO MAINTAIN THE DECEPTION WITHOUT CLOTHES...
...BUT A VISION CAME TO HIM.
A MASTER CHEF...
...CAN ADD A SINGLE PINCH OF SALT TO HOT WATER...
...TO MAKE A DELICIOUS SOUP.

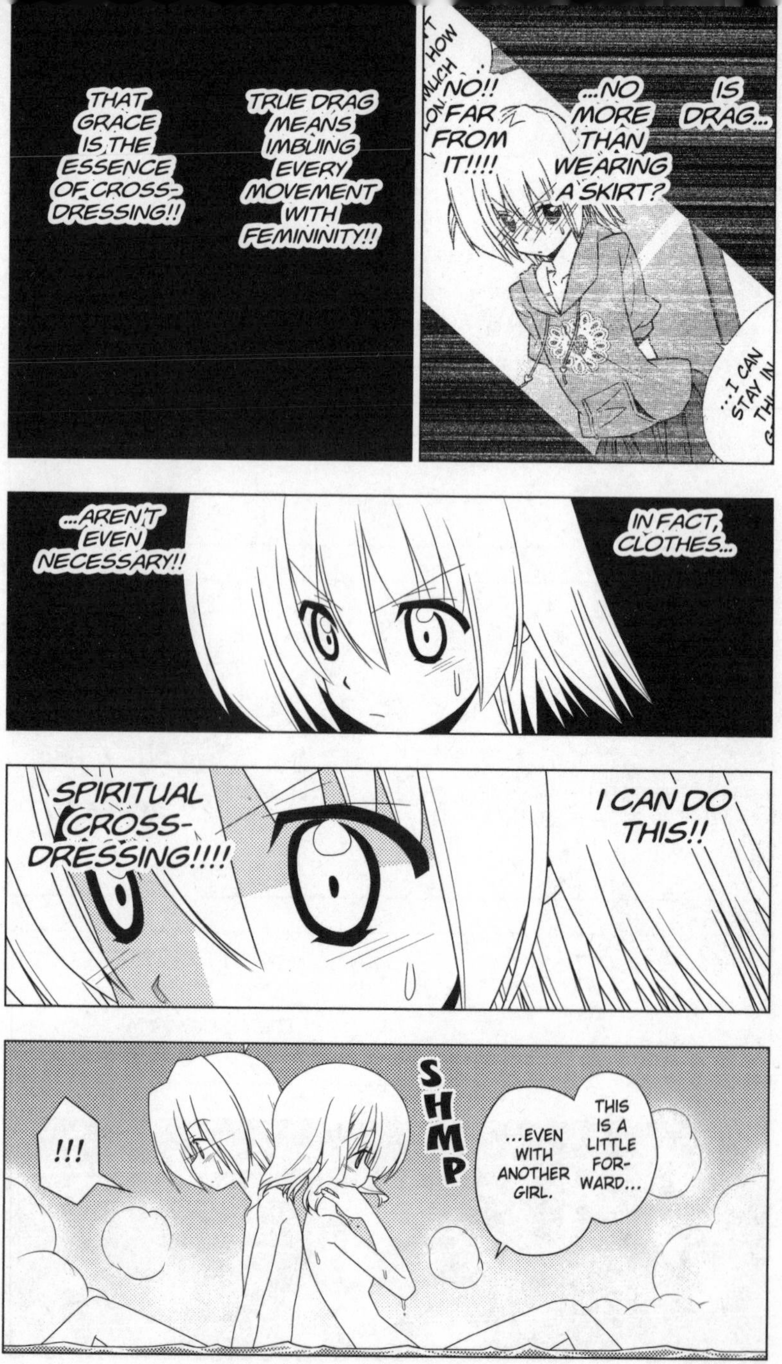
IS DRAG...
...NO MORE THAN WEARING A SKIRT?
NO!! FAR FROM IT!!!!
...I CAN STAY IN
TRUE DRAG MEANS IMBUING EVERY MOVEMENT WITH FEMININITY!!
THAT GRACE IS THE ESSENCE OF CROSS-DRESSING!!
IN FACT, CLOTHES...
...AREN'T EVEN NECESSARY!!
I CAN DO THIS!!
SPIRITUAL CROSS-DRESSING!!!!
THIS IS A LITTLE FOR-WARD...
...EVEN WITH ANOTHER GIRL.
SHMP
!!!

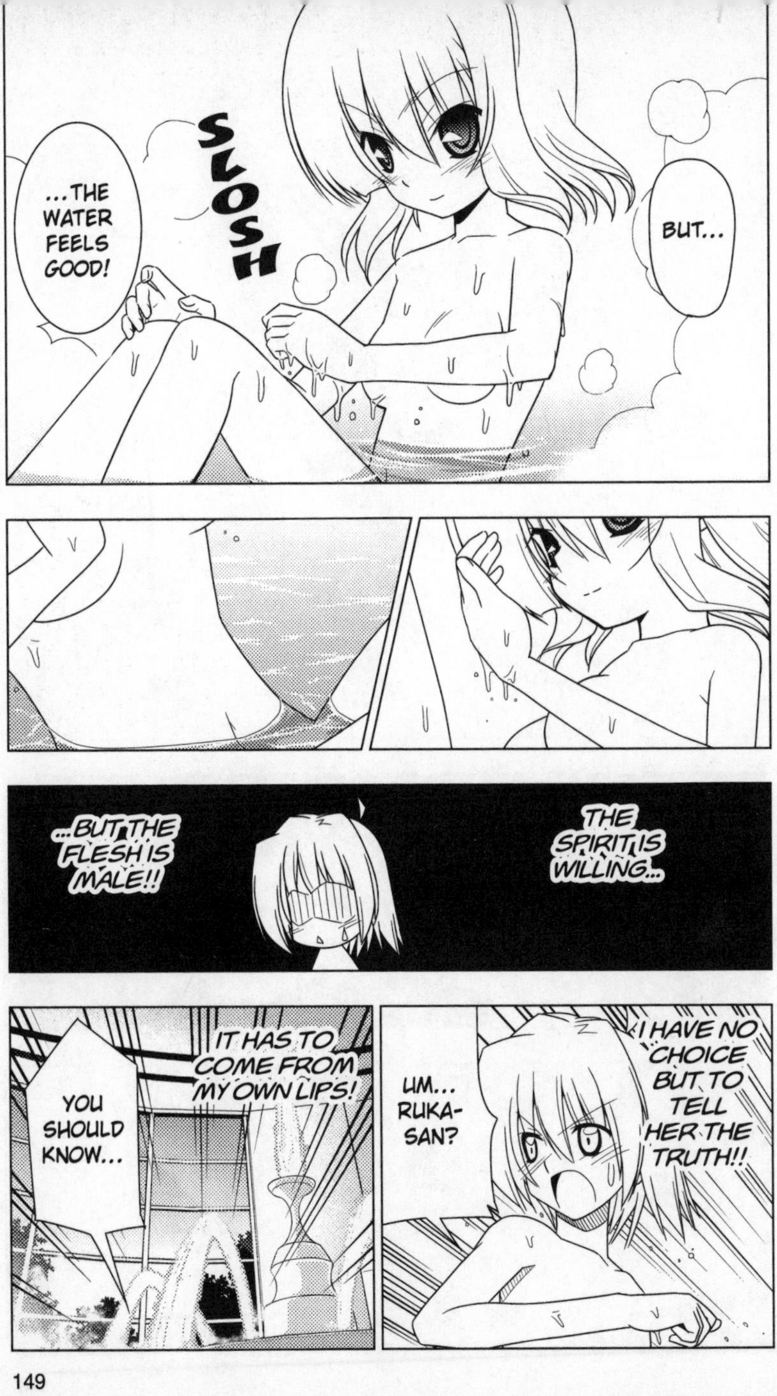
BUT...
SLOSH
...THE WATER FEELS GOOD!
THE SPIRIT IS WILLING...
...BUT THE FLESH IS MALE!!
I HAVE NO CHOICE BUT TO TELL HER THE TRUTH!!
UM... RUKA-SAN?
IT HAS TO COME FROM MY OWN LIPS!
YOU SHOULD KNOW...

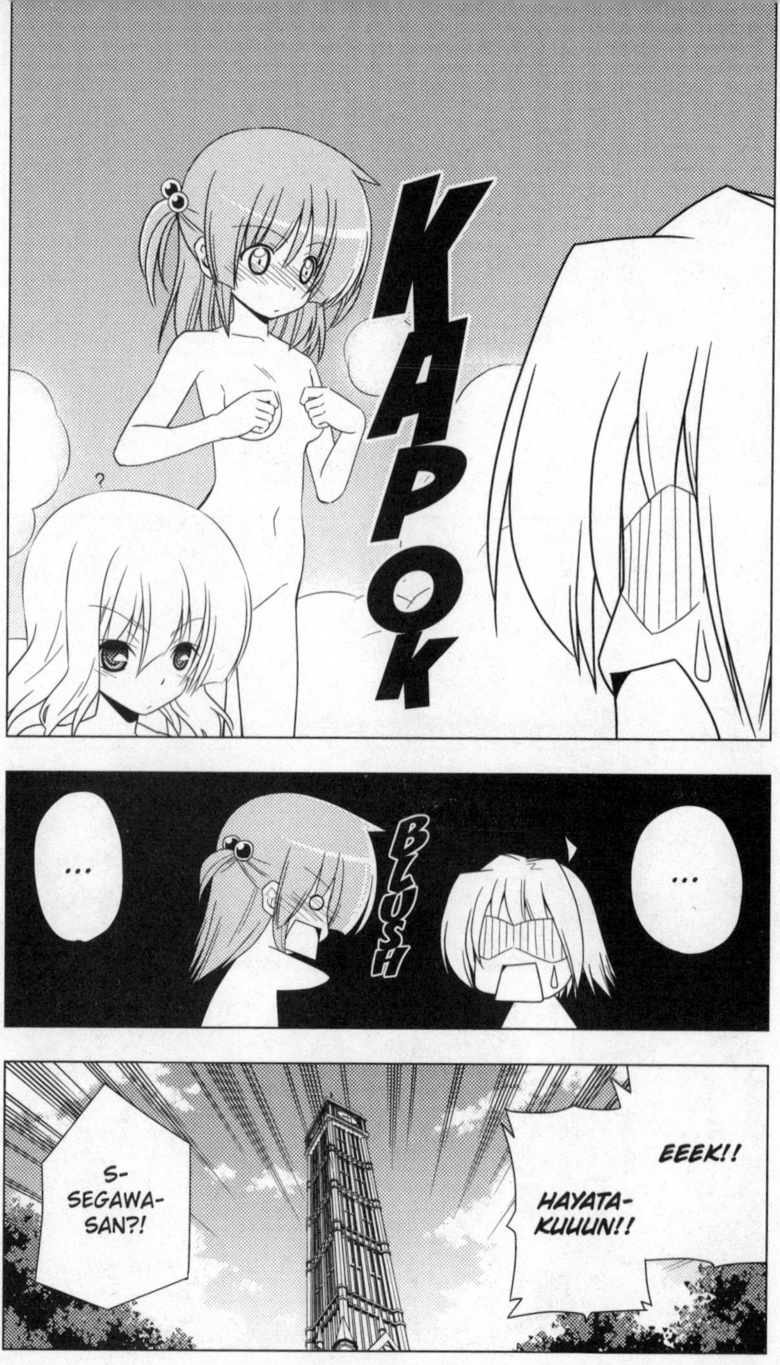
KAPOK
?
...
BLUSH
...
EEEK!!
HAYATA-KUUUN!!
S-SEGAWA-SAN?!

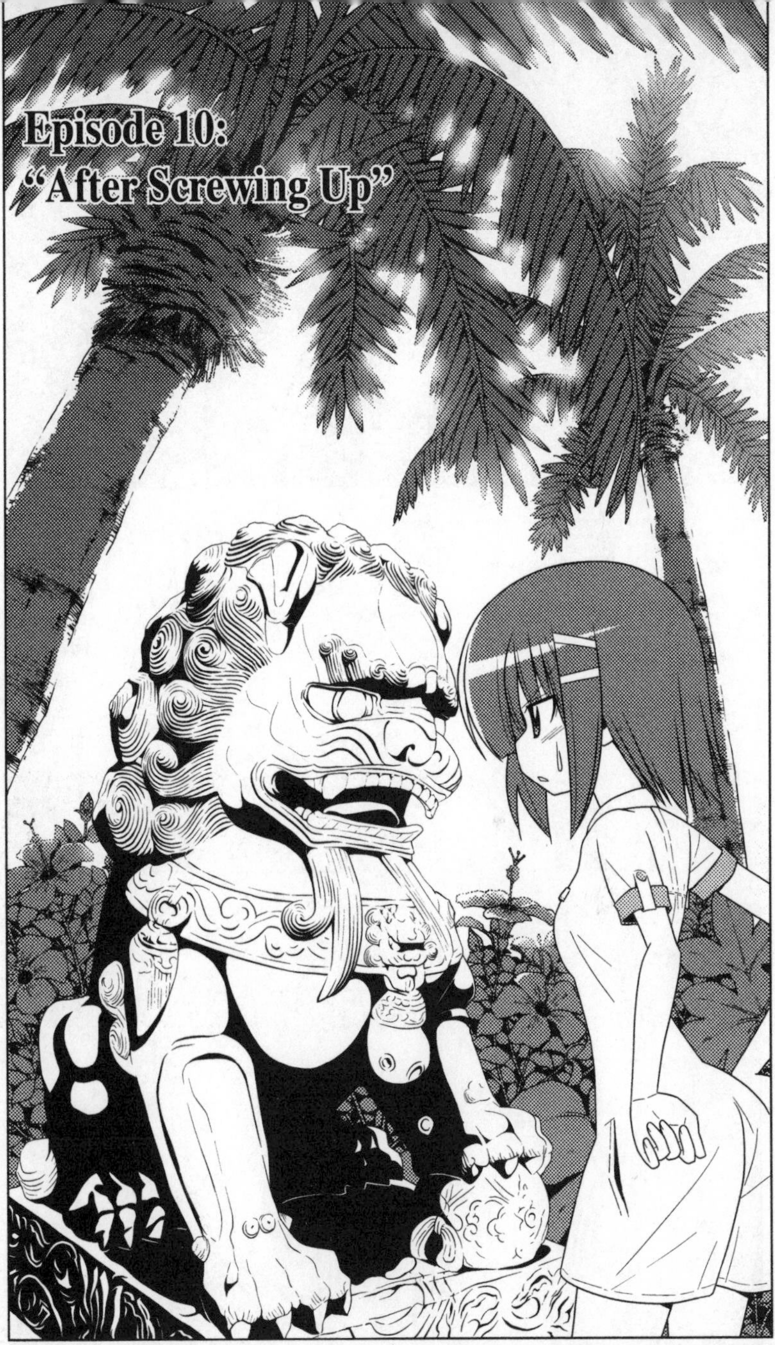
Episode 10:
"After Screwing Up"

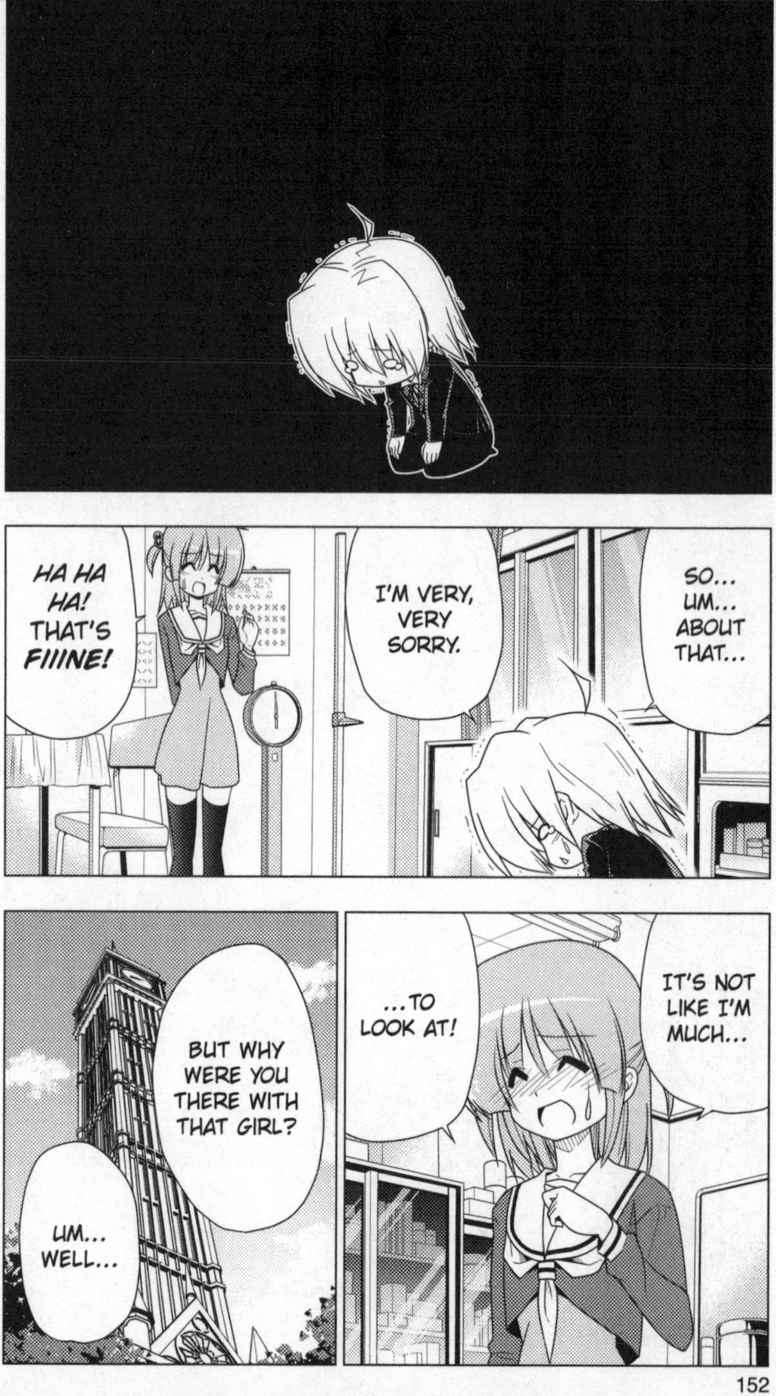
SO... UM... ABOUT THAT...
I'M VERY, VERY SORRY.
HA HA HA! THAT'S FIIINE!
IT'S NOT LIKE I'M MUCH...
...TO LOOK AT!
BUT WHY WERE YOU THERE WITH THAT GIRL?
UM... WELL...

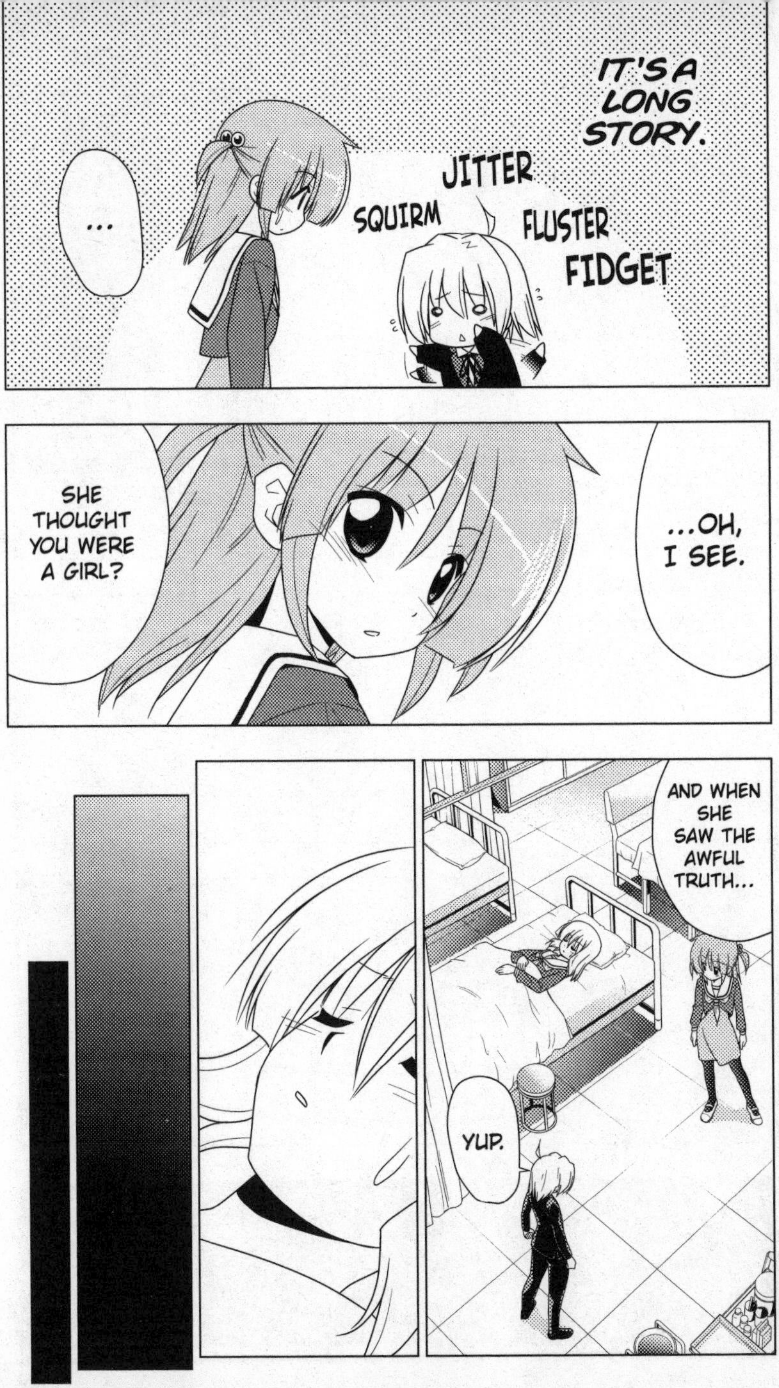
IT'S A LONG STORY.
JITTER
FLUSTER
SQUIRM
FIDGET
...
...OH, I SEE.
SHE THOUGHT YOU WERE A GIRL?
AND WHEN SHE SAW THE AWFUL TRUTH...
YUP.

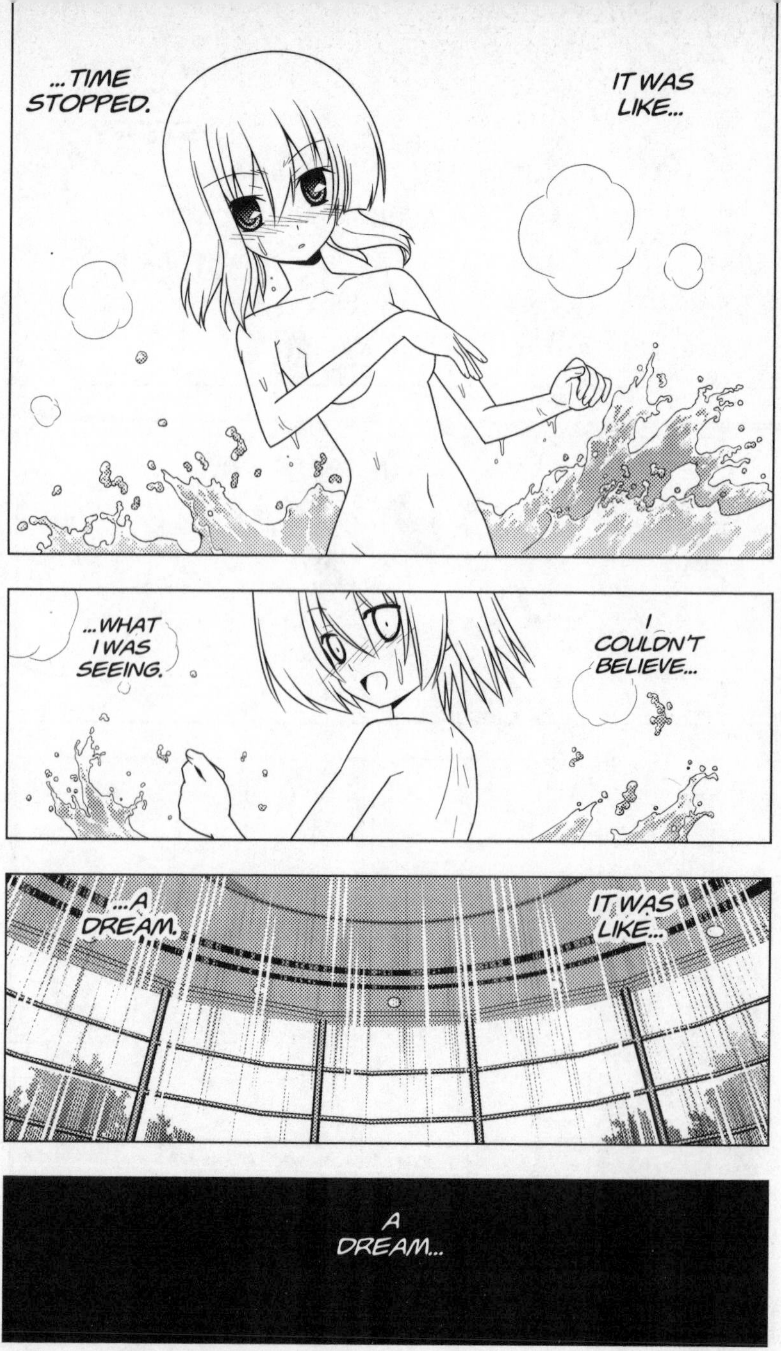
IT WAS LIKE...
...TIME STOPPED.
I COULDN'T BELIEVE...
...WHAT I WAS SEEING.
IT WAS LIKE...
...A DREAM.
A DREAM...

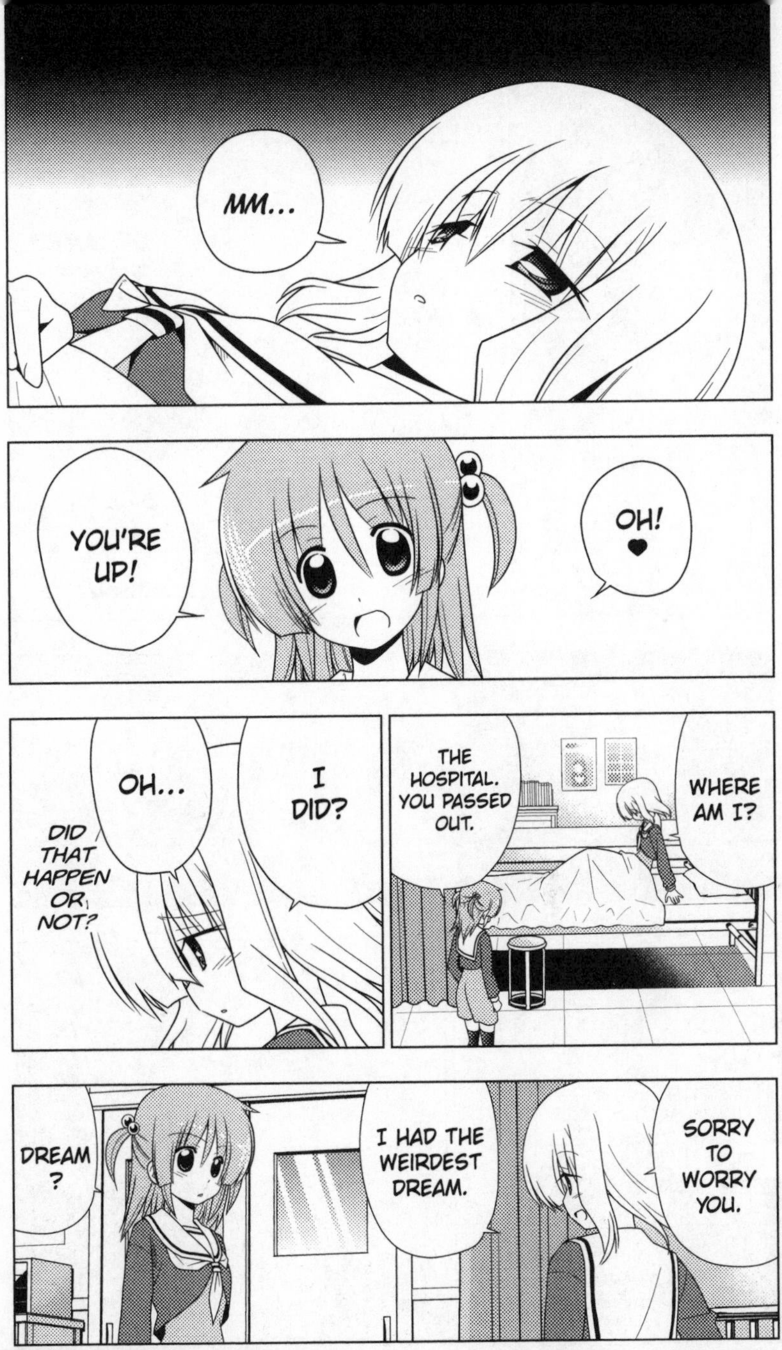
MM...
OH! ♥
YOU'RE UP!
WHERE AM I?
THE HOSPITAL. YOU PASSED OUT.
I DID?
OH...
DID THAT HAPPEN OR NOT?
SORRY TO WORRY YOU.
I HAD THE WEIRDEST DREAM.
DREAM?

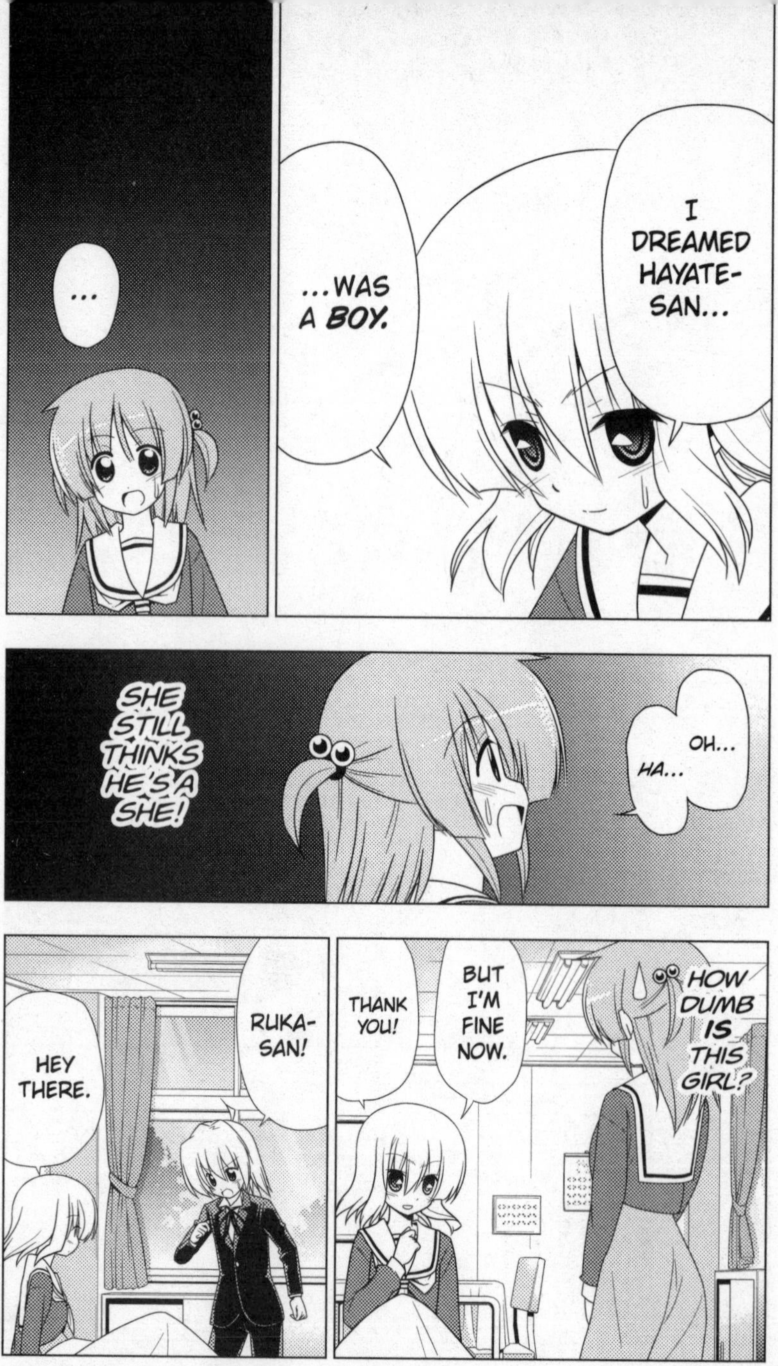
I DREAMED HAYATE-SAN...
...WAS A *BOY.*
...
OH... HA...
SHE STILL THINKS HE'S A SHE!
HOW DUMB IS THIS GIRL?
BUT I'M FINE NOW.
THANK YOU!
RUKA-SAN!
HEY THERE.

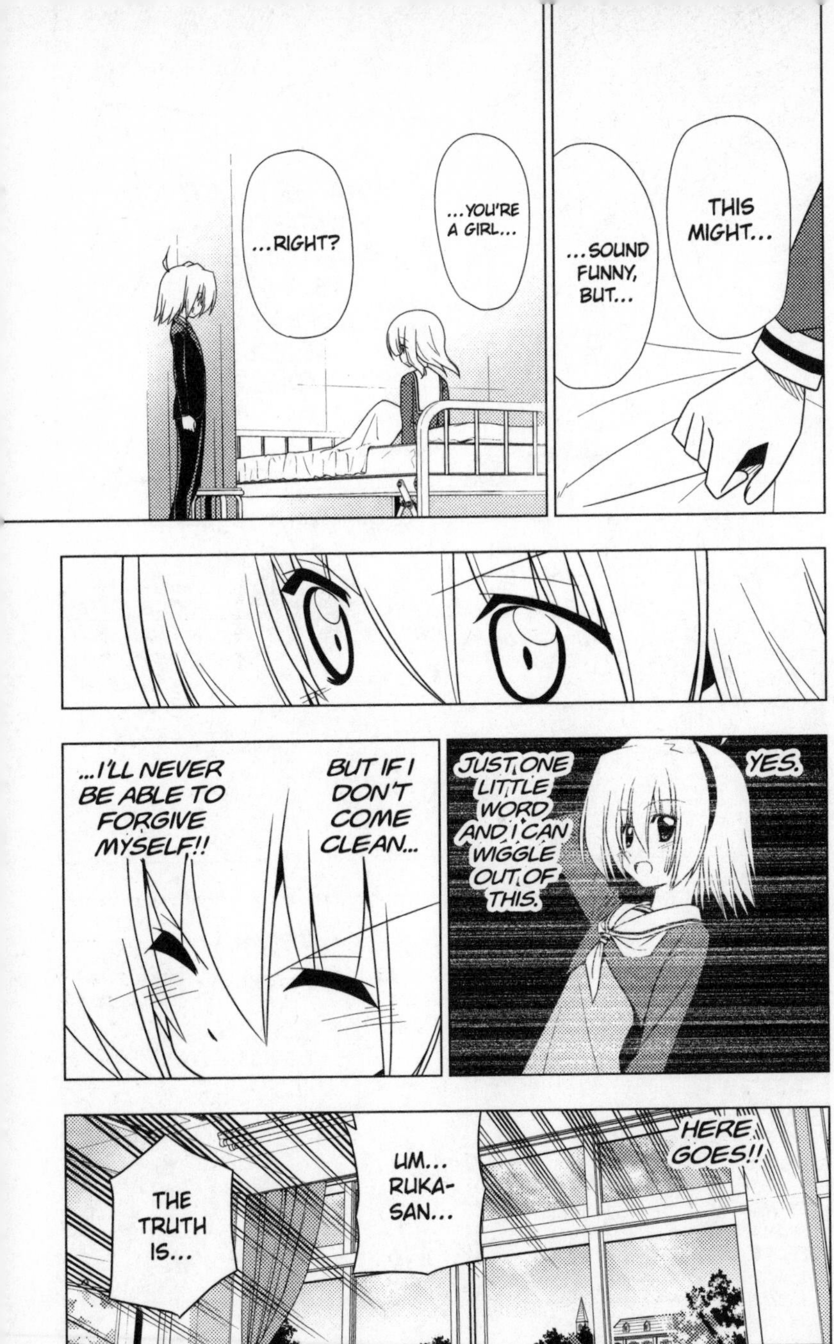
THIS MIGHT...
...SOUND FUNNY, BUT...
...YOU'RE A GIRL...
...RIGHT?
YES.
JUST ONE LITTLE WORD AND I CAN WIGGLE OUT OF THIS.
BUT IF I DON'T COME CLEAN...
...I'LL NEVER BE ABLE TO FORGIVE MYSELF!!
HERE GOES!!
UM... RUKA-SAN...
THE TRUTH IS...

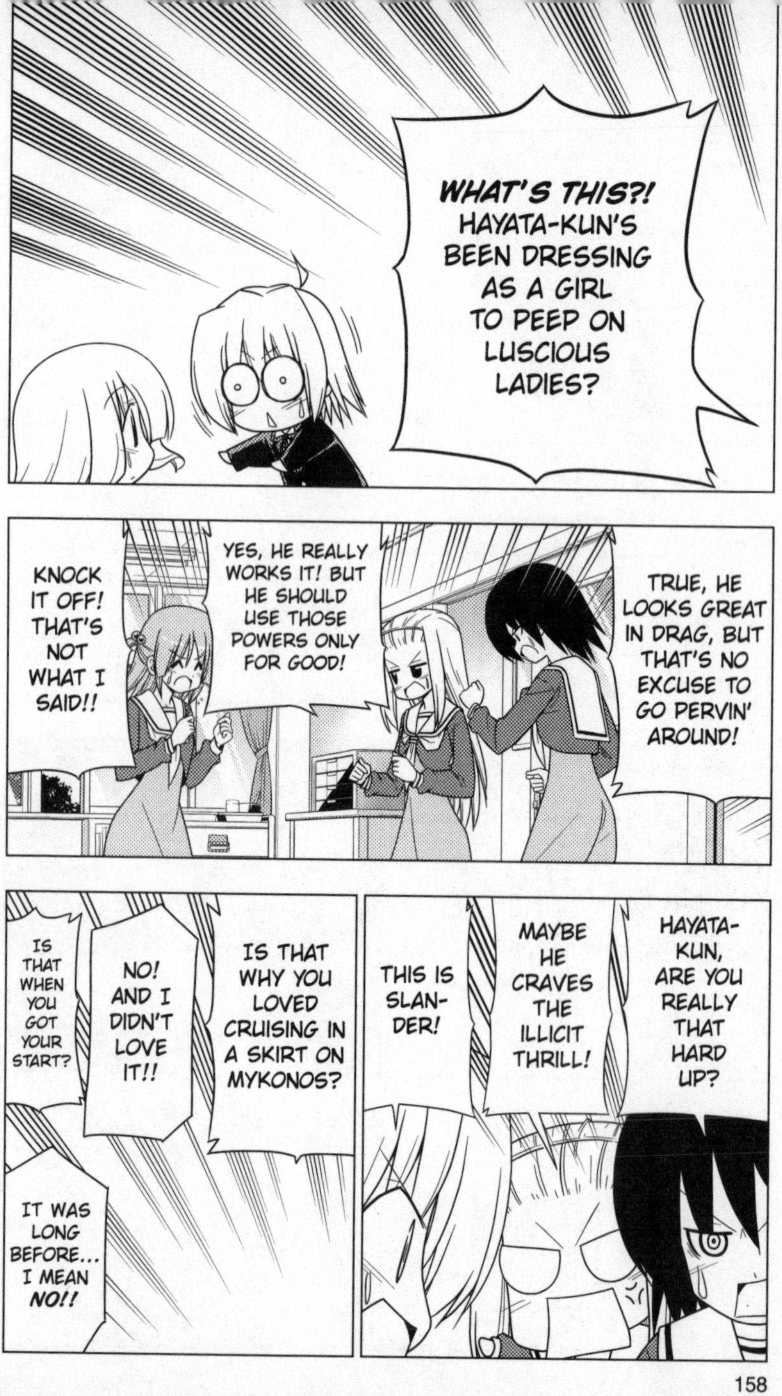
WHAT'S THIS?! HAYATA-KUN'S BEEN DRESSING AS A GIRL TO PEEP ON LUSCIOUS LADIES?
TRUE, HE LOOKS GREAT IN DRAG, BUT THAT'S NO EXCUSE TO GO PERVIN' AROUND!
YES, HE REALLY WORKS IT! BUT HE SHOULD USE THOSE POWERS ONLY FOR GOOD!
KNOCK IT OFF! THAT'S NOT WHAT I SAID!!
HAYATA-KUN, ARE YOU REALLY THAT HARD UP?
MAYBE HE CRAVES THE ILLICIT THRILL!
THIS IS SLAN-DER!
IS THAT WHY YOU LOVED CRUISING IN A SKIRT ON MYKONOS?
NO! AND I DIDN'T LOVE IT!!
IS THAT WHEN YOU GOT YOUR START?
IT WAS LONG BEFORE... I MEAN NO!!

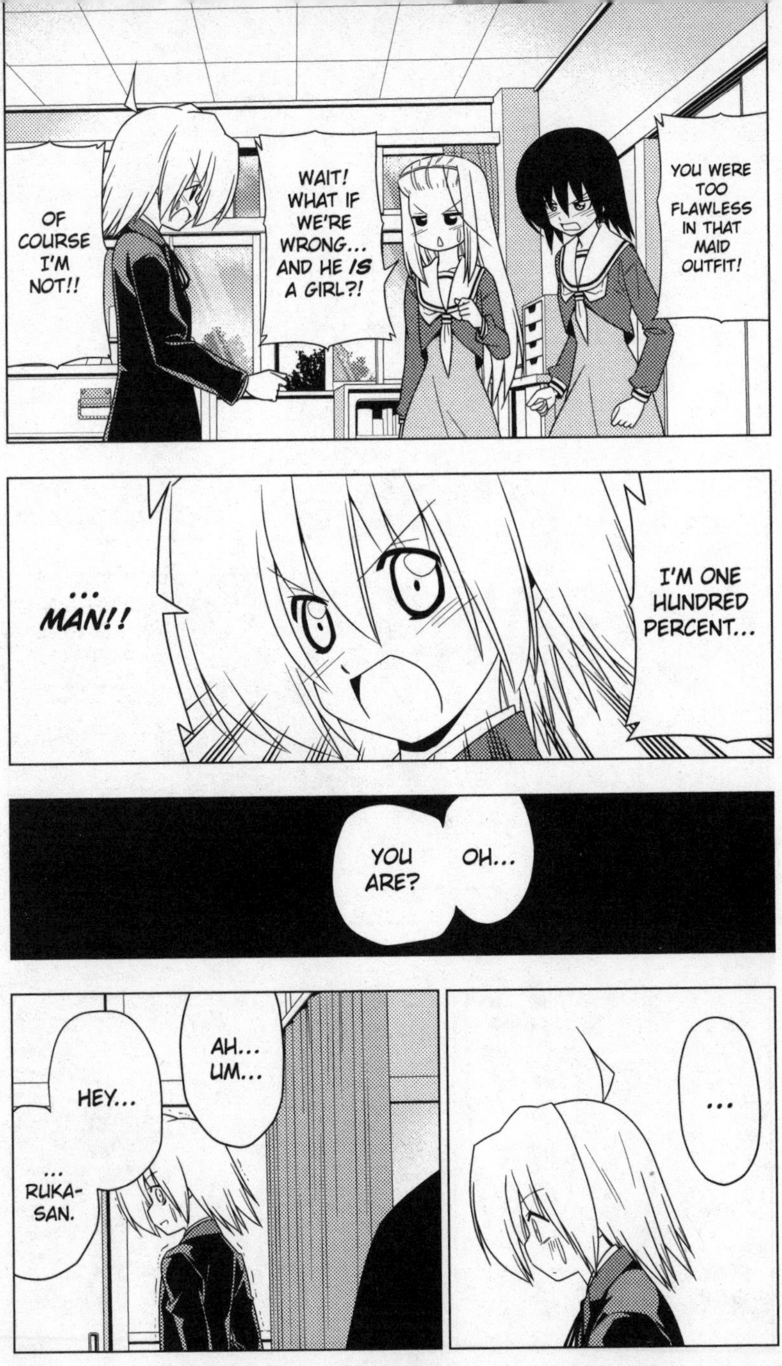
YOU WERE TOO FLAWLESS IN THAT MAID OUTFIT!
WAIT! WHAT IF WE'RE WRONG... AND HE *IS* A GIRL?!
OF COURSE I'M NOT!!
I'M ONE HUNDRED PERCENT...
...*MAN!!*
OH...
YOU ARE?
...
AH... UM...
HEY...
...RUKA-SAN.

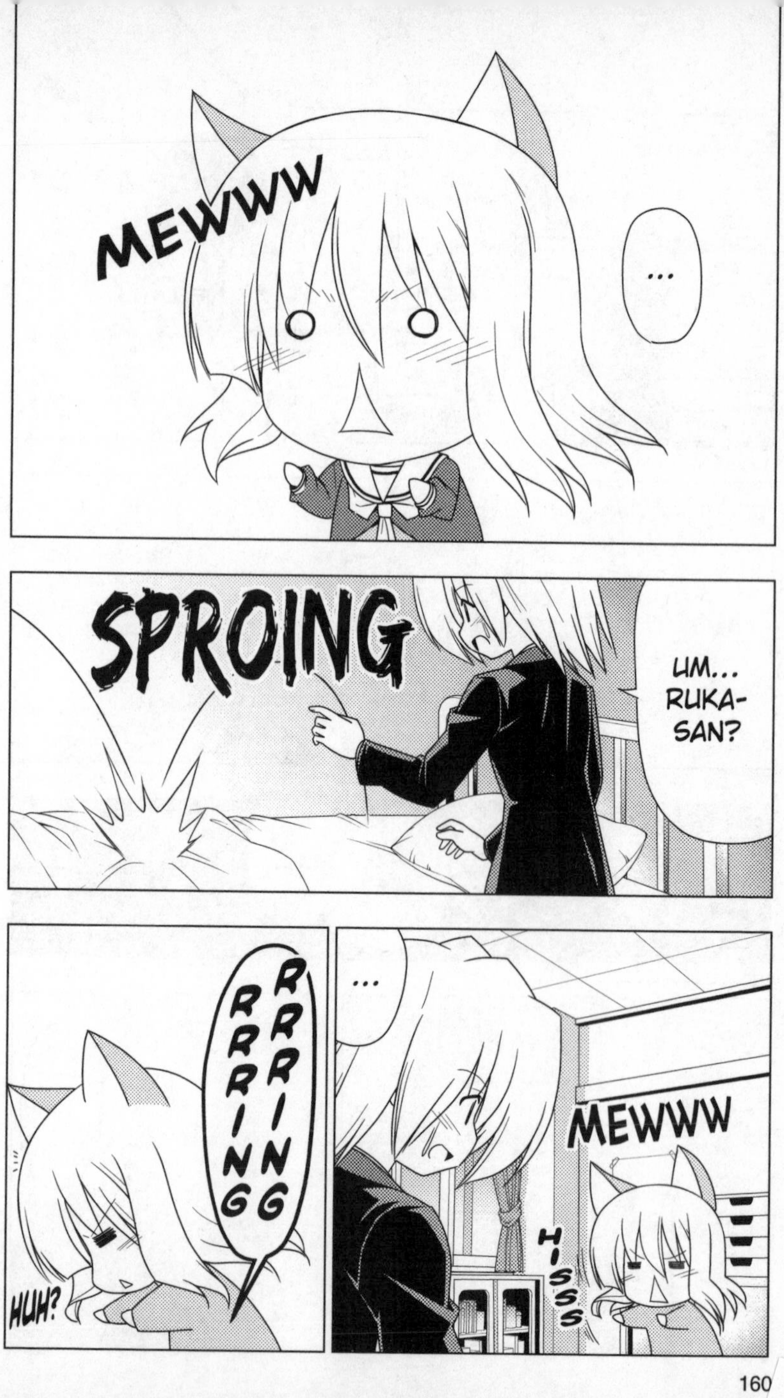

...
MEWWW
UM... RUKA-SAN?
SPROING
...
MEWWW
HISSS
RRRING RRRRING
HUH?

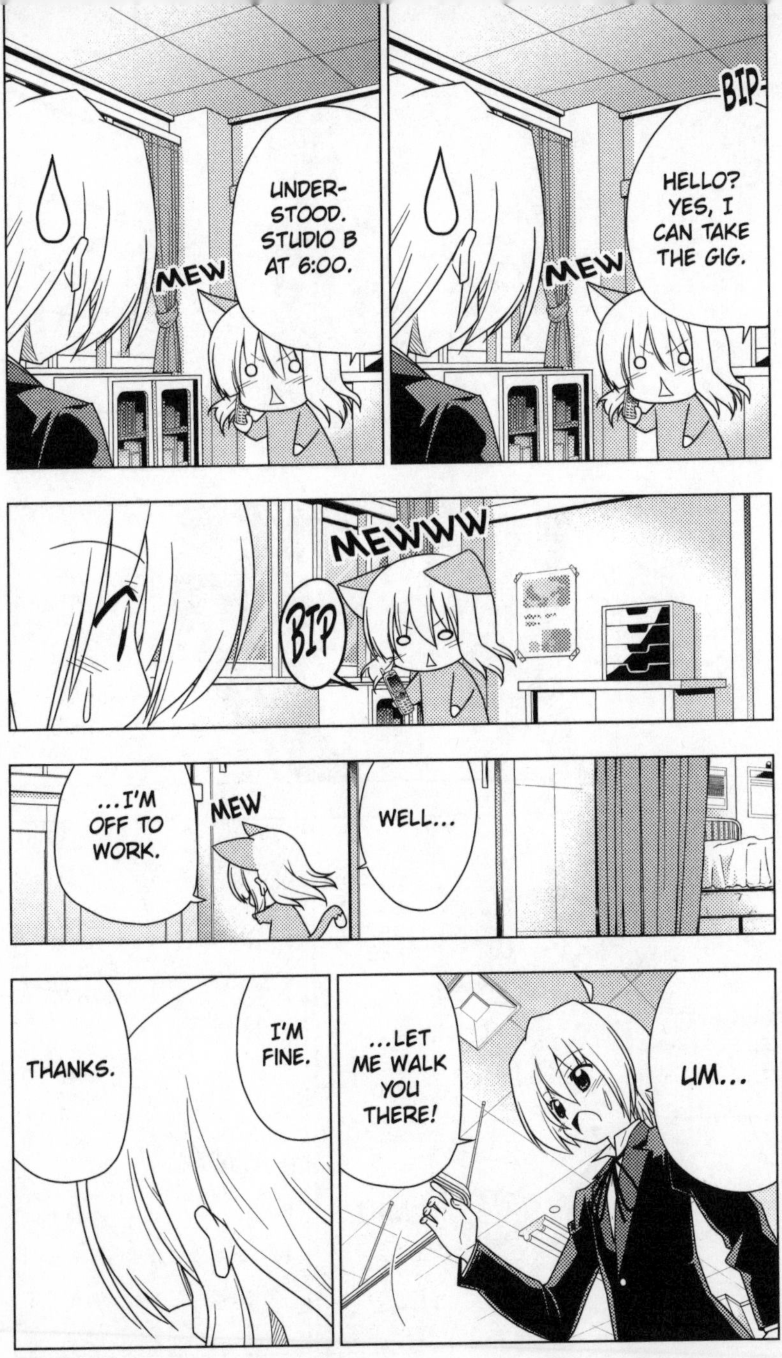
BIP-
HELLO? YES, I CAN TAKE THE GIG.
MEW
UNDER-STOOD. STUDIO B AT 6:00.
MEW
MEWWW
BIP
WELL...
MEW
...I'M OFF TO WORK.
UM...
...LET ME WALK YOU THERE!
I'M FINE.
THANKS.

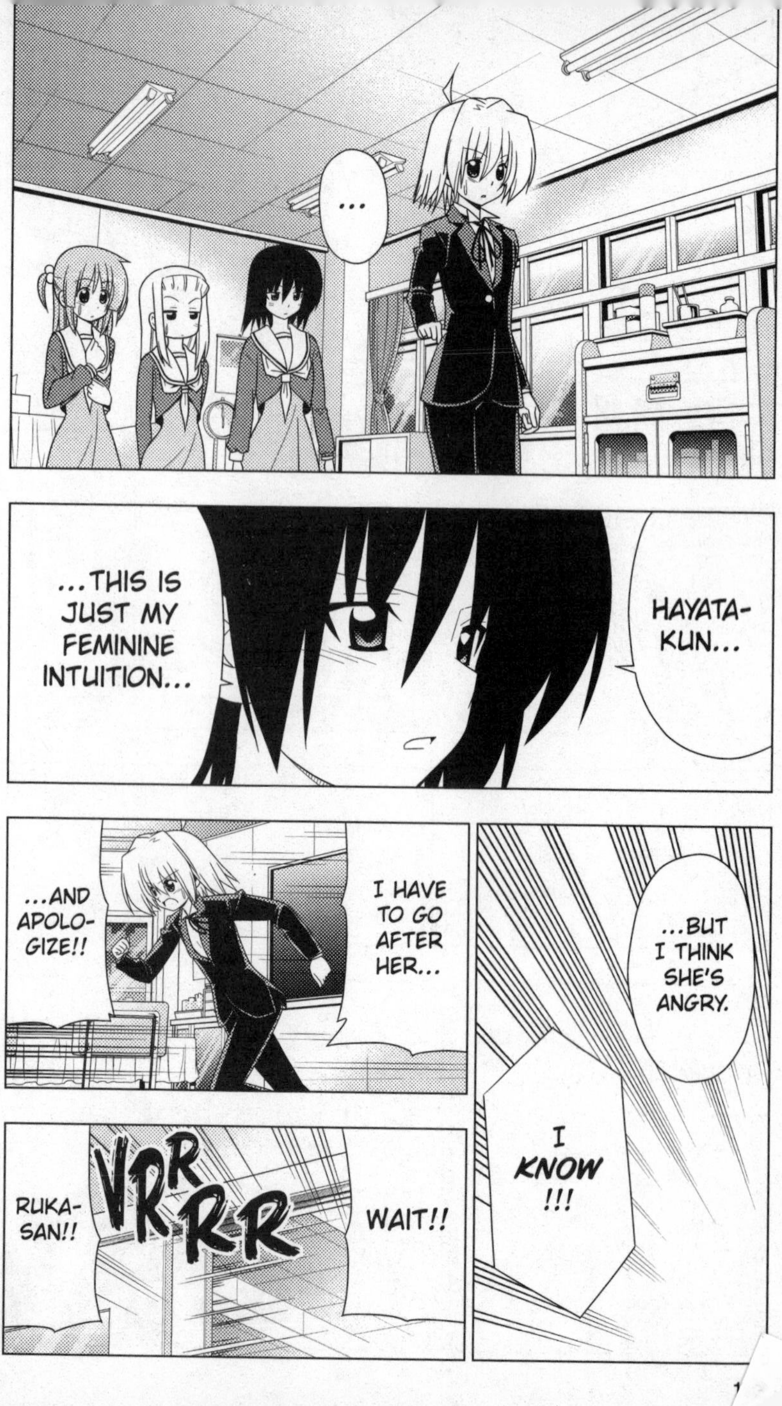
...
HAYATA-KUN...
...THIS IS JUST MY FEMININE INTUITION...
...BUT I THINK SHE'S ANGRY.
I KNOW!!!
I HAVE TO GO AFTER HER...
...AND APOLOGIZE!!
WAIT!!
VRRRR
RUKA-SAN!!

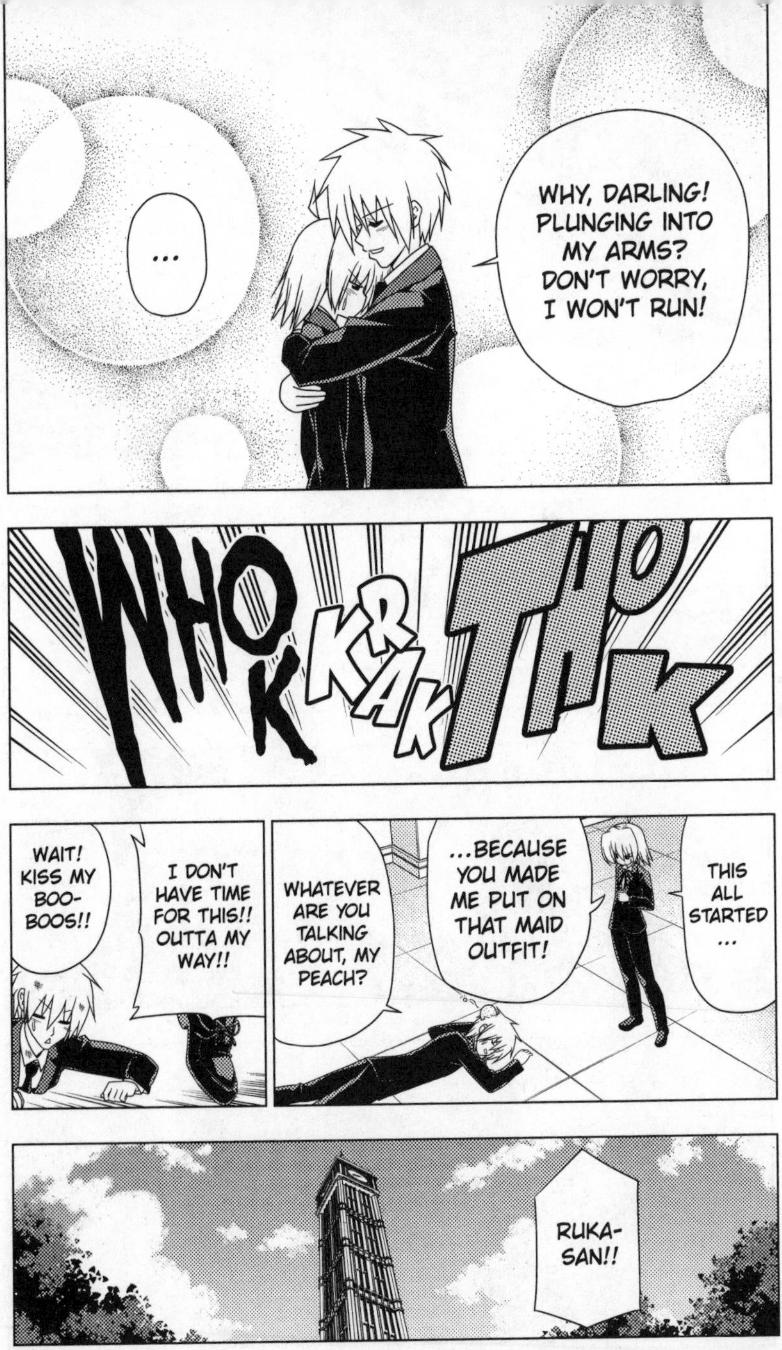
WHY, DARLING! PLUNGING INTO MY ARMS? DON'T WORRY, I WON'T RUN!
...
THOK
KRAK
WHOK
THIS ALL STARTED ...
...BECAUSE YOU MADE ME PUT ON THAT MAID OUTFIT!
WHATEVER ARE YOU TALKING ABOUT, MY PEACH?
I DON'T HAVE TIME FOR THIS!! OUTTA MY WAY!!
WAIT! KISS MY BOO-BOOS!!
RUKA-SAN!!

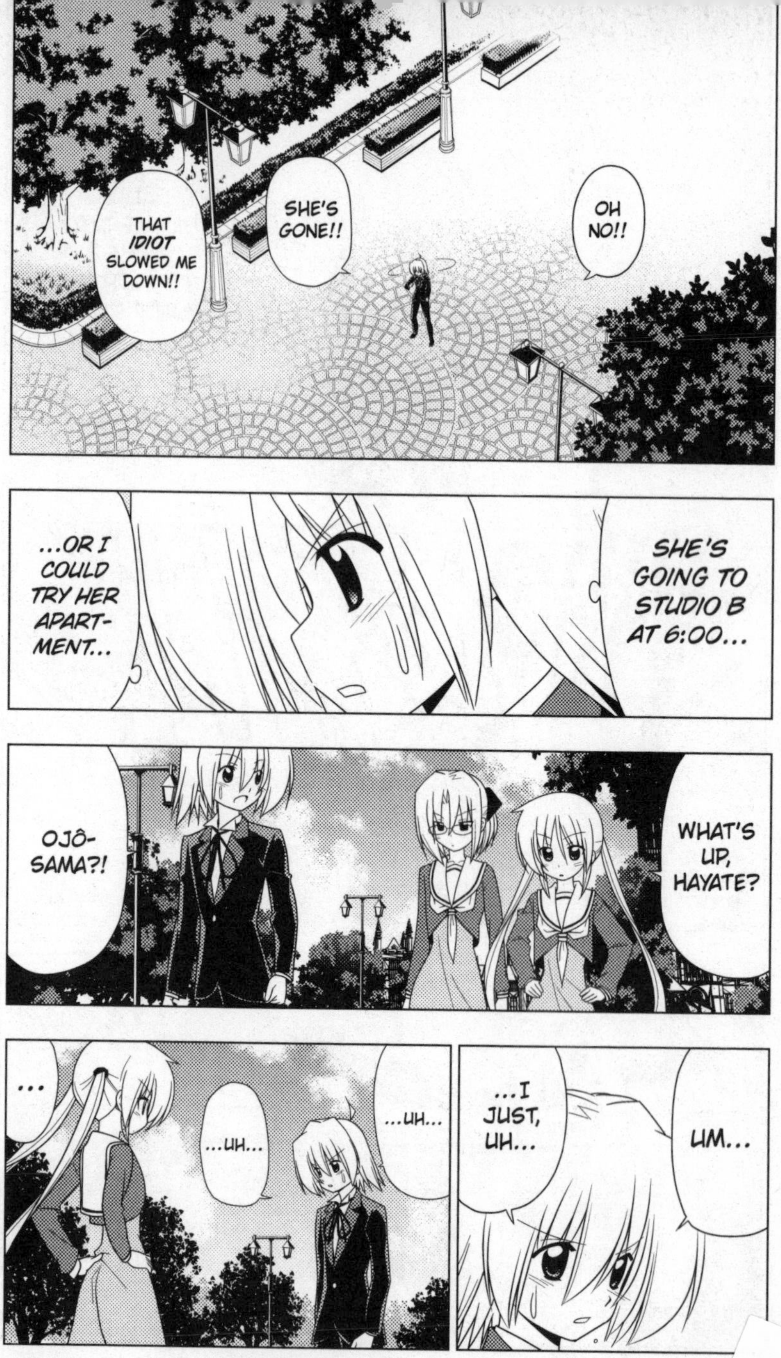
OH NO!!
SHE'S GONE!!
THAT *IDIOT* SLOWED ME DOWN!!
SHE'S GOING TO STUDIO B AT 6:00...
...OR I COULD TRY HER APART-MENT...
WHAT'S UP, HAYATE?
OJÔ-SAMA?!
UM...
...I JUST, UH...
...UH...
...UH...
...

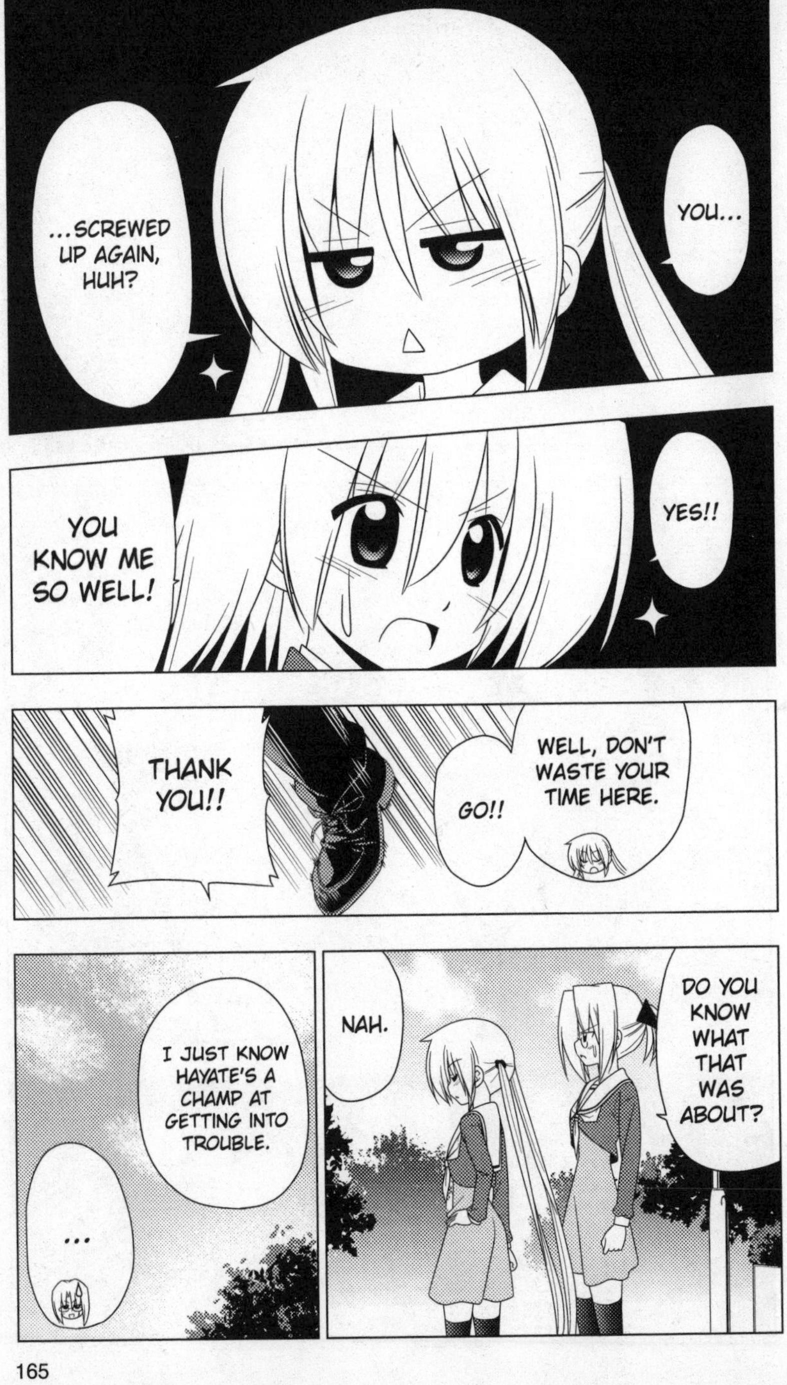
YOU...
...SCREWED UP AGAIN, HUH?
YES!!
YOU KNOW ME SO WELL!
WELL, DON'T WASTE YOUR TIME HERE.
GO!!
THANK YOU!!
DO YOU KNOW WHAT THAT WAS ABOUT?
NAH.
I JUST KNOW HAYATE'S A CHAMP AT GETTING INTO TROUBLE.
...

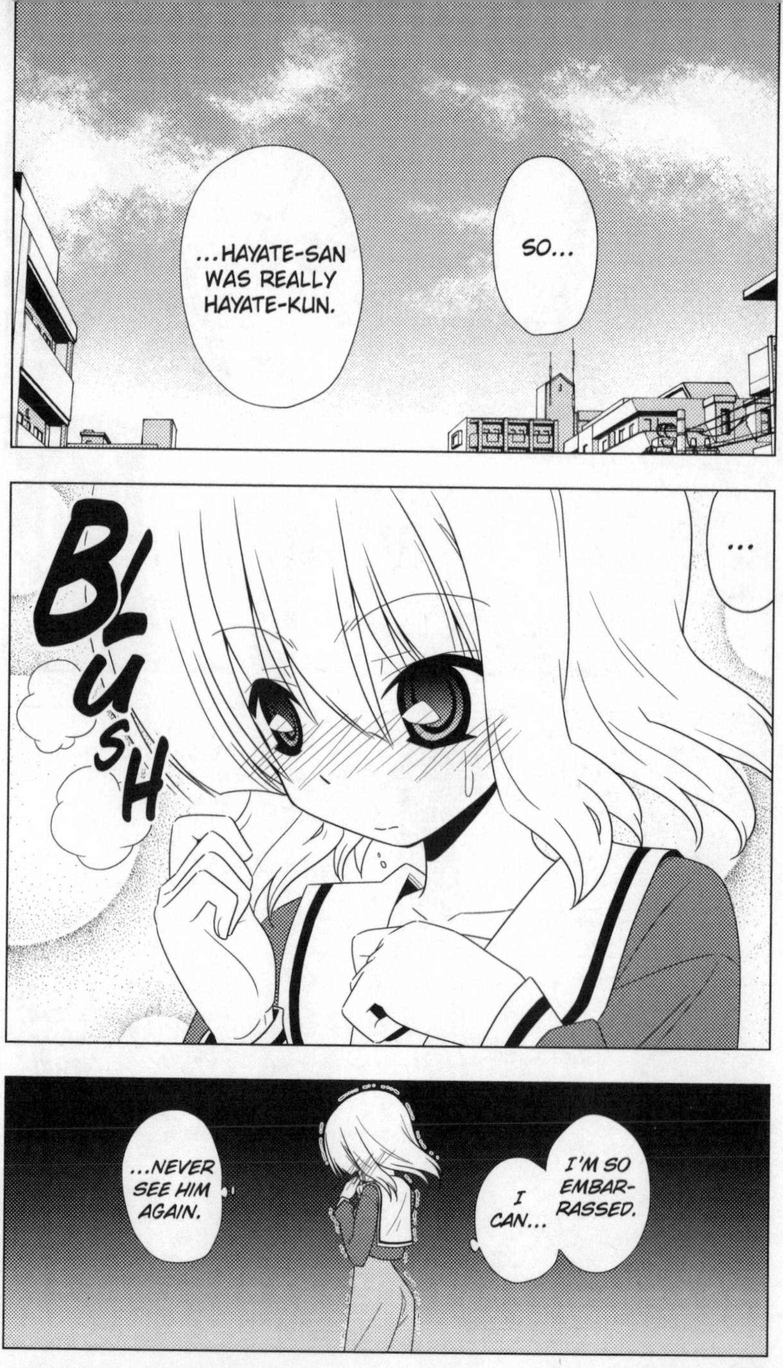
SO...
...HAYATE-SAN WAS REALLY HAYATE-KUN.
...
BLUSH
I'M SO EMBARRASSED.
I CAN...
...NEVER SEE HIM AGAIN.

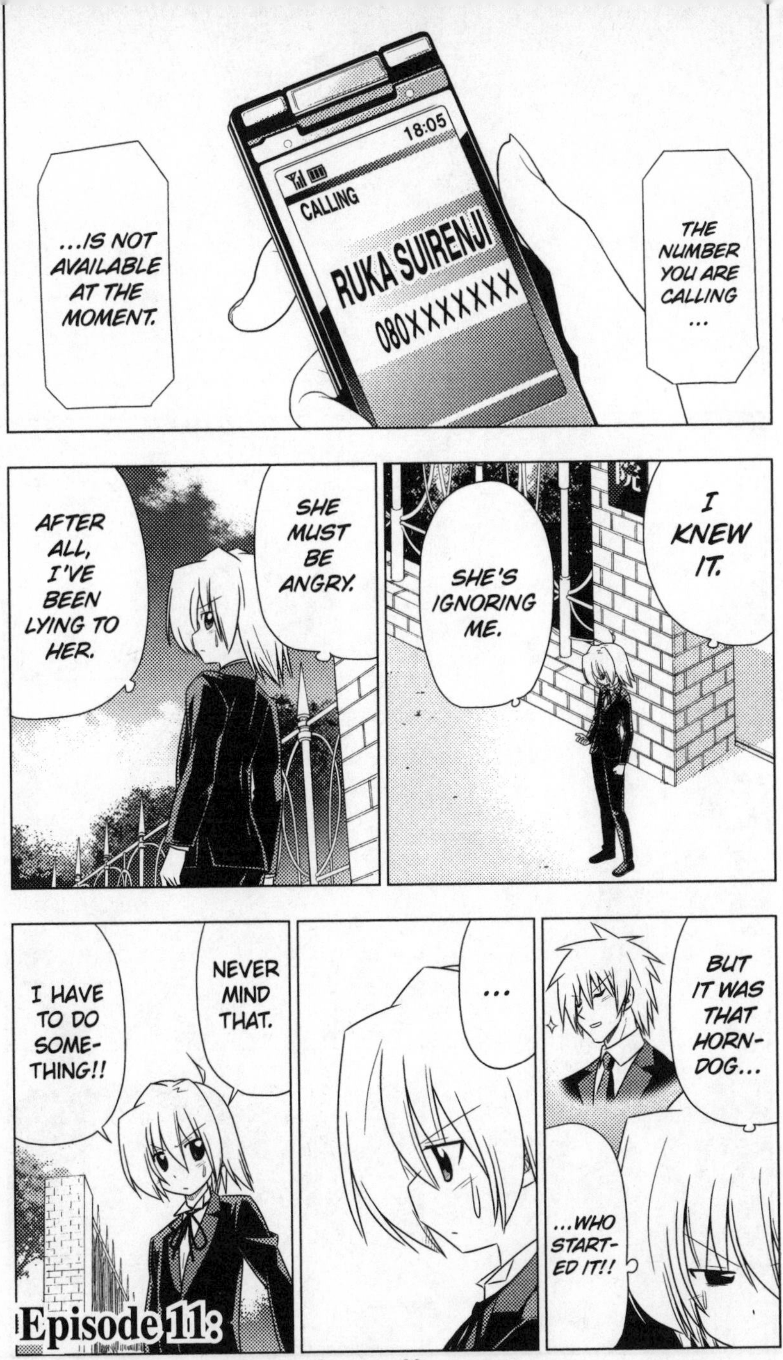
THE NUMBER YOU ARE CALLING...
18:05
CALLING
RUKA SUIRENJI
080XXXXXXX
...IS NOT AVAILABLE AT THE MOMENT.
I KNEW IT.
SHE'S IGNORING ME.
SHE MUST BE ANGRY.
AFTER ALL, I'VE BEEN LYING TO HER.
BUT IT WAS THAT HORN-DOG...
...WHO STARTED IT!!
...
NEVER MIND THAT.
I HAVE TO DO SOMETHING!!

Episode 11: "Goodbye, Happiness"

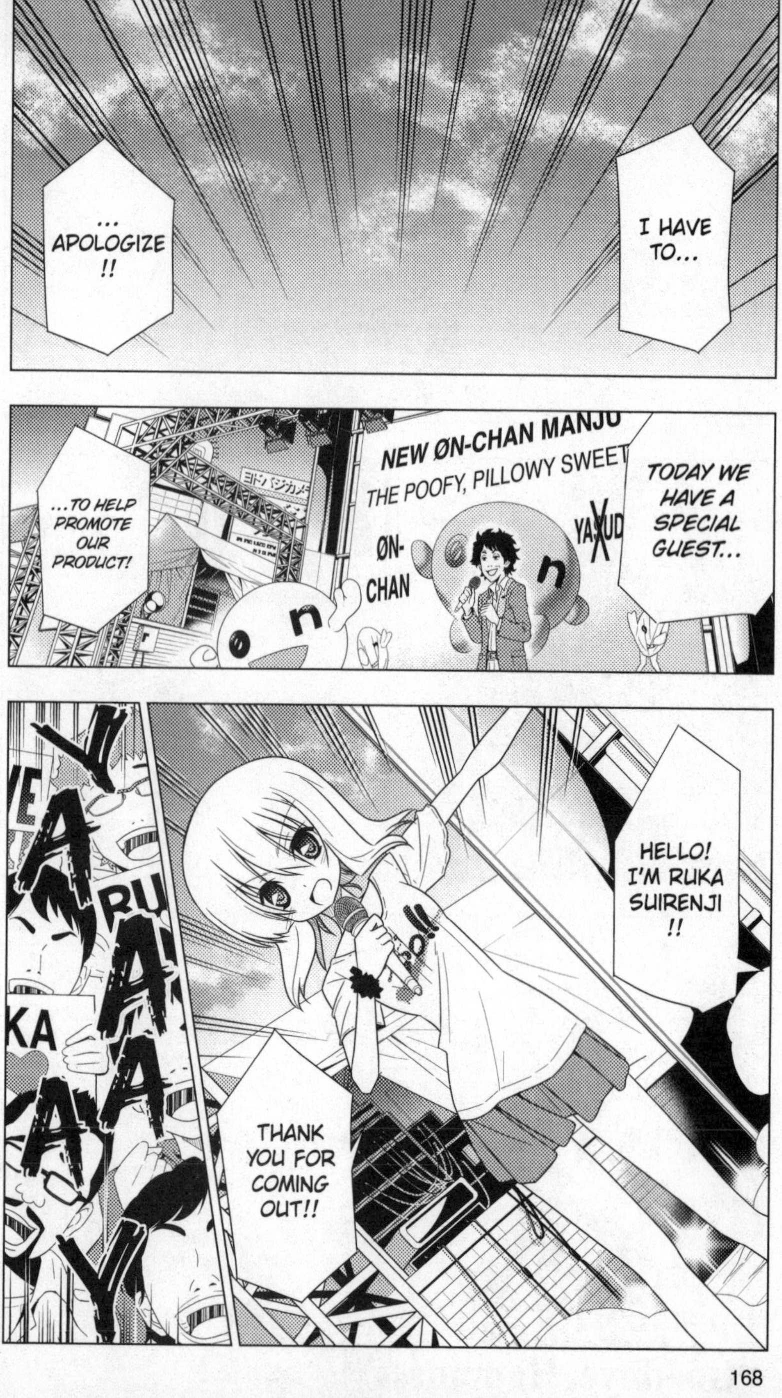
I HAVE TO...
... APOLOGIZE !!
TODAY WE HAVE A SPECIAL GUEST...
NEW ØN-CHAN MANJU
THE POOFY, PILLOWY SWEET
ØN-CHAN
...TO HELP PROMOTE OUR PRODUCT!
HELLO! I'M RUKA SUIRENJI !!
THANK YOU FOR COMING OUT!!

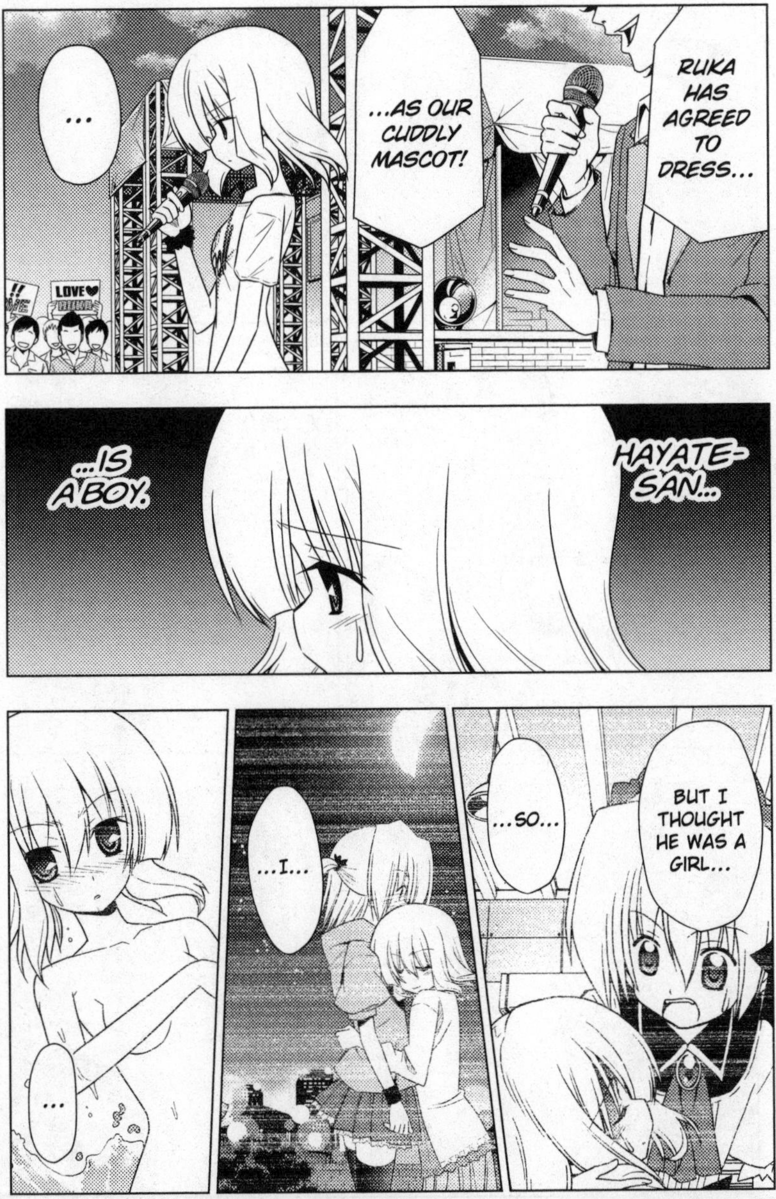
RUKA HAS AGREED TO DRESS...
...AS OUR CUDDLY MASCOT!
...
LOVE
HAYATE-SAN...
...IS A BOY.
BUT I THOUGHT HE WAS A GIRL...
...SO...
...I...
...

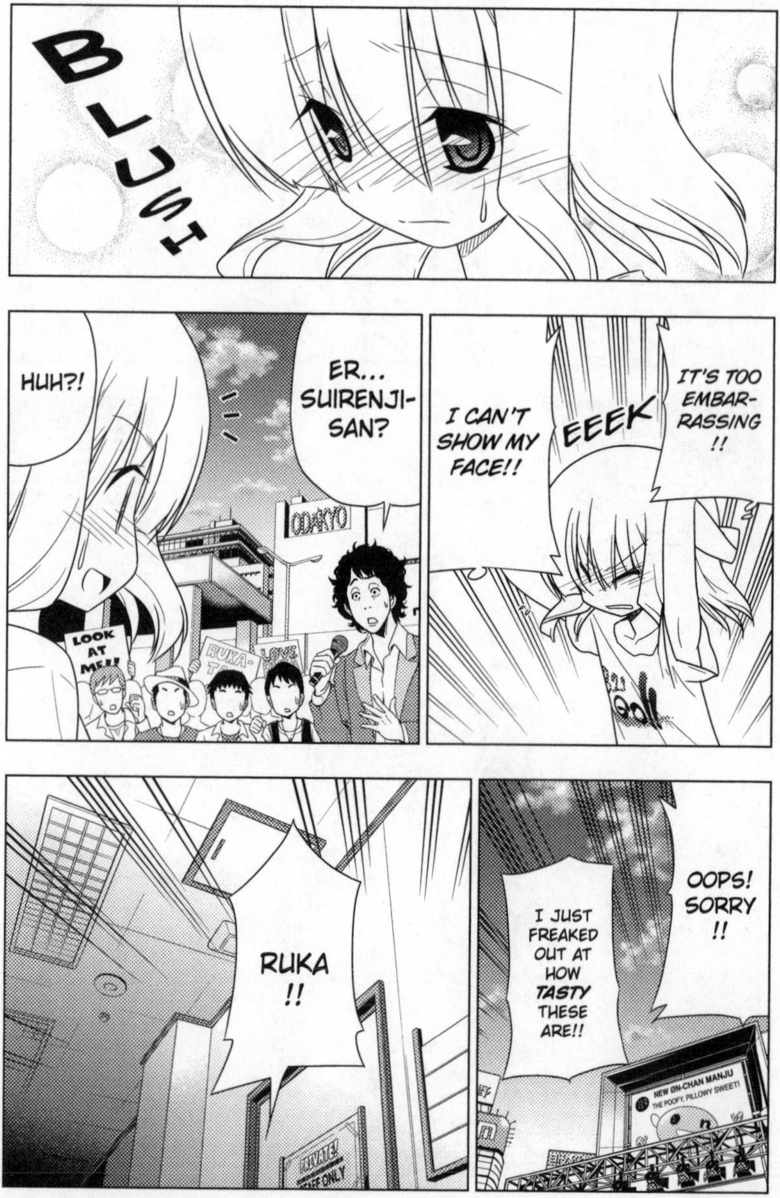
BLUSH
IT'S TOO EMBARRASSING!!
EEEK
I CAN'T SHOW MY FACE!!
ER... SUIRENJI-SAN?
HUH?!
ODAKYO
LOOK AT ME!!
OOPS! SORRY!!
I JUST FREAKED OUT AT HOW *TASTY* THESE ARE!!
NEW ØN-CHAN MANJU
THE POOFY, PILLOWY SWEET!
RUKA!!

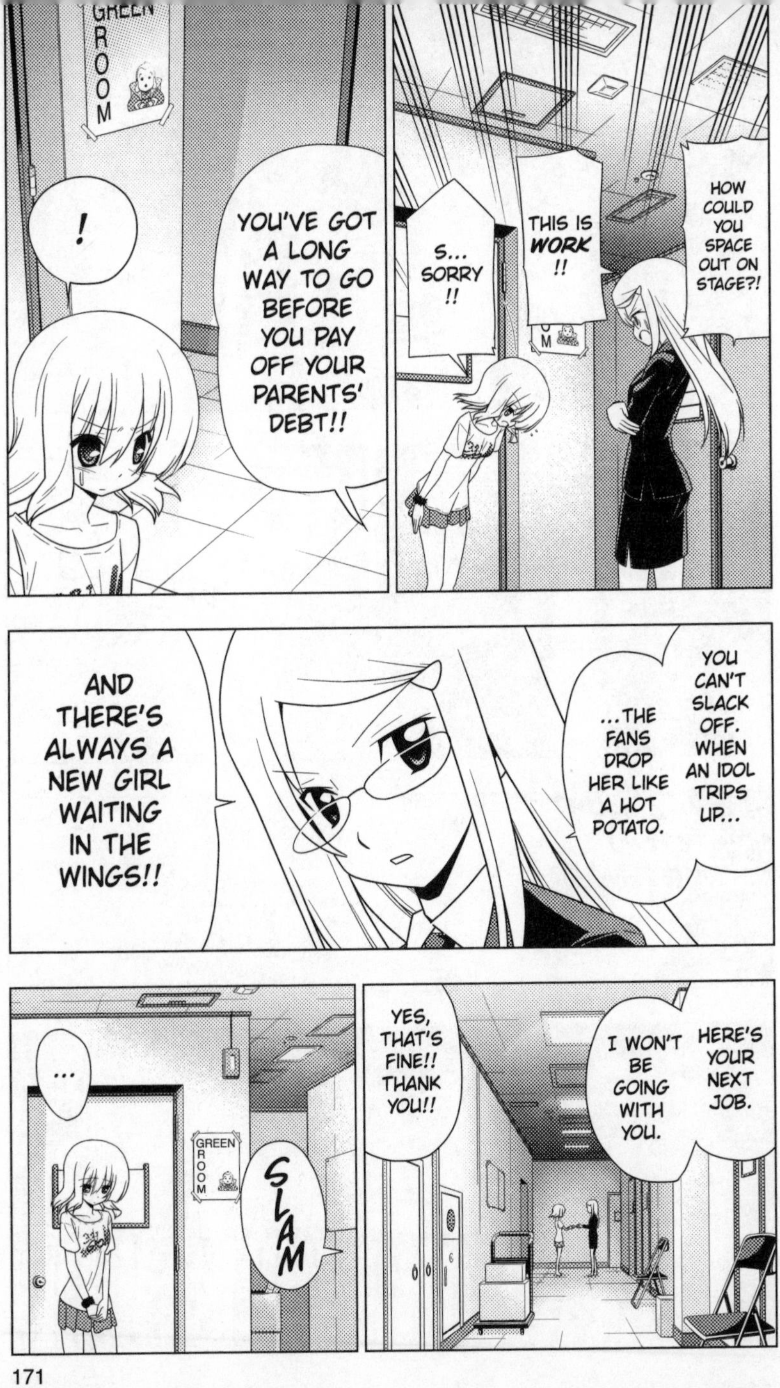
HOW COULD YOU SPACE OUT ON STAGE?!
THIS IS *WORK* !!
S... SORRY !!
GREEN ROOM
YOU'VE GOT A LONG WAY TO GO BEFORE YOU PAY OFF YOUR PARENTS' DEBT!!
!
YOU CAN'T SLACK OFF. WHEN AN IDOL TRIPS UP...
...THE FANS DROP HER LIKE A HOT POTATO.
AND THERE'S ALWAYS A NEW GIRL WAITING IN THE WINGS!!
HERE'S YOUR NEXT JOB.
I WON'T BE GOING WITH YOU.
YES, THAT'S FINE!! THANK YOU!!
SLAM
GREEN ROOM
...

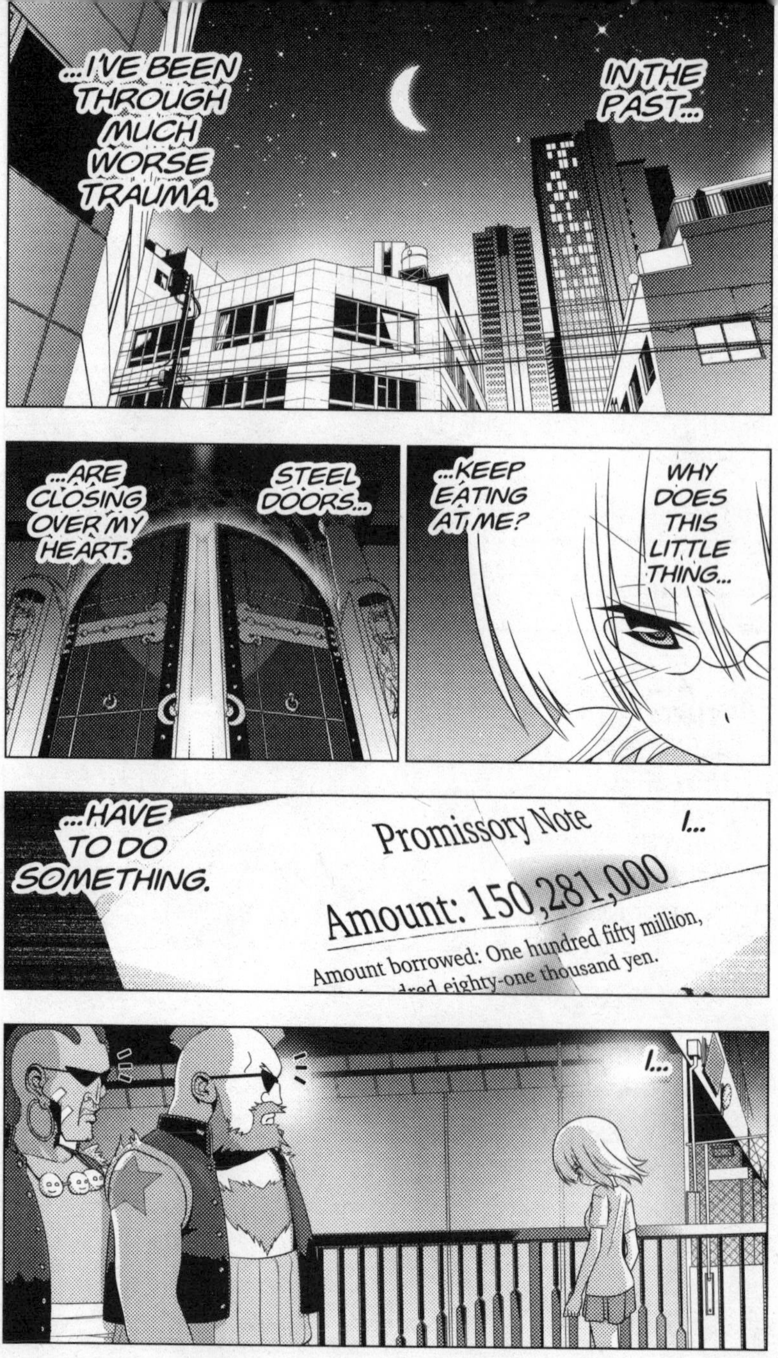
IN THE PAST...
...I'VE BEEN THROUGH MUCH WORSE TRAUMA.
WHY DOES THIS LITTLE THING...
...KEEP EATING AT ME?
STEEL DOORS...
...ARE CLOSING OVER MY HEART.
I...
Promissory Note
Amount: 150,281,000
Amount borrowed: One hundred fifty million,
...HAVE TO DO SOMETHING.
I...

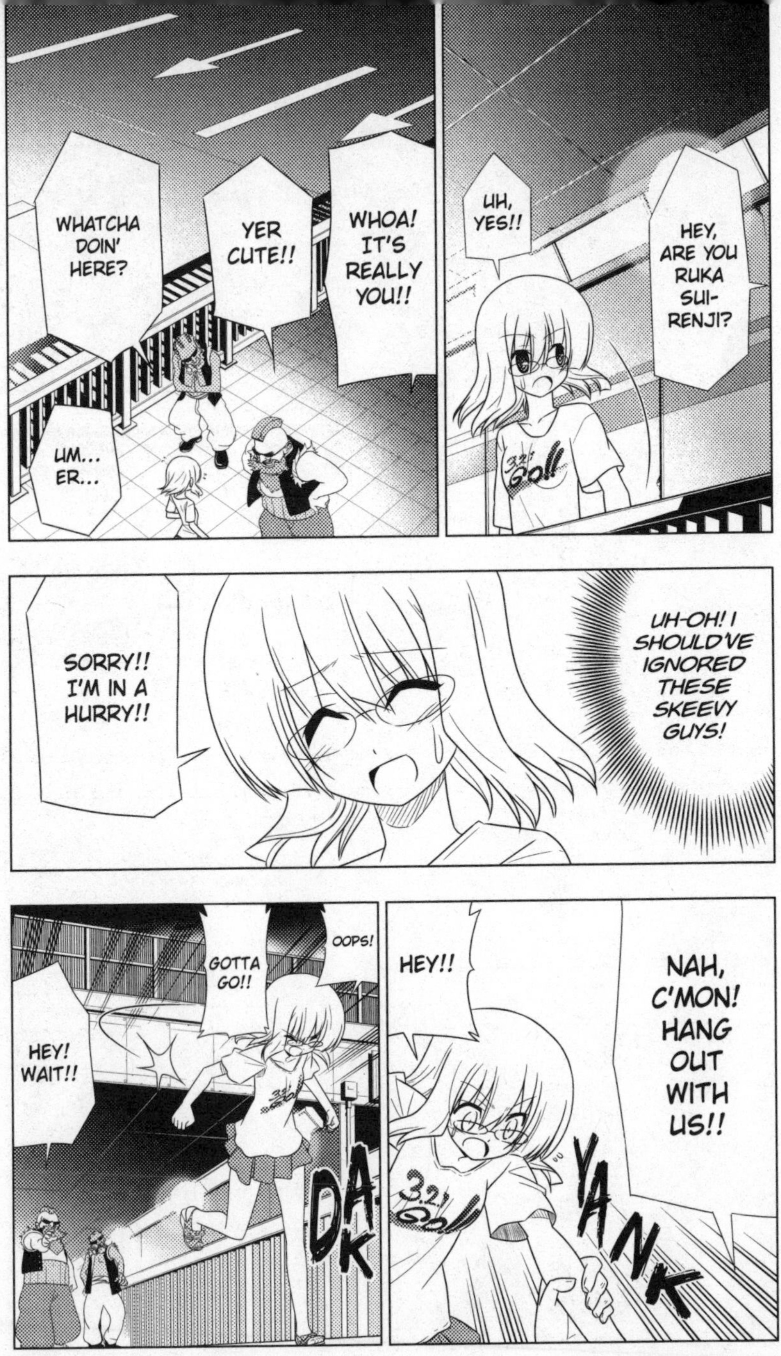
HEY, ARE YOU RUKA SUI-RENJI?
UH, YES!!
WHOA! IT'S REALLY YOU!!
YER CUTE!!
WHATCHA DOIN' HERE?
UM... ER...
UH-OH! I SHOULD'VE IGNORED THESE SKEEVY GUYS!
SORRY!! I'M IN A HURRY!!
NAH, C'MON! HANG OUT WITH US!!
YANK
HEY!!
OOPS!
GOTTA GO!!
DAK
HEY! WAIT!!

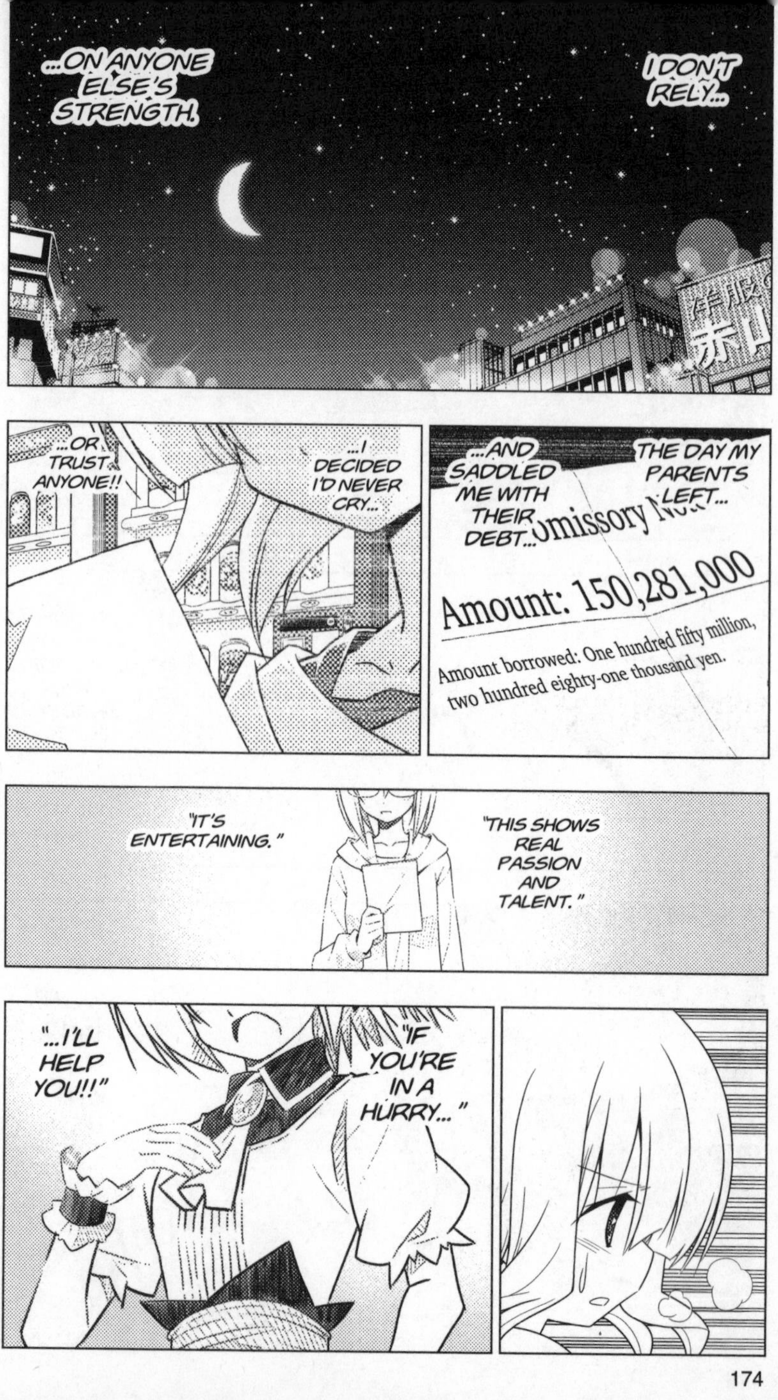
I DON'T RELY...
...ON ANYONE ELSE'S STRENGTH.
THE DAY MY PARENTS LEFT...
...AND SADDLED ME WITH THEIR DEBT...
omissory N
Amount: 150,281,000
Amount borrowed: One hundred fifty million, two hundred eighty-one thousand yen.
...I DECIDED I'D NEVER CRY...
...OR TRUST ANYONE!!
"THIS SHOWS REAL PASSION AND TALENT."
"IT'S ENTERTAINING."
"IF YOU'RE IN A HURRY..."
"...I'LL HELP YOU!!"

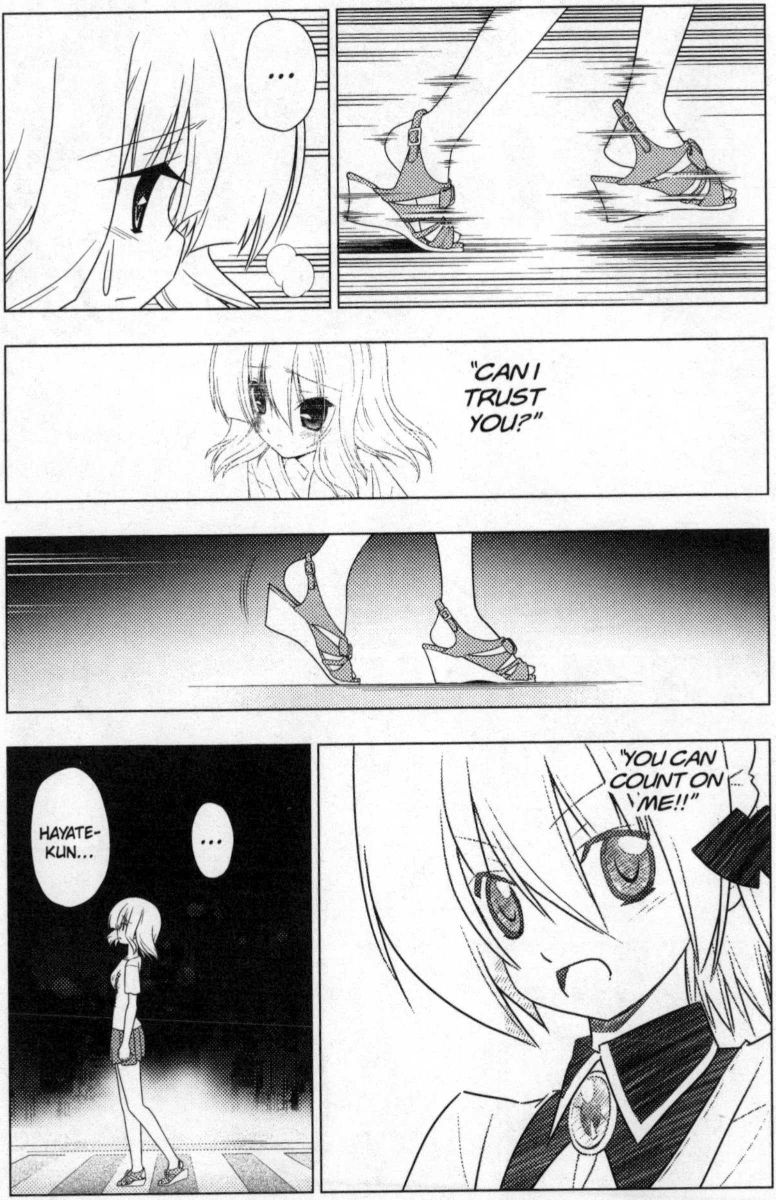
...
"CAN I TRUST YOU?"
"YOU CAN COUNT ON ME!!"
...
HAYATE-KUN...

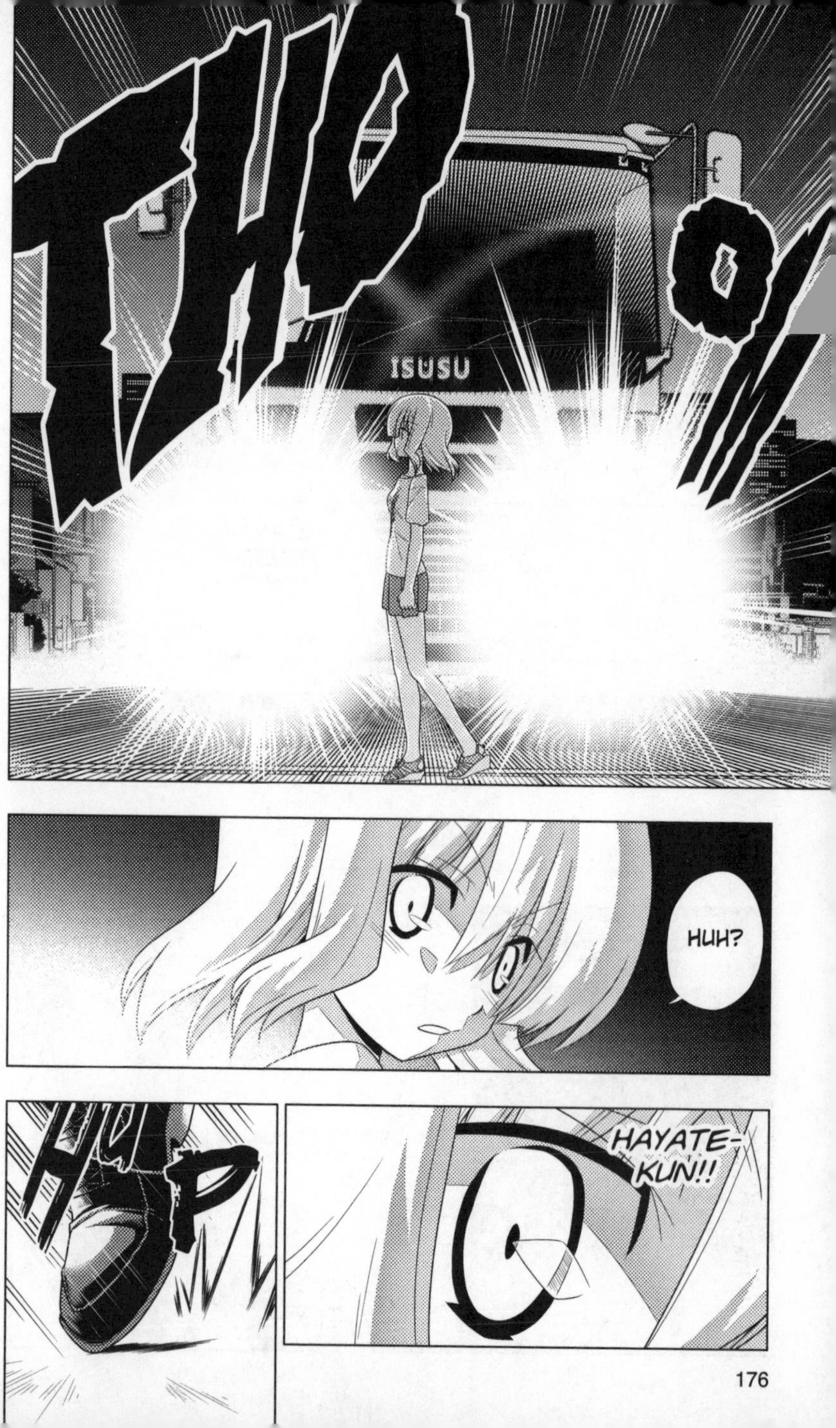
ISUSU
HUH?
HAYATE-KUN!!

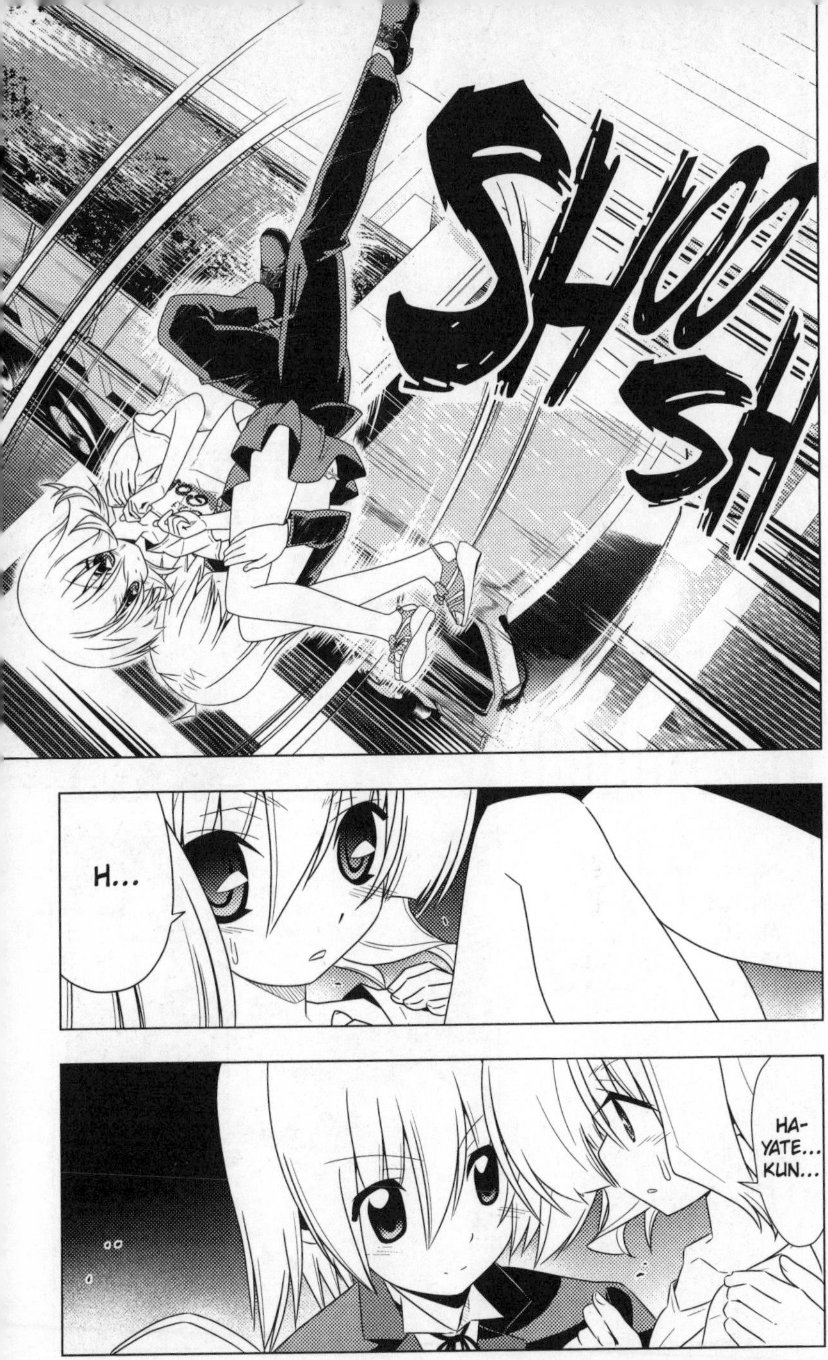
SHOO
SH
H...
HA-YATE... KUN...

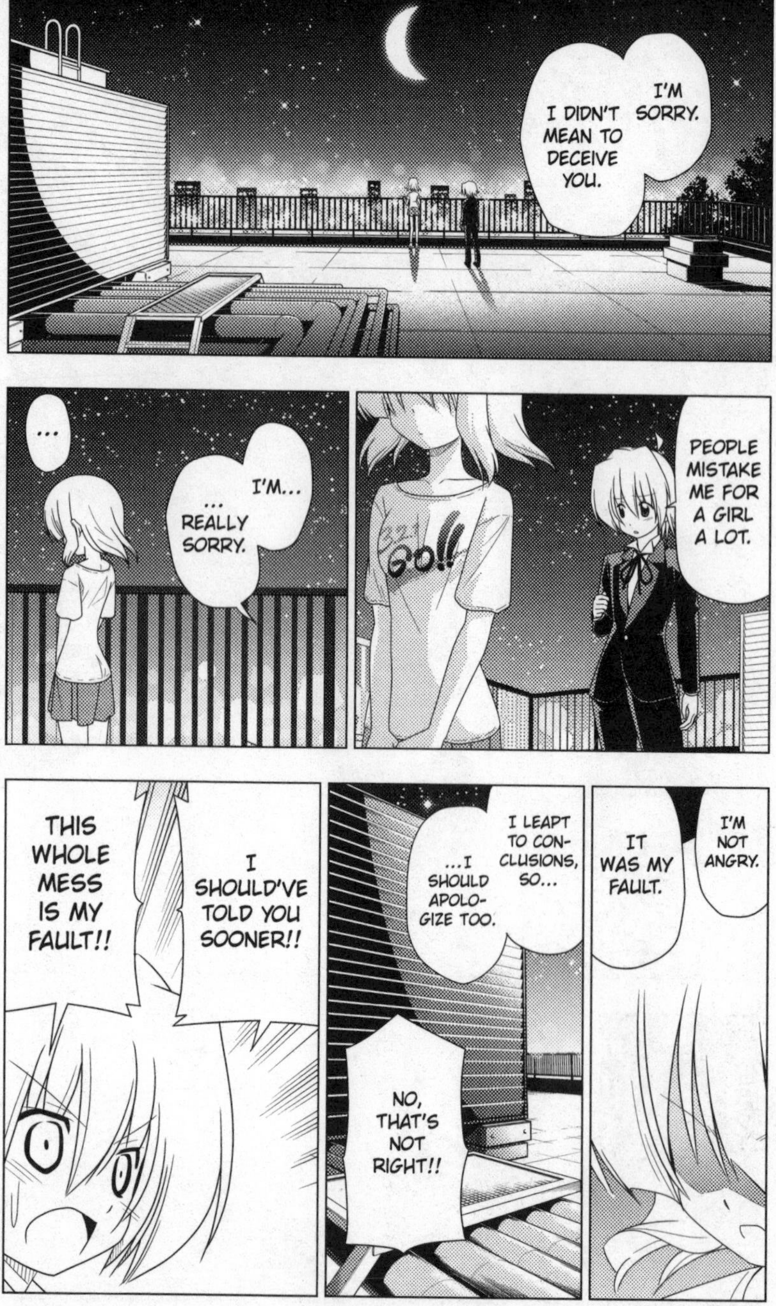
I'M SORRY.
I DIDN'T MEAN TO DECEIVE YOU.
PEOPLE MISTAKE ME FOR A GIRL A LOT.
I'M... ...REALLY SORRY.
...
I'M NOT ANGRY.
IT WAS MY FAULT.
I LEAPT TO CON-CLUSIONS, SO...
...I SHOULD APOLO-GIZE TOO.
NO, THAT'S NOT RIGHT!!
I SHOULD'VE TOLD YOU SOONER!!
THIS WHOLE MESS IS MY FAULT!!

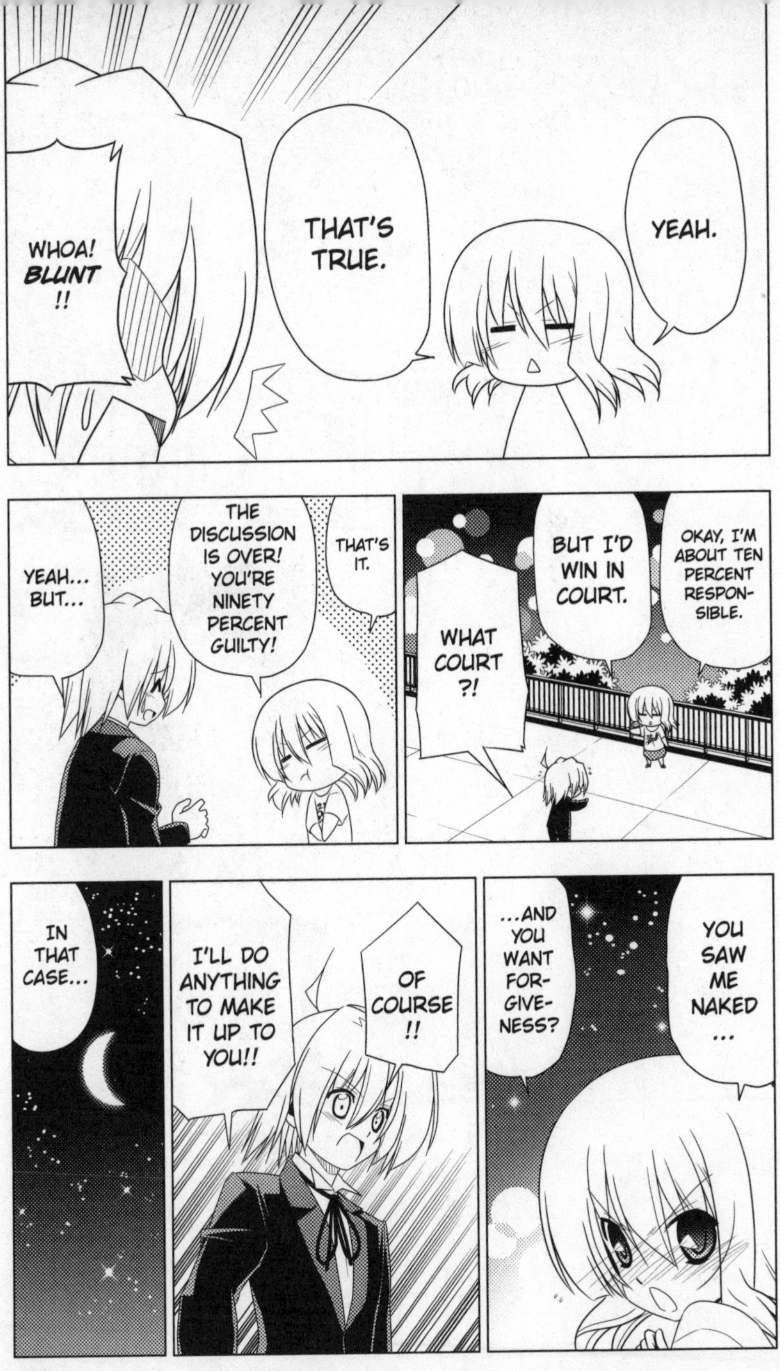
YEAH.
THAT'S TRUE.
WHOA! BLUNT!!
OKAY, I'M ABOUT TEN PERCENT RESPONSIBLE.
BUT I'D WIN IN COURT.
WHAT COURT?!
THAT'S IT.
THE DISCUSSION IS OVER! YOU'RE NINETY PERCENT GUILTY!
YEAH... BUT...
YOU SAW ME NAKED...
...AND YOU WANT FORGIVENESS?
OF COURSE!!
I'LL DO ANYTHING TO MAKE IT UP TO YOU!!
IN THAT CASE...

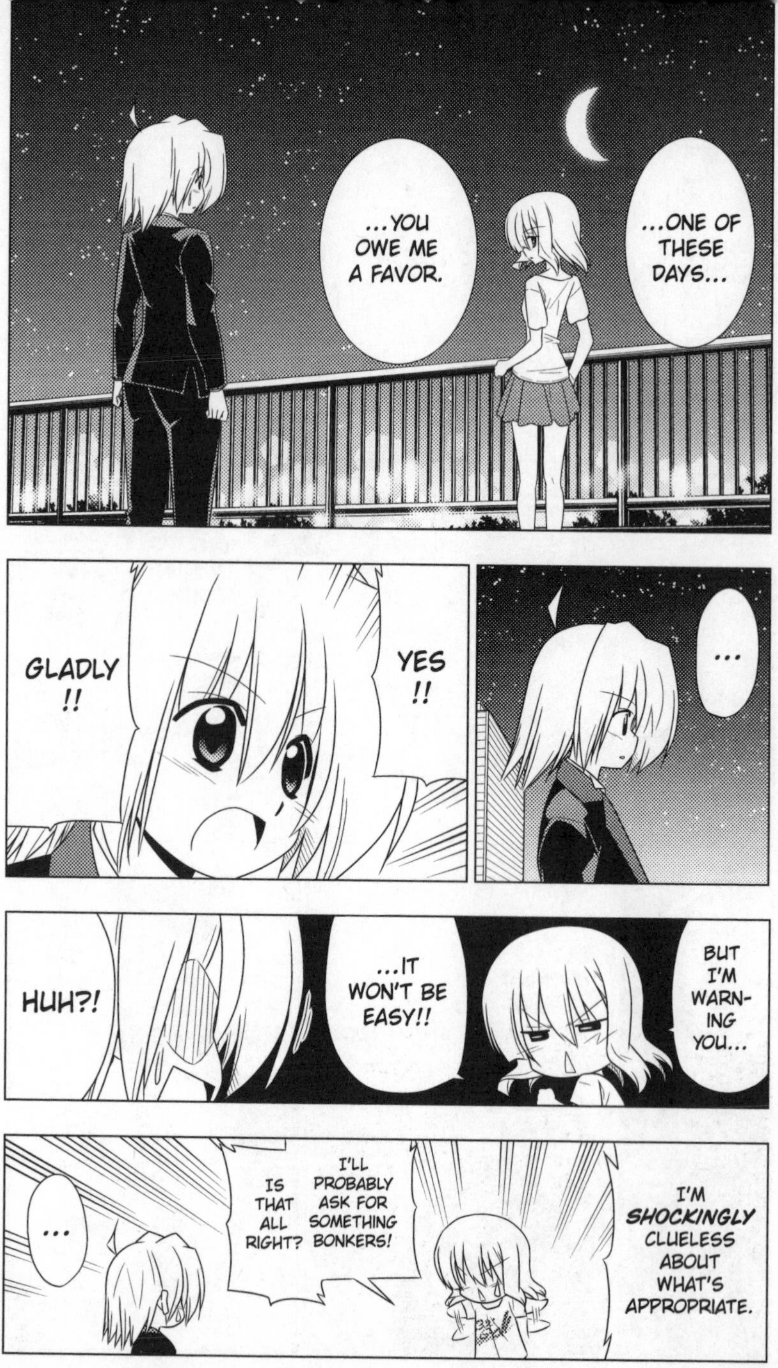
...ONE OF THESE DAYS...
...YOU OWE ME A FAVOR.
...
YES!!
GLADLY!!
BUT I'M WARNING YOU...
...IT WON'T BE EASY!!
HUH?!
I'M *SHOCKINGLY* CLUELESS ABOUT WHAT'S APPROPRIATE.
I'LL PROBABLY ASK FOR SOMETHING BONKERS!
IS THAT ALL RIGHT?
...

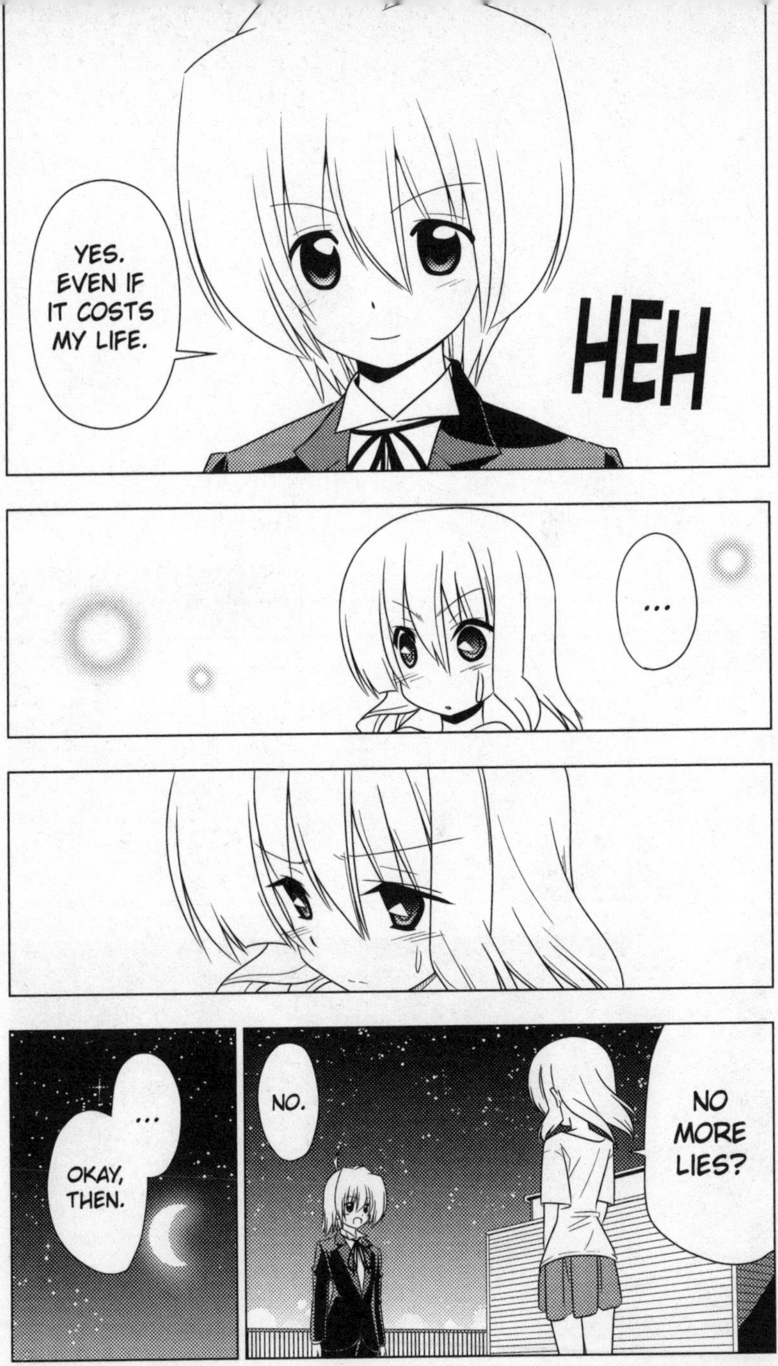
HEH
YES. EVEN IF IT COSTS MY LIFE.
...
NO MORE LIES?
NO.
... OKAY, THEN.

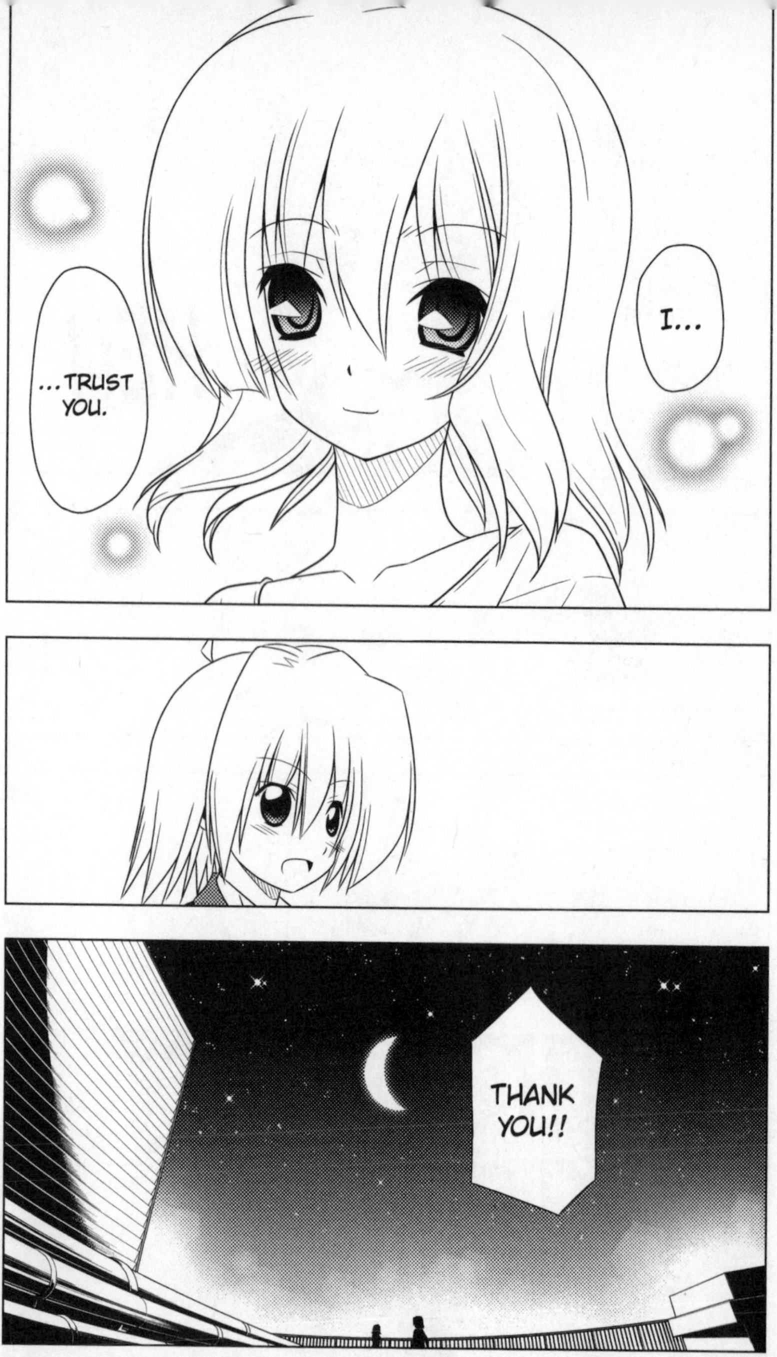
I...
...TRUST YOU.
THANK YOU!!

TO BE CONTINUED

HAYATE THE COMBAT BUTLER

BONUS PAGES

TITLE CALLIGRAPHY BY RITSUKO HATA
(WHOSE EYES ARE BETTER AFTER A CATARACT OPERATION)

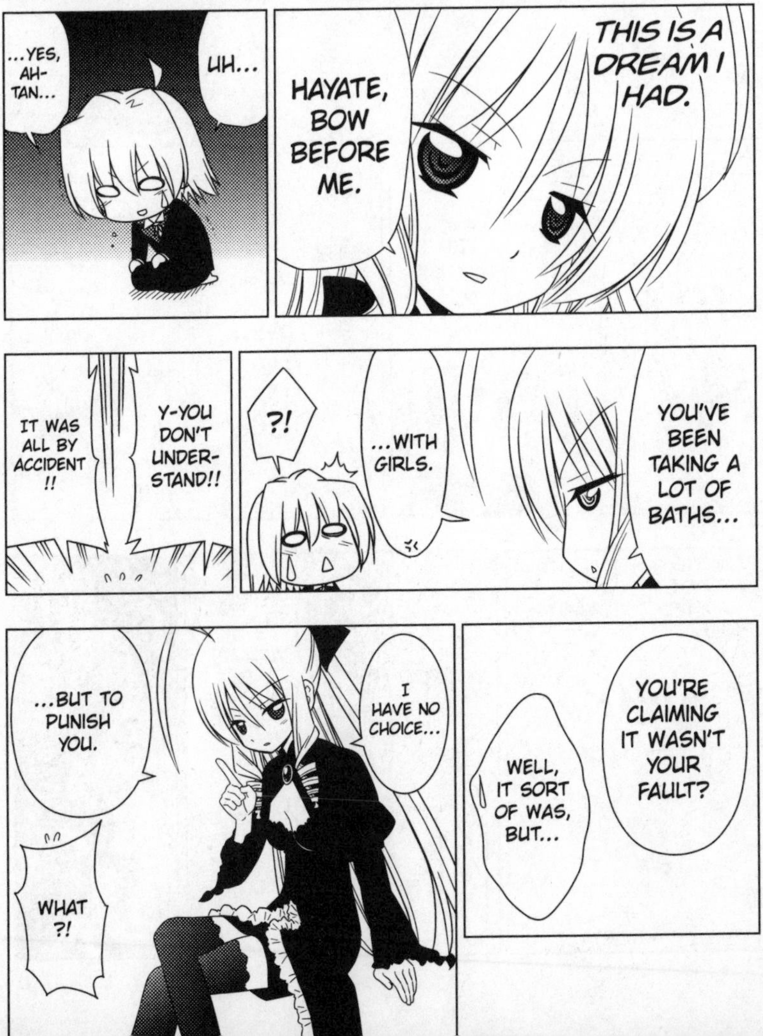
THIS IS A DREAM I HAD.
HAYATE, BOW BEFORE ME.
UH...
...YES, AH-TAN...
YOU'VE BEEN TAKING A LOT OF BATHS...
...WITH GIRLS.
?!
Y-YOU DON'T UNDER-STAND!!
IT WAS ALL BY ACCIDENT!!
YOU'RE CLAIMING IT WASN'T YOUR FAULT?
WELL, IT SORT OF WAS, BUT...
I HAVE NO CHOICE...
...BUT TO PUNISH YOU.
WHAT?!

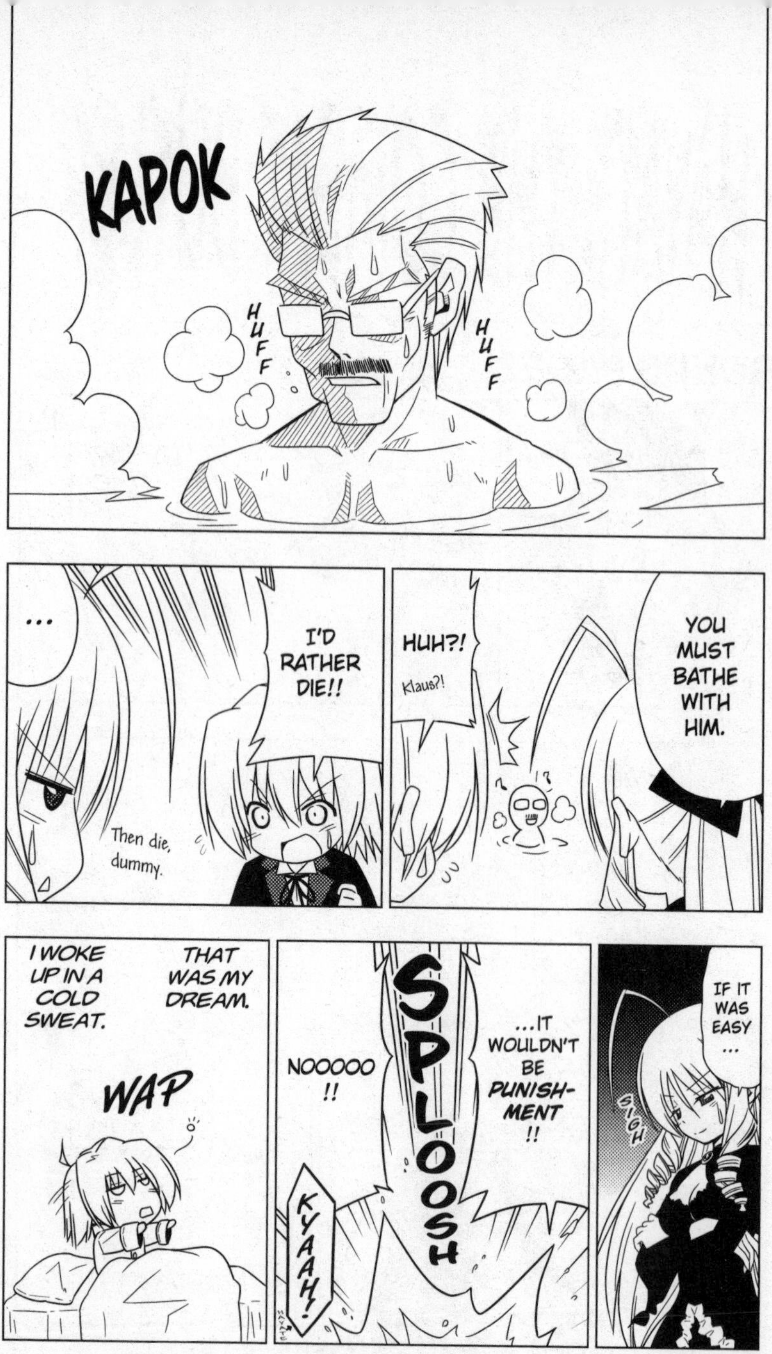
KAPOK
HUFF
HUFF
YOU MUST BATHE WITH HIM.
HUH?!
Klaus?!
I'D RATHER DIE!!
...
Then die, dummy.
IF IT WAS EASY...
SIGH
...IT WOULDN'T BE PUNISHMENT!!
SPLOOOSH
NOOOOO!!
KYAAAH!
THAT WAS MY DREAM.
I WOKE UP IN A COLD SWEAT.
WAP

HERE WE ARE AT VOLUME 30! SEVEN YEARS HAVE PASSED SINCE THE SERIES BEGAN, AND I OWE IT ALL TO YOU READERS. THANK YOU VERY MUCH!

THE MUCH-ANTICIPATED *HAYATE* THEATRICAL MOVIE CAME OUT THIS SUMMER. I WAS OVERJOYED THAT SO MANY PEOPLE WENT TO SEE IT.

HOW DID YOU LIKE IT? WE PUSHED OURSELVES TO THE LIMIT TO MAKE IT. I HOPE IT PROVIDED *GOOD SUMMER MEMORIES*. IF YOU HAVEN'T SEEN IT YET, I'D LOVE FOR YOU TO PICK UP THE DVD OR BLU-RAY WHEN THEY COME OUT.

HERE IN JAPAN, A SPECIAL EDITION OF *HAYATE THE COMBAT BUTTLER* VOLUME 31 WILL COME PACKAGED WITH THE DVD FOR THE LOW, LOW PRICE OF 2,980 YEN!*

LET ME EMPHASIZE ONCE MORE THAT IT'LL BE JUST 2,980 YEN!!!

THAT'S THE MANGA PLUS THE MOVIE! MY PUBLISHER AND THE FILM PRODUCERS HAVE AGREED TO OFFER THIS AS A THANK-YOU TO THE MANY FANS WHO WENT TO SEE IT IN THE THEATER! THAT'S AMAZING!

THEY'RE NOT LIKELY TO MAKE THIS OFFER AGAIN, SO IF YOU DEFINITELY WANT THE MOVIE, GO FOR IT.

NOW THAT THE MANGA HAS REACHED VOLUME 30 AND IS ENTERING ITS EIGHTH YEAR, I PLAN TO WORK WITH RENEWED SPIRIT. STARTING NEXT YEAR, I THINK YOU'LL BEGIN TO SEE THE RESULTS.

IN THE MEANTIME, I HOPE YOU'LL KEEP READING!! SEE YOU IN VOLUME 31! ☆ BYE!

*ABOUT $29.80.

A World Unknown to the Butler

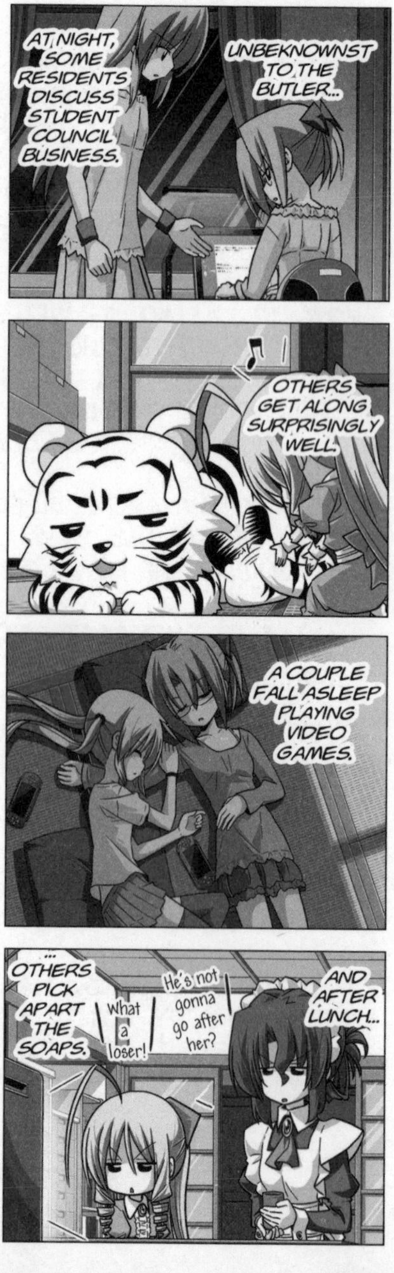
UNBEKNOWNST TO THE BUTLER...
AT NIGHT, SOME RESIDENTS DISCUSS STUDENT COUNCIL BUSINESS.
OTHERS GET ALONG SURPRISINGLY WELL.
A COUPLE FALL ASLEEP PLAYING VIDEO GAMES.
AND AFTER LUNCH...
He's not gonna go after her?
What a loser!
...OTHERS PICK APART THE SOAPS.

A World Unknown to the Butler

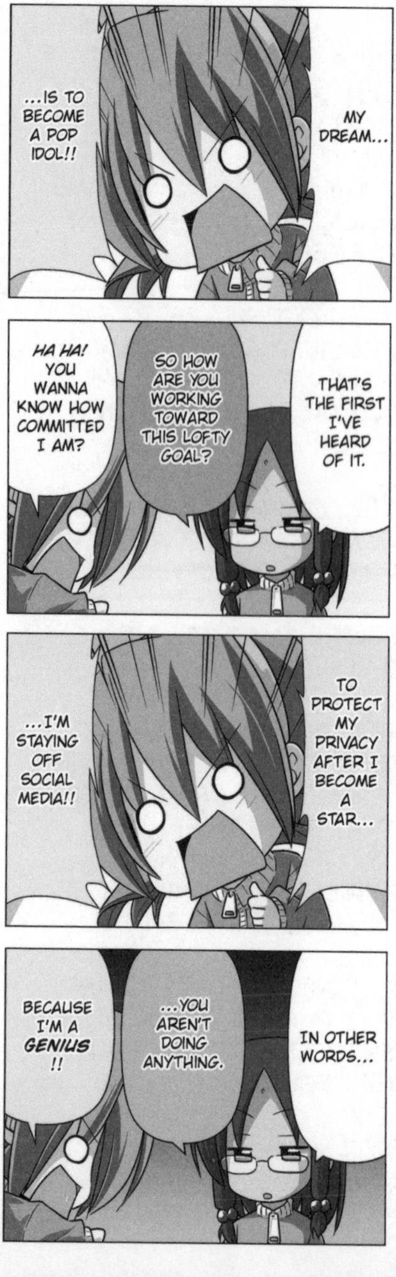
MY DREAM...
...IS TO BECOME A POP IDOL!!
THAT'S THE FIRST I'VE HEARD OF IT.
SO HOW ARE YOU WORKING TOWARD THIS LOFTY GOAL?
HA HA! YOU WANNA KNOW HOW COMMITTED I AM?
TO PROTECT MY PRIVACY AFTER I BECOME A STAR...
...I'M STAYING OFF SOCIAL MEDIA!!
IN OTHER WORDS...
...YOU AREN'T DOING ANYTHING.
BECAUSE I'M A GENIUS !!

HAYATE THE COMBAT BUTLER

<BAD END 15>

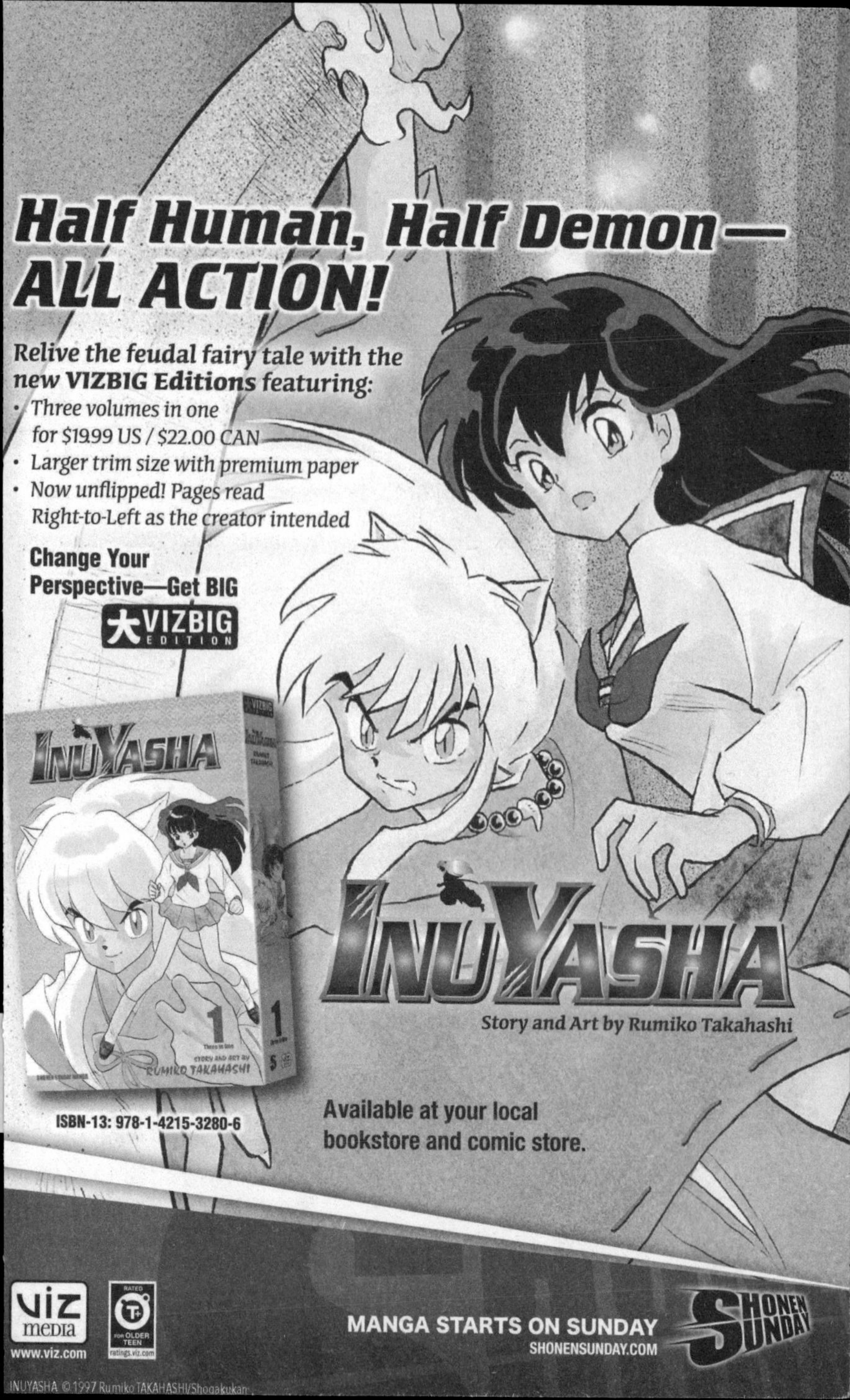
Half Human, Half Demon—
ALL ACTION!
Relive the feudal fairy tale with the new VIZBIG Editions featuring:
• Three volumes in one for $19.99 US / $22.00 CAN
• Larger trim size with premium paper
• Now unflipped! Pages read Right-to-Left as the creator intended
Change Your Perspective—Get BIG
大 VIZBIG EDITION
INUYASHA
1
STORY AND ART BY RUMIKO TAKAHASHI
ISBN-13: 978-1-4215-3280-6
INUYASHA
Story and Art by Rumiko Takahashi
Available at your local bookstore and comic store.
viz media
www.viz.com
RATED T+ FOR OLDER TEEN
ratings.viz.com
MANGA STARTS ON SUNDAY
SHONENSUNDAY.COM
SHONEN SUNDAY
INUYASHA © 1997 Rumiko TAKAHASHI/Shogakukan

Hey! You're Reading in the Wrong Direction!

This is the **end** of this graphic novel!

To properly enjoy this VIZ graphic novel, please turn it around and begin reading from **right to left.** Unlike English, Japanese is read right to left, so Japanese comics are read in reverse order from the way English comics are typically read.

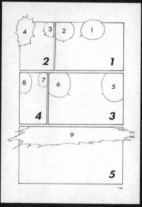

Follow the action this way

This book has been printed in the original Japanese format in order to preserve the orientation of the original artwork. Have fun with it!